The Management of Health
and Well-being in the Workplace

RMS Publishing Limited

Suite 3, Victoria House, Lower High Street, Stourbridge, DY8 1TA

© ACT Associates Limited.

First Published October 2011.

Cover by Smudge Creative Design.

Printed and bound in Great Britain by Stephens and George Print Group, Merthyr Tydfil.

Crown Copyright material is reproduced with the permission of the Controller of HMSO and the Queen's Printer for Scotland.

ISBN-13: 978-1-906674-14-4

Contents

Preface

Publication users

This essential guide provides an excellent reference for those who have responsibility for, or involvement in, health and well-being in the workplace. The guide provides an understanding of this important topic and assists those involved in health and well-being at work to minimise absence, encourage people back to work where possible, and deal effectively with the health issues of employees.

It provides an insight into work-related health problems, how this affects the individual and the impact on the family and wider community. The practical and informative approach will provide managers, human resource staff and health and safety practitioners with a perspective of the significance of health and well-being in the workplace and an understanding of what is involved in managing it. This publication would also be useful for GPs, Practice Nurses and those health professionals undergoing training for Community or Social work.

The guide is an excellent source of information for those undergoing the following learning programmes:

- To meet the requirements of the NEBOSH National Certificate in the Management of Health and Well-being at Work syllabus, in particular.
- To develop knowledge of occupational health practice for nurses working in OH situations.
- To develop and enhance competency and skills needed of occupational health technicians.
- Chartered Institute of Personnel and Development (CIPD) qualifications and certificates.
- Chartered Institute of Managers (CIM) qualifications and certificates.

Topics included in the publication include:

- Identifying risks to health at work.
- The effects of health on work and work on health.
- Learning how to manage sickness absence and implement a return to work programme
- Dealing with mental health at work.
- Prevention and management of work related stress.
- Management of people with musculoskeletal disorders.

Reference is made to clinical issues and the prevalence of ill-health in the working age population. It contains an emphasis on practical management solutions to workplace health, full colour photographs, schematics and case studies are provided to enable an understanding of how these solutions contribute to the prevention of ill-health and promote rehabilitation. The publication contains a sample questionnaire that may be used as a basis of a health and well-being review for organisations.

"Staff with the skills and competencies signified by NEBOSH's new Health and Well-being qualification should be highly valued by employers and employees alike. They add force to the commitment of employers and business managers to strengthen the essential elements of safety, health and well-being management."

Dame Carol Black, National Director for Health and Work

Scope and contents

Syllabus

The Essential Guide reflects the common aspects of health and well-being in the workplace and embraces the scope of the syllabus for the NEBOSH National Certificate in the Management of Health and Well-being at Work award. Though the publication will suit those interested in the topic in general and studying for other awards, it has be structured to reflect the order and content of the NEBOSH National Certificate in the Management of Health and Well-being at Work syllabus in particular. In this way, the student studying for this award can be confident that the Essential Guide reflects the themes of the syllabus and forms an excellent Study Book for that purpose. Each element of the Essential Guide has an overview that sets out the learning outcomes of the element, the content and any connected sources of reference and relevant statutory provisions.

Assessment

In order that users may check their understanding of the topic expressed in the Essential Guide and in particular the syllabus for the NEBOSH National Certificate in the Management of Health and Well-being at Work award, a number of examination questions have been included.

In addition, the publication contains a sample health and well-being review questionnaire that may be used as a basis for an evaluation of an organisation's performance. The questionnaire has been produced by NEBOSH as part of their practical assessment of the above award, their origination and copyright is acknowledged. In order to understand how the questionnaire may be used and the type of report produced by candidates studying this award, a completed questionnaire and report is provided.

Legal requirements

The Essential Guide has at its heart best practice in the management of health in the workplace. Legislation is referred to in context in the various elements that comprise the Essential Guide, reflecting the syllabus of the NEBOSH National Certificate in the Management of Health and Well-being at Work and the important legislation affecting health and well-being in the workplace. The publication also benefits from a section that brings together the main features of all this important legislation.

Diagrams and photographs

We have taken particular care to support the text with a significant number of photographs, diagrams and schematics. Where diagrams/text extracts are known to be drawn from other publications, a clear source reference is shown and RMS Publishing wishes to emphasise that reproduction of such diagrams/text extracts within the Essential Guide is for educational purposes only and the original copyright has not been infringed.

The study book

Acknowledgements

RMS Publishing wish to acknowledge the following contributors and thank them for their assistance in the preparation of the Management of Health and Well-being in the Workplace study book:

Cynthia Atwell OBE, RN, FRCN, RSCPHN (OH), Hon. FFOM, Hon. FIOSH, Occupational Health Consultant with over 40 years experience of occupational health (OH) practice in a range of organisations. Previously Senior Teaching Fellow, University of Warwick set up the OH Diploma and taught on the HSE PG Diploma in Regulatory OH & Safety.

Caroline Whittaker RRC, RN, BSc, RSCPHN (OH), Senior Lecturer in Public Health, University of Glamorgan, where she leads the OH Diploma. Over 20 years experience in OH practice in a range of organisations. Also a Lieutenant Colonel in the TA, has served in Bosnia, Iraq and is presently in Afghanistan.

Marie John MSc. Health Promotion and Health Education, DipN London, RNT, RCNT, FETC, RN, Senior Lecturer, University of Glamorgan (retired Nov 2010 now invited lecturer). Special interest in health promotion and public health and is former Senior Nursing Adviser to Health Promotion Wales. Wide range of nursing experience including working in RSA and passenger liners.

Ian Coombes, Managing Director ACT, CMIOSH; Member of NEBOSH Council, former Board member and examiner. Former member of IOSH Professional Affairs Committee and chairman of the Initial Professional Development sub-committee. Member of the management committee of Safety Groups UK.

Barrie Newell, Director ACT, FCIM; current member of the NEBOSH Certificate Panel, former senior manager in the chemical industry with over 20 years experience of the management of toxic chemicals, waste disposal, energy recovery and recycling.

Julie Skett, senior project development and coordinator. Nick Attwood, Kris James and Andy Taylor layout and formatting.

Publications also available from RMS:

Publication	*Edition*	*ISBN*
Controlling skin exposure (BOHS)	First	978-1-906674-00-7
A Study Book for the NEBOSH National General in Occupational Health and Safety	Sixth	978-1-906674-07-6
A Study Book for the NEBOSH National Certificate in Construction Safety and Health	Third	978-1-906674-15-1
A Study Book for the NEBOSH National Certificate in Fire Safety and Risk Management	Third	978-1-906674-05-2
A Study Book for the NEBOSH National Certificate in Environmental Management	First	978-1-906674-03-8
Study Books for the NEBOSH National Diploma in Occupational Safety and Health:		
■ (Unit A) Managing health and safety	Fourth	978-1-906674-08-3
■ (Unit B) Hazardous agents in the workplace	Fourth	978-1-906674-09-0
■ (Unit C) Workplace and work equipment safety	Fourth	978-1-906674-10-6
A Study Book for the NEBOSH International General Certificate	First	978-1-900420-90-7
Study Books for the NEBOSH International Diploma in Occupational Safety and Health:		
■ (Unit IA) International management of health and safety	First	978-1-906674-11-3
■ (Unit IB) International control of hazardous agents in the workplace	First	978-1-906674-12-0
■ (Unit IC) International workplace and work equipment safety	First	978-1-906674-13-7

Foreword

I welcome this Study Book which in a compact but comprehensive way mirrors the syllabus of the new NEBOSH Certificate in the Management of Health and Wellbeing. But its value reaches beyond candidates who are preparing themselves for the Certificate. The Study Book provides a handy, clearly ordered source of reference for occupational health and human resources personnel in any organisation, indeed for all staff, but especially line mangers with a direct concern and responsibility for the health and well being of employees.

The book is not simply an academic guide, though it is scholarly in approach. It brings together the statutory, legal, economic and cultural aspects of the workplace and working life. Its tone and content and lively illustrations declare long familiarity with countless workplace scenes, operations and tasks. The book conveys a sense of what in the diverse conditions of work people actually do and the problems they deal with each day. It rings true.

Building on long-established legal requirements in respect of a range of health and safety practices we see the importance of maintaining, safeguarding and promoting the physical and mental health and wellbeing of all people of working age. It brings out strongly the modern concept of occupational health and its place within the overarching domain of public health. This has grown out of recognition of the burden and costs of impaired health in relation to working life and the impact upon personal and family life, upon the larger community, and upon economic productivity. And for employers there is persuasive evidence that the health and well-being of employees are critical determinants of the success of their enterprise and service.

Such concerns have brought increasing attention to the role of the workplace in shaping and providing the conditions necessary for healthy and fulfilling working lives. Employers, whether in the public or private sectors, in businesses or other kinds of organisation, have a major role in safeguarding and enhancing the health and well-being of their staff. This is highlighted when people are injured, unwell or distressed - when they need support to remain confident and effective, whether they continuing working through the episode or look to return without delay, from sickness absence. The employer has a crucial role in recognising and addressing the problem of presenteeism, where people who are not well and should be enabled to recover feel bound to attend though cannot perform at their best.

Staff who are familiar with and practised in the knowledge and skills brought together in this Study Book should be valued by employers and employees alike. They add force to the commitment of employers and business managers to strengthen the essential elements of safety, health and wellbeing management.

Dame Carol Black
National Director for Health and Work

February 2011

Figure List (including tables and quotes)

Element 8

Relevant statutory provisions

List of abbreviations

LEGISLATION

AMRA	Access to Medical Reports Act 1988
CAOR	Control of Artificial Optical Radiation at Work Regulations 2010
CAR	Control of Asbestos Regulations 2006
CHIP	Chemical (Hazards Information and Packaging) Regulations 2009
CMA	Computer Misuse Act 1990
CLAW	Control of Lead at Work Regulations 2002
CNWR	Control of Noise at Work Regulations 2005
COSHH	Control of Substances Hazardous to Health Regulations 2002
CVWR	Control of Vibration at Work Regulations 2005
DPA	Data Protection Act 1998
DSER	Health and Safety (Display Screen Equipment) Regulations 1992
EA	Equality Act 2010
EERAR	Employment Equality (Repeals of Retirement Age Provisions) Regulations 2011
ELCIA	Employers' Liability (Compulsory Insurance) Act 1969
EMA	Employment Act 2008
ERA	Employment Rights Act 1996
HASAWA	Health and Safety at Work etc Act 1974
HSCER	Health and Safety (Consultation with Employees) Regulations 1996
IRR	Ionising Radiation Regulations 1999
MDA	Misuse of Drugs Act 1971
MHOR	Manual Handling Operations Regulations 1992
MHSWR	Management of Health and Safety at Work Regulations 1999
NCTECR	Notification of Cooling Towers and Evaporative Condensers Regulations 1992
PPE	Personal Protective Equipment Regulations 1992
RIDDOR	Reporting of Injuries, Diseases and Dangerous Occurrences Regulations 1995
RSCR	Railways (Safety Case) Regulations 2000
RTA	Road Traffic Act 1988
RTSA	Railways and Transport Safety Act 2003
SRSC	Safety Representatives and Safety Committees Regulations 1977
TWA	Transport and Works Act 1992
WHSWR	Workplace (Health Safety and Welfare) Regulations 1992
WTR	Working Time Regulations 1998

GENERAL

ACAS	The Advisory, Conciliation and Arbitration Service
ACD	Allergic Contact Dermatitis
ACOP	Approved Code of Practice
AFARP	As Far As Reasonably Practical
AFOM	Associate of the Faculty of Occupational Medicine
AIDS	Acquired Immune Deficiency Syndrome
AOHNP	Association of OH Nurse Practitioners
ART	Assessment of Repetitive Tasks
ASPR	Age Standardised Prevalence Rate
CBH	Constructing Better Health
CBT	Cognitive-behavioural therapy
CIPD	Chartered Institute of Personnel and Development
CMO	Chief Medical Officer
COHPA	Commercial Occupational Health Providers Association
COPD	Chronic Obstructive Pulmonary Diseases
CSP	Chartered Society of Physiotherapy
CSR	Corporate Social Responsibility
CVD	Cardiovascular Disease
DSE	Display Screen Equipment
DVLA	Driver and Vehicle Licensing Authority
DWP	Department for Work and Pensions
EAA	Extrinsic Allergic Alveolitis
EAP	Employee Action/Assistance Programmes
EAU	Economic Analysis Unit
EAV	Exposure Action Value
EHRC	Equality and Human Rights Commission
ELCI	Employers' Liability Compulsory Insurance
ESRC	Economic and Social Research Council
FFOM	Fellow of the Faculty of Occupational Medicine

FOM	Faculty of Occupational Medicine
GMC	General Medical Council
GP	General Practitioner
HAVS	Hand-arm Vibration Syndrome
HIV	Human Immunodeficiency Virus
HNA	Health Needs Assessment
HPC	Health Professions Council
HSE	Health and Safety Executive
ICD	Irritant Contact Dermatitis
IIDB	Industrial Injuries Disablement Benefit
ILO	International Labour Organisation
LA	Local Authorities
LEV	Local Exhaust Ventilation
LGV	Large Goods Vehicles
LLD's	Lower Limb Disorders
MDMA	3,4-Methylenedioxymethamphetamine
MFOM	Member of the Faculty of Occupational Medicine
MRO	Medical Review Officer
MSDs	Musculoskeletal Disorders
NDDP	New Deal for Disabled People
NHS	National Health Service
NICE	National Institute for Health and Clinical Excellence
NMC	Nursing and Midwifery Council
OCD	Obsessive-compulsive disorder
OH	Occupational Health
ONIHL	Occupational Noise Induced Hearing Loss
OTC	Over the Counter
PCV	Passenger Carrying Vehicles
PHC	Primary Health Care
PPE	Personal Protective Equipment
PTSD	Post-traumatic Stress Disorder
QOF	Quality and Outcome Framework
RN	Registered Nurse
RNIB	Royal National Institute for the Blind
RPE	Respiratory Protective Equipment
RSCPHN.OH	Registered Specialist Community Public Health Nurse
RSI	Repetitive Strain Injury
SARS	Severe Acute Respiratory Syndrome
SME's	Small and Medium sized Enterprises
SSP	Statutory Sick Pay
TB	Tuberculosis
ULDs	Upper Limb Disorders
UVL	Ultra Violet Light
WBV	Whole Body Vibration
WELs	Workplace Exposure Limits
WHO	World Health Organisation
WRMSD's	Work Related Musculoskeletal Disorders
WRULDs	Work Related Upper Limb Disorders

Introduction to workplace health

Learning outcomes

On completion of this element, candidates should be able to demonstrate understanding of the content through the application of knowledge to familiar and unfamiliar situations. In particular they should be able to:

1.1 Outline the scope and nature of health and well-being at work.

1.2 Outline the benefits of maintaining and promoting the health of the working population.

1.3 Outline the role and benefits of effective management in workplace health.

Content

Sources of reference

Black, C. (2008) - Working for a Healthier Tomorrow, ISBN: 978-0-11-702-13-4, London TSO.

Business in the Community - Business Action on Health (2009), healthy people = healthy profits, published by BITC and available online at http://www.workingforhealth.gov.uk/Case-Studies/Healthy-People-Healthy Profits/4647_Healthy_Profits%20FINAL.pdf.

Department of Health (2006) - Health, Work and Well-being - Caring for our Future. London: Department of Health.

DWP (2007) - Ready for Work: Full Employment in our Generation, Chapter 4. ISBN: 978-0-10-172902-4, published by TSO and available online www.tsoshop.co.uk or www.dwp.gov.uk.

HSC (2004) - A Strategy for Workplace Health and Safety in Great Britain to 2010 and Beyond, Suffolk - HSE Books.

International Labour Organisation website www.ilo.org.

Lewis, J. and Thornberry, G. (2006) - Employment Law and Occupational Health Oxford: Blackwell Publishing.

World Health Organisation website www.who.org.

Relevant statutory provisions

Access to Medical Reports Act (AMRA) 1988

Control of Substances Hazardous to Health Regulations (COSHH) 2002 (as amended)

Data Protection Act (DPA) 1998

Employment Equality (Repeals of Retirement Age Provisions) Regulations (EERAR) 2011

Equality Act (EA) 2010

Health and Safety at Work Act (HASAWA) 1974

Management of Health and Safety at Work Regulations (MHSWR) 1999

Reporting of Injuries, Diseases and Dangerous Occurrences Regulations (RIDDOR) 1995

1.1 - Scope and nature of health, work and well-being at work

The extent of work related ill-health and disability in the UK

The Health and Safety Executive (HSE) provides data on formally reported work related ill-health on an annual basis. The HSE annual report for the period 2009/10 showed that 2,249 people died of mesothelioma in 2008, in the same period asbestosis was the underlying cause of 117 deaths and there were 147 deaths due to pneumoconiosis. The annual report confirmed that in 2009 the number of new industrial injuries disablement benefit (IIDB) cases was around 7,100. The largest categories included vibration white finger, carpal tunnel syndrome and respiratory diseases. The Labour Force Survey is a survey of households in the UK and provides information on the amount of self-reported work related health and disability in the UK. The HSE reported that data obtained from the Labour Force Survey confirmed that of the 28.5 million working days lost in the period (1.2 days per worker) 23.4 million were due to work-related ill-health and 5.1 million were due to workplace injury.

This illustrates the importance and scale of work related ill-health. The HSE also reported that 1.3 million people who worked during the period suffered from an illness (long-standing as well as new cases) they believed was caused or made worse by work. Of these 555,000, approximately 43% were new cases. The Chartered Institute of Personnel and Development (CIPD) absence survey for 2010 reported that 3.4% (3.3% for 2009) of working time was lost due to absence, equivalent to 7.7 (7.4 for 2009) working days per employee, resulted in a cost to the employer of £600 for each person annually.

The meaning of health and well-being terms

HEALTH

The World Health Organisation (WHO) established the following definition for the term health. This definition established the ideas that feeling content in one's mind with the social aspects of life and feeling physically well were important aspects of health.

"A state of complete physical, mental and social well-being and not merely the absence of disease or infirmity".

Figure 1-1: Definition of health.   *Source: WHO 1946.*

OCCUPATIONAL HEALTH

The WHO and International Labour Organisation (ILO) issued this definition of occupational health jointly in 1995:

"Occupational health should aim at: The promotion and maintenance of the highest degree of physical, mental and social well-being of workers in all occupations. The prevention amongst workers of departures from health caused by their working conditions. The protection of workers in their employment from risks resulting from factors adverse to health. The placing and maintenance of the worker in an occupational environment adapted to his physiological and psychological capabilities; and, to summarize, the adaptation of work to man and of each man to his job".

Figure 1-2: Definition of occupational health.   *Source: WHO and ILO.*

WELL-BEING

The definition by the Economic and Social Research Council (ESRC) highlights the importance of quality of life. It underpins the concept that physical aspects are only part of well-being, that self-fulfilment and the need for social contact are included.

"Well-being is a state of being with others, where human needs are met, where one can act meaningfully to pursue one's goals, and where one enjoys a satisfactory quality of life".

Figure 1-3: Definition of well-being.   *Source: ESRC.*

"The subjective state of being healthy, happy, contented, comfortable and satisfied with one's quality of life. It includes physical, material, social, emotional ('happiness'), and development and activity dimensions".

Figure 1-4: Definition of well-being.   *Source: Waddell and Burton, 2006.*

Well-being is generally understood to include the whole person, as well as their satisfaction with their life circumstances and their 'quality of life'. In relation to the workplace, it also includes the quality of their working life.

"It should be stressed that definitions of health are very subjective and are often subject to individual feelings and experiences. Health in particular is not merely an absence of disease. Well-being is a particularly poorly defined term and is often linked to feelings of happiness, fulfilment and life satisfaction. On occasions the meanings of health and well-being can clash in that a person can do something which makes them happy, but is intrinsically unhealthy, for example, smoking".

Figure 1-5: Discussion of health and well-being.   *Source: NEBOSH.*

All the elements of an individual's health and well-being experience can affect performance in the workplace.

"Bullying" is an example of a workplace condition that can threaten the health and well-being of the worker, as it can result in physical, psychological and social effects. The results of bullying can include:

- Loss of appetite.
- Substance abuse.
- Family problems.

- Sleeplessness.
- Lack of self-esteem.
- Absenteeism.

Support from the employer to ensure a sense of health and well-being of the worker will ensure a greater engagement of the worker with their employer's business and motivation to achieve the organisational goals of the business. The scope and nature of health and well-being acknowledges that the interrelationship of body, mind, spirit and the social aspects of an individual within the workplace influences the ability of the employer to meet the goals of the organisation.

1.2 - Building the business case for maintaining and promoting the health of the working population

The benefits of building the business case

The recruitment and training of members of the workforce represents an investment by an organisation in that individual and in their overall contribution to achieving the goals and objectives that make that organisation successful. Absence of workers means a greater burden on colleagues and a disruption of the team's ability to meet expectation, which can lead to dissatisfaction and a loss of motivation. If the absence of the worker makes it necessary to provide a temporary replacement, the additional cost to the organisation will affect budgets and/or profitability.

"Health and well-being programmes have a positive impact on intermediate and bottom-line benefits. Intermediate business benefits include reduced sickness absence, reduced staff turnover, reduced accidents and injuries, reduced resource allocation, increased employee satisfaction, a higher company profile, and higher productivity".

Figure 1-6: Economic costs. *Source: TSO, Working for a Healthier Tomorrow.*

Dame Carol Black's Review of the Health of Britain's working age population, "Working for a Healthier Tomorrow", highlights that 175 million working days were lost to illness in 2006. This represented an economic cost to the country of £13 billion, a loss of social standing and a risk of social exclusion for the worker.

"The annual economic costs of sickness absence and worklessness associated with working age ill-health are estimated to be over £100 billion. This is greater than the current annual budget for the NHS and equivalent to the entire GDP of Portugal. There is, therefore, a compelling case to act decisively in order to improve the health and well-being of the working age population - to help ensure a healthy, active retirement, to promote social inclusion and to deliver prosperity to individuals, employers and the nation as a whole".

Figure 1-7: Economic costs. *Source: TSO, Working for a Healthier Tomorrow.*

Following a survey conducted in conjunction with Pfizer, the CBI reported that the UK economy lost 190 million working days to absence in 2010, with each employee taking an average of 6.5 days off sick. The CBI state that 190 million days cost employers £17 billion and that nearly a third of the absences were of a long-term nature, this shows a significant increase since 2006.

Evidence suggests that families without a working member are more likely to suffer "low income and poverty". The consequences of worklessness affect the physical, social and mental health of all members of the family. In particular, children's health, education and life chances are adversely affected. The workplace is a key setting for influencing the health and well-being of employees. Health messages and the working environment can support behavioural change, for example, smoking and eating. Worklessness can lead to a family not feeling part of their community (socially excluded) this leads to added burdens in relation to benefit payments and a reduction in tax revenues, which affects all public expenditure.

"Many common diseases are directly linked to lifestyle factors, but these are generally not the conditions that keep people out of work. Instead, common mental health problems and musculoskeletal disorders are the major causes of sickness absence and worklessness due to ill-health. This is compounded by a lack of appropriate and timely diagnosis and intervention. The costs to the taxpayer - benefit costs, additional health costs and forgone taxes - are estimated to be over £60 billion".

Figure 1-8: Sickness absence and worklessness. *Source: TSO, Working for a Healthier Tomorrow.*

There is a strong business case for maintaining and promoting the health of the working population. This is true on a national basis and on an organisational basis. Reducing the costs due to sickness absence and worklessness enable a lower cost base for the country, and this allows lower national insurance and taxation burden on organisations. Organisations benefit from reduced consequential costs covering work or disruption of services.

Issues increasing the significance of health and well-being at work

CORPORATE SOCIAL RESPONSIBILITY

A definition of corporate social responsibility (CSR) refers to how organisations manage their work processes to produce an overall positive impact on society. This agenda raises awareness of the role that employment plays in not only the life and well-being of the individual worker, but in the prosperity of the country as a whole.

Corporate social responsibility includes the need to consider the issues of sustainability in relation to the work processes and the impact on the local environment of the operation of the organisation. The influence of an organisation reaches out beyond the confines of its immediate operation. It is important to accept the need to consider the effects on the community at a local level and the influence on wider issues, including the contribution of employment to the life of the nation. Organisations in the UK that are embracing their corporate social responsibility are placing greater significance on the extended perspective of health and the additional issues that create strong well-being. This includes programmes of health that extend the healthy life of the worker, addressing lifestyle issues such as smoking, diet and exercise. This is in addition to health risk programmes that minimise the risk to workers' health caused by work. Well-being programmes include an acceptance that the organisation can influence and support a worker's well-being when the worker is dealing with such things as dependents.

THE "AGEING WORKFORCE"

People are living longer than at any previous time, which means more people are available to work at an older age. The Employment Equality (Repeals of Retirement Age Provisions) Regulations (EERAR) 2011 removes the general right of the employer to operate a compulsory retirement age, unless it can be objectively justified. Men and women can now work past the age when the state pension is normally paid. This could lead to an increase in older workers and, as the number of younger workers entering employment reduces, will lead to an 'aging workforce'. This will require employers to take account of the work risks related to the worker's age, which should be done in a positive way. A good workplace policy should be able to incorporate the individual needs of all groups without making them feel discriminated against or singled out. The workplace should be an enabling environment where flexibility and good workplace design meet the needs of the workers. A positive approach to age and inclusiveness will ensure that the older worker will feel comfortable with asking for an adjustment to any aspect of their working life.

The Equality Act (EA) 2010 prohibits the discrimination, harassment or victimisation of workers with regard to their age. This means employers will need to continue to provide support and training for older workers, in the same way that they might younger workers.

Over a million people are working beyond State Pension age, which, moreover, is set to rise to 68 for both men and women by 2046. This is likely to increase the average retirement age, which is currently around 62 years for women and 64 for men.

Figure 1-9: Retirement age.   *Source: TSO, Working for a Healthier Tomorrow.*

Statements by Government officials indicate that the State Pension age will rise to 66 for both men and women by 2020.

INCREASING NUMBERS OF MIGRANT WORKERS

The United Nations definition of the term "migrant worker" refers to the worker who engages or has been engaged in remunerated activity in a state in which he or she is not a national. The term is also used in a general sense in relation to seasonal workers who may move within their own country to seek work for a period. In the UK the term is generally used in relation to the former group, who may have specific challenges in relation to their health and well-being related to integrating in an alien environment. In addition, the introduction of workers from outside the UK may bring workplace contact with people that have not had the benefit of a strong national health programme and could lead to increased contact with communicable diseases such as tuberculosis (TB). The accession of new countries within the European Union has led to an increase of workers from these European countries into the workplace.

INCREASING ECONOMIC SIGNIFICANCE OF SERVICE INDUSTRIES

A service industry is one that does not produce tangible products, but is engaged in meeting the needs of the population. Examples of service industries include entertainment, food, retail, banking and distribution industries. Their significance in the daily life of the nation has grown due to increasing prosperity and the fact that the disposable income of workers in the nation has increased, which has been helped by an increase in the availability of credit. Employment in these industries invariably involves the worker in engagement with customers, often in a direct sales encounter. Many of the industries are characterised by the need for the workers to be available to provide a service when the customer wants it.

This has led to an increase in the number of workers working extended or what are sometimes referred to as 'unsocial' hours. The features of this type of employment provide specific challenges to health and well-being, in particular musculoskeletal, stress and broad social issues.

It is important that these are addressed, as a worker who is satisfied and feels valued by their employer will usually offer a better service and be more engaged in the fulfilment of the service objective.

RECOGNITION OF THE IMPORTANCE OF HEALTH AND WORK-LIFE BALANCE

Those that work in the media often work extended or 'unsocial' hours, which has made them particularly aware of health and the work-life balance. The media tends to reflect the wider recognition by individuals of the importance of health and the work-life balance. Some aspects of health, such as diet, have been considered important for a long time and have been reported on by the media. More recently, topics such as drinking alcohol and the pursuit of fitness are also being focused on. Work-life balance has gained greater significance as the number of women in the workforce has increased, and is often thought of in relation to the needs of mothers and the demands that childcare makes on the worker. Men are also effected if there is a lack of appreciation of their role within the family and the need for them to spend time with their wife and children. The concept of work-life balance is a complex one, particularly as where the balance lies is largely a matter of subjective perspective. The benefits of a flexible approach and the recognition of the wider world in which the workplace exists bring benefits in terms of higher productivity, higher morale and engagement and commitment of the workforce. The employer can become the 'employer of choice' by recognising the needs of all and going beyond the legal requirements, making recruitment and retention of workers easier.

Costs to business of work-related and non-work related ill-health

REDUCING THE COSTS TO BUSINESS

Work related ill-health should be addressed through the systematic management of this risk. This will involve risk assessment and implementation of policies and procedures to meet health and safety legislation. It is necessary for employers to review and update policies and procedures in relation to protecting the workforce from untoward events. This approach to limiting work related ill-health should include risk assessing all new processes, procedures and equipment, as well as proposed changes in organisational structure.

Through this approach, the employer should be able to reduce the costs of work-related ill-health by firstly managing its prevention and secondly managing its effects. The management system should include early diagnosis of the effects of health risks and strategies to retain the worker within work or to return them to work in an effective manner that minimises their absence. Diagnosis within a structured management system could include health screening and health surveillance.

Non-work related ill-health is less within the control of the employer to manage as it is less predictable, but nonetheless good human resource policies should enable employees to seek help at an early stage of any personal health problem occurring. Active steps can then be taken to intervene at an early stage and an appropriate link can be initiated with outside agencies that can support the worker during this period. In some cases, it may be the vigilance of an employer that identifies a non-work related illness and then raises it to the attention of the worker.

Symptoms like shortage of breath and depression may be observed by the employer while the person is working. It is not uncommon for the person not to recognise the symptoms themselves and the illness to go un-diagnosed and treated. This vigilance may help to avert a long-term absence from work by helping to identify ill-health at the earliest opportunity. Organisations will always experience costs related to sickness absence, whether the cause is directly work-related or from a pre-existing condition. The challenge is to intervene as early as possible to minimise the incapacity and thus limit the cost.

INSURED AND UNINSURED COSTS

In 2005/06, a HSE study showed the combined costs to the employer for workplace ill-health to be between £1.7-2.0 billion, more than workplace injuries, which were £1.2-1.3 billion. This included sick pay, administrative costs, recruitment costs and compensation/insurance costs. One of the significant parts of the costs of ill-health is the lost productivity related to the absence of the individual. The amount that this constitutes will usually depend on the ease at which the employees work can be covered and the bearing of their absence on the service being provided.

A highly skilled person that is critical to the provision of service will have a particularly high effect and therefore cost on productivity, for example, this may be a construction engineer or social worker with particular skills. The cost to productivity may be 11 times the cost of salary of the worker. The HSE study showed that the costs of sick pay for work related ill-health were between £1.25-1.49 billion. Administrative costs for ill-health for the period were estimated to be between £19-21 million and recruitment costs were £7.6 million. The study identified that compensation and insurance costs amounted to £440 million.

A study conducted by South West Water determined that, at the time of the report in 2000, the average cost of a case of work-related illness was £8,650. The study recognised that few of the cases in the study included costs of Employer's Liability claims and as workers become more litigious this figure would increase. In November 2008, the Economic Analysis Unit (EAU) of the HSE provided revised figures for an average case of ill-health. They established the cost by considering:

- The human costs estimate is calculated as a weighted average of the human costs of different cases of ill health categorised by length of absence.

- The definition of lost output for a case of ill health is calculated using the length of absence as the average number of days lost due to ill health.
- The resource costs for a case of ill health include administration, recruitment and medical treatment.

This analysis derived an average cost of the three component costs to be approximately £6,700 in human cost, £2,700 in lost output and £800 in resource cost, making the average cost of a case of ill-health to be £10,100 (The costs of the components are rounded making the total cost different to the sum of the components).

Studies by Norwich Union Healthcare and Confederation of British Industry/PPP Healthcare identified that the indirect costs of absence due to ill-health are 1-2 times the direct costs. If we consider the indirect costs of ill-health to equate to the uninsured costs we can see that they are significant. Insurance policies do not cover all costs related to ill-health and may only pay for serious cases of ill-health. Studies conducted by the HSE suggest that the uninsured costs of incidents involving injury, ill-health and damage are typically between 8 and 36 times the uninsured costs. Some of the uninsured costs can be related to equipment and materials damaged in an incident, these factors do not tend to be so significant in ill-health incidents. However, ill-health often involves long periods of absence of the worker. The following 'Ill-health Costs Iceberg' represents the ratio of insured to uninsured costs of work-related ill-health incurred by a typical organisation.

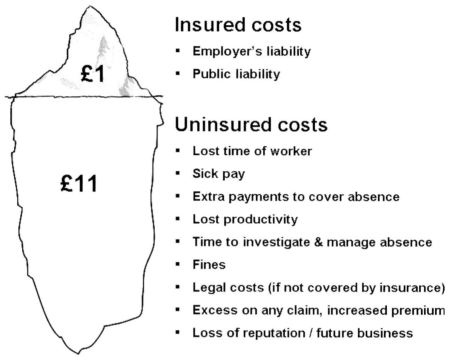

Insured costs

- **Employer's liability**
- **Public liability**

Uninsured costs

- **Lost time of worker**
- **Sick pay**
- **Extra payments to cover absence**
- **Lost productivity**
- **Time to investigate & manage absence**
- **Fines**
- **Legal costs (if not covered by insurance)**
- **Excess on any claim, increased premium**
- **Loss of reputation / future business**

Figure 1-10: Insured and uninsured costs of ill-health.   *Source: RMS.*

EMPLOYERS' LIABILITY INSURANCE

Employers' liability compulsory insurance (ELCI) enables employers to meet the costs of compensation and legal fees for employees who are injured or made ill at work through the fault of their employer.

Under the Employers' Liability (Compulsory Insurance) Act 1969 an employer must have ELCI and be insured for at least £5 million per individual claim. Most insurers automatically provide cover of at least £10 million. ELCI must cover all employees in England, Scotland, Wales and Northern Ireland.

An employer who has been issued with an insurance certificate must display one or more copies of it at each place of business where they employ any employee of the class or description to which the certificate relates and keep copies for at least 40 years. This period reflects the long gestation of some work-related ill-health. It is necessary to establish that insurance was held at the time ill-health could have been caused and who was the insuring organisation at the time.

The purpose of employer's liability insurance is to satisfy a legal requirement for employers to carry such insurance, so that an employee who is harmed due to the fault of their employer is assured of receiving compensation that the employer might otherwise have insufficient resources to pay. At a time of increases in the number of claims and size of awards, and the consequent rise in premiums, this type of insurance is exerting significant pressure on employers to improve their standards of health at work.

The Health and Safety Executive (HSE) is responsible for enforcing the law on ELCI. Employers can be fined up to £2,500 for each day that they do not have appropriate insurance.

ELCI is designed to protect employees who have suffered a personal loss. Separate provision will need to be considered for the many uninsured costs associated with workplace ill-health that may not, depending on the policies carried, be covered by insurance.

Compensation to employees suffering ill-health is covered as a legal requirement, although any excess agreed between the employer and the insurance company will have to be paid, as will any increase in the insurance premium that could follow a claim.

Benefits to the employer

REDUCED ABSENTEEISM

By maintaining and promoting health the employer will reduce the causes of workplace ill-health and in turn the consequences, in particular absenteeism. The employer's management of workplace ill-health cases will ensure that absence is reduced to a minimum, which will control direct and indirect costs arising from the ill-health. The management of ill-health related absence cases should aspire to as early a return to work as is possible. Often the positive co-operation that such programmes provide can make the worker feel more valued. A workforce that feels valued is more likely to enjoy their work and feel loyalty to their employer. Being part of a team and not wishing to let that team down will have an effect on the attendance behaviour of the workers. Clarifying the role and function the individual has within the overall goals of the organisation increases the feeling of being part of the end product and wanting to remain in work to contribute to this.

REDUCTION IN STAFF TURNOVER, LEADING TO INCREASED SKILL RETENTION

Organisations that maintain and promote health are seen as 'positive employers', with values that workers can relate to. This can encourage people to want to work for the organisation and can lead to reduced turnover of workers, as they feel valued and recognise what they may lose by moving to another organisation. This can lead to an increase in long-term loyalty to the organisation and the associated increase in skill retention.

Retained workers become more useful to the organisation and able to contribute to its goals as they gain the skills needed in their role. They also have the potential to develop and encourage others acting as a positive role model to younger and inexperienced recruits within the business.

REDUCTION IN RECRUITMENT AND TRAINING COSTS

The cost of recruitment in advertising the vacancies and then dealing with applications is quite considerable. By retaining workers and making the organisation a desirable place to work these recruitment costs will be reduced. Instead of advertising, the method of recruitment may become by worker recommendation to others and the use of waiting lists of potential applicants. New workers need to learn what is expected of them and in their induction period time is spent helping them integrate into the workforce. This process usually involves the participation of other members of staff who will be not performing their usual role at the time they are helping with the induction of new workers. Reduced turnover will mean that direct and indirect costs of training will not be required.

> *"A successful health and well-being programme will result in reduced absenteeism and a reduction in staff turnover, leading to increased skill retention, and a reduction in recruitment and training costs. It's not all about cost reduction though. A successful health and well-being programme, where employee physical and mental well-being is protected and improved, results in sustained staff morale leading to greater workplace engagement, which in turn drives increased productivity. The benefits are significant, whatever the economic climate".*

Figure 1-11: Healthy people = healthy profits. *Source: Working for Health, Case Studies.*

SUSTAINED STAFF MORALE LEADING TO GREATER WORKPLACE ENGAGEMENT, WHICH IN TURN DRIVES INCREASED PRODUCTIVITY

By maintaining and promoting health, organisations establish a positive workplace where health and well-being are normal. This can establish a strong staff morale, which leads workers to feel valued and more willing to engage with the goals and objectives of the organisation. This in turn creates a reciprocal value of the organisation's goals and objectives leading to increased productivity.

New additions to teams can be beneficial, but they can also upset the dynamics of the long established team. Morale and staff engagement with the goals of the organisation will affect the overall effectiveness of the organisation. The team that is constantly disrupted, with people leaving the organisation and new members joining, is less likely to function well and achieve the overall objectives of the organisation. As a result, efficiency and effectiveness will be reduced.

SEEN AS A CARING EMPLOYER

An organisation that continually appears in the press advertising to recruit employees will arouse questions about why there is such a high turnover. A 'caring employer' label will mean that the best recruits are drawn to the organisation. By this process the quality of work and the volume of output should be increased, with evident increase in success and worker satisfaction.

The lack of early interventions for people off work on sickness absence

Work-related rehabilitation is not generally available within the National Health Service (NHS) in the UK where all patients/clients are treated equally, with access to services based on clinical need not on their occupational status.

This leads to delays in primary care treatment and restorative interventions that would have the potential to return workers to their normal job in a more timely fashion, for example, counselling and physiotherapy have long waiting times. Worklessness over an extended period, 3 to 6 months being a critical duration, can result in the employee losing confidence in their ability to carry out their job and there becomes a risk of them being permanently unable to rejoin the workforce.

All members of the workforce should be registered with a General Practitioner (GP), who will be the first point of contact for a worker who is ill and unable to work. The self-certification sickness absence process will mean that the worker can validate to their employer the first week of any absence from work themself. To help support people who become ill to return to work as quickly as possible, the Department for Work and Pensions (DWP) has reformed the Medical Statement (the 'sick note'). The new Medical Statement (Med3), known as the 'Statement of Fitness for Work', or the 'fit note', came into effect on 6 April 2010.

Once the GP has been consulted, the GP will be able to recommend worker capability/limitations for return to work or alternatively refer the worker to other care services, this maybe in secondary care, such as physiotherapy or counselling. There may be a long waiting time for these services in the public sector, which would affect the workers' ability to return to full work capability promptly.

An occupational service may be able to arrange an earlier referral within the private sector, but this of course will incur a cost to either the organisation or the worker. Smaller organisations may not be able to afford to offer the worker additional help to enable early referral.

An extract from Dame Carol Black's review, "Working for a Healthier Tomorrow", published by TSO, showed the importance of early professional interventions. The study related to two demonstration sites working with psychological therapies in Doncaster and Newham.

Impact of improved access to psychological therapies:

- **Well-being and effectiveness:** 56% achieved measurable recovery, no matter how long they had been ill, comparing favorably with the National Institute for Health and Clinical Excellence's evidence from clinical trials, and with natural recovery rates.
- **Demonstrating health gain:** 90% patient outcome data has been recorded, where previously there was very little recording of this kind.
- **Improving access to treatment:** more than 4,800 appropriate referrals to pilot services in 12 months.
- **Savings for the wider economy:** 5% net reduction in patients on Statutory Sick Pay due to return to work, in line with the programme's expectations (range: 4% Doncaster, 11% Newham).

The return to work before the situation results in worklessness is a key goal in early intervention, for example, 4 to 6 weeks absence from work is seen to be a critical period in relation to back pain and in general cases the critical period is 3 to 6 months. Absence for a duration above this can lead to long-term worklessness. The Royal College of Nursing recommends fast track services in counselling and in physiotherapy.

Implications to the wider community

Strong evidence suggests that generally "good work is good for your health and well-being". It provides a structure for day-to-day living, enhances self-esteem and creates opportunities for social interaction. Work is crucial in personal identity terms, for example, through work the individual is able to provide for the needs of their family. In terms of their place in society and within their own community work is a marker of social standing and status. The economic benefits from work-related income allows the individual to have control over economic choice, for example, paying to use leisure facilities and suitable housing provision. Conversely, individuals who are economically inactive have a decrease in life expectancy and many experience an increase in ill-health from issues, such as smoking, obesity and heart disease, resulting in an increase in the need for health care provision.

Many individuals, not working, experience low self-esteem and low financial state, which can have a bearing on the social and economic stability of this country. Many parts of the UK are experiencing the "transgenerational" effect, where there are generations of families who live on benefits in households where no one has ever worked. All these factors place an additional burden on public expenditure, which is not sustainable for future generations and therefore must be addressed to reduce health inequalities and improve health for all.

TO INDIVIDUALS

The worker who does not rejoin the workforce in a short period of time after suffering ill-health may lose their confidence and become reluctant to return. This lack of work can affect their sense of well-being and their role within their own family. Work helps the individual to feel self-worth and to have a certain standing within their own community.

The motivation to provide for their own needs, or for the needs of a family, is a key part of personal identity that contributes to an overall sense of belonging in the community. The person who is working has the knowledge that they are contributing to society as a whole. The realisation that the "biopsychosocial" (biological, psychological and social) or holistic view of health is valuable as a model for the worker within the life of the community is discussed by Dame Carol Black in the review noted previously, "Working for a Healthier Tomorrow".

THE GOVERNMENT AND SOCIETY FROM WORK RELATED ILL-HEALTH

The cost of sickness benefits provided to those not working due to work-related ill-health increases the burden on government expenditure. This means that in addition to the financial cost of supporting worklessness there is also a loss of revenue for the government from tax and national insurance. A lack of income for the government will result in less revenue for the government to use for providing high-class public services, including the National Health Service, which will ultimately affect access to early health intervention services that are essential for a prompt return to work.

DISABILITY AND WORKLESSNESS

Long-term disability and worklessness can result from a delay in returning the worker to a normal pattern of life that includes work. Failure to limit disability and worklessness in the wider community affects society's moral perspective that harm and suffering should be minimised. The moral effects on the individual worker may be from a feeling of guilt as they may feel a burden on society, and have a sense of hopelessness and a loss of confidence. This loss of confidence may affect their relationships within their own family and the community; social exclusion and isolation may result.

In addition, disability and worklessness can result in significant periods of absence from work and the high costs of sickness absence that result from this. By improving disability and worklessness there will be an improvement of the moral position of the wider community as more people will have a positive outlook.

INCAPACITY AND WORKLESSNESS AND THE LINK BETWEEN WORKLESSNESS AND OTHER SOCIETAL PROBLEMS

Incapacity and worklessness can affect the worker experiencing ill-health and their dependents. The reduction in income can result in child poverty, the effects of which may be that children may be bullied at school, may have to accept free school meals and be unable to join in activities at school that need financial contribution in order to participate. Growing up in a home where the parent is not in work can have a negative role model for worklessness. The overall effect can be compounded if bullying makes children not want to attend school, causing their education to be incomplete and resulting in a long-term negative effect on their life chances.

Meeting legal obligations under health and safety and disability discrimination law

Discrimination law, in particular the Equality Act (EA) 2010, provides employees with statutory protection from discrimination at work, including through disability, age or sex. Therefore, all written policies and procedures must demonstrate recognition of fairness as an overarching objective. However, protecting workers against foreseen health and safety hazards identified by risk assessment would take precedence over discrimination requirements, in the context of work practices. For example, someone who suffers from dizziness would not be employed to work at heights. Pregnant women would not be expected to work anywhere that could reasonably foreseeably harm the health of the unborn child. A structured approach to maintaining and promoting workplace health enables organisations to ensure that legal obligations under health and safety and disability discrimination law are met in a balanced and effective way.

The Equality Act (EA) 2010, through its aim of preventing discrimination against people with a disability, provides a more assured route to employment for those with disability. The EA provides those with a form of disability recognised by the EA, those with a 'protected characteristic', with protection from discrimination, harassment and victimisation. The EA also requires employers to make reasonable adjustments to enable a disabled person to work without being at a substantial disadvantage to other workers.

For more detail on 'Disability', see also Element 2 - Effects of health on work - Equality Act and Fitness to work.

The role of health and well-being at work in systems which promote business improvement

The workplace can play an important role in promoting the health and well-being of all employees at work. Organisations should work with all stakeholders, such as trade unions, safety representatives and line managers, to ensure that the workplace is 'health enhancing'. National programmes that focus on heath and well-being in the workplace must be managed in a way that places the worker at the centre of the improvement process.

The demands to achieve recognition by the organisation will, if managed well, enhance the reputation of the organisation and improve job satisfaction and opportunities for the workforce. Programmes like Investors in People require a thoughtful approach to the development of people; this should include health and well-being issues in order to be judged a complete and effective approach.

Investors in People have introduced an award to recognise employers who have strengthened their organisations by investing in the health and well-being of employees. Investors in People worked with over 400 organisations to develop the framework for the award.

"Over the past five years we have worked with some of the UK's leading employers to analyse the role of health and well-being in the workplace. This is not just about fruit and gym membership, and nor is it about benefits or 'nice to haves'. It is about embedding health and well-being into the culture of the business to ensure everyone benefits. The organisations we have worked with recognise these benefits and we believe this new award will help others reap the same rewards".

Figure 1-12: Health and well-being award.   *Source: Jane Jones, acting Chief Executive of Investors in People UK.*

Figure 1-13: Workplace health issues and their impact.
Source: Investors in People.

Figure 1-14: Health and well-being award framework.
Source: Investors in People.

RECOGNITION AND REWARD
People's contribution to the organisation is recognised and valued.

Evidence Requirements

Top managers	**Managers** (includes top managers)	**People** (includes top managers and managers)
	1 Managers can give examples of how they recognise and value people's individual contribution to the organisation.	2 People can describe how they contribute to the organisation and believe they make a positive difference to its performance.
		3 People can describe how their contribution to the organisation is recognised and valued.

Do: Take action to improve performance

Figure 1-15: Health and well-being award framework - sample.   *Source: Investors in People.*

1.3 - Role and benefits of effective management in workplace health

Planning and organising the management of health and well-being

Effective health and well-being management should be demonstrated by board level commitment. Board commitment is best demonstrated through the appointment of a board member assigned with the responsibility to integrate a proactive health and well-being strategy throughout all aspects of the organisation's operations. The role of this individual will be to provide leadership throughout the organisation, ensuring that all policies and practices are considered in relation to the impact that they will exert on the health and well-being of all workers.

The value the organisation places on the health and well-being of their workers will be demonstrated by the degree to which this aspect of their operation is integrated into the core purpose of the organisation. This integration will mean that the occupational health arrangements provided will need to meet the needs of the worker in relation to the work in which they are engaged. An effective health and well-being approach will go beyond meeting the minimum legal requirements, for example, those required by the Control of Substances Hazardous to Health Regulations, providing a philosophy that permeates throughout the organisation, and which identifies the workplace as a caring environment where workers are valued and invited to be part of the success of the organisation.

The role of line management is to manage the activities of the organisation to achieve the desired outcomes or goals. To achieve these goals the three 'Ms' of management - materials, manpower and methods - should be considered.

The most important resource of any organisation is the workforce (manpower); without them, the other two 'Ms', materials and methods, are either not operational or not fully optimised. The management arrangements of an organisation should focus on the importance of the workforce and ensure the workforce remains effective, including the maintenance of their health and well-being.

The general management arrangements of an organisation will include the need to organise, plan, implement and monitor the performance of all departments in relation to the health and well-being of workers. This is best achieved by setting the arrangements within a formal management system for health and well-being. The management system and associated management arrangement for each workplace will vary in size and composition depending on the activities of the organisation, but will tend to reflect the main elements of a successful health and well-being management system, similar to the one expressed in the HSE document HSG 65, "Successful Health and Safety Management".

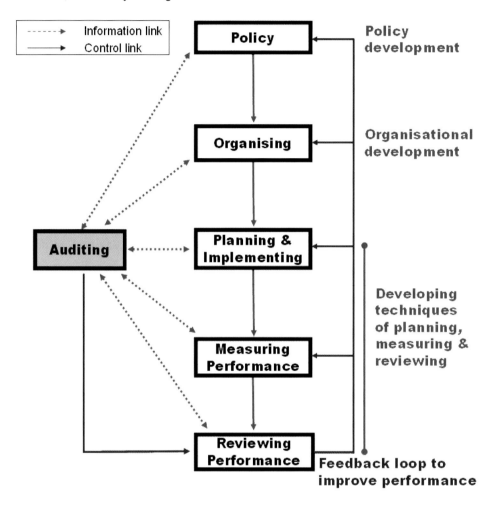

Figure 1-16: Health and well-being management system.   Source: HSE, HSG65.

The management system and arrangements should include mechanisms for representation from the workforce, and where relevant those that represent them collectively, to demonstrate that the views of the workers are valued by senior management. Where provided, the organisation's occupational health services should be represented at the board level. The occupational health team should co-ordinate the health and well-being endeavours and may review their effectiveness and benchmark them in relation to other organisations. An efficient reporting system will need to be in place to ensure senior management know how effective the arrangements are.

Feedback to the board in relation to the benefits of an integrated, systematic approach should include data on incidents that can affect ill-health, sickness absence and adverse workplace conditions. In addition, the results of proactive monitoring and improvements should similarly be included. Staff retention and satisfaction will be an additional indicator of the effectiveness of the organisation's management system and arrangements, for example, high staff turnover could be indicative of poor employee relations because of health issues.

Effects of health on work

Learning outcomes

On completion of this element, candidates should be able to demonstrate understanding of the content through the application of knowledge to familiar and unfamiliar situations. In particular they should be able to:

2.1   Describe the effects of health on work.

2.2   Outline the role of pre-employment screening and fitness to work standards.

2.3   Outline the requirements of the Equality Act (EA) 2010 in relation to fitness for work.

2.4   Outline the potential impact of substance misuse in the workplace.

Content

Sources of reference

Aw, T.C. Gardiner, K. Harrington, J.M (2007) - Occupational Health Pocket Consultant. 5th Edn. Oxford: Blackwell Science Ltd.

Faculty of Occupational Medicine July 2006 - Guidance on alcohol and drug misuse in the workplace. London. FOM.

Lewis, J. and Thornbory, G. (2006) - Employment Law and Occupational Health. Oxford: Blackwell Publishing.

Oakley, Kate. (2008) - Occupational Health Nursing. (Third Edition). Whurr Publications, London.

Palmer, K. Cox, R.A.F. Brown, I (2007) - Fitness for Work - The Medical Aspects. Fourth Edition. Oxford University Press, Oxford.

Waddell, G. Burton, Kim A. (2004) - Concepts of Rehabilitation for the Management of Common Health Problems. The Stationery Office, London.

Waddell, G. Burton, Kim A. (2006) - Is Work Good For Your Health and Well-being? The Stationery Office, London.

Relevant statutory provisions

Employment Equality (Repeals of Retirement Age Provisions) Regulations (EERAR) 2011

Equality Act (EA) 2010

Health and Safety at Work etc Act (HASAWA) 1974

Management of Health and Safety at Work Regulations (MHSWR) 1999

Misuse of Drugs Act (MDA) 1971

Road Traffic Act (RTA) 1988

2.1 - The effects of health on work

Effects of ill-health on a person's ability and performance at work

Someone's state of health could:

- Put their own health and safety at risk.
- Endanger the health and safety of others.
- Affect the person's ability to do their work properly or attend work regularly.

OWN HEALTH AND SAFETY AT RISK

Someone with an existing health problem might be at higher risk of the condition worsening if they were placed in the wrong work environment, for example, for an asthmatic working in a dusty environment inhaling the dust might make the asthma worse. Someone with a heart condition working in a very cold environment may find their blood circulation affected by the cold.

HEALTH AND SAFETY OF OTHERS

A person's health could affect others where a food handler, who had a food borne infection such as gastroenteritis, passed the infection onto others through the food. Similarly, a health care worker, who had a blood borne infection such as Hepatitis 'B', may infect a patient while carrying out procedures like injections or surgery. If a worker had a condition where they may suddenly lose consciousness, such as blackouts, hypoglycaemic attack (diabetic coma) or epilepsy, it could be dangerous for them to operate machinery, drive or work at height. However, these conditions are not automatically a barrier to conducting these 'at risk tasks' as it will depend on how well the condition is controlled or if the individual has prior warning of an event. The Equality Act (EA) 2010 states that employers cannot discriminate against people with health problems that are recognised as a disability, unless there is a serious health and safety risk at work arising from their disability. If a serious health and safety risk exists it is health and safety legislation that takes precedence over disability law, in order to protect the worker and others. *See also - Element 2 – Effects of health on work – Equality Act and Fitness to work - for more detail on 'Disability',*

ABILITY TO DO THEIR JOB PROPERLY OR ATTEND REGULARLY AT WORK

The ability of a worker to do their job properly and their attendance at work must be considered in relation to the Equality Act (EA) 2010, and must not be used to refuse people employment where reasonable adjustments could be made to help the worker to undertake their work in a safe and healthy manner and perform well. *See also - Element 2 – Effects of health on work – Equality Act and Fitness to work - for more detail on 'Disability',*

Temporary loss of ability

Many workers suffer ill-health over the period of their working life. Some health issues may prevent the individual performing their work effective for a short period of time, such as anaemia, which until successfully treated will result in tiredness and possibly poor concentration. When the condition is successfully corrected by medical treatment the individual will then return to normal ability and be able to carry out their work to the same standard as before the illness. One way to address the effect of this temporary condition would be to allow the individual to absent themselves from work or make temporary adjustment to work. An adjustment may be to carry out a less demanding task or work shorter hours. Both the employer and the individual can mutually benefit from this type of temporary adjustment.

Long term loss of ability

Some ill effects will develop over time and may be exacerbated by the age of the individual, for example, rheumatoid arthritis. This initially causes pain and swelling in the joints of the hands and feet and progressively stops them working properly. This disability may eventually prevent the worker being able to do their tasks, either in terms of dexterity or work rate required.

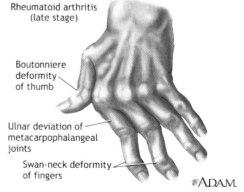

Figure 2-1: Rheumatoid arthritis. *Source: US National Library of Medicine.*

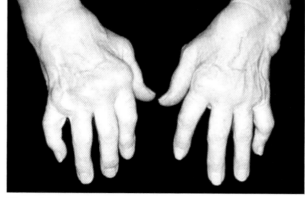

Figure 2-2: Rheumatoid arthritis. *Source: Davidson College.*

The impact of arthritis on the abilities of individuals being able to continue in work will depend on how physically demanding their work tasks are. If the work involves lifting, carrying, walking or standing for long periods then this condition will progressively impact upon their performance level and eventually prevent them carrying out their normal tasks. However, if the individual works seated at a desk, is able to vary their work rate, including taking regular breaks from work, and the tasks do not require high levels of dexterity then their work will be less affected. Employers who recognise these health effects, and where possible look to transfer their workers from the more physically demanding tasks to the less demanding, are able to retain valuable skills and provide continued employment within the organisation. For example, a skilled worker may be retrained as an instructor.

For those involved with desk work, it may be possible to change their work environment or equipment by adaptations, such as providing adjustable height chairs or desks, altering the location and position of supplies to improve reach or access and issuing workers with electric staplers, pencil sharpeners or similar aids.

The UK prevalence and possible effects on work performance of long term health conditions in the working population

DIABETES

Prevalence

People with diabetes mellitus have an abnormally high blood glucose level due to a lack of, or insensitivity to, the hormone insulin, which metabolises glucose. There are two main types of diabetes. Type 1 is more common in children and is caused by destruction of the cells in the pancreas that make insulin by the body's own immune system. Type 2 diabetes is more common in older adults and in adults of Asian and African-Caribbean origin and is usually caused by insensitivity to insulin. Diabetes also occurs more rarely when insulin production is disrupted by certain drugs or other diseases. Diabetes can also occur in pregnancy, known as gestational diabetes. The General Practice Research Database observed in their report "Prevalence of diagnosed diabetes mellitus in general practice in England and Wales, 1994 to 1998", that from 1994 to 1998, the age-standardised prevalence of diagnosed diabetes increased by 18 per cent from 1.89 to 2.23 per 100 males, and by 20 per cent from 1.37 to 1.64 per 100 females. Prevalence increased in most age groups, was higher in males than females in most age groups and peaked in those aged 75 to 84 years in each year. It was reported in Health Statistics Quarterly, produced by the National Statistics Office, that because the population is ageing, the number of males and females with diagnosed diabetes is projected to rise even if there is no further increase in age-specific prevalence. Even with a conservative increase in prevalence of 10 per cent it was predicted that from 1998 to 2023, the number of people with diagnosed diabetes would rise by 44 per cent, from 1.15 million in 1998 to 1.66 million in 2023.

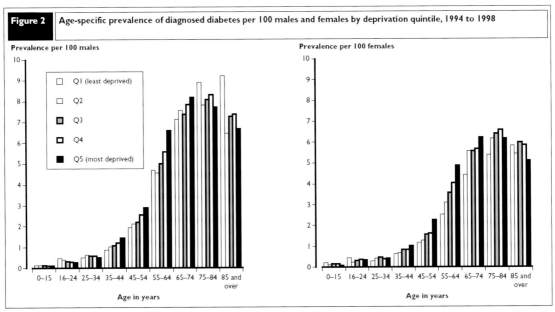

Figure 2-3: Prevalence of diabetes.   *Source: National Statistics Office, Health Statistics Quarterly.*

Symptoms and possible effects on performance

The symptoms of diabetes include excessive thirst and urination. If left untreated, the metabolic disturbances caused by a high blood glucose level can be life threatening. Long term metabolic disturbances caused by high blood glucose level, if untreated, will cause damage to blood vessels and may lead to visual impairment, stokes and heart disease. Progressive effects will result in poor blood supply to the legs leading to increasing incapacity and development of ulcers. Early diagnosis is of importance and health screening is a relatively simple process to diagnose this condition. Many individuals are able to continue to work productively with this condition, except in circumstances where the symptoms may become severe.

People with type 1 diabetes usually need regular insulin injections. Although type 2 diabetes can sometimes be controlled by restricting the dietary intake of glucose, drugs that stimulate production of, or increase sensitivity to insulin and insulin injections are also often used. People with diabetes also need regular check-ups to look for signs of complications so that they can be detected and treated early. Where severe symptoms exist, adjustments in the type of work undertaken will need to be made to accommodate the symptoms, such as deteriorating sight and/or mobility.

EPILEPSY

Prevalence

Epilepsy is a neurological condition which presents in as many as 50 different types. It is the most common chronic disabling neurological condition in the UK. The Joint Epilepsy Council reported in 2004 that approximately 456,000 people in the UK have epilepsy (based on the 2003 census and a total UK population of 59,554,000). This is equivalent to 1 in 131 (0.76%) people. The National Institute for Health and Clinical Excellence (NICE) reported that the Age Standardised Prevalence Rate (ASPR) of Epilepsy in the UK is estimated to be 7.5 per 1,000 (0.75%). Data on the prevalence of diagnosed epilepsy has been derived from the IMS Disease Analyser, which holds data from a sample of GP practices. NICE reported in 2010 that analysis of the data collected between 2006 and 2007 for England suggests that the prevalence of diagnosed epilepsy in people aged 15 years and older is 1.15% (11.5 per 1,000), higher than the ASPR. This provides a good indication of the prevalence of epilepsy in the working age population.

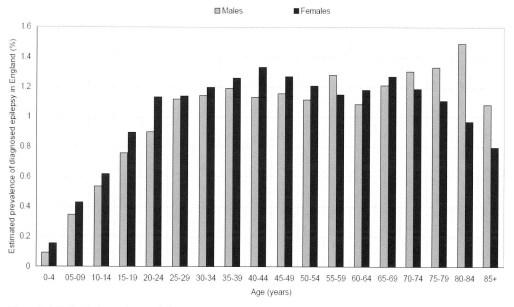

Figure 2-4: Estimated prevalence of diagnosed epilepsy in England, 2006/07.   *Source: IMS Disease Analyzer.*

Symptoms and possible effects on performance

Epileptic attacks, commonly referred to as seizures, result from abnormal electrical activity within the brain, disrupting its normal function. During a seizure, the abnormal electrical activity may cause:

- Muscle spasms.
- Irregular sensations, for example, tingling, unusual taste or smell.
- Emotional symptoms such as fear or joy.
- Unconsciousness.

Partial seizures affect only part of the brain; therefore the symptoms depend on the part of the brain affected. In simple partial seizures the person remains fully conscious and can experience a range of symptoms, such as those related to taste, emotional symptoms and twitches. More complex partial seizures can lead to the person being partially conscious, confused behaviour and repetitive movements.

Generalised seizures affect all or most of the brain; and the person usually loses consciousness. There are generally two phases to seizures, though each phase can occur independently. In the first phase, tonic phase, the person tends to lose consciousness, muscles stiffen, balance may be lost and the person may fall to the ground. In the second phase, clonic phase, muscles jerk and control of bladder or bowel may be lost. During an atonic seizure the persons' muscles suddenly relax and they may fall forwards to the ground, which can lead to injury.

The seizures tend to last from seconds to a few minutes, after which time the individual affected will often return quickly to normal ability. The symptoms for epilepsy are usually treated with prescribed medicines. Most diagnosed patients will go into remission following ongoing treatment and may not experience seizures for a period of time.

Most individuals are able to continue to work productively with this complaint, depending upon the frequency and severity of the seizure. Some work, where the occurrence of a seizure may endanger their person or others, will have to be avoided; typical examples may include driving, working with some types of machinery, work at height and similar.

CORONARY HEART DISEASE

Prevalence

Coronary heart disease is the most common cause of death in the UK, and results in healthcare costs in excess of £1.7 billion per year. The Information Centre, part of the National Health Service, reported data on the prevalence of coronary heart disease derived from the Quality and Outcome Framework (QOF) for 2006 to 2007. They found that the data, derived from actual diagnosis, suggests that 3.5% (35 per 1,000) of the population in England suffer from coronary heart disease. The QOF data for 2008 to 2009 suggests that there are approximately 2.3 million people suffering from coronary heart disease in the UK. The prevalence of coronary heart disease was determined in this survey to be higher in Scotland, at 4.4% (44 per 1,000), than England. The prevalence of coronary heart disease in the population is greatly influenced by age and is higher in men than women.

The British Heart Foundation reported that in 2003 coronary heart disease was the cause of one in five deaths in men and one in six deaths in women. Deaths from coronary heart disease in that year totalled 114,000.

The HSE reported the estimated prevalence of 19,000 for self-reported heart disease/attack or other circulatory illness caused or made worse by work during 2009/10. They also reported a rate of reporting of 63 per 100,000 people that were employed in last 12 months.

Symptoms and possible effects on performance

Coronary heart disease happens when fatty deposits build up on the walls of the coronary arteries. The fatty deposits are called atheroma and the process of it building up is known as atherosclerosis.

In atherosclerosis, fat and cholesterol in the blood builds up on the artery walls. The atheroma can cause the arteries to become narrow preventing the heart muscle from getting the blood supply it needs. This can cause the condition known as angina (chest pains). The reduced blood flow combined with the rough edges of the atheroma may cause a blood clot to form, blocking the artery. This can lead to part of the heart muscle being starved of oxygen and cause a heart attack, myocardial infarction.

Coronary heart disease develops slowly over many years. In some people, breathlessness or chest tightness (angina) when exercising is the only symptom. Most individuals do not show symptoms until they develop chest pains or have a heart attack.

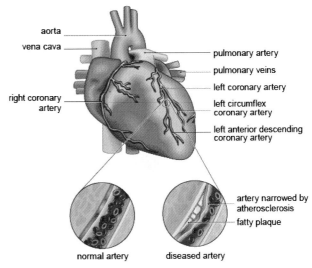

Figure 2-5: Coronary heart disease. *Source: Bupa.*

Medicines are available that can prevent coronary heart disease getting worse, including reducing the likelihood of further heart attacks. With the assistance of treatments and surgery, such as heart bypass or insertion of stents, many people with a heart condition will be able to continue a 'normal' life. Even without treatment or surgery, many individuals are able to continue to work productively with this condition, depending upon the frequency and severity of the attacks and the type of work they do.

After diagnosis, treatment or surgery it is necessary for a risk assessment to be conducted and this compared with the individual's capabilities. For those diagnosed with this disease some work should be avoided, where the attack may endanger the worker or others; typical examples may include driving, working with some types of machinery and work at height.

In addition, there may be limitations on specific tasks that may involve high levels of exertion, for example, manual handling of heavy loads and repeated movement between levels. This will mean that workers with this condition may need to have their usual work adapted to reduce heavy work; the heavy work may be able to be done by someone else or where a job requires the worker to stand doing repetitive work handling objects, analysis might show that the job could be done sitting down, with regular job rotation to reduce fatigue. The need to consider work adaptations may also provide an opportunity to make changes that could benefit other workers. For example, the need to adapt manual handling tasks might lead to the introduction of mechanical aids that assist a wider group of workers.

CANCER

The office for national statistics reported in their statistical bulletin that nearly 300,000 people were diagnosed with cancer each year in the UK, during 2005-07.

This represents 415 cases per 100,000 (0.415%) males and 359 per 100,000 (0.359%) females. Cancer is predominantly a disease of older people - only 0.5 per cent of cases registered in 2007 were in children (aged under 15) and 25 per cent were in people aged under 60. Breast cancer accounted for 31 per cent of cases among women and prostate cancer for 25 per cent among men.

Over one in four people die from cancer. Cancer accounted for 30 per cent of all deaths in males and 25 per cent in females. For the majority of cancers, a higher proportion of women than men survived for at least five years after diagnosis. For almost every cancer among adults, the younger the age at diagnosis, the higher the likelihood of survival.

Symptoms and possible effects on performance

There are over 200 types of cancer. A cancer may cause specific symptoms because of where it is located in the body and what it affects. Symptoms may include a lump somewhere in the body, a cough or hoarseness that will not go away, abnormal bleeding, changes in bowel or urination habit, unexplained weight loss, unexplained pain and feeling very tired.

Some of the above symptoms may have an effect on someone's work, for example, feeling very tired. In addition, the treatment for cancer may have severe debilitating effects, in particular chronic fatigue. The effects of treatment can last for a considerable time after treatment. Naturally, this can have a significant effect on a worker's performance.

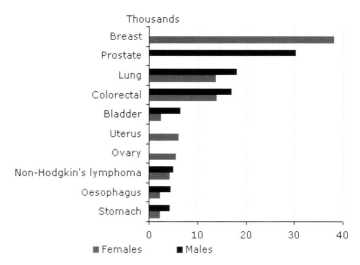

Figure 2-6: Occurrence of cancer.   *Source: National Statistics Office.*

It is usual to make adjustments to the work in order to accommodate the condition and the effects of any treatment. This may include phased return to work, reduced hours, frequent breaks and alternative duties.

 Case Study - High security observer

A 48 year old man had been appointed to a job as an observer for a high security firm. This job involved viewing computer screens for adverse situations, covering 24 hours in shifts, and it required a high level of concentration. Three weeks into his new job he was diagnosed with cancer of the bowel; he was otherwise very healthy. Although the manager was concerned about his health and ability to continue in work, he was allowed to do so. He was having chemotherapy treatment every Tuesday. The company agreed that he could take Wednesdays off to recover and for the first two months he worked only day shifts. He was monitored by his General Practitioner (GP) doctor who communicated well with the company and the man was able to do the job. This helped him to maintain his self esteem and mental health, whilst he was going through a very difficult time in his life. He also stated that his colleagues were supportive, which gave him hope for the future. He made a good recovery and after 3 months was working normal shifts, and was a good reliable worker.

Workers with long term health conditions can generally be accommodated in the workforce, though it may be necessary to make adjustments to their work. In jobs classed as higher risk, fitness criteria should be developed, based on the findings of a risk assessment, and any potential worker assessed against that criteria. People with known long term ill-health conditions may require careful assessment by a health professional who understands the workplace, who will liaise with the person's General Practitioner (GP) doctor if necessary.

This is so that all relevant information regarding the ill-health condition can be obtained and a full assessment made of their suitability to undertake the work or what adjustments may be necessary. *(See also - section 2.2 - 'Fitness for work').*

MENTAL ILL-HEALTH

Prevalence

Mental ill-health is very common in the UK and affects one in four of the population. A report commissioned by the Royal College of Psychiatrists, *Mental Health and Work*, reported that five million people of working age have a common mental health disorder and just under a million a severe condition.

Analysis of sick notes in the Merseyside area showed that one in four people were diagnosed as having mental ill-health. Mental ill-health accounted for over 40% of the time certified by the sick notes issued. The average time of certification was 15 weeks, being nearly twice as long as other conditions.

Mental ill-health can take a number of forms, including depression, anxiety and schizophrenia. *See also - Element 5 - Management of mental health at work.*

Depression

Depression affects a person's mood; they may feel worthless, unmotivated and often tired. Sleep patterns are often disturbed and loss of appetite and interest in daily activities and routines usually follows. Sometimes physical health will be affected resulting in skin disorders, hair loss and stomach ulcers. Often this will result in a downward cycle increasing depression with its associated effects. Depression often goes hand in hand with anxiety.

Anxiety

Anxiety is essentially unrealistic worry about any aspects of daily life.

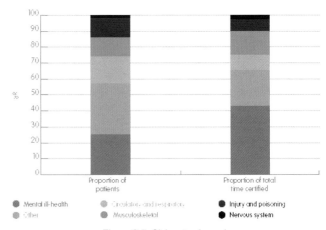

Figure 2-7: Sick notes issued.
Source: TSO, Working for a healthier Britain.

It often manifests its self in restlessness, sleeping problems sometimes with associated physical problems such as increased heart beat, stomach upset, including bowel disorder resulting in diarrhoea. Extreme anxiety may result in panic attacks, a phobia or obsessive compulsive disorder.

Schizophrenia

Schizophrenia is extremely debilitating and can severely interfere with someone's ability to perform everyday tasks and activities. Symptoms often include hearing voices and seeing things that other people cannot see resulting in confusion and withdrawal from social interaction.

Symptoms and possible effects on performance

Mental ill-health symptoms can include problems in thinking, including concentration and distraction; unusual behaviour, including irrational gestures or comments; and accentuated personal feelings, such as lack of self esteem. Mental ill-health will significantly affect interpersonal relationships both at home and at work. It is important in diagnosis and provision of intervention not to focus singularly on the symptoms, but to give consideration to the person as a whole and their work life situation.

One estimate for the UK suggests that, for those with mental ill-health conditions, reduced productivity accounts for 1.5 times as much working time lost as sickness absence.

Despite good practice amongst some employers, the cost to the economy of mental illness is enormous. It has been estimated that a total of 12.8 million working days were lost to stress, depression and anxiety in 2004/5. This costs the country billions of pounds each year.

Figure 2-8: Effects of mental ill-health.   *Source: Shift, Line Managers' Resource.*

Many individuals are able to continue to work productively with mental ill-health conditions, depending on the form and severity of the condition. The most common type of treatment for mental health is prescription medication which may be used to calm an individual or to lift depression or to control disturbing thoughts. Many are helped with medication which enables them to cope with each day, both in terms of their domestic and work life balance. Without medication many would not work or may have become separated from their families. The medication may present work related risks and may limit work performance due to their cognitive effects on the person that takes them.

Medication, of itself, does not cure mental ill-health, and a societal holistic approach needs to be taken to address the many issues that often are manifested by the various symptoms of mental ill-health. (This includes social interaction, continuance of work, family co-operation and support, better working relationships between the employer and the employee). It is usually helpful that workers with mental ill-health are retained in the workforce as it can contribute to improvement of their condition.

Gender specific health issues

Males and females are biologically susceptible to certain common illnesses, but to different degrees. It is increasingly evident that the social and biological nature of being female and male carries certain risks. Until recently there was little attention paid to the impact of gender on men's health.

Throughout the world it has been identified that men are more likely to die than women at almost all ages, including in the womb before birth. Underpinning all of the explanations for these differences are both social (gender) issues and biological (sex) factors. Social (gender) causative issues include, for example, cardiovascular disease (CVD) and diabetes often related to poor diet, obesity and lack of physical activity. Biological (sex) factors are often related to protection for pregnant or nursing mothers. Restrictions are placed by society, often through legislative requirements, which prohibit females, particularly of child bearing age, from certain work activities.

Gender factors, such as a males 'unwillingness to appear weak', is thought to be a significant factor in why many males are unwilling to seek help for physical or mental health problems. Anxiety and depression are reported more often by women than by men in most parts of the world, yet there is no evidence of any biological basis for such differences.

Men are diagnosed with the majority of cancers and have a greater rate of premature death across nearly all disorders, except those of the musculoskeletal system, skin and connective tissue, where women's death rate is higher across all age groups.

Social influences, such as the increased high expectations for achievement of young people, often with inadequate support networks, has resulted in an exceptionally high increase in suicide rates among young men during the last 30 years, and it is now the major cause of death in men under 44 in the UK. There is evidence that young gay men form a significant proportion of these suicides, reflecting an increase in homophobia among young people, which can result in bullying and social exclusion, both during education and in the workplace.

PREGNANCY

Early reporting of pregnancy to the worker's employer is essential in order to allow arrangements to be made for the well-being of the mother and foetus. This is particularly important in the first 3 months of pregnancy, when the foetus is developing. It is at this time that the foetus, if exposed to chemicals classed as teratogenic (an agent which causes malformation of an embryo), may not develop properly and the baby could be born with abnormalities. Work to be avoided would include work with lead or its compounds and work with ionising radiation. Risks to the newly born child continue after childbirth and similar precautions are necessary if the mother is breast feeding.

Health care workers are at specific risk from communicable diseases, such as Rubella (German measles); the baby could be born with physical disabilities such as blindness or deafness.

It is therefore necessary to ensure that women working in health care or with children are vaccinated for Rubella, and other contagions, in order to prevent such life changing events that may impact on the worker's ability to return to work when the child is born. Well-being initiatives should therefore include the importance of workers informing their employer at the earliest time they know they are pregnant, so that the work being carried out by the worker can be re-assessed to ensure that she is not exposed to any harmful agents that could affect her unborn child.

Pregnant workers will have reduced lifting and postural capacity before and for a period after birth so the employer has a duty, when in knowledge of the pregnancy, to make appropriate adjustments.

Figure 2-9: Guide for new and expectant mothers.
Source: HSE, INDG373.

This may include such issues as changes to day work from shift working, prohibition of high risk lifting tasks and increased rest facilities. Regulation 16 of the Management of Health and Safety at Work Regulations (MHSWR) 1999 requires a specific risk assessment for women of child bearing age where they could be exposed to agents that may affect a new or expectant mother or her baby. The regulations require the alteration of hours of work or work conditions if it is reasonable to do so and it will avoid these types of risks. In some cases suspension of the worker may be necessary as a safeguard.

Other health related issues that may have an effect on work

YOUNG PERSONS

Young persons can be at higher risk than the average worker due to their immaturity; their bodies are still developing and can be more susceptible to exposures to chemicals and dusts. Their inexperience in life and work in particular can mean they are more likely to have accidents and need closer supervision and education.

Regulation 19 of the Management of Health and Safety at Work Regulations (MHSWR) 1999 requires that unless the young person is under training, under competent supervision and risks are reduced:

No employer shall employ a young person for work:

(a) *That is beyond his physical or psychological capacity.*

(b) *Involving harmful exposure to agents which are toxic or carcinogenic, cause heritable genetic damage or harm to the unborn child or which in any other way chronically affect human health.*

(c) *Involving harmful exposure to radiation.*

(d) *Involving the risk of accidents which it may reasonably be assumed cannot be recognised or avoided by young persons owing to their insufficient attention to safety or lack of experience or training.*

(e) *In which there is a risk to health from:*

    i) *Extreme cold or heat.*

    ii) *Noise.*

iii) Vibration, and in determining whether work will involve harm or risks for the purposes of this paragraph, regard shall be had to the results of the assessment.

OLDER PERSONS

There is no official 'retirement age' in the UK, although by tradition most pension schemes have entry at the age of 65 years for men and 60 years for women. However, recent problems with company pension schemes, an increased ageing population and the introduction of the Equality Act (EA) 2010 has meant that some organisations are now actively recruiting and encouraging older workers to continue in employment. This Act made it unlawful to discriminate against employees, job seekers and trainees on the grounds of age. In addition, following the introduction of the Employment Equality (Repeals of Retirement Age Provisions) Regulations (EERAR) 2011, workers will be able to retire when they are ready; enforced retirement will only be possible if it is objectively justified. This means that a greater number of workers are likely to be in employment beyond the age of 65.

Employers increasingly see the benefits of employing older workers, including their commitment to working and attendance rates. The health and fitness of older people has improved over the past decades, with better access to health care, improved diet, housing and social activity and therefore it does not necessarily mean that older workers will have more ill health or accidents. They will, however, have special needs as they may not be as fast or agile, but they are likely to be more accurate and reliable. Older workers will require risk assessments of their work as the work or their individual capabilities change (as they may for any other worker), and may require additional adjustments, such as seating to be available when required or frequent changes in activity.

DISABLED PERSONS

See also Element 2 - Effects of health on work - Equality Act and Fitness to work - for more detail on 'Disability'.

2.2 - Pre-employment screening and fitness to work standards

The meaning of fitness to work standards

Fitness to work standards are those standards set out by government, industry groups and organisations to establish the minimum health capabilities a worker would need to conduct a job. Standards are adopted or defined by organisations to assist them when selecting new employees, by using these standards during pre-employment health screening processes. The Equality Act (EA) 2010 prevents the use of unreasonable health standards when selecting employees if this would unreasonably limit the ability of a disabled person from being selected.

For example, it may be determined that it is essential that a train driver has a high standard of visual capability, which may be written into the fitness to work standard for the job; however to set high standards of fitness for someone carrying out a simple packing job may be considered unreasonable.

The fitness to work standards should be derived by careful analysis of the job, considering the hazards and demands of the job. The standards may relate to both the physical and psychological capabilities of the individual. Some jobs may have demands on physical dexterity, others may require high levels of mental reasoning.

The 'health risk assessment' used to derive the fitness to work standards needs to consider a number of factors:

- Nature of the work, and the work demands, for example, physical and psychological.
- How the work might affect the health of the worker.
- How health of the worker might affect work.
- Is there a recognised specific fitness standard.
- The potential hazards.

With any fitness standard, there may be some room for 'professional clinical judgement' regarding new employees who, through ill health or reduced fitness through ageing, may be able to do the job providing additional safe systems of work are put in place. An example of this is where railway trackside workers, whose hearing has diminished with age, may be able to continue to work trackside if the team they are working with are aware of their limitations and the worker can be warned of danger by other means than sound, for example, lights, flags, buddy system. This type of decision should be made by an occupational health professional (doctor or nurse), in conjunction with health and safety practitioners, who are aware of the work and hazards associated with it. This decision may be supplemented by actively monitoring the worker to ensure the measures in place provide safety and the decision was appropriate. The outcome of any health assessment conducted as part of pre-employment screening should address the question: "Is this person fit/suitable to do the job?" The following should be considered if there is not clear conformity with the fitness standards:

- Are modifications to the workplace required? *(See also - section 2.3. for more details).*
- Is there alternative work?
- Is a safe system of work required for this person to do the job?

Setting and judging fitness to work standards

THE ROLE OF PRE-EMPLOYMENT HEALTH ASSESSMENT

The role of pre-employment (pre-placement) health assessment is to:

■ Ensure someone is fit to do the job - assessed against specific fitness standards.

■ Ensure that those with known health problems are not put at risk, or they put others at risk. *(see also - section 2.1).*

■ Provide a reference profile (baseline) of health for the worker entering the workplace, for example, hearing, lung function, vision. This is important for the worker and organisation, especially if there has been previous exposure to noise or dust and the individual may already have impaired hearing or lung function. Both the worker and organisation need to know this, in case there are any future claims and to prevent further harm, for example, due to noise induced hearing loss or occupational asthma.

■ Support an organisation's overall positive health strategy and provide an opportunity for early health education. It can also be used to inform workers of any specific health requirements and/or the positive health initiatives the organisation has in place that the workers can access.

■ Provide an opportunity to review the current fitness standards by actively considering the standards in the context of assessing the health of real people. This enables fitness to work to be set that remain relevant and effective.

THE BENEFIT OF PRE-EMPLOYMENT HEALTH ASSESSMENT

The benefit of pre-employment health assessment is that it enables an employer to:

■ Judge a new worker's fitness to work against pre-defined standards.

■ Not expose a new worker to hazards that may exacerbate a health condition.

■ Make adjustments to work to accommodate a new worker's health condition.

THE USE OF PRE-EMPLOYMENT HEALTH ASSESSMENT

A pre-employment health assessment should be undertaken once the individual has been offered the job and they have met all the other criteria for undertaking the work.

Pre-employment health assessment, means applying appropriate procedures and test in examining an individual to enable a competent person to decide whether the individual is fit for the specific work applied for.

Figure 2-10: Pre-employment health assessment. *Source: RMS.*

The majority of organisations use pre-employment health questionnaires to assess fitness; against fitness to work standards, however, they are sometimes used to screen out those individuals who disclose a health problem to avoid employing them. This practice is unlawful under the Equality Act (EA) 2010. The Equality and Human Rights Commission (EHRC) has the power to investigate the use of prohibited questions and take enforcement action. Pre-employment assessments must not be used to screen out those with health problems unless there is a specific health and safety reason for doing so.

Section 60 of the EA 2010 relates to pre-employment screening. In general, an employer must not ask questions about the health of an applicant (including sickness absence) until a job offer is made, the job offer can be conditional on medical clearance. The EA 2010 allows questions to be asked about health before a job offer is made where:

■ The question is for the purpose of establishing whether reasonable adjustments need to be made to the selection process to accommodate the applicant.

■ The question is for the purpose of establishing whether the potential employee will be able to carry out a *function intrinsic to the work,* for example, where eyesight, hearing, physical fitness, or colour vision standards need to be met by the applicant.

■ The question is for the purpose of monitoring diversity in the range of persons applying for work.

The EA 2010 provides protection for those that have a disability that is recognised as a 'protected characteristic'. Asking pre-employment health questions will not automatically amount to discrimination against an applicant, but acting on the answers may well do. If an unsuccessful job applicant brings a direct disability discrimination claim against an organisation, and a pre-employment health question was asked without good reason, the onus will be on the organisation to show that no discrimination took place. It is acceptable to ask health questions of an applicant when they have been selected for employment and been offered a job. It may be essential to ask questions in order to take action in readiness for employment of a person with a disability.

Questionnaires are useful tools to provide health information on entering employment. This, followed by a physical assessment by an occupational health nurse (or an Occupational Health Technician working under the supervision of an Occupational Health Nurse), would provide the organisation with a reference health profile (baseline) at the start of a person's employment.

Many jobs do not require specific fitness to work standards and could be classed as low risk, for example, some office work, and it may only be necessary to ask the person to complete a basic health questionnaire, which requires a declaration regarding their health capabilities. The information provided could be designed to be medically non-confidential and could be administered by authorised human resources staff. This would enable the employer to make appropriate adjustments to accommodate a disabled worker and would support the requirements of the Equality Act (EA) 2010.

Understanding that most jobs do not require "100% fitness"

There is a misconception by some managers that all the workers they employ should be 100% fit. This is unrealistic, unnecessary and would be unlawful in disability discrimination terms. The main objective of pre-employment assessments is to assess the individual's capabilities, but too often the focus is on the negative 'what they cannot do'. Even in organisations where there is a requirement for workers to be flexible and work anywhere, this should not be used to deny employment to someone who has a health problem or disability, without consideration to making 'reasonable adjustments' or justification for health and safety reasons. *(See also – section 2.3 – for further information)*.

Occupations requiring specific fitness standards and why these are necessary

There are jobs that require strict fitness standards and some that are supported by legal standards such as:

- Drivers of large goods vehicles (LGV's) and passenger carrying vehicles (PCV's) have specific fitness standards that they must comply with. All other drivers must comply with the requirements of the Driver and Vehicle Licensing Authority (DVLA) standards of general fitness to drive.
- Railway workers - such as train drivers, signalling operators and trackside workers.
- Pilots and air traffic controllers.

In the above examples, it is clear that if an individual had certain health problems, for example, where they may suddenly lose consciousness, this would pose a serious safety problem. The consequences of such an event could be catastrophic for the individual, the general public and environment.

 Case Study - Chemical tanker driver

A chemical tanker driver may have a health condition that may affect their ability to drive safely. For example, they may be suffering from narcolepsy, which may cause the driver to fall asleep suddenly without any prior warning.

Should the driver fall asleep whilst driving, the vehicle could crash into other vehicles, the contents of the tank could be spilt or explode, killing or injuring the general public and/or polluting the environment.

Setting fitness to work standards that are non-discriminatory

Any fitness to work standard should not discriminate unnecessarily against someone with a health problem, disability or age, without good cause. The fitness standard should set out requirements that identify conditions that could prevent the worker doing the job safely, for example, not having insulin dependant diabetes, which is not well controlled, would be an acceptable fitness standard for a large goods vehicle (LGV) driver. The fitness standards should also identify specific fitness requirements necessary for the job, for example, a train driver who does not meet the vision standard. Fitness standards need to be specific, based on the actual job, and the hazards to health and safety which have been identified through the risk assessment process. Fitness standards should be set by an occupational health physician, who is familiar with the workplace and associated hazards to health and safety, and should be agreed in consultation with management, the workforce and human resources department. All prospective workers should be assessed against the same criteria, which should be fair and non-discriminatory. *(See also - Element 2.3 - Equality Act and fitness to work)*.

The Employment Equality (Repeals of Retirement Age Provisions) Regulation (EERAR) 2011 removes the general right of the employer to operate a compulsory retirement age, unless it can be objectively justified. To justify a compulsory retirement age, the employer must be able to show that it is a proportionate means of achieving a legitimate aim.

"Proportionate" means that:

- What the employer is doing is actually achieving its aim.
- The discriminatory effect should be significantly outweighed by the importance and benefits of the legitimate aim.
- The employer should have no reasonable alternative to the action that it is taking.

An aim could be "legitimate" if it relates to, for example:

- The health, welfare and safety of the individual (including protection of older workers).
- The particular training requirements of the job.
- Economic factors such as the needs of and the efficiency of running a business.

The aim of saving money by getting rid of older workers (who might, for example, be paid more than a younger worker for doing the same job) is not, by itself, a legitimate aim. It can therefore be seen that setting a compulsory retirement age may be acceptable if an older worker can no longer meet fitness to work standards.

2.3 - Equality Act and fitness for work

The meaning of disability and its relationship to capability, impairment and capacity for work

The definition of 'disability' is set out under the Equality Act (EA) 2010. A person has a disability if:

- They have a physical or mental impairment.
- The impairment has a substantial and long-term adverse effect on their ability to perform normal day-to-day activities.

Capability to perform normal day-to-day activities includes everyday things like eating, washing, walking and going shopping. This will involve such things as:

- Mobility, for example, moving around, walking, standing.
- Manual dexterity, for example, dressing, picking up objects, doing up buttons.
- Physical co-ordination, for example, pouring a cup of tea.
- Continence.
- Ability to lift, carry or otherwise move everyday objects.
- Speech, eyesight and hearing.
- Ability to learn or understand memory or ability to concentrate.
- Perception of the risk of danger.

'Substantial' means more than minor or trivial. A severe disfigurement is to be treated as having a substantial adverse effect on the ability of the person concerned to carry out normal day-to-day activities. This includes impairments controlled by measures that mean, but for the measure, the impairment would prevent them conducting day to day activities; this includes medical treatment or prosthetics.

Long term impairment is defined as:

- Has lasted at least 12 months.
- Is likely to last 12 months or more.
- Is likely to last for the lifetime of the individual.
- Has ceased to have substantial effect, but is likely to recur. Likely means 'may well happen', not 'more likely than not'.

People who have had a disability in the past that meets this definition are also protected by the Equality Act (EA) 2010. There are additional provisions relating to people with progressive conditions. People with HIV, cancer or multiple sclerosis are protected by the Equality Act (EA) 2010 from the point of diagnosis. People with some visual impairment are automatically deemed to be disabled.

Some conditions are specifically excluded from being covered by the disability definition:

- Alcohol, nicotine or drug dependency.
- Pyromania, kleptomania.
- Exhibitionism.
- Disfigurement from tattooing or piercing.
- Hay fever.
- Physical/sexual abuse.
- Voyeurism.

However, the consequences of some of these conditions are covered by conditions like cirrhosis of the liver caused by alcohol misuse or lung cancer from smoking, which could lead to a recognised disability.

People with a disability are not necessarily ill and want to be assessed on their 'capability', rather than on their 'incapability', and the Equality Act (EA) 2010 addresses this.

For example, where an applicant for a job has a visual impairment they may be the best person for the job, but will need adjustment to their display screen equipment (DSE) so that they can do the job. They are not ill, but physically impaired and 'fit' in every other aspect.

20% of the workforces, 6.9 million people, have some form of disability or impairment. Only 17% of people with a disability are born with that disability; the majority acquire their disability during their working life.

Figure 2-11: Prevalence of disability. *Source: National Statistics Office, Labour Force Survey 2005.*

The Equality Act (EA) 2010 also provides rights for people not to be directly discriminated against or harassed because they have an association with a disabled person. This can apply to a carer or parent of a disabled person. In addition, people must not be directly discriminated against or harassed because they are wrongly perceived to be disabled. A person without disability cannot be discriminated against merely because an employer treats someone with disability more favourably with regard to their disability.

Under the Equality Act (EA) 2010, section 138, there is a process for people to obtain information from the person or organisation they think may have discriminated against them. The process involves working through the 'discrimination and other prohibited conduct' forms. They are offered as a guide; there is one form for the person's questions and another form for the organisation's answers. Other forms or a letter may be used to set out the questions, if preferred. Answers are expected within eight weeks of the questions being asked, the answers are admissible in evidence in proceedings and a tribunal may draw an inference from failure to answer questions effectively.

What may constitute a reasonable adjustment

Identifying the need for adjustments to the workplace is essential and must be paramount if organisations are to comply with the requirements of the Equality Act (EA) 2010. Adjustments are important when enabling disabled people to work or when considering the rehabilitation of an employee back to work following a period of sickness absence. Under the Equality Act (EA) 2010 an employer has a duty to make 'reasonable adjustments' for disabled applicants and employees. Adjustments should be made to avoid them being put at a substantial disadvantage compared to non-disabled people. The need to make reasonable adjustments can apply to the working arrangements or any physical feature of the workplace. Adjustments to working arrangements include adjusting working hours. Adjustments to physical features might include replacing steps with a ramp. In addition, if the person is at a substantial disadvantage and it is reasonable, the employer should provide an auxiliary aid, for example, a visual or personal vibration fire alarm for the deaf.

The Equality Act (EA) 2010 defines a physical feature as:

a) *A feature arising from the design or construction of a building.*
b) *A feature of an approach to, exit from or access to a building.*
c) *A fixture or fitting, or furniture, furnishings, materials, equipment or other chattels, in or on premises.*
d) *Any other physical element or quality.*

Action to deal with a physical feature causing a substantial disadvantage is prescribed as:

a) *Removing the physical feature in question.*
b) *Altering it.*
c) *Providing a reasonable means of avoiding it.*

The Equality Act (EA) 2010 prohibits the employer from requiring payment for the reasonable adjustments provided. 'Reasonable adjustments' may include:

■ Adjustments to premises, for example, installing ramps for wheelchair access, providing visual warning signals for the deaf.
■ Allocating some of the disabled persons work to another person, for example, someone who has had a heart attack may be unable to move heavy objects which could be done by a colleague.
■ Transferring to another vacancy. (This does not mean that the business has to 'make a job' for a disabled person, but to see if there are any other suitable vacancies).
■ Altering working hours, for example, not undertaking shift work, whilst undergoing a period of treatment. Changing work start and finishing times. Part time working.
■ Assigning to a different workplace, for example, someone with reduced mobility following an accident may not be able to work in an area where there is a lot of traffic activity.
■ Allowing absence for treatment, assessment or rehabilitation, for example, someone who is able to return to work, but requires continuing treatment such as cancer treatment, or someone requiring physiotherapy or counselling, should reasonably expect to be allowed time off for this.
■ Acquiring or modifying equipment, for example, an employee operating a computer and DSE with visual impairment, might reasonably expect an employer to make modifications to the DSE. This might be achieved by making contact with outside organisations such as the Royal National Institute for the Blind (RNIB), or the local Disability Adviser who would be able to offer advice and support.
■ Training. People with disabilities should be given opportunities for re-training and/or developing new skills.
■ Modifying instructions or work manuals, for example, Braille, or larger font size.
■ Modifying procedures for testing or assessment, for example, someone with learning or reading difficulties may require a more practical assessment or testing and/or be given more time.
■ Providing a reader or interpreter, for example, the visually impaired may require a reader and/or voice activated equipment.
■ Providing supervision.

Reasonableness is difficult to define and causes many legal arguments. When considering what is 'reasonable' for an employer to do, the following factors will be considered:

■ The employer's resources - can the employer afford it and is it reasonable to spend that money. This is particularly an issue for small organisations.
■ The practicability of what is needed.
■ The cost and disruption to the employer.
■ The effect of the steps taken.

📄 **Case Study - Call centre operative**

A call centre in Sunderland identified the need to display large characters on a call centre operator's screen; they acquired and installed suitable software to enable this. Following the change, the operator reached the same efficiency levels as the best of all the other centre operators and commented that "it enabled me to feel I was making a real contribution to the overall team effort".

Relationship between health and safety and disability legislation

The Equality Act (EA) 2010 requires that a worker's disability must not be used to refuse them employment where reasonable adjustments could be made to help the worker to undertake their work in a safe and healthy manner and perform well. However, health and safety legislation requires that an employer and the worker have regard for the health and safety of the worker and others that may be affected by the presence of the worker in the workplace and what they do. Where allowing the worker to conduct specific work would present unacceptable risks to the worker and others, health and safety legislation would be seen as superior to the worker's right to work under the EA 2010. In these circumstances it would have to be proved that the risks of employing the person were high and that it was not 'reasonable' to put in special resources (make reasonable adjustments) to protect the individual and others from harm in that given situation. For example, healthcare workers with blood borne virus infections must not be employed in work that involves invasive surgical procedures.

Risk assessment, taking account of disability

The main factors to consider regarding the employment of workers with disabilities have been outlined above.

However, in any work situation the first approach must be to undertake a risk assessment, bearing in mind the needs of the individual and their capabilities. The five steps to risk assessment should be applied:

Step 1   Identify the hazard.

Step 2   Decide who might be harmed and how.

Step 3   Evaluate the risks and decide on precautions.

Step 4   Record the findings and implement them.

Step 5   Review the assessment and update if necessary.

The main risk considerations regarding disabled workers is whether they create or are at a higher risk than able bodied workers, and whether this risk depends on their disability.

 Case Studies - Disability

A worker with Multiple Sclerosis working in a warehouse may not be as mobile as others working in the warehouse. Additional warning methods may be needed to warn the person of moving vehicles and those driving fork lift trucks should be additionally warned of the presence of a person with limited mobility working in the area.

A worker who has recently returned to work following heart surgery might be at higher risk working in a cold environment. They might require additional protection in the form of thermal clothing and to be afforded additional breaks and changes of activity in order to maintain a good core temperature and limit strain on their heart.

Health and safety must not be compromised, but conversely neither should 'health and safety' be used to prevent a disabled person from working in a role that they could safely carry out, without harming themselves or others.

2.4 - The potential impact of substance misuse in the workplace

Legal requirements on employers

HEALTH AND SAFETY AT WORK ETC ACT (HASAWA) 1974

Section 2.1 of the Health and Safety at Work etc Act (HASAWA) 1974 requires the employer to ensure the health, safety and welfare at work of employees. This requires the employer to ensure, as far as is reasonably practicable, a workplace where there is no risk of accidents, for example, caused by an employee being under the influence of drugs or alcohol.

Section 7 of HASAWA 1974 makes employees responsible for the health and safety of themselves and others affected by their acts or omissions. Therefore if an employee reports for work under the influence of drugs or alcohol they would not be complying with this section. Additionally, section 7 requires the employee to co-operate with the employer on all matters of health and safety. This means complying with policies, which could include substance misuse testing.

It is important to emphasis that a worker who is under the influence of drugs or alcohol whilst working is likely to be a danger to themselves and others. Both the employer and employee have a duty prevent this danger. Therefore the risks related to drugs and alcohol must be managed like any other health and safety risk.

MANAGEMENT OF HEALTH AND SAFETY AT WORK REGULATIONS (MHSWR) 1999

Regulation 3 of the Management of Health and Safety at Work Regulations (MHSWR) 1999 requires the employer to assess risks to health and safety - this would include assessing the risks of the consequences of substance misuse.

Regulation 4 requires the employer to prevent or control the risk; therefore a substance abuse policy is needed and, depending on the level of risk, testing may be required.

Regulation 14 sets out employees duties:

- To inform employers of any dangers or situations likely to cause harm. This means that any employee who thinks someone is working under the influence of drugs or alcohol should report this to their manager. However, it is often the case that workers will cover up for each other, especially if alcohol abuse is suspected. Managers will also try to do the same, but a good 'Substance misuse policy' should address this and allow managers to manage the situation.
- Employees are required to follow instructions by using machinery, substances, transport etc in accordance with instructions and training that they have received. This could include instructions not to operate machinery while under the influence of drugs and alcohol.

TRANSPORT AND WORKS ACT (TWA) 1992

The Transport and Works Act (TWA) 1992 states that it is a criminal offence for certain safety related work to be undertaken whilst being 'unfit for work' as a result of drugs or alcohol. This applies to rail and other rail based systems.

Employers are required to ensure 'Due Diligence'; therefore testing for substance misuse is required.

ROAD TRAFFIC ACT (RTA) 1988

It is an offence to drive or attempt to drive a motor vehicle whilst being unfit though drugs or alcohol.

There is a statutory legal limit for blood alcohol levels, and this applies to all drivers; therefore employers should ensure their drivers - LGV, PCV, van and car drivers are under this limit.

Some companies have introduced a lower alcohol tolerance level as part of their substance misuse policy, which can be done provided the policy is agreed and set up by consultation and is applied to all drivers.

MISUSE OF DRUGS ACT (MDA) 1971

The Misuse of Drugs Act (MDA) 1971 stipulates that it is an offence for any person knowingly to permit the production, supply or use of controlled substances on their premises, except when prescribed by a doctor. This means that if an organisation is aware that drugs abuse or drug supplying is going on within the organisation and does nothing about it, they could be prosecuted.

Section 8 - Misuse of Drugs Act (MDA) 1971

A person commits an offence if, being the occupier or concerned in the management of any premises, the person knowingly permits or suffers any of the following activities to take place on those premises:

a) Producing or attempting to produce a controlled drug in contravention of section 4(1) of this Act.
b) Supplying or attempting to supply a controlled drug to another in contravention of section 4(1) of this Act, or offering to supply a controlled drug to another in contravention of section 4(1).
c) Preparing opium for smoking.
d) Smoking cannabis, cannabis resin or prepared opium.

There are also other industry specific regulations covering particular sectors, for example, the Railways (Safety Case) Regulations (RSCR) 2000 (as amended April 2003) and the Railways and Transport Safety Act (RTSA) 2003 - Aviation. These specific regulations within the transport industry require employers and operators to use all due diligence to ensure that their workers are not 'unfit' for work through alcohol or substance abuse.

Substance misuse policy and disciplinary procedures

Organisations should consider their policy on drugs and alcohol abuse and make it clear to employees, contractors and others who may be required to attend or work at its premises the policy requirements. This is particularly important if it is decided to have a zero tolerance for some or all of its work activities. The policy must state the requirements and be communicated to all staff and third parties, particularly if there is a random testing procedure. It should set out what the outcome will be if anyone is found to be in breach of the policy, for example, stopped from working, suspended, dismissal. The policy must take account of those who may be on prescribed medication and how they should make this known to the organisation, i.e. to whom this should be communicated and how. It is common knowledge that an increasing number of people use illegal substances or drink alcohol in excess, particularly at the weekends and it should be the goal of the policy to deal with such abuse in the interests of both the organisation and the individual. Many organisations encourage their employees to declare if they have taken substances or alcohol before the start of a work period; arrangements are then made to send them home or to reassign them to other duties. This arrangement will normally be linked to a requirement to attend counselling sessions to control or remove their dependence on the substance.

ROLE OF A SUBSTANCE MISUSE POLICY AND PROCEDURES

The role of a substance misuse policy and procedures is:

- To ensure workers do not report for work unfit through drugs or alcohol, nor consume them at work.
- To comply with health and safety requirements in respect of safety critical jobs.

■ To support/assist with treatment and rehabilitation of workers with addiction problems.

BENEFITS

The benefits of a substance misuse policy and procedures are:

■ When there is an incident of substance misuse, management know what to do, roles are clearly defined.
■ It safeguards the business with reduced costs of recruitment and training.
■ Reduced absence and accidents, therefore improved productivity and reduced insurance premiums.
■ Safeguards health, safety and the environment.
■ Improved employee health and well-being.
■ Improves the organisation's image.
■ Contributes to society's battle against drug and alcohol abuse.

It is estimated that in the UK 1 in 20 people are dependent on alcohol, as well as those who 'binge drink' at the weekend and on days off. Millions of working days are lost each year due to alcohol related absences.

Adults in households classified as 'managerial and professional' drank more alcohol than 'routine and manual' households - 13.8 units compared with 10.6 units as a weekly average. Furthermore, around a fifth (19 per cent) of people in managerial and professional households had an alcoholic drink on five or more days in the week before interview. In routine and manual households this was much lower at 11 per cent.

Figure 2-12: Prevalence of alcohol use.   Source: The annual report, smoking and drinking among adults, 2008 (the general lifestyle survey).

The report highlights the fact that on average adults in 2008 consumed 12.2 units of alcohol a week compared to 13.5 units in 2006, reflecting a continuing downward trend since 2002. Heavy drinking exceeding 8 units for men and 6 units for women was most common in the 16-24 (27%) and 25-44 (23%) age groups. Those 45 and over were twice as likely to drink every day of the week as those under 45. It is estimated that the cost to the UK economy is several £billions per year for drug and alcohol related absenteeism and associated poor work performance.

DEVELOPING A SUBSTANCE MISUSE POLICY

It is good practice to have a policy even if there is no evidence of current substance misuse. An established policy will enable the organisation to deal with any future problems that may arise and help to monitor the situation.

In order to achieve clarity and consistency in dealing with what is a difficult issue, it is advisable to have a policy that covers alcohol and all other substances of abuse, including illegal drugs and issues such as 'glue sniffing' and 'solvent abuse', as they should all be managed in a similar way. However, it must be remembered that the use of drugs (other than those prescribed by a doctor) is illegal, whereas alcohol consumption is not; therefore, there should be a specific reference to illegal drug use by employees and how this will managed. The policy must be developed to meet the needs of the specific organisation, and might include testing workers for the presence of drugs and alcohol in their system.

The first action when establishing a substance misuse policy must be for management to undertake a 'risk assessment', bearing in mind the need to prevent and control adverse health and safety incidents, particularly in activities involving chemicals, electricity, radiation, rail, large goods vehicles (LGV), forklift truck, dangerous machines, working at heights and working in confined spaces. Once the risk assessment has been carried out the company should set up a working group to develop the policy, based on the findings of the risk assessment.

This group should include management, and worker representative(s), human resources department, occupational health nurse and/or doctor (if the organisation has one or another health professional from outside the company) who has knowledge of substance misuse. It will be the role of this group to develop the policy and work together to successfully implement and monitor the policy. The policy must be 'open' and 'caring', with all parties signing up to it.

Scope of the policy

The substance misuse policy should cover:

■ How it will operate, who is responsible for its implementation and management.
■ Who it will apply to - it should include everyone in the business; otherwise it could be seen to be discriminatory such as, if it allows certain people to consume alcohol whilst at work, for example, sales representatives or managers lunchtime entertainment. Contractors should also be included.
■ When it will apply - if the organisation decides that at certain times alcohol consumption is permitted, for example, special occasions, Christmas parties, then this should be stipulated and how it will be controlled.
■ If testing is included and how it will be done - this will depend on the findings of the risk assessment and if there are safety critical situations. Details of the process and procedures for testing should be included.
■ What will be the disciplinary and appeals procedures - this must set out what is expected of the worker and what the consequences of non-compliance will be. Will the organisation have a limit of tolerance such as an alcohol limit or is 'just smelling of alcohol' sufficient for suspension from work? Will suspension be on full pay whilst there is an investigation? It will also be necessary to detail what is the organisation's stance on positive tests (if testing is carried out), what will happen - would it mean instant dismissal or a second chance?

■ Procedures for support, including counselling and treatment - every policy of this type must include procedures to support workers who may have an addiction problem. However, the circumstances of this support must be specified in the policy, so that it is clear what will happen, and what would be the consequences of failing to complete a treatment or counselling programme.

Main substances misused and their effects on the individual

ALCOHOL

Even at low levels of consumption the body is affected by alcohol, reducing reaction time and impeding co-ordination. It also affects thinking, judgement and mood and can have a significant effect on behaviour when conducting routine work. Whilst large amounts of alcohol in one session can put a strain on the body's functions, in particular the liver, it can also affect muscle function and stamina.

Drinking alcohol raises the drinker's blood pressure and this can increase the risk of coronary heart disease and some kinds of stroke. Regularly drinking more than the 'daily benchmarks' also increases the risk of cirrhosis of the liver. The effect of alcohol is not limited to physical effects - people who drink very heavily may develop psychological and emotional problems, including depression.

Alcohol is absorbed into your bloodstream within a few minutes of being drunk and carried to all parts of your body including the brain. The concentration of alcohol in the body, known as the 'blood alcohol concentration', depends on many factors, but principally, how much you have drunk, how long you have been drinking, whether you have eaten, and your size and weight. It is difficult to know exactly how much alcohol is in your bloodstream or what effect it may have. It takes a healthy liver about 1 hour to break down and remove 1 unit of alcohol. A unit is equivalent to 8 gm or 10 ml (1cl) of pure alcohol. The following all contain one unit of alcohol: A half pint of average strength beer, lager or cider (3.5%ABV), a single 250ml measure of spirits (40%ABV), a small glass of wine (9%ABV). If someone drinks 2 pints of ordinary strength beer at lunchtime or half a bottle of wine (i.e. 4 units), they will still have alcohol in their bloodstream 3 hours later. Similarly, if someone drinks heavily in the evening they may still be over the legal drink drive limit the following morning. Black coffee, cold showers and fresh air won't sober someone up. Only time can remove alcohol from the bloodstream.

Figure 2-13: The effects of alcohol.   *Source: HSE "Don't mix it!" IND(G)240L 11/96.*

Many organisations reflect the national limit for driving when deciding if an individual has too much alcohol in their system to be allowed to work. Other organisations that are involved in safety critical work have established a zero level of alcohol approach for those involved in safety critical work. The legal limit of alcohol in the body is:

■ 35 micrograms (μg) per 100 millilitres of breath.

■ 80 milligrams (mg) per 100 millilitres of blood.

■ 107 milligrams per 100 millilitres of urine.

This limit is often equated to two pints (4 units) of ordinary strength beer. For an average weight male this is said to be a rough approximation, but should not be used as a general rule. There are significant differences between male and female absorption rates and many physiological factors combine to affect the amount of alcohol showing in the system.

PRESCRIBED AND 'OVER THE COUNTER' (OTC) DRUGS

It may be appropriate for the substance misuse policy to include a requirement for workers to declare if they are taking medication prescribed by a doctor or bought from retail outlets or pharmacies without prescription. Workers should be advised that it might not be safe to take prescribed or freely available medication; for safety reasons; this will depend on the safety critical nature of the work.

They should be advised to seek advice from the prescribing doctor or pharmacist regarding any possible side effects likely to affect their ability to work.

In the rail sector, workers in safety critical roles, for example, train drivers, signalling staff, trackside workers have to report to their line manager if they have been prescribed or are taking medication that is likely to affect their ability to do their job safely. The manager then may have to make reasonable work adjustments to allow the person to work or the worker may be prohibited from carrying out their safety critical role until any effects have been monitored.

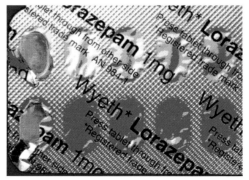

Figure 2-14: Example of Benzodiazepines. *Source: RMS.*

ILLEGAL (CONTROLLED) DRUGS

The effects on the workplace of some drugs can be catastrophic if a worker is a regular user, and even the casual user may not be fully fit for work on a Monday morning, or any other day. The effects of cannabis can continue for up to 3 weeks in the heavy user. It is imperative that organisations take the issue of substance misuse seriously in order to protect health and safety, especially in high risk activities such as chemical, nuclear and transport etc.

Cannabis

Cannabis is a resinous substance usually presented as lumps, leaves, stalks or seeds. It is usually taken rolled with tobacco into a 'spliff', 'joint', 'reefer' and smoked. It can alternatively be smoked in a pipe or 'bong' (which is a homemade implement normally made from a can); it is sometimes eaten. The common street names for cannabis are Marijuana, Pot, Hash, Ganga, Grass, Blow, Weed, Resin, Dope.

According to some studies, cannabis has more than 400 different chemical compounds and contains even more cancer-causing agents than are found in tobacco. Even low doses of the drug can interfere with coordination, perception of time, reasoning and judgment, making driving under its influence extremely dangerous.

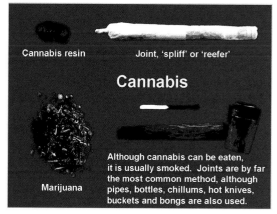

Figure 2-15: Cannabis. *Source: RMS.*

The effects on the individual are as follows:

- Euphoria.
- Slow reactions.
- Poor co-ordination.
- Short term memory affected.
- Distortion in perception of space and time.
- Drowsiness.
- Inability to think clearly.
- Anxiety and depression.

Depressants

Substance	Name and street names	Effects
Alcohol (not illegal, included for comparison only).	Beer, wine, spirits.	Drunkenness. Hangovers.
Opiates.	Morphine, heroin - Smack, Scag, Stuff.	Drowsiness. Inability to concentrate.
Tranquillisers.	Barbiturates, Benzodiazepines - Benzo's, Downers.	Poor co-ordination. Slow reactions. Anxiety and depression. Overdose.

Opiates

Heroin, Opium, Morphine, and Codeine are used legally by the medical profession to relieve pain, but they are taken illegally for their mood-altering effects. Opiates will begin to affect the central nervous system almost immediately after use. Because the drug suppresses the central nervous system the user experiences 'cloudy' mental function, breathing slows and may reach a point of respiratory failure. They are extremely physically and psychologically addictive drugs. Health issues that may arise from their use can include congested lungs, liver disease, tetanus, infection of the heart valves, skin abscesses, anaemia and pneumonia. Death can occur from overdose.

Tranquilisers

Tranquilisers act by enhancing the effects of a brain chemical transmitter that depresses or calms the central nervous system, slowing down mental activity. As the brain gets used to the drug more of it is required to obtain the same level of effect, and this can lead to an addiction to the drug.

Stimulants

Substance	Name and street names	Effects
Amphetamines.	Speed, Whiz, Billy, Amph, Pep Pills.	Aggression. Increased confidence.
Cocaine.	Coke, Snow, Charlie.	Tendency to take risks.
3,4-Methylenedioxymethamphetamine.	Ecstasy, E's, Doves, XTC, MDMA.	Post stimulation fatigue.

Amphetamines

Amphetamines increase levels of the neurotransmitters dopamine and noradrenaline in the brain, and prevent these chemicals from being re-absorbed. This leads to their stimulant effects, making people feel more lively, awake, energetic and confident. Improved focus, concentration and wakefulness mean they are a useful treatment for narcolepsy. There may be a mild euphoria (more intense if the drug is injected) and ability to stay awake for hours without feeling tired. Amphetamines have powerful health effects, increasing breathing, heart rate and temperature, dilating the pupils and suppressing the appetite. When amphetamines are snorted they produce effects within three to twenty minutes, with effects lasting for up to about eight hours. As the drug wears off, the person may become anxious, irritable and restless, but even when they feel desperate for sleep the drug may continue to keep them awake. Finally, exhaustion and often intense mood swings affect the user. Taking large amounts of amphetamines, especially over a short space of time, can lead to marked psychological problems, especially a sense of panic and paranoia and extreme exhaustion. In the long term, there may be chronic sleep deprivation with reduced performance of work and disruption of relationships.

Cocaine

Cocaine can be snorted, injected and even smoked in some forms of the drug. In all cases cocaine is a strong central nervous system stimulant that affects the brain's processing of dopamine. Cocaine is very addictive, as it is hard to resist the craving and strong psychological dependence due to changes in the brain. Cocaine can be snorted, injected and even smoked in some forms of the drug. In all cases cocaine is a strong central nervous system stimulant that affects the brain's processing of dopamine. When cocaine is used it interferes with the re-absorption of dopamine, a brain chemical associated with pleasure and movement, producing a euphoric effect. Shortly after cocaine is taken the user may experience symptoms such as constricted blood vessels, dilated pupils, increased body temperature, increased heart rate and higher blood pressure.

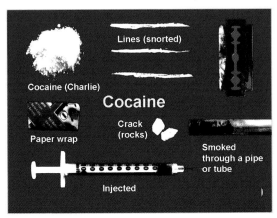

Figure 2-16: Cocaine.   *Source: RMS.*

During the euphoric period after cocaine use, which can last up to 30 minutes, user will experience hyperstimulation, reduced fatigue, and mental alertness. However, some users also experience restlessness, irritability, and anxiety. When cocaine is taken repeatedly over a short period users may experience increasing restlessness, irritability and paranoia. Repeated, long term cocaine use can cause irregular heart beat, heart attack, chest pain, respiratory failure, stroke, seizures, headaches, abdominal pain and nausea. Chronic users of cocaine can become malnourished due to the drug's ability to decrease appetite. Each method of taking cocaine can produce specific health effects, for example, snorting can lead to a chronically runny nose, nosebleeds, loss of smell, hoarseness, and problems swallowing.

3,4-Methylenedioxymethamphetamine (MDMA)

MDMA has both stimulant and psychedelic properties. It is often taken for the feelings of well-being (including emotional warmth, empathy toward others, decreased anxiety) and stimulation (mental and physical), as well as the distortions in time and sensory perceptions that it produces. Some users report undesired effects like anxiety, agitation and recklessness. Specific adverse health effects include nausea, chills, sweating, involuntary teeth clenching, muscle cramps and blurred vision. In the hours after taking MDMA it causes significant reduction in mental abilities that can last for a week, particularly those affecting memory. The fact that MDMA impairs information processing could present dangers for those involved in safety critical work requiring complex or skilled activities, such as driving a car or train, while under the influence of the drug.

Effects on other workers and their reluctance to report misuse

The effects of substance misuse in the workplace can affect everyone. Workers suffering from the effects of substance misuse may be in safety critical jobs, which may lead to the lives of other workers and the public being put at risk. In addition, the affected worker's behaviour, manner and attendance may put additional pressure on the existing workforce to do their job for them.

Fellow workers may feel reluctant to report observed misuse because they feel it would not be in the best interests of the person misusing or because they misuse substances occasionally and it would reflect badly on themselves.

Care should be taken to emphasise to the workforce that it is their duty to report fellow workers who may be under the influence of substances at work and it is in the long term best interest of the individual affected and those who may be affected by their work. In order to minimise the reluctance of people to report substance misuse it may be necessary to have confidential reporting. It should be emphasised that those reporting should not feel guilty for bringing it to the organisation's attention.

Looking for signs of substance misuse

All members of the workforce and management should know what is expected of them when applying the substance misuse policy. This will include developing skills to identify the symptoms of substance misuse, for example, poor attendance, particularly following week-ends or behavioural changes, such as lethargy or mood swings. When changes occur in workers that might indicate substance misuse it is important not to make presumptions without confidential analysis. The changes may not be as a result of substances misuse. For example, changes may be due to:

- Increased work demands that have become a stressor and affect the workers' behaviour adversely.
- Work life issues, such as the need to care for a highly dependant family.
- Relationship or family changes, such as divorce, separation or bereavement.
- Personal health problems, such as anaemia.

There should be careful documentation of these changes as part of the analysis. The following may be indicators of a worker with a substance misuse problem.

CHANGES TO THE INDIVIDUAL'S BEHAVIOUR

Changes to the individual's behaviour that might indicate substance misuse include:

- Sudden mood changes.
- Unusual irritability or aggression.
- Tendency towards confusion.
- Fluctuations in concentration and energy.
- Impaired job performance.

- Poor time keeping.
- Increased sickness.
- Deterioration in relationships - colleagues, managers, customers, family.
- Dishonesty and theft.

DRUG PARAPHERNALIA

The presence of the following drug paraphernalia in an individual's possessions in the workplace might indicate substance misuse, including:

- Syringes and needles.
- Bloodstained cotton wool or handkerchiefs.
- Ligatures.
- Scorched tin foil or spoons with the base burnt.
- Small pipes or bongs.
- Small mirror, razor blades or straws.
- Can, bottle with tubes.
- Lemon juice containers.

- Small twists and squares of polythene, cling film or paper used for holding powder.
- Home rolled cigarettes and papers.
- Rolled up cardboard filters.
- Alcohol cans and bottles.
- Alcohol smells, particularly on the breath or in atmosphere of confined areas where workers work alone.

If time keeping and/or absenteeism is an issue, this should be carefully documented as 'evidence', as when the individual is confronted with the managers concerns, they are likely to deny there is a problem. The management of this should be closely linked to the businesses 'Management of Attendance policy'. *(See also - Element 4 - Management of attendance).*

Requirement for risk assessment to include substance misuse

General risk assessment, as required under the Management of Health Safety at Work Regulations (MHSWR) 1999 and specific legislation such as the Electricity at Work Regulations (EWR) 1989, require the employer to consider all factors that influence risk to workers and others affected by their work. This will require the employer to identify safety critical posts and safety critical tasks that may be unduly affected by the influence of substance misuse or medication taken by workers.

Drug and alcohol testing in the workplace

The decision to carry out drug and alcohol testing must be a well thought through decision, based on a risk assessment to establish why it is needed. Consideration should be made as to its purpose, how it is to be carried out and legal implications. Issues that need to be addressed include:

- The people the testing policy cover will cover and why - safety critical posts alone or the whole workforce.
- The penalties of a positive test - this must be stated within the substance misuse policy.
- Systems to educate and inform the workforce of the policy and how it applies to them.
- The help available to workers who have a substance misuse addiction problem.
- Confidentiality and human rights assurances.

The Human Rights Act (HRA) 1998 confers a right to privacy and has been used as a defence against testing employees for substance misuse. However, case law has implied that where there are justifiable safety grounds for testing this will not violate the HRA 1998.

ROLE OF DRUG AND ALCOHOL TESTING

The role of drug and alcohol testing is to establish if workers are under the influence of drugs and alcohol and to what extent. Testing has a role at the following times:

- Pre-employment.
- Following an accident or incident as part of the investigation.
- Where the behaviour of an individual gives cause for concern.
- Unannounced and/or random testing, particularly for safety critical workers.
- As part of the rehabilitation programme.

TESTING FOR SUBSTANCES OF MISUSE

Workplace testing must be carried out by a competent person, who is trained in the correct procedures. There are a number of laboratories and companies who specialise in this work. Any testing provider should be confirmed to be accredited to the ISO 17025 for laboratory quality and also participate in the UK National Quality Assurance Scheme. Testing can be carried out in several ways:

- Point of contact testing, for example, breath analysis or mouth swab for alcohol, or dipstick to detect misuse of drugs.
- Laboratory testing of urine, blood or hair samples. Urine testing is the preferred method as it is less invasive. Laboratory testing should always be used to confirm the positive results of point of contact testing.

Chain of custody

Chain of custody is a secure method for tracking and auditing the sample from donation, through laboratory analysis, to the final report. It is also a mechanism for notifying the laboratory of specific information related to the analysis, such as use of medication by the person being tested. It also ensures anonymity. The collected sample is normally split into 2 samples at the point of collection. If a positive result is reported on the first sample, the individual can challenge the result and have the second sample tested independently. Every stage of the procedure must be audited to enable complete tracking of the sample from collection, so that the integrity of the sample can be validated.

Managing the results

In order to ensure that testing is fair and results are accurate a Medical Review Officer (MRO) is required. The MRO's role is to interpret results, determine if there is evidence of misuse and whether there are other factors affecting the evidence, like use of prescribed or over the counter (OTC) medication. The MRO is an independent doctor who will review positive results to remove the risk of reporting 'false positive's'.

This is done by:

- Reviewing declared medication - if an individual has taken prescribed or OTC medication it can be assessed by the MRO. The MRO will consult with the laboratory toxicologist to assess if the level of drug found is in keeping with the declared medication taken. The toxicologist will inform the MRO of the safe 'cut off levels', which are the levels above which it would indicate drug misuse.
- The MRO will review the medical history of the individual to assess if they are on medication likely to produce a positive result.
- Liaising with the laboratory toxicologist as required.

Facilitating the care, treatment and support of workers with substance misuse problems

The treatment and support of workers with substance misuse problems must be included within the main policy and must include the following:

- A written procedure about what the organisation will provide, such as detoxification treatment or counselling, and how this will be managed.
- What is involved - most organisations that provide support and treatment will expect the individual to sign an agreement for support and will be expected to comply. This is in order that the organisation can see the worker is committed to and wants help.
- The issue of confidentiality of the information must be secured and only relevant information given to the manager, with the worker's consent.
- What time off will be given for treatment and counselling - normally organisations treat substance misuse problems as they would other health problems and this should be reflected in the 'managing attendance policy'.

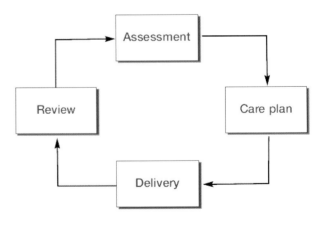

Figure 2-17: The cycle of care. *Source: SCAN.*

- Details of what will happen if someone has a relapse of treatment, how long can the treatment last and what will be the outcome of failure to comply.
- What the disciplinary procedures will be - what, when and how will they be implemented.

The 'care' element of the substance misuse policy is important to its success. Otherwise the policy will be seen only as a 'disciplinary tool' and will not achieve its aim of providing a safer and healthier workplace and workforce. For its ongoing success it will require the individual to be periodically reviewed by an occupational health specialist to ensure no remission in their progress.

Effects of work on health

Learning outcomes

On completion of this element, candidates should be able to demonstrate understanding of the content through the application of knowledge to familiar and unfamiliar situations. In particular they should be able to:

3.1 Identify the scope and nature of possible detrimental effects of work on health.

3.2 Identify emerging workplace health risks which may have an increasing significance in the future.

3.3 Outline the positive benefits of work on health.

3.4 Outline how patterns of work can affect health and what control measures can be adopted.

3.5 Outline the role and function of health surveillance.

3.6 Outline the procedure for formal reporting of diagnosed occupational diseases.

3.7 Identify the role and benefits of exposure monitoring to hazardous agents.

3.8 Outline what may constitute a healthy working environment.

Content

Sources of reference

Aw, T.C. Gardiner, K. Harrington, J.M (2007) - Occupational Health Pocket Consultant. (Fifth edition). Oxford: Blackwell Science Ltd.

Black C. (2008) - 'Working for a Healthier Tomorrow: a review of the health of Britain's working age population'. TSO London.

DWP, DH (Nov 2008) - 'Improving health and work: changing lives'. The Government's response to Dame Carol Black's review of the health of Britain's working age population. TSO London.

Lewis Joan, Thornbory Greta (2006) - 'Employment Law and Occupational Health'. A practical handbook. Blackwell, Oxford.

Lewis, J. and Thornbory, G. (2006) - Employment Law and Occupational Health. Oxford: Blackwell Publishing.

Oakley, Kate. (2008) - Occupational Health Nursing. (Third Edition). Whurr Publications, London.

Palmer, K. Cox, R.A.F. Brown, I (2007) - Fitness for Work - the Medical Aspects. Fourth Edition. Oxford University Press, Oxford.

Waddell Gordon, Burton A Kim (2006) - 'Is work good for your health and well-being?' The Stationery Office (TSO) London.

Waddell, G. Burton, Kim A (2004) - Concepts of Rehabilitation for the Management of Common Health Problems. The Stationery Office, London.

Relevant statutory provisions

Control of Asbestos Regulations (CAR) 2006

Control of Lead at Work Regulations (CLAW) 2002 Third edition

Control of Noise at Work Regulations (CNWR) 2005

Control of Substances Hazardous to Health Regulations (COSHH) 2002 (as amended)

Control of Vibration at Work Regulations (CVWR) 2005

Management of Health and Safety at Work Regulations (MHSWR) 1999

Working Time Regulations (WTR) 1998 (as amended)

Workplace (Health Safety and Welfare) Regulations (WHSWR) 1992

3.1 - Scope and nature of the detrimental effects of work on health

Causes, effects and management of work-related ill-health issues

INTRODUCTION

This section is intended to provide an introduction to the effects of work on health and performance. The hazards outlined were chosen to represent the most prevalent work-related ill-health issues. However, the main causes of work -related ill-health, namely stress and musculoskeletal disorders, are covered in detail in separate sections. *(See also - Element 5 - Management of mental health at work and Element 6 - Management of people with musculoskeletal disorders).* In order to understand the effects of work on health it is necessary to understand the working environment and how this might impact on the individual's health.

Physical hazards

These are hazards that cause physical effects on the body:

- Noise - from grinding, cutting or pneumatic powered equipment, which may cause occupational noise induced hearing loss (ONIHL).
- Vibration - from vibrating tools/equipment such as drills, chain saws, grinders and concrete breakers, which may cause hand-arm vibration syndrome (HAVS), or whole body vibration syndrome affecting seated drivers of heavy rough terrain vehicles used on construction sites or farms.
- Heat/cold - excessive heat or cold, from work in laundries, foundries, cold storage warehouses, may have detrimental effects on the body temperature regulating mechanism, leading to heat stroke, or in the case of a cold environment affect the circulation and heart.
- Radiation - is a form of energy and comes in different types, ionising and non-ionising, which may, depending on the type of radiation, cause cataracts, dermatitis, cancer and genetic damage.

Chemical hazards

These are hazards that bring about a chemical reaction by the body.

Some examples are set out in *figure ref 3-1*.

Hazard	Source	Type of work	Effect on the body
Dust.	Wood.	Forestry. Wood processing.	Irritation of the eyes, nose, asthma. Nasal cancer.
	Asbestos.	Asbestos removal.	Asbestosis, lung cancer.
	Silica.	Quarrying. Foundry.	Pulmonary fibrosis.
Fume/vapour.	Lead.	Manufacture of pipes. Sheet metal, foil. Soldering.	Anaemia, lethargy, kidney damage.
	Solvents.	Painting and decorating, degreasing. Dry cleaning.	Skin and liver damage, narcotic.
	Isocyanates.	Car body repair. Polyurethane production.	Occupational asthma.

Figure 3-1: Chemical hazards.   *Source: RMS.*

Chemicals can enter the body through inhalation, ingestion or skin absorption and can affect the lungs, gastrointestinal tract or skin directly or, after absorption, affect other parts of the body that are known as 'target organs'.

For example, mercury can be inhaled or absorbed through the skin, but affects the central nervous system; cadmium salts can be absorbed through the skin or ingested, resulting in damage to the kidneys and leading to renal failure. Inhalation of cadmium fume is particularly hazardous.

Five workers died from exposure to cadmium fume. The men were dismantling a frame of girders in a confined space by cutting bolts with an oxyacetylene burner. They were unaware at the time that the bolts were cadmium-plated or that this presented a serious industrial hazard. Cadmium salts are toxic by mouth, producing marked gastro-intestinal upset, but the oxide, by inhalation, is at least 60 times as toxic (Macfarland, 1960).

Figure 3-2: Effects of cadmium.   *Source: British Journal of Industrial Medicine.*

Biological hazards

Biological hazards are infections that are typically derived from human, environmental or animal sources. Biological hazards include bacteria and viruses.

Hazard	Source	Type of work	Affect on the body
Blood borne infections.	Blood.	Health care. Laboratory.	Infections, for example, Hepatitis B, C, HIV.
Orf.	Infected sheep.	Farming.	Infected lesions on the hands.
Salmonella.	Food.	Food handlers.	Salmonella/ typhoid infections.
Typhoid.	Sewers.	Sewer workers.	
Legionnella.	Cooling towers in hospitals, hotels.	Health care. Patients. Hotel workers and residents.	Pneumonia.
Psittacosis.	Infected birds and poultry.	Poultry workers, pet shop workers, zoo workers.	Flu-like symptoms, pneumonia.

Figure 3-3: Biological hazards.

Source: RMS.

Psychosocial hazards

Psychosocial hazards relate to workplace factors that may cause psychological or social harm or distress. The most common of these is 'stress', which can affect anyone and its occurrence will depend on a number of issues such as job content, organisation of work, work role, relationships, workplace culture, control of work, the work environment and the home-work interface. The effects on health may be sleeplessness, fatigue, depression, anxiety, increase in smoking and alcohol intake, drug misuse, eating disorders.

See also - Element 5 - Management of mental health at work - for more detail.

Ergonomic hazards

'Ergonomics' is defined as an applied science that considers the physical and psychological capabilities of the individual and that of human limitations, in other words 'fitting the task to the person'.

Poor ergonomics, like workplace design and layout, may cause individuals to carry out repetitive tasks and lift heavy weights in poor postures. This can lead to musculoskeletal disorders (MSD's), such as upper limb disorders and back pain. Examples of such work are using display screen equipment (DSE), handling and lifting, using poorly designed machinery and using poorly designed hand tools.

See also - Element 6 - Management of people with musculoskeletal disorders - for more detail.

OCCUPATIONAL HEARING LOSS

Most people who are exposed to workplace noise suffer from prolonged exposure rather then sudden loud surges. Exposure to noise may be intermittent or continuous, but generally takes place over a prolonged period of time.

If the noise is sufficiently intense and prolonged it can damage the hair cells located in the cochlea of the ear, this damage causes sensory loss and may be temporary or permanent. Hearing loss is gradual, reflecting the prolonged exposure to noise. Those exposed will often say "I am used to the noise". This is not a good sign and could be an indication that the worker has occupational noise induced hearing loss (ONIHL).

Permanent hearing loss cannot be corrected and the occurrence of ONIHL will affect the worker's ability to hear normal speech. This might mean that their family and friends complain about the worker having the television or radio too loud, and/or the worker will have problems hearing conversation in a group and may have difficulty using the telephone.

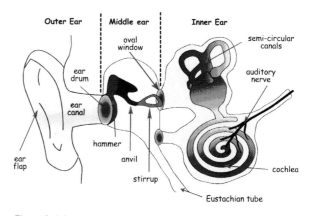

Figure 3-4: Inner ear diagram.   *Source: www.echalk.co.uk.*

This loss of hearing is very isolating for the individual who will not be able to take part in normal day to day communication.

Noise is defined as 'unwanted sound'. As well as noise from work processes noise can be introduced into the workplace in the form of continuous loud music played in the workplace which this may contribute to the overall environmental noise and push the noise level that workers are exposed to over the legal action levels. As well as causing ONIHL workers can develop tinnitus (ringing, buzzing or whistling in the ears), a distressing condition, which can lead to sleep disturbance and lack of concentration. Exposure to noise can be distracting and interfere with warning signals and work processes. The HSE reported the estimated prevalence of 21,000 for self-reported hearing problems caused or made worse by work during 2009/10. They also reported a rate of reporting of 70 per 100,000 people that were employed in last 12 months.

The Control of Noise at Work Regulations (CNWR) 2005

The Control of Noise at Work Regulations (CNWR) 2005 establishes the legal requirements for employers to reduce and control exposure to noise in the workplace; the main emphasis is on elimination and control of exposure at source, with personal protective equipment (PPE) being the last resort. These Regulations set out the exposure limit values and action values that employers must respond to. These are the noise levels at which action must be taken to control or reduce exposure.

The management of occupational noise induced hearing loss (ONIHL)

The CNWR 2005 require the employer to assess the risks to health and safety of exposure to noise at work, to record the findings and take action to eliminate and/or control exposure by engineering means, or alter work methods so as to reduce exposure to noise. Employers have a duty to provide hearing protection if they are unable to reduce exposure to noise by other means.

The identification, elimination and reduction of noise at source must be the first priority. Appropriate prevention and control measures include good design and selection of equipment, maintenance of equipment to ensure noise is controlled as equipment wears out and replacement strategy to remove equipment that is or becomes noisy. Some processes may have to be adapted, for example, where items fall onto hard surfaces from height the surface may have to be coated with sound absorbent material and means found to reduce the height. Personal hearing protection may have to be provided to workers to supplement action to minimise noise at source. This noise limiting programme should be supported by provision of health surveillance and medical advice on the symptoms of ONIHL, as well as the importance of limiting personal noise exposure by wearing personal hearing protection.

Health surveillance

Hearing tests (audiometry) must be provided for all employees who are likely to be regularly exposed to the upper exposure action values or if they are at higher risk for other reasons, such as they are already deaf or they are more sensitive to damage. Regulation 9 of the Control of Noise at Work Regulations (CNWR) 2005 requires:

"(1) If the risk assessment indicates that there is a risk to the health of his employees who are, or are liable to be, exposed to noise, the employer shall ensure that such employees are placed under suitable health surveillance, which shall include testing of their hearing.

(2) The employer shall ensure that a health record in respect of each of his employees who undergoes health surveillance in accordance with paragraph (1) is made and maintained and that the record or a copy thereof is kept available in a suitable form.

(3) The employer shall:

(a) On reasonable notice being given, allow an employee access to his personal health record.

(b) Provide the enforcing authority with copies of such health records as it may require".

The purpose of the audiometric hearing tests is to:

- Warn if an employee has early signs of ONIHL.
- Provide an opportunity to take action to prevent any identified hearing loss getting any worse.
- Assist with the evaluation of control measures, through the collection of the hearing test results, with the aim of bringing about improvements in the working environment through the reduction of the exposure of employees to noise.

Audiometric hearing tests conducted for health surveillance are normally carried out annually for the first 2 years and then 3 yearly, unless there are indications that it is required more frequently, for example, adverse test results, or where the risk of hearing damage is high. This will be decided by the doctor or nurse managing the testing programme and will depend on the results of the tests. Health surveillance for exposure to noise normally involves:

- New workers being tested prior to taking up a post in a potentially noisy environment to provide a reference measurement of their hearing on entering the company. This is important as the worker may already have ONIHL due to exposure in a previous job. If that is the case, then the employer will have a duty to protect that worker to ensure the hearing is not damaged further. The reference measurement also provides data on the level of hearing the worker had on entering the workplace, which would provide vital information for any future claims for ONIHL.

- New workers should be retested at an interval of 3 and 6 months in their first year of employment to determine any detrimental change in hearing that might indicate they have a higher susceptibility to noise damage than would normally be expected. Such individuals may not be suitable for continued work in the noisy environment with the existing levels of control.
- Regular audiometric hearing tests in special controlled conditions, for example, an acoustic (sound proof) booth.
- Keeping records of the results and acting on any adverse results.
- Informing employees of the results of their hearing tests.
- Ensuring employees are referred to a doctor if hearing damage is identified.

Regulation 9 of the Control of Noise at Work Regulations (CNWR) 2005 also requires:

"(1) Where, as a result of health surveillance, an employee is found to have identifiable hearing damage the employer shall ensure that the employee is examined by a doctor and, if the doctor or any specialist to whom the doctor considers it necessary to refer the employee considers that the damage is likely to be the result of exposure to noise, the employer shall:

(a) *Ensure that a suitably qualified person informs the employee accordingly.*

(b) *Review the risk assessment.*

(c) *Review any measure taken to comply with regulations 6, 7 and 8, taking into account any advice given by a doctor or occupational health professional, or by the enforcing authority.*

(d) *Consider assigning the employee to alternative work where there is no risk from further exposure to noise, taking into account any advice given by a doctor or occupational health professional.*

(e) *Ensure continued health surveillance and provide for a review of the health of any other employee who has been similarly exposed.*

(2) *An employee to whom this regulation applies shall, when required by his employer and at the cost of his employer; present himself during his working hours for such health surveillance procedures as may be required for the purposes of paragraph (1)".*

All employees should be given advice regarding the effect of noise on hearing and the correct use of hearing protection as part of the health surveillance programme. Where an employee's hearing falls within category 2 for the level of ONIHL that a formal notification should be given to that employee regarding the presence of hearing damage. Arrangements and procedures should be put in place for medical referral of those employees falling into categories 3 and 4 and where unilateral hearing loss is identified.

Category	Calculation	Action
1. Acceptable Hearing Ability Hearing within normal limits.	Sum of hearing levels at 1, 2, 3, 4 and 6 kHz.	None
2. Mild Hearing Impairment Hearing within 20th percentile, i.e. hearing level normally experienced by 1 person in 5. May indicate developing NIHL.	Sum of hearing levels at 1, 2, 3, 4 and 6 kHz. Compare value with figure given for appropriate age band and gender in Table 14.	Warning
3. Poor Hearing Hearing within 5th percentile, i.e. hearing level normally experienced by 1 person in 20. Suggests significant NIHL.	Sum of hearing levels at 1, 2, 3, 4 and 6 kHz. Compare value with figure given for appropriate age band and gender in Table 14.	Referral
4. Rapid Hearing Loss Reduction in hearing level of 30 dB or more, within 3 years or less. Such a change could be caused by noise exposure or disease.	Sum of hearing levels at 3, 4 and 6 kHz.	Referral

Figure 3-5: HSE categorisation scheme for hearing loss.   *Source: HSE, L108 Controlling Noise at Work.*

Managing an audiometric hearing testing programme

Before introducing any testing programme it is important to ensure that workers understand the purpose and implications of the programme.

They need to be fully aware of:

- The aims and objectives of the programme.
- Procedures regarding confidentiality of the test results.
- The method used to carry out the tests.
- The way adverse results will be managed, including medical referral.
- The need to collate and keep anonymous (results not specific to any individual) statistical data and how this will be used to assess the control measures in place.

There should be a 'designated person' in charge of the testing programme. This person should be fully conversant with the technical and ethical aspects of conducting audiometric hearing tests and should be responsible for:

■ Ensuring the tests are carried out properly and maintain standards.
■ The maintenance of records.
■ Referring individuals for further advice.
■ Ensuring the quality of the testing, which must include calibration of audiometric equipment and competence of the individuals carrying out the tests.

A suitable person would be an occupational health physician or nurse who has special knowledge and training in audiometry, or an audiologist. It must be noted however, that the employer has the ultimate responsibility to ensure that the audiometric hearing testing programme is carried out on employees exposed to noise, and the employer must make clear the responsibilities of the 'designated person'. There should be a clearly stated policy and agreement signed, which sets out the procedures and protocols for medical referral and feedback to employees, unions and the employer. The quality of the testing programme must be assured to ensure confidence when comparing results year on year.

HAND-ARM AND WHOLE BODY VIBRATION SYNDROME

Vibration is oscillation around a point (rapid and continuous movement to and fro). In the workplace workers may be exposed to two types:

■ Hand transmitted vibration - when vibration passes to the hands from a source of vibration, such as hand held tools, for example, drills, hand saws, grinders, polishers, mowers, shears.
■ Whole body vibration - when the body is supported on a surface that is vibrating, such as sitting on a seat that is vibrating, for example, a tractor cab driver's seat, helicopter seats, or seats in earth moving vehicles.

Vibration is measured in two ways - acceleration in metres per second squared (ms^{-2})) and the frequency in hertz (Hz). Hand-arm vibration syndrome (HAVS) may be caused where exposure is in the frequency range of 2 - 1,000 Hz, the most damaging being between 5 and 20 Hz. The most significant range for whole body vibration (WBV) is 0.1 - 1.0 Hz and 1 - 20 Hz. The effects of WBV will vary and will depend on the direction of the vibration (vertical or lateral), as well as the acceleration and duration of exposure.

It is estimated that up to 300,000 working days are lost each year in the UK due to hand-arm disability related absences (HSE statistics). Hand-arm vibration syndrome (HAVS) is a prescribed disease A11, covered by industrial injuries disablement benefit. Other problems associated with hand-arm vibration are carpal tunnel syndrome (pain and numbness in the hands and fingers), painful joints and muscle weakening, and damage to bones in the hand and arms. HAVS is a chronic progressive disorder, also known as Raynaud's syndrome 'vibration white finger' and 'dead finger'. It is characterised by:

■ Episodes of finger blanching (white finger). This is usually precipitated by exposure to cold and starts at the tips of the fingers closest to the vibration transmission. It affects the index and or middle fingers, which can last several minutes or up to an hour. This is usually followed by redness and pain. If exposure continues then blanching can spread to the base of fingers and affect other fingers.
■ Episodes of numbness and tingling. Often these are noticed before vascular symptoms and can progress to become permanent and the most disabling of the symptoms.
■ Pain.
■ Reduced temperature sensation.
■ Reduced strength.
■ Impaired manual dexterity/clumsiness with difficulty picking up small items. This can be very disabling and can affect the individual's ability to undertake everyday tasks.

Workers suffering from HAVS can experience difficulty in carrying out tasks in the workplace that involve fine or manipulative work, such as assembling components, and are less able to work in cold conditions, such as deep freeze warehouses and outside working.

The disease may have an impact on earnings and on a worker's social and family life. Everyday tasks may become difficult, for example, tying shoe laces, fastening small buttons on clothes.

Attacks of 'white finger' will take place not only at work, but during other activities, especially if people get cold, such as when washing the car or watching outdoor sports.

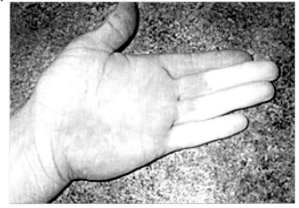

Figure 3-6: Finger blanching due to vibration.
Source: HAVS Screening Ltd.

Prolonged exposure to whole body vibration (WBV) can lead to considerable back pain and may result in permanent injury and having to give up work.

Other effects of WBV can include headaches, motion sickness, visual disturbances and in some cases abdominal discomfort.

Control of Vibration at Work Regulations (CVWR) 2005

These regulations require the employer to carry out a risk assessment where there is a risk of exposure to vibration, and, where vibration is identified as an issue it must be eliminated or exposure reduced to a minimum. There is a requirement for employees to be provided with information and training. There is also a duty for the employer to provide health surveillance where the risks are significant. For hand-arm vibration a daily exposure action value (EAV) rate of 2.5 ms^{-2} is set, above which exposure must be reduced as far as reasonably practical (AFARP) and health surveillance provided. For whole body vibration the daily exposure action value is 0.5 ms^{-2} and similar action must be taken as for hand-arm vibration.

The Reporting of Injuries, Diseases and Dangerous Occurrences Regulations (RIDDOR) 1995 place a duty on the employer to report any cases of HAVS arising from certain work activities or of carpal tunnel syndrome associated with exposure to vibration. The duty comes into effect when a formal written diagnosis from a doctor has been made confirming that the employee has either of these conditions, and that there is reason to believe that the disease is likely to have an occupational origin.

The management of hand arm vibration syndrome (HAVS)

The main principle is that exposure to vibration must be reduced at source by engineering means, i.e. good maintenance of machinery and tools, selection of appropriate tools and good information, instruction and training for workers exposed to vibration. The emphasis of the prevention strategy must be to prevent any new cases of HAVS and to ensure that existing cases do not become worse. A detailed policy for HAVS and vibration exposure is required. Health surveillance is also required where the risk assessment has identified significant exposure and a risk to the workers health.

The management of whole body vibration (WBV)

Elimination and reduction of exposure at source must be the first priority. Appropriate prevention and control measures include good design and selection of seats for vehicles (for example, mining and quarrying machines, agricultural and forestry machinery, earth movers), maintenance of seating and consideration of the ergonomic design of seats to provide good posture for the drivers. The management of WBV should include provision of medical advice on the symptoms of WBV, which might include low back pain, headaches, motion sickness, sleep disturbance, visual disturbances and in some cases abdominal discomfort.

Health surveillance

Health surveillance is required for any worker exposed to vibration levels above the exposure action value (EAV) rate. It should also be implemented for workers with existing HAVS, even if they are not regularly exposed to the daily EAV, as a means to identify whether the condition is getting worse.

Regulation 7(2) of the Control of Vibration at Work Regulations (CVWR) 2005 requires:

"(2) Health surveillance, which shall be intended to prevent or diagnose any health effect linked with exposure to vibration, shall be appropriate where the exposure of the employee to vibration is such that:

(a) A link can be established between that exposure and an identifiable disease or adverse health effect.

(b) It is probable that the disease or effect may occur under the particular conditions of his work.

(c) There are valid techniques for detecting the disease or effect".

An effective health surveillance programme for HAVS includes annual checks by an occupational health nurse, who is competent and familiar with the symptoms of HAVS and, where conditions indicate the need, can refer the person to a doctor for advice. The Health and Safety Executive (HSE) recommend a 'tiered' system for health assessment, (www.hse.gov.uk/vibration/hav) which is a simple and cost effective approach that requires different levels of assessment:

- **Tier 1** is a short questionnaire, an example of which can be downloaded from the HSE's website *(initial screening questionnaire)*. This is used as a first check for people moving into jobs involving exposure to vibration. The replies to the questionnaire will indicate whether they need to be referred to Tier 3 for a HAVS health assessment.

- **Tier 2** is a short questionnaire, an example of which can be downloaded from the HSE's website *(annual screening questionnaire)* that can be used once a year. It is issued to employees exposed to vibration risks to check whether they need to be referred to Tier 3 for a HAVS health assessment. It is a self-administered questionnaire.

- **Tier 3** involves a HAVS health assessment by a qualified person, such as an occupational health nurse or an occupational health technician who is competent and working under the supervision of a qualified occupational health nurse. If the assessment shows that the employee has HAVS, Tier 4 assessment will apply and the employee would be referred to an occupational health physician for further diagnostic tests.

- **Tier 4** involves a formal diagnosis and is carried out by a qualified occupational health physician. The occupational health physician will advise on the employee's fitness for work.

- **Tier 5** is optional and involves referral of the employee for certain tests for HAVS. The results may help the doctor assess fitness for work.

This 'tiered' approach helps to ensure assessment is focused and keep costs to a minimum, as it uses the appropriate skilled people to carry out the particular tier of assessment, not all employees will require full clinical and diagnostic assessment.

It is important to ensure that the health surveillance is carried out by occupational health professionals who are competent, understand the workplace issues and can advise management accordingly. Certification for both doctors and nurses from a Faculty of Occupational Medicine approved training course in HAVS (see Appendix 6 of "Hand-arm vibration - The Control of Vibration at Work Regulations (CVWR) 2005"; Guidance on Regulations (L140)) or equivalent level of competency may be appropriate.

(Further details can be found on the faculty of occupational medicine website www.facoccmed.co.uk).

A health record for each individual must be maintained for as long as they are under health surveillance, and it is good practice to keep them for longer. It is also good practice to offer individual employees a copy of their health records when they leave their employment. The record should be kept up to date and should include:

- Details of the employee, for example, name, age, national insurance (NI) number, type of work.
- The employee's history of exposure to vibration.
- The results of previous health surveillance in terms of fitness for work, and any restrictions required.
- The Tier 1 and Tier 2 questionnaire results (as long as they are not confidential) even if an employee has said they have no symptoms.

See also - section 3.5 on health surveillance and record keeping - for more details.

Training and education of employees

When training and educating employees it is important to:

- Ensure the employee understands the purpose of health surveillance, how this is managed and what will happen with the results, including referral for medical assessment if indicated.
- Educate the worker to wear adequate clothing to keep the entire body warm, especially the hands and feet.
- Outline of the early symptoms of HAVS/WBV and emphasise the importance of reporting the symptoms early so that action can be taken to ensure the symptoms do not get worse.
- Provide health education to encourage employees to avoid or minimise the smoking of tobacco, which can have adverse affects on circulation.
- Instruct employees in the correct use of tools and machinery, so as to reduce the incidence of exposure.

OCCUPATIONAL SKIN DISEASE

The skin is the largest organ of the body (1.4-1.85 square metres or 15-20 square feet), which forms a barrier between the external environment and vulnerable body tissue. It is an organ that is exposed to all types of hazardous agents at work and in every day life, being a major route of entry to the body for many chemicals, and is susceptible to trauma, irritation, sensitisation, infections and cancer. The skin consists of two basic layers the outer epidermis, which acts as a protective layer and the dermis, which gives it its strength. The epidermis is waterproof with an oily surface, but can be affected by the absorption of agents such as solvents that break down this protective barrier.

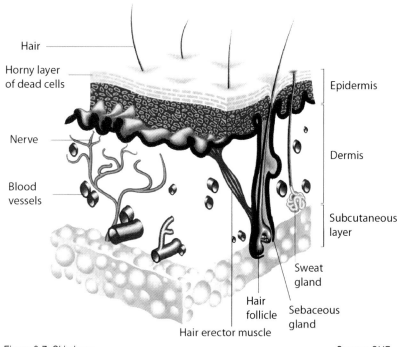

Figure 3-7: Skin layer. *Source: SHP.*

The functions of the skin are:

- Provides a mechanical protection - dermis, epidermis.
- Waterproofing, due to the oily nature of the skin, this acts as protection.
- Defence against harmful agents, for example, chemicals, bacteria.
- Insulation to keep the body warm - subcutaneous fat.
- Regulates temperature by helping to regulate blood flow and sweating through the actions of the hair follicles and sweat glands.
- Excretion - sweat secretion.
- Organ of sense: it has receptors of touch, temperature, pain and vibration and the nerve endings help to prevent further injury.
- Helps with the production of Vitamin D, which occurs as a result of exposure to sunlight. However, this needs to be controlled as over exposure to sunlight (ultra violet light UVL) can cause skin cancer (melanoma).

Agents that can cause skin conditions:

Mechanical	Friction, pressure, trauma	for example, callosities.
Physical	Heat, cold, radiation	for example, rashes, chilblains, frostbite, burns, cancer.
Chemical	Acids, alkalis, solvents, oils, pitch, tar	for example, dermatitis, rashes, dry skin, blistering.
Plants	Flowers, wood	for example, dermatitis, rashes.
Biological	Organisms, insects, mites, scabies	for example, infection, infestation.

There are two main types of occupationally related skin disease, irritant contact dermatitis (ICD) and allergic contact dermatitis (ACD).

Irritant contact dermatitis

The majority of work related dermatitis is irritant contact dermatitis (ICD). With this form of dermatitis irritants cause a direct effect on the skin and the amount of damage will depend on the dose and length of exposure. The degree to which damage occurs will depend on a number of factors:

- Dryness of the skin.
- Sweating of the hands.
- Type and pigmentation of the skin.
- The health of the epidermis, for example, damage such as cuts abrasions.
- Skin cleanliness.
- Pre-existing skin conditions and the individuals' susceptibility.
- The environment such as temperature, humidity, friction.

Almost any chemical can cause ICD in susceptible individuals and it can be a number of different chemical agents that together cause the problem. Even soap and water can cause ICD in people who carry out frequent hand washing such as food handlers, nurses, and doctors.

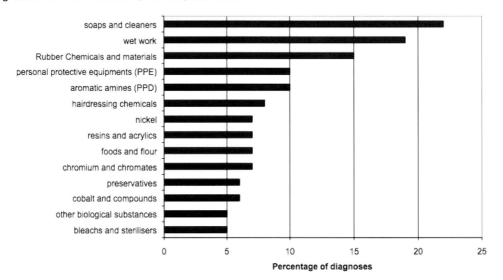

Figure 3-8: Causative agents for contact dermatitis, 2006-08.   *Source: HSE.*

A person's skin is unique and has its own threshold of resistance to irritant exposures. One person may develop ICD after a short exposure whilst in another it may take many months or even years to develop. This makes diagnosis difficult, as it is assumed that if a worker has carried out a job for several years, it cannot be work related, when in fact it is the build up of exposure over the months or years that may have triggered the irritant reaction of the skin.

This further places difficulty in identifying any work exposures likely to cause ICD, as other exposures to irritants may have taken place at home or whilst undertaking a hobby such as DIY, car maintenance and gardening. High risk occupations for chronic ICD include:

- Cleaning.
- Catering.
- Construction.
- Hairdressing.
- Metal working.
- Nursing.
- Painting.
- Printing.
- Vehicle repair and maintenance.
- Horticulture.
- Forestry.

Allergic contact dermatitis

Allergic contact dermatitis (ACD) accounts for around 15-20% of occupationally related skin disease. It is usually caused by one specific agent and the skin reaction can be immediate or may be delayed for up to a week or more after exposure. The initial reaction is normally following exposure to high concentrations and/or long exposure to a substance.

Following this initial reaction it may then only take small, short exposures to get a reaction to the same or similar substances. With ACD it is the effect on the immune system that triggers a reaction to the substance when the body forms antibodies. These bind with mast cells and form granules containing histamine, which are released and cause a rash to occur. Once this sensitisation has occurred, an individual will react to any future exposure to the substance and will normally have to avoid any contact with the offending substance. Commonly used examples of contact allergens include:

- Epoxy resins, for example, found in adhesives, cement and surface coating agents.
- Rubber latex, for example, found in rubber gloves, tubes - affecting health care workers, hairdressers.
- Gluteraldahyde, for example, used as a sterilising agent in health care work.
- Nickel salts, for example, used to coat other metals to prevent rusting as in electroplating.
- Dyes, for example, used in hairdressing.

The diagnosis of ACD can be made by carrying out 'patch testing' where the individual has a number of patches containing the suspected agents placed onto the skin and left for 48-72 hours. An assessment of the reaction is made after removal. These tests are carried out under controlled conditions, by a doctor, who has knowledge of the workplace and work processes.

Typical signs of dermatitis:

- Redness, soreness and rash visible on the skin.
- Irritation of the skin.
- Raised patches, blistering.
- Cracking and flaking.
- Skin discolouration.
- Weeping of the skin.
- Pain.
- Swelling.

The HSE reported the estimated prevalence of 22,000 for self-reported skin problems caused or made worse by work during 2009/10. They also reported a rate of reporting of 73 per 100,000 people that were employed in last 12 months.

Legislation applicable to occupational skin disease

The main legislation applicable to occupational skin disease is:

- Health and Safety at Work Act (HASAWA) 1974.
- Control of Substances Hazardous to Health Regulations (COSHH) 2002 (as amended).
- Chemical (Hazards Information and Packaging) Regulations (CHIP) 2009 (requires 'risk phrases' to be used and the main ones for skin are R34 - causes burns; R38 - irritating to the skin; R43 - possible sensitisation to the skin).
- Management of Health and Safety at Work Regulations (MHSWR) 1999.
- Workplace (Health Safety and Welfare) Regulations (WHSWR) 1992.
- Personal Protective Equipment Regulations (PPE) 1992.

These set out explicit or implied requirements for the employer to carry out a risk assessment to identify any risks to health then take action to prevent and/or control exposure.

The management of occupational skin disease

The hierarchy of control for managing the risks related to occupational skin disease includes:

- *Avoid* contact with the skin - prevention, eliminating the use of the chemical as far as possible.
- *Change the method* of working, consider safer alternative methods, automate the system, or change the work method to avoid skin contact, for example, obtain pre-packed and ready mixed.
- Use the substance/chemical in a *different form*, for example, paste instead of liquid or powder.
- **Enclosure** of the process to reduce the need for handling.
- Limit the number of people exposed by **segregating** the work and stopping people walking through the work area.
- Consider the use of *local exhaust ventilation (LEV)* to reduce any residual environmental skin exposure.

- Correct use and provision of **personal protective equipment (PPE)** which is suitable for the work, to provide appropriate protection. The PPE must take account of all aspects of the work carried out as there may be more than one hazard, such as a mixture of chemicals, other mechanical hazards and handling issues. The gloves should provide protection from the specific substance. Consideration should be made of the 'break-through time' (when the barrier becomes permeable to the agent) of the protection. The PPE should also be suitable for the worker, affording the correct fit. A system should be in place to ensure gloves are inspected and changed when necessary and new ones available.

- Ensure there is good **housekeeping** - ensure spillages are removed and routine cleaning schedules are in place.

- A programme of **health surveillance** and environmental monitoring to ensure the controls in place are working and adequate. Where identified through the risk assessment, set up a health surveillance programme. This can be a 'tiered' system, starting with self skin checks, followed by a questionnaire and, where adverse health effects are suspected, referral to an occupational health nurse or physician for further assessment, treatment and advice on preventive action.

- Set up a system to ensure good **personal hygiene** standards are implemented, for example, washing facilities, use of suitable skin cleaners and use of suitable after work creams to ensure the skin is kept healthy.

- Set up a programme of **education** for all workers at risk so that they understand the risks of skin disease, how to use the control systems and how to care for their skin. This should include special training on correct hand washing procedures, how to use barrier and after work creams and how to use PPE, for example, putting on and taking off gloves. Workers should also be educated in how to examine their own skin for early signs of damage, the importance of early reporting of any problems and how the health surveillance programme will be managed.

- Managers should be educated regarding their **responsibilities** to maintain the control systems and ensure that workers adhere to correct work procedures and skin hygiene programmes.

OCCUPATIONAL LUNG DISEASE

The main function of the lungs is to proved oxygen to the body through the blood and capillaries and to facilitate the removal of carbon dioxide as a waste product. Occupational lung diseases remain a significant problem within the workplace. The lungs are particularly vulnerable to hazardous agents as the average resting adult breathes 10-20,000 litres of air daily and the lungs act as a 'sponge' for the air we breathe. If there are significant hazardous substances in the air they will be inhaled and this is greatly enhanced where the worker is carrying out strenuous work, as respiration rate is increased at this time. The substances may not only damage the lungs directly, but can be absorbed through the lungs blood capillaries and taken to other parts of the body. An example of this is the inhalation of lead fume, which does not directly damage the lungs, but it is absorbed by the capillaries and deposited elsewhere in the body causing ill health, such as anaemia and brain damage.

Types of occupationally related lung disease:

- Asbestos related diseases, such as pneumoconiosis, lung cancer and mesothelioma.
- Legionellosis.
- Work-related chronic obstructive pulmonary diseases (COPD) such as pneumoconiosis.
- Occupational asthma.

Asbestos related diseases

Asbestos related diseases include pneumoconiosis, lung cancer and mesothelioma. The term "pneumoconiosis" refers to a group of lung diseases caused by the inhalation and retention in the lungs of dusts. Pneumoconiosis derived from exposure to asbestos is statistically significant and incidence is often reported separately from other diseases in the group. Asbestos fibres are a particular form of fibrous dust that readily become airborne when disturbed and may enter the lungs, where they cause fibrosis (scarring and thickening) of the lung tissue (asbestosis) or pleura (diffuse pleural thickening). The pleura is a two-layered membrane that surrounds the lungs and lines the inside of the rib cage.

Whilst asbestos fibres may have a direct effect on the lungs, some asbestos fibres inhaled into the lungs work their way out to the pleura and may cause fibrosis or scarring to develop there, which causing the pleura to thicken. These forms of pneumoconiosis typically take more than 10 years to develop.

The HSE reported that there were 117 deaths in 2008 where asbestosis is described as the underlying cause of death on the death certificate and there were 460 new cases of disablement benefit for diffuse pleural thickening in 2009.

> "The annual number of new cases of asbestosis according to the Department of Work and Pensions (DWP) Industrial Injuries and Disablement Benefit (IIDB) scheme (which compensates workers for prescribed occupational diseases) has risen erratically since the early 1980s, with the trend strongly increasing since the early 1990s reaching the current level of 825 in 2009. This is likely to be an underestimate of the total number of cases".

Figure 3-9: Annual incidence of asbestosis.

Source: HSE.

The HSE also reported that the trend in diffuse pleural thickening cases has increased over recent years, although this may due to the acceptance of claims under the IIDB scheme for unilateral (affecting only one lung) cases and other changes in data collection methods.

In addition, exposure to asbestos can lead to lung cancer and mesothelioma (cancer of the pleura). Mesothelioma is a type of cancer that affects the mesothelial cells. These cells cover the outer surface of most of our internal body organs, including the lungs and abdomen, forming a lining that is sometimes called the mesothelium. Cancer affecting the lining of the lungs is known as pleural mesothelioma and may arise out of exposure to asbestos. Lung cancers or mesotheliomas may not appear until 20 to 50 years after exposure.

The HSE reported that the annual number of mesothelioma deaths had increased since 1968, where annual recorded deaths were 153, reaching 2249 deaths in 2008. The expected number of deaths amongst males is predicted to increase to a peak of 2038 in the year 2016. The HSE also reported that there it was likely that there were around as many asbestos related lung cancer deaths in Great Britain annually as there are mesothelioma deaths. In the majority of cases mesothelioma is rapidly fatal following diagnosis so mesothelioma death statistics give a clear indication of the disease incidence.

Diagnosis for asbestos related diseases is generally made on the basis of clinical features, X-ray appearances or CT scan and a history of asbestos exposure. It is generally recognised that heavy asbestos exposures are required in order to produce clinically significant asbestosis within the lifetime of an individual. Current trends of identified cases of asbestosis therefore still largely reflect the results of heavy exposures in the past. This may not reflect the occurrence of mesothelioma as it is asserted that it could result from a single fibre, though risks are greater if the worker is exposed to large amounts of asbestos over a period of time. Cancer Research UK reported that approximately 1 in 10 people exposed to asbestos develop mesothelioma in the pleural membranes.

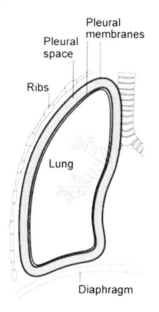

Figure 3-10: Diagram of lung showing pleura. *Source: Cancer Help UK.*

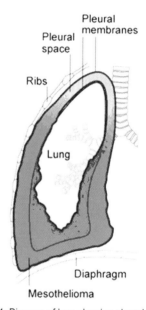

Figure 3-11: Diagram of lung showing pleural mesothelioma. *Source: Cancer Help UK.*

The HSE identified that the ten male occupations found to have the highest risk of asbestos related diseases were carpenters, plumbers, electricians, labourers in other construction trades, metal plate workers, pipe fitters, construction operatives, managers in construction, construction trades and energy plant operatives.

Legionellosis

Legionellosis is the effect the legionella pneumophila bacterium has on the lungs, which has a similar effect as pneumonia. The bacteria is transferred to people by inhaling small droplets of water suspended in air that contains the bacteria. The bacteria is widespread in nature. The bacteria will grow in water systems at temperatures of between 20-45°C, particularly where there is a source of nutrient for the bacteria, for example, sludge, rust, algae and other organic matter.

Exposure to the bacteria is made more likely in situations where breathable droplets of water containing it are created or spread, for example, aerosols created by cooling towers, spa pools, hot water shower systems and some air conditioning systems.

The incubation period in the lungs is between 2 to 10 days, it causes pneumonia type symptoms such as difficulty in breathing, a high temperature, fever, chills, muscle pain and headaches. The disease affects susceptible individuals and the major concern is with outbreaks in hospitals, where patients, already susceptible due to illness may be affected. The fatality rate in the UK is about 12%. Smoking, age and alcohol may increase susceptibility.

In August 2002, seven members of the public died and 180 people suffered ill health as a result of an outbreak of legionella at a council-owned arts and leisure facility in the town centre of Barrow-in-Furness, Cumbria. This report allows others to learn what caused the outbreak and what changes have been made since.

Figure 3-12: Large occurrence of legionellosis in Barrow-in-Furness. *Source: HSE.*

Work-related chronic obstructive pulmonary diseases (COPD)

Chronic obstructive pulmonary disease (COPD) is the name for a collection of lung diseases, including chronic bronchitis and emphysema. The largest cause of COPD is due to smoking. However, work-related COPDs include pneumoconiosis, caused by exposure to coal or silica dust and byssinosis, caused by exposure to cotton, flax or hemp dust.

As the condition develops the worker's lungs become inflamed due to irritation, caused by exposure to the substance. Over many years, the inflammation leads to permanent changes in the lung. In response to the inflammation mucus is produced and the walls of the airways become fibrosed, hardened and thicker. Damage to the delicate walls of the alveoli means the lungs loose their normal elasticity. It then becomes much harder for the worker to breathe, especially when they exert themselves. The changes in the lungs cause the symptoms of breathlessness, cough and phlegm that are associated with COPD. Once COPD develops the damage to the lungs cannot be reversed. However, reducing exposure to the dust, fume and irritating gases at work that are causing the problem can stop the condition getting worse.

A wide range of occupations are linked with COPD, including miners, quarry workers, sand blasters, and foundry workers, welders, textile workers, stone masons, flour and grain workers.

Research findings reported by the HSE on their website suggest that for Great Britain:

- Around 15% of COPD may be caused or made worse by work.
- 4,000 COPD deaths every year may be related to work exposures.
- 4 in every 10 COPD patients are below retirement age.
- A quarter of those below retirement age are unable to work at all.

Occupational asthma

Occupational asthma is an allergic reaction that can occur in some workers when they are exposed to substances in the workplace, for example, flour or wood dust. These substances are called 'respiratory sensitisers' or asthmagens. They can cause a change in the worker's airways, known as the 'hypersensitive state'. Not everyone who becomes sensitised goes on to get asthma. But once the lungs become hypersensitive, further exposure to the substance, even at quite low levels, may trigger an asthma attack.

Whilst the larger airways have cartilage in their walls to prevent their collapse, the smaller bronchi and bronchioles do not have this support; they are muscular tubes and their lining contains many mucus secreting cells. During an asthma attack the muscle wall contracts and the lining of the airways becomes swollen and inflamed. These changes cause a narrowing of the airways, which is further aggravated by an increase in secretions from the mucus membrane that are capable of blocking the smaller airways. All these effects combine to create an obstruction to airflow. This leads to a significant increase in the effort needed to move air in and out of the lungs, giving rise to breathlessness.

Symptoms of occupational asthma therefore include severe shortness of breath, wheezing, coughing and chest tightness. Other associated conditions may arise, for example, rhinitis (sneezing/runny nose), conjunctivitis (itchy and inflamed red eyes). The symptoms can develop during exposure to a workplace substance or may appear several hours later, possibly at night. This can make any link with workplace activities unclear.

Some of the main examples of agents that can sensitise are:

- Flour/grain.
- Colophony (pine resin).
- Epoxy resins.
- Animal fur/urine.
- Fish and egg proteins.
- Soybean and coffee bean dusts.
- Some hardwood and softwood dusts.
- Isocyanates.
- Glutaraldehyde.
- Metals such as platinum, chromium, nickel.
- Spores from moulds related to various materials, for example, hay, straw, malt and mushroom compost.

Extrinsic allergic alveolitis (EAA) is a specific form of occupational asthma that triggers an allergic response of the alveoli to exposure to sensitising agents. The inflammation of the alveoli gives rise to a lowering of the ability of the alveoli to transfer gases to the bloodstream.

It is mostly caused by exposure to organic materials such as fungal spores in materials such as mouldy hay, mouldy sugar cane, mouldy grain, flour, cork. The most commonly known condition of this type is 'Farmer's Lung', as a result of contact with mouldy hay.

Legislation applicable to occupational lung disease

The main legislation applicable to occupational lung disease is:

- Control of Substances Hazardous to Health Regulations (COSHH) 2002 (as amended).
- Management of Health and Safety at Work Regulations (MHSWR) 1999.
- Control of Asbestos Regulations (CAR) 2006.
- The Notification of Cooling Towers and Evaporative Condensers Regulations (NCTECR) 1992.

These regulations require the employer to carry out suitable and sufficient risk assessments to assess levels of exposure to biological hazards, dusts, fumes and gases.

Once these have been carried out, the employer must then take action to remove the hazard, as far as reasonably practicable.

Figure 3-13: The control of legionella bacteria in water systems. *Source: HSE.*

If this is not possible, then exposure must be reduced at source and other control measures put in place. In addition the Personal Protective Equipment (PPE) Regulations 1992 set out requirements related to the management of personal protective equipment. The legionella bacteria is a substance covered by the Control of Substances Hazardous to Health Regulations, but has its own Approved Code of Practice (ACOP); "The control of legionella bacteria in water systems and guidance, L8".

The management of occupational lung disease

The hierarchy of control for preventing, managing and controlling exposure to fibres, dust, fumes and gases that cause occupational lung diseases is as follows:

- ***Eliminate, substitute or change*** the process for something less harmful, for example, where there is a dusty process a liquid or pellet form of the substance may be used instead of powder.
- ***Enclose and isolate*** the process, for example, working in a fume cabinet or enclosing the machine with the operator working outside the enclosure.
- ***Segregate*** the process to reduce the number of people exposed, for example, stop people walking through work areas.
- Improve the ***ventilation***, for example, provide local exhaust ventilation (LEV) to extract the dust, fume or gas at source and prevent it getting into the environment. For example, when using a solder gun a nozzle is attached to remove solder fume directly from the tip of the solder gun and when controlling wood dust local exhaust ventilation can be fixed to the cutting tool, for example, hoods over a circular saw to remove and contain the dust.
- Implement a ***safe system of work:*** can the work be done in a better way to reduce exposure? Processes are often carried out without considering the impact they can make, for example, when emptying bags containing powdered substances like flour, the bags may be shaken and then folded up; this process creates additional dust that may not be captured by the extraction system.
- Suppress the dust by ensuring ***cleaning*** is carried out by vacuuming and damping, not sweeping, which causes more dust.
- Improve the ***housekeeping*** and disposal of waste. Keep the workplace clean and tidy, remove waste regularly and correctly.
- Ensure that correct ***personal protective equipment (PPE)*** is provided and worn correctly. This should be the last resort, when all other methods of prevention and control have been exhausted or may be necessary, in addition to other controls, where highly toxic substances may be controlled by extraction, but there is a risk of extraction failure, such as with the manufacture of isocyanates. Suitable respiratory protective equipment (RPE), which complies with British Standards, is required to protect workers; advice on this should be sought from a competent person. It is important to ensure the RPE provides suitable protection in the circumstances in which it is being used.
- Health ***surveillance***, which will help to protect the health of workers by early detection of any adverse health effects. It also helps to evaluate the control methods in place, through the collection of data, which should be used to inform management of any changes in the health of the workers, bringing about improvements in the working environment, by reducing exposure.

Employers must also ensure that workers are educated regarding:

- How to use the control measures in place, for example, LEV systems, RPE.
- The correct use of RPE, cleaning, maintenance and replacement.
- How and to whom to report early symptoms such as cough, wheezing, flu-like symptoms.
- The purpose of health surveillance, what will happen if there are any adverse test results, with referral for medical assessment, and what will happen to the results.

Local exhaust ventilation

General applications and principles

Various local exhaust ventilation (LEV) systems are in use in the workplace, for example:

- Receptor hoods such as are used in fume cupboards and kilns.
- Captor hoods (used for welding and milling operations).
- High velocity low volume flow systems, for example, as used on a grinding tool.

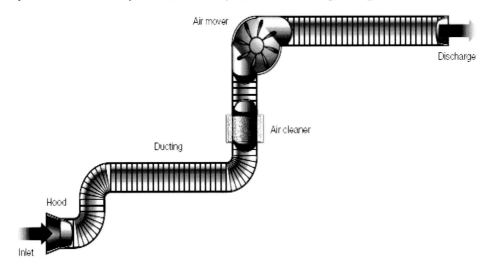

Figure 3-14: Common elements of a simple LEV system.   *Source: HSE indg408.*

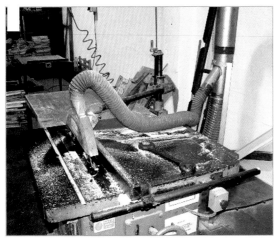

Figure 3-15: Captor system on circular saw. Clearly shows the fixed captor hood, flexible hose and rigid duct. *Source: RMS.*

Figure 3-16: Fan and motor on large LEV system.   *Source: RMS.*

Figure 3-17: Flexible hose showing how captor hood can be repositioned to suit the work activity. *Source: RMS.*

Figure 3-18: Self contained unit which can be moved around the workplace. *Source: RMS.*

Health surveillance

A programme of health surveillance and environmental monitoring should be implemented, depending on the findings of the risk assessment, to ensure the controls in place are working and adequate. This could start with a questionnaire asking about symptoms of respiratory problems, for example, cough, wheezing, sleeplessness through coughing, runny nose.

Where adverse health effects are suspected, the worker affected should be referred to an occupational health nurse or physician for further assessment, treatment and advice on preventive action. Depending on the results of the questionnaire, it may be necessary to carry out spirometry (lung function testing), but this will be decided by the occupational health professional carrying out the health surveillance, considering the type of hazard and the individual exposed.

For example, it is known that flour dust, isocyanates and latex exposure can cause asthma; therefore employees exposed to these substances would require spirometry tests to be carried out.

The Health and Safety Executive (HSE) recommend that, where it is required, for example, exposure to flour dust and isocyanates, respiratory health surveillance should be carried out as follows:

- Pre-employment to provide a reference measurement when starting the job.
- After 3 months into employment.
- Every 6 months for the first 2 years of employment, with annual reviews thereafter if there are no problems. If problems are identified then this may be increased, depending on the advice of the occupational health professional managing the health surveillance programme.

OCCUPATIONAL CANCER

There are a number of causes of occupational cancer and there is still much to learn regarding the effect of exposure to hazardous substances, especially multiple exposures.

Occupationally related cancer was first identified by Percival Potts, a surgeon at a London hospital in 1775. He noticed an increase in the incidents of scrotal cancer amongst chimney sweeps, which he had attributed to contact with soot.

Since then much research has been carried out on the effects of fossil fuel based substances and the links to scrotal cancer. Many of these substances continue to be used, for example, benzene, vinyl chloride. One of the main problems associated with the diagnosis of occupational cancer is the long latency period from exposure to symptoms, which can be up to 40 years.

In the 1970's and 80's there were a number of recognised cases of scrotal cancer, associated with exposure to mineral oils. It was caused by workers carrying dirty oil soaked rags in their pockets, which resulted in the oil soaking through overalls onto the scrotum. The use of vegetable oils, together with changes in work practice and improved personal hygiene has greatly reduced this risk.

A study conducted for the HSE estimates that 8,000 cancer deaths (5.3% of all cancer deaths in 2005) and 14,000 cancer registrations (4% of all cancer registrations in 2004) per year in Great Britain could be attributed to past occupational exposure to known carcinogens.

Some well recognised agents that can cause cancer (known as carcinogens) include:

- Ultra violet light (UVL) - skin exposure, which can cause skin cancer in workers exposed to high level of sunlight, for example, construction and farm workers.
- Asbestos - the inhalation of asbestos fibres, which can cause mesothelioma (cancer of the pleura, lining of the lung) and lung cancer in workers in contact with asbestos, for example, asbestos removers, demolition workers and facilities maintenance staff.
- Ionising radiation - may cause bone cancer, leukaemia, cancer of the glands (lymphoma) in radiologists and radiographers working in health care or those working in the nuclear industry.
- Naphthylamine - a substance used to make dyes and benzene, used in rubber manufacturing - which can cause bladder cancer in workers using the substances in manufacturing processes.

One major source of skin cancer is exposure to the sun and this is particularly relevant to outside workers such as those on construction, farming, road maintenance, sportsmen and women. The management of this must be through avoiding exposure by where possible, ensuring the skin is covered at all times.

Consideration should be given to restricting the wearing of shorts and ensuring that shirts are worn. Consideration should be given to scheduling outdoor work to avoid the heat of the day between 1100 hrs and 1500 hrs; this may be best achieved by starting work at an earlier time during the summer months. High factor skin creams can help to reduce exposure, but must not be relied upon to provide adequate protection.

Workers should be trained to report early cancer symptoms, for example, the appearance of irregular moles (possible melanomas) to the skin resulting from exposure to ultraviolet radiation from sunlight whilst working outdoors.

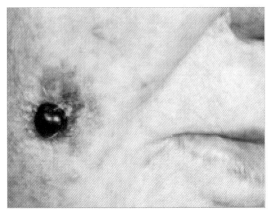

Figure 3-19: Lentigo malignant melanoma. *Source: Guy's and St Thomas NHS Foundation.*

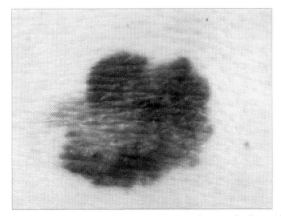

Figure 3-20: Superficial malignant melanoma. *Source: Guy's and St Thomas NHS Foundation.*

Legislation applicable to occupational cancer

The main legislation applicable to occupational cancer is:

- Health and Safety at Work Act (HASAWA) 1974.
- Control of Substances Hazardous to Health Regulations (COSHH) 2002 (as amended).
- Chemical (Hazards Information and Packaging) Regulations (CHIP) 2009 (requires 'risk phrases' to be used.
- Management of Health and Safety at Work Regulations (MHSWR) 1999.
- Ionising Radiation Regulations (IRR) 1999.
- Control of Asbestos Regulations (CAR) 2006.
- Control of Artificial Optical Radiation at Work Regulations (CAOR) 2010.
- Workplace (Health Safety and Welfare) Regulations (WHSWR) 1992.
- Personal Protective Equipment Regulations (PPE) 1992.

The management of occupational cancer

There are strict controls for the use and removal of asbestos. The Control of Asbestos Regulations (CAR) 2006 sets out requirements for this. They set out standards for the management of asbestos, working with asbestos and asbestos removal. Training of workers that may be exposed to asbestos is also mandatory, as is medical surveillance of workers. Medical surveillance must be carried out by an approved doctor appointed by the HSE and will include:

- Advice on fitness to work with asbestos.
- The provision of information to the employee on their current state of health - particularly the respiratory system.
- Alert and educate the employee to the early signs of disease.
- Chest x-rays may also be carried out.

It is important to note that medical surveillance is not preventive as, if there has been exposure above the recommended safe limits, there could be damage which cannot be cured. However, symptoms may take many years to manifest themselves, typically 20-50 years after exposure.

Education of both management and workers will be vital, workers need to know how to protect themselves and management need to understand the importance of ensuring that the prevention and control methods are working. Workers must understand how controls work and how to report breakdowns or deficiencies of any kind immediately.

Exposure to carcinogens must be prevented and controlled at source as, once the cancer has started to develop, it will not be able to be cured easily and may be fatal. The main hierarchy of control previously discussed for prevention of occupational lung diseases also applies for prevention of occupational cancer.

BLOOD BORNE VIRUSES

The main blood borne viruses that can be encountered during occupational exposure are hepatitis B and C and human immunodeficiency virus (HIV). The people at risk are healthcare workers such as nurses, nursing assistants, doctors, laboratory and research staff, those working in prisons, and the emergency services.

Health care workers are at risk from exposure to infected blood and from 'sharps' injuries, for example, injection needles, scalpels, and from inadvertent contact with large blood spillages and other body fluids. However, the highest risk of contracting blood borne infections is not occupational, but from unprotected sex and sharing needles.

Hepatitis

Hepatitis occurs when there is inflammation (swelling) of the liver, often caused by a virus. Hepatitis 'B' is not very common in the UK, approximately 1,000 are thought to have the virus.

Though the hepatitis 'B' virus is described as being 100 times more infectious than HIV it can remain viable in the environment for weeks, is resistant to common antiseptics and is not affected by boiling for les than thirty minutes. Most people infected with the hepatitis 'B' virus are able to fight the virus and a full recovery can be made within two months. However, there is a small risk that a person may develop chronic carrier status, and also liver failure may result, which can cause death. There is a vaccine available to prevent this infection.

Hepatitis 'C' is similar to hepatitis 'B'; however for a significant number of those infected the disease can progress to chronic liver disease, including cirrhosis (severe scarring of the liver) and liver cancer. Unlike hepatitis 'B', there is no available vaccine for this infection. Hepatitis 'C' is a notifiable condition: the doctor making the diagnosis must inform the local authority. It is estimated that approximately 200,000-500,000 people are infected with hepatitis 'C' in England and Wales; many would not know they were infected.

HIV

HIV is a virus that breaks down the body's immune system. It can remain dormant with no clinical symptoms or it can develop into acquired immune deficiency syndrome (AIDS). AIDS manifests itself with increased susceptibility to infections, such as general lung infections and TB (tuberculosis), there is also a risk of increased incidence of skin and lymphatic cancers. The incidence of occupationally contracted HIV is very small and it has mainly been transmission to a patient from an infected health care worker, for example, a dentist or surgeon may infect a patient during medical treatment. HIV is a delicate virus and does not live very long outside the body. Contamination is more likely from direct contact with fresh blood. Medication is available that can slow down the effects of HIV and the development of AIDS, but there are side effects to the treatment. There is no known cure at present for HIV/AIDS, but extensive research is being carried out to find one. There is no vaccine available.

Legislation applicable to blood borne viruses

- Health and Safety at Work Act (HASAWA) 1974.
- Control of Substances Hazardous to Health Regulations (COSHH) 2002 (as amended).
- Management of Health and Safety at Work Regulations (MHSWR) 1999.
- Workplace (Health Safety and Welfare) Regulations (WHSWR) 1992.
- Personal Protective Equipment Regulations (PPE) 1992.

The Control of Substances Hazardous to Health Regulations (COSHH) 2002 (as amended), require the employer to carry out risk assessments to identify potential hazards to health, and this includes identifying risks related to blood borne viruses and ensuring that suitable prevention and control methods are in place.

The management of blood borne viruses

Prevention and control of blood borne infections:

- Vaccination programme for Hepatitis 'B', with blood tests to check the vaccine has provided adequate cover. It is recommended that only high risk groups should be vaccinated for Hepatitis 'B'. Care should be taken to ensure that those provided with vaccinations do not develop the impression that once vaccinated they are protected against all blood borne infections, which is not the case. It is important that employees are educated about this and supervised to ensure they follow the prevention and control strategies in place.
- Prohibiting workers who are infected from carrying out exposure prone procedures (operations where the hands are in contact with sharp objects inside a patients open body cavity or wound).
- Care using sharp instruments and needles, for example, no re-sheathing of used needles.
- Correct hand washing procedures.
- Safe disposal of sharps in suitable robust containers, which are not overfilled.
- Safe disposal of clinical waste, which should be separated from ordinary waste and incinerated.
- Safe systems of work especially during exposure prone procedures.

There should be a detailed written policy regarding blood borne infection, which should include procedures for vaccinations, disposal of sharps and clinical waste, reporting of injuries, procedures to deal with sharps injuries and blood spillages including counselling services for staff that have been exposed.

Figure 3-21: Blue top, yellow body. Unspecified NOS (National Occupational Standards).

Figure 3-22: Orange top, yellow body. Infectious waste fully discharged sharps **not** cycotic/cyclostaic medicines.

Figure 3-23: Yellow top, yellow body. Infectious waste partially discharged sharps **not** cycotic/cyclostaic medicines.

Figure 3-24: Purple top, yellow body. Cytotoxic/cytostatic waste. For sharps contaminated with cytotoxic and cytostatic medicines.

Source: cleanroomshop.co.uk.

Cycotic/cyclostaic means any medicinal product or chemically contaminated biological waste that possesses one or more of the hazardous properties toxic, carcinogenic, toxic for reproduction or mutagenic. This may include drugs from a number of medicinal classes, for example, antineoplastic agents, antivirals, immunosuppressants, a range of hormonal drugs and others.

All workers at risk of blood borne infections should receive training and education on the risks to their health, safe systems of working, disposal of clinical and sharps waste, how to use control measures, including the use of PPE and hand washing.

1) Wet hands with warm water.

2) Lather to hands with soap completely.

3) Scrub hands thoroughly for 20 seconds.

4) Rinse hands.

5) Dry hands with a single use towel.

6) Use towel to turn off the tap.

7) Use towel to open the door.

8) Discard towel into pedal operated bin after exit.

Workers will also need to be educated in the procedures in place for reporting incidents, the treatment and advice that is available and how to access counselling services.

There should also be strict disciplinary procedures in place for those people who do not follow the safe systems of work and control procedures, as the implications of exposure are serious and could prove life threatening.

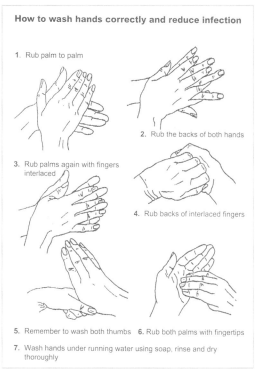

How to wash hands correctly and reduce infection

1. Rub palm to palm

2. Rub the backs of both hands

3. Rub palms again with fingers interlaced

4. Rub backs of interlaced fingers

5. Remember to wash both thumbs   6. Rub both palms with fingertips

7. Wash hands under running water using soap, rinse and dry thoroughly

Figure 3-25: Hand washing techniques.   *Source: Ayliffe et al 2000.*

There is often concern expressed by first-aiders that they are at high risk of blood borne infections, however the risk is minimal if they follow the procedures they are taught on their training courses and report any incidents of blood spillages or splashes.

3.2 - Emerging workplace health risks

Potentially significant emerging health issues

Over the past decade there has been a number of emerging health risks that have the potential to impact on the workplace by causing high absence levels due to infections. Because these emerging health issues, by their nature, are new or present where prevention has not been established they represent a significant threat to the health of workers and the population at large. Recent examples of significant emerging health issues are set out below. Though TB is not a new health condition the way in which it is presenting itself and its re-emergence after a period of strong prevention and control is setting new challenges. The new health issues, like SARS, present themselves to a population that has little or no immunity to them and this means the scale of the potential impact on the workplace is highly significant. As a consequence it is important to be aware of them and plan for potential outbreaks in order to reduce the impact on the workplace and community at large. The advice on planning and prevention relating to flu pandemics, set out below, is indicative of the type of response necessary for all the emerging health issues.

NOROVIRUS

This is named after a town in Ohio (Norwalk) where there was an outbreak in 1968. Norovirus causes a form of gastroenteritis, the symptoms being sickness, diarrhoea, stomach pains, raised temperature and tiredness. The incubation period is 12-72 hours and the illness is of short duration, with recovery normally within 2 days. It is highly contagious and the main effects of the virus are found in institutional settings such as hospitals, schools and prisons. Due to the high infection rate, it has caused many wards to be closed in hospitals as many patients will be more vulnerable due to their reduced ability to fight infections. Good personal hygiene and deep cleaning is required to prevent and control norovirus as it is transmitted by the faecal - oral route (for example, using the toilet and not washing the hands properly). Where institutions have been closed due to the presence of the virus, for example, hospital wards or schools, there is likely to be high absence levels amongst staff, who may also contract the illness through hand to infected hand or hand to surfaces contact.

SARS (SEVERE ACUTE RESPIRATORY SYNDROME)

SARS (severe acute respiratory syndrome) was first identified in 2002 in the Far East. It affected mainly health care workers and air travellers. The incubation period for the infection is around 1 week and symptoms include high temperature, dry cough, severe muscular pains (Myalagia) and severe respiratory disease, which can lead to pneumonia and can be fatal. Prevention is by controlling non-essential travel to affected areas and the provision of appropriate personal protective equipment (PPE) for health care workers, along with isolation of infected patients.

AVIAN FLU (BIRD FLU)

This virus has caused outbreaks of chest infections amongst chickens and wild migratory birds. A highly infectious strain of this disease was responsible for a major outbreak in Hong Kong in 1997, which resulted in the culling of millions of chickens. The infection symptoms include high temperature, cough, difficulty in breathing, reduction in the production of white blood cells (cells that help to fight infection). Transmission has occurred from birds to humans, but there is very little evidence of transmission from human to human. However, there are concerns that as new strains of the virus develop, it may become a potential for a new flu pandemic, which again could cause high absence levels within businesses.

PANDEMIC FLU

Flu (influenza) refers to a number of different flu viruses. Every year a percentage of workers will get flu. Pandemic flu is different from ordinary flu because it occurs when a new flu virus emerges into the human population and spreads from person-to person worldwide. As the emerging virus is a new virus no one will have established an immunity to it, therefore it has potential to affect everyone.

The Faculty of Occupational Medicine (FOM) published a guidance document for employers on pandemic flu and the following information is provided based on their recommendations. The guidance leaflet can be downloaded from the FOM website www.facoccmed.ac.uk.

Planning for a pandemic flu outbreak

- Consider how to deal with cuts in supplies, transport and technical help - how will this affect the business.
- Plan if work could be carried out remotely, for example, working from home.
- Consider the need for back up staff for key roles, for example, training up others to take on additional tasks and responsibilities, if required.
- Consider those in the workforce who may be affected if schools and day centres are closed, for example, how could this be managed if workers are unable to find child care, or if day centres for the elderly are closed?
- Consider modifying shifts to allow for increased absenteeism, due to illness or unforeseen child or elderly care problems.

Prevention and reducing the risk of pandemic flu

- Reduce the risk of infection by isolating those infected, for example, remove from the workplace.
- Inform employees not to come to work if they have any symptoms, and that they should let their manager know if this is the case.
- Encourage frequent thorough hand washing with the use of alcohol gels.
- Educate employees to use disposable tissues and to dispose of them appropriately.
- Improve cleaning of hard surfaces, preferably by damp cleaning.

TUBERCULOSIS (TB)

Tuberculosis (TB) is an infectious condition that is spread by 'droplets' (coughing, sneezing) and mainly affects the lungs. It manifests as a chronic persistent cough. There is usually loss of weight and those affected suffer night sweats. TB can also affect other parts of the body such as the bones and brain, but this is more unusual.

TB has been fairly well controlled in the UK and western countries; however it is still prevalent in developing countries such as Africa and parts of Asia. It tends to affect people who live in poor living conditions; also people with AIDS are at increased risk due to their reduced immune status. Workers at risk are those who have contact with potentially infected people and infected human samples, for example, immigration officials, health care workers, laboratory, mortuary and post-mortem room staff. Vets and farmers can also be affected by a similar strain of TB found in cattle.

Prevention and control of TB includes:

- Checking the TB status of at risk workers by the Mantoux test, (which replaced the Heaf test in the UK in 2005). This involves the injection between the layers of the demis of a small amount of Tuberculin. The area on the arm is examined after 46 hours to assess what type of reaction has taken place. A positive reaction would result in a raised hardened area. Provided the Mantoux test is negative a BCG Vaccination (a live strain of Mycobacterium bovis known as bacillus Calmette-Guérin (BCG) used to stimulate the development of cross-immunity to tuberculosis) may be given.
- Tests should be carried out at pre-employment and form part of the pre-employment health assessment.
- Isolation of infected people, for example, infected patients nursed in separate rooms.
- Infected cadavers placed in sealed containers and during post-mortem procedures staff to wear appropriate respiratory protection equipment (RPE), which would normally be self contained breathing apparatus.
- Long term prevention is to improve living conditions and educate people regarding personal hygiene and diet.

3.3 - Positive benefits of work on health

Benefits to an individual's health through work

A study published in 2006 by Gordon Waddell and A Kim Burton 'Is work good for your health and well-being?' found that it had a positive effect on the individual's physical and psychosocial well-being.

"Employment is generally the most important means of obtaining adequate economic resources, which are essential for material well-being and full participation in today's society. Work meets important psychosocial needs in societies where employment is the norm. Work is central to individual identity, social roles and status. Employment and socio-economic status are the main drivers of social gradients in physical and mental health mortality. Various physical and psychosocial aspects of work can also be hazardous and pose a risk to health".

Figure 3-26: Benefits of work on health.   Source: Gordon Waddell and A Kim Burton 'Is work good for your health and well-being'?

Their study also found the opposite applied to those unemployed, and that the unemployed were likely to have poorer physical and mental health. They also identified positive factors for "the right work" on the sick and disabled, which included being therapeutic, aiding recovery, reduced long term absenteeism, promoted self esteem and inclusion into society, and reduced poverty.

BENEFITS TO THE INDIVIDUAL BOTH PHYSICALLY AND PSYCHO-SOCIALLY

There have been a number of studies that have indicated that work is beneficial to people. People who are healthy and in work are likely to lead full and satisfying lives and will be more productive. They are financially secure and will have higher self-esteem. Work also affords companionship and status. When we meet people for the first time we normally ask "what is your job" and no one likes to say 'unemployed' or 'off sick'. There is anecdotal evidence that working enhances a person's life. People who have been made redundant and have been out of work for a significant time will say how relieved they are when they find employment. Redundancy shatters lives; the feeling of not being wanted and 'sacked' on an individual will be difficult psychologically for them to cope with. There will also be the financial pressures to find work, especially if there is a mortgage/rent to pay, a family to feed and support, and this may lead to depression if work is not found for some time. An individual who has been off sick for a long time will also experience the same problems.

BENEFITS TO AID REHABILITATION

Assisting and supporting people back to work following injury or illness is beneficial to both the individual and the organisation. Research studies have found that employing someone with a disability will often show that:

- They are able to carry out work as well as able bodied colleagues.
- They have less time off sick.
- They tend to stay longer in their jobs; they are loyal to the company who supports them.
- Have fewer work accidents.

There is also evidence that rehabilitation aids recovery. With the right work and gradual introduction back into the workplace workers are less likely to go off 'sick' again. When someone has been off work for an extended period, it is very difficult to go straight back into 'normal working'; there is the fear of changes and how colleagues will react to you and whether you can manage to do the job.

 Case Study - Rehabilitation after surgery

A woman who had been off work for 8 weeks following abdominal surgery, wanted to return to work, but her job involved a great deal of standing and walking. Her manager arranged for her to return on an alternative job, where she was able to sit some of the time, also returning on reduced hours, gradually building up over a period of 6 weeks. She used her job to undertake some of her exercises that the physiotherapist had advised, for example, whilst standing she carried out abdominal tightening, and increased her walking distance. Within the 6 weeks she was back to her normal work. She was pleased with her progress and her manager was content that he had been able to support her return. Being at work had helped her recovery. If she had remained at home, she would probably not have been able to make such good progress as there would be less motivation to try to do more.

NEGATIVE EFFECTS OF UNEMPLOYMENT

The Health Development Agency have reviewed the literature relating to unemployment and health and concluded:

- There is a relationship between unemployment and poor health, although causation is not proven.
- There is a strong association between deprived areas, poor health, poverty and worklessness, although the exact relationship is not clear.
- Given the potential differences on morbidity and life expectancy within local authorities, there may be an argument to examine the geographical dimension on worklessness and health at local authority ward level.

In some parts of the UK there are areas where three generations of people have not worked, for example, South Wales, following the closure of coal mines. These areas have increased poverty, poor health and lower life expectancy.

There are many reasons for this, including expectations for employment and the lack of opportunity to re-train for a different job. There is also the psychological impact this has on communities, who in the past had relied on the mining industry for their livelihood, as had their parents and grandparents before them.

Characteristics of what constitutes "good work"

There are no definitive studies that have identified what is 'good work'. However, anecdotal evidence suggest the factors likely to influence this include:

- A safe and healthy working environment.
- Secure work, without fear of redundancy.
- Feeling valued, with opportunities to develop potential and 'get on'.
- Fair payment.
- Having control of work, autonomy and being able to take appropriate breaks.
- Management who are supportive, accommodating and non-discriminatory.
- Job satisfaction and fulfilment.
- Good communications - knowing what is going on, for example, how well the business is doing, being praised when you do well.

In terms of health and well-being, in addition to the above, 'good work' would be work which:

- Focuses on the capabilities of the individual rather than their limitations.
- Can be adapted to reflect reduced or improved capabilities.
- Where a worker is recovering from work-related ill-health, work that supports this recovery.
- Is good for both the individual's physical and psychosocial health.
- Provides suitable breaks in order to maintain performance, reduce fatigue and provide rest.
- Establishes an appropriate work life balance.

"Good work is work that is rewarding for employees, employers and society. For employees, good work provides secure and interesting jobs; choice, flexibility and control over working hours; autonomy and control over the pace and timing of work and the working environment; a say in the critical decisions that affect their futures; and an appropriate balance between effort and reward.

From a business perspective, good work is productive and efficient; aims to involve and engage employees; and to encourage their contribution to organisational success. And from a society perspective, good work is socially aware, ethical, and sustainable".

Figure 3-27: 'Good work'. *Source: The Work Foundation.*

3.4 - Patterns of work

Effects on physical and mental health from patterns of work

When looking at the health effects of 'patterns of work' there are six main aspects to consider:

- Shift working.
- Night working.
- Extended hours.
- Part-time working.
- Remote working.
- Patterns of work related to pregnancy.

The first three of these patterns of work would usually be labelled 'working unsociable hours'; however, many people choose to work this way. For example, some people will choose to work nights because it fits in with their lifestyle and family commitments.

With the changes in society and our increased expectations, more and more organisations are now working 24 hours a day, 7 days a week (24/7). This is due to the demands that society makes relating to the provision of emergency services, being able to shop when people want and access to assistance through call centres that provide help-lines. There are also other considerations, such as industries with continuous processing that, from an economic point of view, need to use plant and equipment to maximum effect, as the cost of closing down the plant is too high.

SHIFT WORKING

There is no specific definition of shift work in law, but it is usually taken to mean a work activity scheduled outside standard daytime hours, where there may be a handover of duty from one individual or work group to another; a pattern of work where one employee replaces another on the same job within a 24-hour period.

Figure 3-28: Definition of shift work. *Source: HSE, Managing Shift Work.*

There are many types of shift working patterns, which include 2 or 3 shifts in 24 hours and rotating shifts, for example, one week the individual works days, one week the individual works afternoons/evenings and one week the individual works nights. A typical shift rotation system might use shifts of 6am to 2pm, 2pm to 10pm and 10pm to 6am. Typically 6 days on one shift (say 6am to 2pm) 2 days rest, and then 6 days on the next shift (which would be 2pm to 10pm) such that the individual works each shift in turn. With this system hours will be accumulated and every six weeks the worker will take 6 days rest.

The effects on health of rotating shift working are fairly well documented and include heart disease, stomach disorders and fatigue, due to sleep loss. There are also factors to consider that affect the psychosocial aspects of work, leading to reduced performance and the potential for increased accidents, as well as family and social life, putting strain on family relationships.

There are also shift working patterns that involve long hours, where people work 12 hour shifts for 3 days and then have time off. The problem with this shift working pattern is that some people working these hours will often take on second jobs, which will increase the incidence of their tiredness and fatigue.

> The number of shift workers in the UK has gradually increased over the last 25 years reaching a peak in 2000, when around 15% of the working population (approximately 3.8 million people), worked shifts for 'most of the time'. Since then, numbers have stabilised, with around 14% of the working population (3.6 million people) now doing shift work 'most of the time'.

Figure 3-29: Number of people involved in shift work. *Source: HSE, Managing Shift Work.*

Shift working may result in:

- Disruption of the internal body clock.
- Fatigue.
- Sleeping difficulties.
- Disturbed appetite and digestion.
- Reliance on sedatives and/or stimulants.
- Social and domestic problems.

All of which in turn can affect performance, increase the likelihood of errors and accidents at work and might have a negative effect on health or exacerbate a pre-existing health condition, such as diabetes or epilepsy.

Individuals vary in their tolerance to shift working for a variety of reasons, including:

- Some find it easier to fall asleep, sleep for longer and adapt more easily to changes in sleep patterns.
- Some have a tendency to be more alert at particular times of the day, early in the morning or late at night.
- Some organise their domestic duties and social activities in line with their shifts.
- Some use different behaviours or coping strategies.
- Differing ability to adapt to shift work; it tends to decrease with age.
- People have differing degrees of health and fitness.

NIGHT WORKING

Night working is generally taken to be work conducted between 11pm to 6am, which reflects the Working Time Regulations (WTR) 1998. Night work is normally part of a shift rotation system; though some jobs involve permanent night working, for example, underground railway workers, some postal staff and security staff. Many who work shifts find that it disturbs sleep and eating patterns greatly; not many people enjoy eating a main meal at 2am in the morning. Sleep is often difficult in the day, especially in the summer months when children are off school or keen home owners are carrying out DIY or using lawn mowers or just chatting with one another. This is exacerbated if the weather is hot and it is necessary to have windows open to keep cool whilst they sleep. Night working can therefore lead to 'sleep debt' and fatigue. There is a small to moderate risk of premature birth and low birth rates for pregnant women working shifts or long hours.

The Working Time Regulations (WTR) 1998 as amended, make special provision for night workers. Regulation 6 limits the length of night work to an average of eight hours for each 24 hours worked in a reference period (17 week period including rest days). For a night worker whose work involves special hazards, heavy physical work or significant mental strain, the employer must ensure workers do not work for more than eight hours in any 24-hour period.

Such work may be identified through a:

- Collective (National) agreement.
- Workforce (local) agreement.
- A risk assessment made by the employer under Regulation 3 of the Management of Health and Safety at Work Regulations (MHSWR) 1999.

When the work is of a kind that would involve risk to a new or expectant mother or her baby, the assessment required by Regulation 3 should take this into account.

If the risks cannot be avoided, then the employer should take reasonable steps to:

- Adjust the hours worked.
- Offer alternative work.
- Give paid leave for as long as is necessary.

Regulation 7 of WTR 1998 requires that the employer offers the opportunity for a free health assessment before the worker is assigned to night work for the first time. In addition, the employer must provide a health assessment on the request of a night worker, this is in addition to any ongoing assessment the employer have determined necessary.

If, following such an assessment, a medical practitioner determines a night worker is suffering from night work related health problems, and there is available day work which is within the capability of the worker; the employer must transfer the night worker to day time working.

The employer must not assign a young worker to work during the "restricted period" (typically 10am to 6am) unless a health and capacities assessment has been carried out and the employer has no reason to believe that that assessment is no longer valid. Each young worker employed and assigned to work during the restricted period has the right to an assessment of their health and capacities for night working at regular intervals.

See also - Scope and application of the main implications of the Working Time Regulations (WTR) 1998 - later in this element.

EXTENDED HOURS

Many businesses now work longer periods than an eight hour shift over a five day working week, for example, twelve hours over a three day period. Rest days vary considerably depending upon the shift system applied and where relatively long periods, three to five days of rest, occur there can be a temptation for workers to seek other employment.

 Case Study - Driving after extended hours working

Following a traffic accident, involving an Large Goods Vehicle (LGV) in the West Midlands, it was found that the LGV driver was not only driving long distances in connection with the LGV licence, but was working in between time, on a three day twelve hour shift system in a factory carrying out heavy industrial grinding work. The reason for the accident was that the driver fell asleep at the wheel.

In addition to long shift systems, extended hours can occur due to 'overtime' working, either on a prescribed paid basis or just working longer to ensure things get done. This can happen at relatively short notice, such as where maintenance engineers, care workers or security staff are asked to cover for the absence of other workers. This can mean them working their usual period and then working extended hours to ensure the other person's work is covered. It is predictable that fatigue could lead to errors, particularly if the extended hours take place without a suitable break between the usual periods of working. Employers should reduce long working hours for women in the later stages of pregnancy, as it is normal for the woman to become fatigued as pregnancy progresses.

PART-TIME WORKING

Part-time working is often carried out by parents with dependant children or relatives or those looking towards retirement. If the culture of the organisation in which they work recognises the need to embrace flexible working then often the process is beneficial to both parties.

Part-time working is often difficult to implement for certain jobs, for example, where there are few workers able to carry out essential tasks such as personnel or maintenance functions. Workers in critical functions may be put under pressure to work longer or take work home because the work has to be done within a similar time frame to that which would normally be required of a full-time worker. Job sharing similarly can have its own strengths and weaknesses.

 Case Study - Part-time working as job share

Two administration assistants were employed on a job share. Mary worked 9am to 1pm. Tom worked 1pm to 5pm. Tom was always early and started at 12.45pm in order to hand over with Mary before she left for the day. Tom found that he was increasingly under greater pressure to complete the day's work because Mary did not complete all her tasks before she left promptly at 1pm and this meant that he did not leave until after 5pm.

The potential imbalance of workload and pressures to work longer than agreed to complete work could lead to one of the workers developing stress. Before implementing job sharing it is important to run a provisional scheme before agreeing to the change; consideration should be given to rotation of individuals, am to pm to avoid any imbalance in work load. Absence for sickness or holidays will also need to be covered by some mutual agreement of the parties involved or by transfer of labour to cover the job.

REMOTE WORKING

Remote working may have both physical and mental risks to health associated with it. Workers may find themselves exposed to physical risks due to not having available to them resources that can prevent physical harm, for example, musculoskeletal risks may arise due to having to lift something or someone without mechanical or human assistance. In addition, the isolation of remote working can limit communications and other social interaction, which may lead to anxiety about work issues and lead to stress.

Remote or peripatetic workers such as social workers and district nurses are a special risk and as such should be managed to the level of risk that is necessary for their daily routine. It is important for their managers to require them to work to a strict rota so that it is known where they are at any moment in time. This usually requires the establishment of a central control to monitor them throughout the working day.

Where risk is high they should notify control before each attendance at a household and immediately after leaving the household. Means of raising the alarm in a hostile situation should be an essential part of the procedure and training.

PATTERNS OF WORK RELATED TO PREGNANCY

Pregnancy is not an illness and the majority of women keep healthy during their pregnancy. There is much 'scare-mongering' about the affects of work on pregnant women and it is important to keep this in perspective. There are a number of non-occupational factors that are more likely to influence pregnancy outcomes, such as young maternal age, obesity, smoking, and low social economic status. Occupational risks can be controlled and modified to accommodate the pregnant woman. There is a small to moderate risk of premature birth and low birth rates for pregnant women working shifts or long hours; conversely there is evidence that confirms that women who work are healthier during their pregnancy. Women should not be removed from work, if the risks have been explained and they choose to continue, as there may be insufficient evidence to enforce restrictions that may be classed as discriminatory. However, the health of the individual woman must be taken into consideration and advice sought from an occupational health professional, where there are doubts. Employers should reduce long working hours for women in the later stages of pregnancy, as it is normal for the woman to become fatigued as pregnancy progresses.

(More information and a guidance leaflet are available to download from www.nhsplus.uk).

Scope and application of the Working Time Regulations (WTR) 1998

In 1998 the Working Time Regulations (WTR) were introduced as a result of the European Commission Directive to control working hours. There have been a number of amendments, the last being in 2009. As these regulations are developing and changing, it is recommended regular checks are made to obtain updates, which are available from a number of websites, including the HSE, business link and www.legislation.gov.uk.

The main principles of the Working Time Regulations (WTR) 1998 (as amended) are:

- Workers cannot be forced to work more than 48 hours a week on average.
- Employees can choose to 'opt out' of the 48 hour week, and employers are required to keep a record of all employees who have opted out.
- Employers must provide adequate rest breaks where a ***pattern of work*** organised by the employer puts the health and safety of a worker employed by them at risk, for example, where the work is uninterruptible or monotonous. The provision of breaks is in order to reduce the risk caused by this type of work, for example, due to fatigue.
- There must be regular ***rest breaks***.
  - Where the adult worker works more that six hours the rest break must be not less than 20 minutes.
  - Where a young worker works more than four and a half hours the rest break must be at least 30 minutes.
- ***Daily rest*** must be provided.
  - An adult worker is entitled to a daily rest period of not less than eleven hours in each 24 hour period.
  - A young worker is entitled to a daily rest period of not less than twelve hours in each 24 hour period.
  - The minimum rest period may be interrupted where the pattern of work is broken up into short periods over the 24 hours.
- ***Weekly rest*** periods must be provided (conditions not explained here apply to this provision).
  - An adult worker is entitled to an uninterrupted rest period of not less than 24 hours in each seven day period.
  - A young worker is entitled to an uninterrupted rest period of not less than 48 hours in each seven day period.
- Workers are entitled to a minimum of 4 weeks paid leave per year.
- ***Night workers*** have special rules. Night time is defined as between 11pm and 6am. A night time worker has been defined by a High Court of Northern Ireland to be a worker who works at least three hours during the night time as a "regular feature of their employment". The rules state that night workers should not work more than 8 hours in 24 hours, on average referenced over a 17 week period. In general, young workers should not work at night time. Where the work involves special hazards, or heavy physical strain, or mental strain, no night worker may work for more than eight hours in a 24 hour period. Overtime hours are included in this calculation. This is an absolute limit and is not subject to averaging over a reference period.
- Subject to the provision of compensatory rest, the night work limits do not apply in the circumstances listed in Regulation 21. This includes:
  - Where the worker is engaged in security and surveillance activities and a permanent presence is required.
  - Where there is a need for continuity of service or production, for example, health care; work at docks and airports; press, radio, television etc; gas, water and electricity production; industries in which work

cannot be interrupted on technical grounds; research and development activities, the carriage of passengers on regular urban transport services.

- Where the worker's activities are affected by an unusual and unforeseeable circumstances/exceptional events; or an accident or the imminent risk of an accident.

■ Employers must offer a health assessment to night workers before they commence night working. This can be in the form of a questionnaire, with a follow up medical assessment if required. The employee does not have to take up this offer.

Health questionnaire to assess if you are fit to work nights

The purpose of this questionnaire is to make sure that you are suited to working at night. All the information you provide will be kept confidential.

About you

Job Title:

Surname:

First and second name/s:

Sex: M [   ]   F [   ]

Date of birth:

Permanent address:

Job title:

National Insurance number:

Health conditions

Do you suffer from any of the following health conditions?

Diabetes	Yes [ ]	No [ ]
Heart or circulatory disorders	Yes [ ]	No [ ]
Stomach or intestinal disorders	Yes [ ]	No [ ]
Any condition which causes difficulties sleeping	Yes [ ]	No [ ]
Chronic chest disorders (especially if night-time symptoms are troublesome)	Yes [ ]	No [ ]
Any medical condition requiring medication to a strict timetable	Yes [ ]	No [ ]
Any other health factors that might affect fitness at work	Yes [ ]	No [ ]

If you have answered 'yes' to any of the above questions, you may be asked to see a doctor or nurse

I, the undersigned, confirm that the above is correct to the best of my knowledge

Signed: ………………………………… Date: …………………………………

Figure 3-30: Sample health questionnaire for night work.   *Source: Business Link.*

■ Employers also have a duty to transfer a night worker from night work to more suitable work which is not night work, if a registered medical practitioner has advised the employer that the worker is suffering health problems considered by the practitioner to be connected with night work. This duty is qualified by the phrase 'where it is possible'.

■ There are special rules for the employment of *young people*; they may not work more than 8 hours a day or 40 hours a week, and are entitled to regular work rest breaks. Young workers must not work between 10pm and 6am, known as the restricted period, unless the work is allowed by an exception. The limits relating to young workers can be relaxed if all of the following conditions apply:
- Their employer requires him to undertake work which is necessary either to maintain continuity of service or production or to respond to a surge in demand for a service or product.
- No adult worker is available to perform the work.
- Performing the work would not adversely affect the young worker's education or training.

In these circumstances the following exemptions are allowed.

Possible exemption	Young workers to whom it applies
Disapplication of eight hour daily and 40 hour weekly working limit. To be replaced by 48 hour limit as for adult workers.	Any.
Disapplication of prohibition on work during restricted hours. To be replaced by eight hour limit as for adult workers.	Employed in a hospital or similar establishment, or in connection with cultural, artistic, sporting or advertising activities.
Restricted hours for night work reduced to between midnight and 4 am.	Employed in agriculture, retail trading, postal or newspaper deliveries, catering businesses, hotels, public houses, restaurants, bars, bakeries.

Figure 3-31: Exemptions from prohibition of young workers doing night work.   Source: HSE.

Where the night work exceptions apply and the young worker is required to work during a period that would otherwise be a rest period or rest break:

- The young worker should have adult supervision where this is necessary for their protection.
- They should be given an equivalent period of compensatory rest immediately after the end of the work period.

The working time regulations provide information on what is classed as 'working time'; this includes:

- Working lunches, such as business lunches.
- When an employee has to travel as part of their work, for example, sales people, repair/maintenance workers.
- Specific job related training (this does not include non-job related training such as night school or day release).
- Time spent working abroad if the employers' main base is in Great Britain.

3.5 - The role and function of health surveillance

Role and benefits of health surveillance

THE ROLE OF HEALTH SURVEILLANCE

Health surveillance is part of secondary intervention, and its **role** is to provide early detection of work related ill-health. Primary intervention is the elimination and control at source of hazardous agents in the workplace and tertiary intervention is the early treatment of identified work related ill-health.

BENEFITS OF HEALTH SURVEILLANCE

Health surveillance is useful as an additional tool for risk management, where risks cannot be completely eliminated and the benefits include:

- It helps to protect the health of employees by early detection of adverse health effects that might be attributed to exposure to hazardous substances or other workplace hazards.
- It enables early action to be taken to prevent the effects becoming worse.
- It enables the provision of tertiary intervention at the earliest opportunity.
- It aids the collection of data for detecting or evaluating health hazards.
- It will assist with the evaluation of control measures through the collection of measurements and data relating to the exposure of employees to hazards.

BIOLOGICAL MONITORING

- **Biological monitoring** - the measurement and assessment of workplace agents or their metabolites (substances formed when the body converts the chemical) in exposed workers, for example, breath, urine or blood.
- **Biological effect monitoring** - the measurement and assessment of early effects such as reduced lung function in exposed workers caused by absorption of chemicals, for example, isocyanates, flour dust.

Common types of health surveillance

LEGISLATIVE REQUIREMENTS

Regulation 6 of the Management of Health and Safety at Work Regulations (MHSWR) 1999 sets out a general duty with regard to the provision of health surveillance:

"Every employer shall ensure that his employees are provided with such health surveillance as is appropriate having regard to the risks to their health and safety which are identified by the assessment".

Figure 3-32: Regulation 6 of the MHSWR 1999.   Source: MHSWR 1999.

Health surveillance is necessary when:

- The employee is exposed to one of the substances specified in Schedule 6 of Control of Substances Hazardous to Health Regulations (COSHH) 2002 (as amended).
- Where it is known that work can affect the health in some way, for example, noise, vibration, dust, fumes, gases.
- Where there are valid ways to detect the disease or health condition.
- Where it is likely that damage to health may occur under the particular working conditions.
- Where health surveillance is likely to be of benefit to the employees and that the technique for investigation is of low risk to the employee.

CONTROL OF SUBSTANCES HAZARDOUS TO HEALTH REGULATIONS

Regulation 11, of the Control of Substances Hazardous to Health Regulations (COSHH) 2002 (as amended), places a duty on employers to carry out health surveillance for the protection of their employee's health if they are liable to be exposed to certain substances specified in schedule 6 and where:

"The exposure of the employee to a substance hazardous to health is such that:

(i) An identifiable disease or adverse health effect may be related to the exposure.

(ii) There is a reasonable likelihood that the disease or effect may occur under the particular conditions of his work.

(iii) There are valid techniques for detecting indications of the disease or effect".

Employees have to make themselves available for health surveillance during working hours.

Results of health surveillance must be kept available in a suitable form for at least 40 years; if the employer ceases to trade they must make the records available to the HSE.

CONTROL OF NOISE AT WORK REGULATIONS

Regulation 9 of the Control of Noise at Work Regulations (CNWR) 2005 requires that if the assessment of noise risk indicates that there is a risk to the health of the employer's employees, who are exposed to noise, the employer must ensure that the employees are placed under suitable health surveillance, which has to include testing of their hearing (audiometry). If the health surveillance identifies hearing damage, a doctor must examine the employee. If the doctor considers the damage is a result of exposure to noise, the employer must take the following action:

- Ensure a qualified person informs the employee.
- Review risk assessments and controls to prevent exposure.
- Consider re-assignment of the employee to less noisy work.
- Continue health surveillance.

Employees must make themselves available for health surveillance that has to be provided during normal working hours. The results of health surveillance must be recorded.

CONTROL OF VIBRATION AT WORK REGULATIONS

Regulation 7 of the Control of Vibration at Work Regulations (CVWR) 2005 requires that if the assessment of vibration risk indicates that there is a risk to the health of the employer's employees, who are exposed to vibration or are likely to be exposed to vibration at or above an exposure action value, the employer shall ensure that the employees are placed under suitable health surveillance. Surveillance is, however, only appropriate if:

"The exposure of the employee to vibration is such that:

(a) A link can be established between that exposure and an identifiable disease or adverse health effect.

(b) It is probable that the disease or effect may occur under the particular conditions of his work.

(c) There are valid techniques for detecting the disease or effect".

If the health surveillance finds an identifiable disease or adverse effect, a doctor must examine the employee.

If the doctor considers this to be a result of exposure to vibration, the employer must take action as a response to the findings, similar to those required relating to noise exposure:

- Ensure a qualified person informs the employee.
- Consider re-assignment of the employee.
- Continue health surveillance.
- Review risk assessments and controls to prevent exposure.

The results of health surveillance must be recorded and employees have to make themselves available for health surveillance during working hours.

DISPLAY SCREEN EQUIPMENT REGULATIONS

Regulation 5 of the Health and Safety (Display Screen Equipment) Regulations (DSER) 1992 (as amended) requires employees and those about to become employees identified as users to be provided with eyesight testing and corrective eyesight appliances, if requested by the user. After the user or employee about to become a user has been provided with an eyesight test, the employer must ensure that the user is provided with a further eyesight test at regular intervals, whilst they are carrying out work as a user.

Where a user experiences visual difficulties that may reasonably relate to work with display screen equipment, the employer must ensure the user is provided with an appropriate eye and eyesight test by a competent person. The regulations clarify that none of the requirements affecting the employer enable the employer to carry out eye or eyesight tests against the will of the user.

TYPES OF HEALTH SURVEILLANCE

Examples of types of health surveillance include:

Type of health surveillance	Occupation	Hazard	Health effect	Legal requirement
Respiratory questionnaire	Baker	Flour dust	Asthma	COSHH
	Paint sprayer	Isocyanates	Asthma	COSHH
	Farm worker	Mouldy hay	Farmers lung	COSHH
Lung function test (LFT)	Baker	Flour dust	Asthma	COSHH
	Paint sprayer	Isocyanates	Asthma	COSHH
	Farm worker	Mouldy hay	Farmers lung	COSHH
Skin exam	Hairdresser	Shampoo dyes	Dermatitis	COSHH
Audiometry	Forestry worker	Noise	Deafness	Control of Noise at Work Regulations
Questionnaire on symptoms	Forestry worker	Vibration	HAVS	Control of Vibration at Work Regulations

Figure 3-33: Examples of types of health surveillance.   Source: RMS.

Health surveillance is often a 'staged' process and it is usually the type and level of exposure of the worker to the hazard that will determine what suitable health surveillance is.

COSHH 2002 recommends the following:

- **Review of records and occupational history**. In low hazard situations this may be all that is necessary and a record kept of the findings, so that they can be used for future reference and comparison.
- **Inspection by a responsible person** such as a supervisor or manager, for example, for chrome ulceration.
- **Enquires about symptoms and inspection** - use of a questionnaire enquiring about symptoms, testing or examination by a suitably qualified person, for example, occupational health nurse.
- **Medical surveillance** - may be under the supervision of a Health and Safety Executive (HSE) medical inspector, or an appointed doctor for the purpose of Regulation 11(5) of COSHH 2002, and a registered medical practitioner. This may include clinical examination, physiological measurement, for example, lung function, and the psychological effects of exposure to hazardous substances in the workplace.

A number of regulations set out specific requirements for medical surveillance to be conducted, including COSHH 2002, as stated above. Employees to whom the Control of Substances Hazardous to Health Regulations (COSHH) 2002 (as amended), Control of Lead at Work Regulations (CLAW) 2002, Control of Asbestos Regulations (CAR) 2006 and Ionising Radiation Regulations (IRR) 1999, apply must present themselves for medical examination and provide any information concerning their health as the doctor may reasonably require.

Examinations are at the cost of the employer and during their working hours. The regulations require that medical surveillance can only be conducted if it is of low risk to the employee and records must be kept for at least 40 years, some till the worker reaches the age of 80.

Schedule 6 of COSHH 2002 specifies substances and work in processes where medical surveillance is mandatory. CLAW 2002 specifies thresholds of blood-lead and urinary-lead concentrations that require medical surveillance. CAR 2006 requires medical surveillance to be conducted before exposure to asbestos and at intervals of no more than 2 years. IRR 1999 similarly requires medical surveillance prior to being designated as a classified person and at intervals of no more than 1 year.

Initial questionnaire for surveillance of people potentially exposed to substances that cause occupational asthma

To be completed by the responsible person

Company name_____

Address_____

_____

In this workplace substances are in use that have been known to cause allergic chest problems. Following the risk assessment under regulation 6 of the Control of Substances Hazardous to Health (COSHH) Regulations 2002, management have decided to carry out a programme of pre-exposure and periodic health surveillance as required by regulation 11 of the COSHH Regulations.

In some cases further advice may be required from the company occupational health adviser.

I understand that a programme of health surveillance is necessary in this employment and will form part of my management health record.

Signature of employee   Date

Signature of responsible person   Date

Referred for further investigation?

Would you please answer the following questions:

1   Surname Forenames_____

       Date of birth_____

       Home address_____

       _____

       _____

       Tel number_____

2   Have you any chest problems, such as periods of breathlessness, wheeze,
       chest tightness or persistent coughing?   Yes ☐   No ☐

3   Do you believe that your chest has suffered as a result of any previous employment?   Yes ☐   No ☐

4   Do you or have you ever had any of the following? (Do not include isolated colds, sore throats or flu.)

       (a)   Recurring soreness of or watering of eyes   Yes ☐   No ☐
       (b)   Recurring blocked or running nose   Yes ☐   No ☐
       (c)   Bouts of coughing   Yes ☐   No ☐
       (d)   Chest tightness   Yes ☐   No ☐
       (e)   Wheezing   Yes ☐   No ☐
       (f)   Breathlessness   Yes ☐   No ☐
       (g)   Any other persistent or history of chest problems   Yes ☐   No ☐

To be completed by the responsible person

       (a)   No further action required   ☐
       (b)   Refer to company occupational health adviser   ☐

Signed (responsible person)   Date

I confirm that the responses given by me are correct and that I have received a copy of the completed questionnaire.

Signed   Date

Please note: It will be for a health professional to assess the relevance of any respiratory symptoms and to obtain a detailed smoking history as necessary.

Figure 3-34: Respiratory symptoms questionnaire - occupational asthma.   *Source: HSE.*

The difference between health surveillance and health screening

Health surveillance is putting in place systematic, regular and appropriate programmes to detect early signs of work related ill-health among workers exposed to certain health risks; and acting on the results. Health screening is 'good practice' as a means of promoting a healthy lifestyle and identifying early signs of non-occupational disease. This may include lifestyle questionnaires. It is important that the employee and employer know the difference between health surveillance and health screening. Health surveillance is a 'legal requirement'; health screening is a non-statutory 'nice to have'.

Policies and procedures for health surveillance

THE ROLE OF POLICIES AND PROCEDURES

Policy and procedures define how an organisation manages health surveillance. They set out why the organisation is doing it, what is to be done, who is involved and how it is to take place. By establishing formal policies and procedures they set clear expectations and standards of performance. This avoids ambiguity and enables those involved to organise to ensure they are met. They should include:

- What health surveillance is to be carried out and why.
- Who will carry out the health surveillance.
- How workers will be informed of the results of tests, what will happen to the results and the procedure to ensure confidentiality of sensitive personal information.
- What control measures are in place and procedures for maintenance, for example, local exhaust ventilation (LEV).
- Procedure for reporting early symptoms of any adverse health affects.
- Procedures for reporting break down in control measures.
- Details of the management and workers' responsibilities.
- Details of how workers and managers will be educated and trained regarding health surveillance.

THE ROLE OF MANAGEMENT IN HEALTH SURVEILLANCE

Management need to take an active role in ensuring that health surveillance takes place. They need to:

- Identify the need for health surveillance through the risk assessment process. Health surveillance must be based on risk and level of exposure; there should never be a 'blanket' approach, for example, including everyone, just in case. This is bad practice as it causes unnecessary concern to employees, is time consuming and costly.
- Implement a health surveillance policy and procedures.
- Consult with workers so they understand the need for health surveillance and their role and responsibilities.
- Identify a manager who will be responsible for managing the process. This is a manager who will be responsible for ensuring the health surveillance programme is carried out, that results are managed and the findings acted upon - being the main link between the organisation and the occupational health provider carrying out the surveillance.
- Identify a suitable occupational health provider to carry out and/or supervise health surveillance if there is no in-house occupational health service.
- Ensure that line managers are aware of the need for health surveillance and that they know their responsibilities.
- Set up systems for the maintenance of records and recall systems, in conjunction with the occupational health provider. The results of health surveillance should be maintained and available for inspection by enforcing agencies like the HSE, if requested.
- Set up procedures for implementing recommendations from any reported adverse health surveillance results. Ensuring any recommendations made by the occupational health provider are implemented and systems set up for monitoring as required.
- Audit the management system and review processes, making changes as necessary to ensure compliance with the law.

FACILITIES REQUIRED FOR CARRYING OUT HEALTH SURVEILLANCE

Typical facilities required for carrying out health surveillance include:

- Facilities set aside exclusively for health surveillance at the time they are required.
- Enable health surveillance to be conducted in privacy.
- A room that is clean, warm, well ventilated and furnished with a table and seating.
- Washbasin with hot and cold running water, soap and clean towel.
- If required, facility for specimen collection, for example, toilet and hand washing facilities.
- Suitable waiting area.

Figure 3-35: Health surveillance at work. *Source HSE, HSG61.*

RECORD KEEPING AND CONFIDENTIALITY

- Employers must keep an up to date health record for each worker. Some workers may also have a medical record.
- Results of all health surveillance procedures must be recorded, including date and by whom it was carried out.

- Health records should only contain the information on fitness for work, for example, the decision of the doctor or conclusions of the doctor, occupational health nurse or other responsible person.
- Health records should not include confidential clinical information.
- Medical records are confidential records and would include clinical information derived from medical examinations. This clinical information would be used to support decisions on fitness to work. The decisions on fitness to work would be recorded in the health record.
- To comply with COSHH 2002 Regulation 11(3) employers must keep records for 40 years (that is 40 years from the last entry to the record); other legislation requires them to be retained for longer, for example, IRR 1999.
- Workers are allowed to see their own records.
- Employers may, with the worker's consent, allow a worker representative to see the worker's records.
- If a business ceases to trade, its records should be offered to the HSE for safe keeping.

Dealing with adverse effects identified during health surveillance

MANAGING ADVERSE HEALTH SURVEILLANCE RESULTS

The management of adverse health results is vital to the success of the health surveillance programme. There is no point in implementing a programme if the results are not acted upon.

Therefore, it is essential that any adverse health surveillance results are acted upon. What should be done will depend on the findings and effect on the individual. It may be necessary to remove a worker from a specific job, for example, when high lead levels are found in their blood. Advice will be given by the occupational health provider doctor or nurse, who should specify what action needs to be taken. With the example given of high lead levels in blood, it would be necessary to find out why this worker's levels were higher than other workers - it could be due to poor procedures or poor personal hygiene by the worker, or they might not be wearing personal protective equipment (PPE) correctly, PPE may be broken or they could be doing a job no one else is doing. All the control systems in place must be checked. In addition, some employees will be more susceptible to exposures; this depends on the individual's genetic makeup and is out of their personal control. How long the worker is kept away from the work causing the problem will depend on how well the lead in blood levels reduce when they are away from exposure, but advice on this should be provided by the occupational health provider and they should follow this up.

There must be a procedure in place to deal with and manage any adverse health surveillance results, whether it is exposure to a chemical agent, such as lead, or a physical cause, such as noise or vibration. Together with the employer the occupational health provider should set up systems for referral for additional medical investigation where required, for example, noise induce hearing loss should be referred to the worker's general practitioner doctor and/or a hearing specialist. Someone with a reduced lung function might need further investigation by a chest physician, so that specific tests can be carried out to identify the root cause of the condition.

Workers who acquire a chronic ill-health condition due to exposure at work to health risks, for example, occupational asthma due to exposure to isocyanates, flour, or latex, may need to be permanently taken away from the work hazard causing the problem. If this is the case, account may have to be taken of the Equality Act (EA) 2010 *(see also - Element 2 - Effects of health on work - Equality Act (EA) 2010 and fitness for work)*. The employer should always try to re-deploy the worker to another suitable job where possible. Alternatively special arrangements may need to be made to protect the worker by the provision of specific PPE, such as positive pressure respiratory protection. If this is not possible, the worker may have to leave the company on grounds of ill-health. It will be important to ensure that all possible alternative work opportunities are explored and special additional protection provided before the option to dismiss the worker on grounds of ill-health is taken.

At all stages in the management of adverse health surveillance the affected worker should be kept informed. Where possible, the worker should be involved in the changes to their work and the provision of special protection measures. Depending on the nature of the results of the surveillance the effects on the individual may be significant and require them to be provided with support and counselling in order to cope with the health condition and its effects.

See also - Element 3.1 for details of what health surveillance is needed for specific situations.

RELATIONSHIP TO FITNESS FOR WORK

When adverse effects are identified the workers affected should be assessed to determine their fitness for work. The adverse effect may involve consideration of defined fitness standards and some work restrictions may result. This may be a temporary situation or permanent. It is important that the managers involved work with occupational health staff to adjust the work situation for the person affected, where this is possible. Occupational health staff should inform managers of the nature of the range of fitness for work and any work restriction related to the adverse effect in such a way that the manager can take action to manage the situation. Where fitness to work is not the full range required for the worker's job occupational health staff must make it clear what the likely duration of this change is. Where this duration is until the next time the worker undergoes further health surveillance and assessment this date should be made known to managers.

3.6 - Reporting of diagnosed occupational diseases

Procedure for formal reporting of diagnosed occupational diseases

The Reporting of Injuries, Diseases and Dangerous Occurrences Regulations (RIDDOR) 1995 require employers to report to their enforcing authority (HSE or Local Authority) certain incidents and diseases that arise out of, or in connection with work. These are listed by RIDDOR 1995 as follows:

■ Death or major injuries from accidents.

■ Minor injuries resulting in the individual being off work, or being unable to carry out their normal work for 3 days or more.

■ A specified work related disease, which has been diagnosed and confirmed in writing by a doctor.

■ Dangerous occurrences, where there has been an incident, which has not necessarily caused injury, but potentially could have done so. Needle stick injuries are included in this.

The report can be made to the Incident Contact Centre by telephone or online using the online form F2508A. The HSE prefer reporting online for reporting situations that are not urgent. The reporting requirement for work-related diseases is that they must be reported without delay (forthwith); the online system of reporting would meet this requirement.

"The responsible person shall forthwith send a report thereof to the relevant enforcing authority on a form approved for the purposes of this regulation".

Figure 3-36: Requirement for reporting diseases.   *Source: RIDDOR 1995.*

Reporting of work-related diseases in accordance with RIDDOR 1995 requires more than the confirmation that the worker has been diagnosed by a doctor as having the disease. It is also necessary for the worker to be engaged in a prescribed work activity. The diseases and the work activities are set out in Schedule 3 to RIDDOR 1995; only if both requirements are met is reporting required. The range of diseases that are reportable includes:

■ Conditions due to physical agents and physical demands of work, for example, cataracts, carpal tunnel syndrome and hand-arm vibration syndrome (HAVS).

■ Infections due to biological agents, for example, hepatitis and legionellosis.

■ Conditions due to substances, for example, poisoning by lead, mesothelioma, asbestosis, occupational dermatitis, occupational asthma.

Disease	*Activities*
Hand-arm vibration syndrome	"Work involving: (a) The use of chain saws, brush cutters or hand-held or hand-fed circular saws in forestry or woodworking. (b) The use of hand-held rotary tools in grinding material or in sanding or polishing metal. (c) The holding of material being ground or metal being sanded or polished by rotary tools. (d) The use of hand-held percussive metal-working tools or the holding of metal being worked upon by percussive tools in connection with riveting, caulking, chipping, hammering, fettling or swaging. (e) The use of hand-held powered percussive drills or hand-held powered percussive hammers in mining, quarrying or demolition, or on roads or footpaths (including road construction). (f) The holding of material being worked upon by pounding machines in shoe manufacture".
Hepatitis	"Work involving contact with: (a) Human blood or human blood products. (b) Any source of viral hepatitis".
Asbestosis	(a) The working or handling of asbestos or any admixture of asbestos. (b) The manufacture or repair of asbestos textiles or other articles containing or composed of asbestos. (c) The cleaning of any machinery or plant used in any of the foregoing operations and of any chambers, fixtures and appliances for the collection of asbestos dust. (d) Substantial exposure to the dust arising from any of the foregoing operations.

Figure 3-37: Sample reportable diseases and work activities.   *Source: RIDDOR 1995.*

To comply with RIDDOR 1995 it is necessary for the employer to put in place a system for identifying and reporting any incidents of work related ill health, listed in the regulations. It is the employer's responsibility to do this; however, the task may be delegated to the occupational health provider, and if this is the case the employer should ensure they are kept informed of any reported cases. This means the employer will need to have a written agreement with the occupational health provider, stating who is responsible for what, which should be referred to in the employer's 'health surveillance policy'.

With potential occupationally related ill-health it will be prudent for the organisation to work closely with their occupational health provider, to ensure there is an effective system in place for reporting. The organisation will need to have access to appropriate occupational health advice and in turn the occupational health doctor/nurse will need to develop good working relationships with local general practitioner doctors and hospitals, so that early diagnosis can be made and the disease reported to the appropriate enforcing authority as required. The employer should ensure there is a system in place, monitor and audit it.

3.7 - Monitoring exposure to hazardous agents

The role of and benefits of environmental monitoring

The *role* of environmental monitoring is to identify workplace conditions that may present a significant risk to the health of workers.

The *benefits* of environmental monitoring to organisations include:

- Enables the identification and assessment of health risks in the workplace.
- Enables compliance with Workplace Exposure Limits (WELs).
- Helps towards the design of exposure control measures.
- Enables the correct selection of personal protective equipment.
- Enables the effectiveness of control measures to be checked.
- Enables the informing of workers of their pattern of exposure and level of risk.
- Indicates the need for health surveillance.
- Helps to establish in-house exposure standards, where necessary.
- Provides evidence in civil claims and for insurance purposes.
- Contributes to organisational, industry group and national epidemiological studies.

The HSE have published Workplace Exposure Limit's (WEL's) which are limits that have been set at a level at which there are no known affects to human health (based on research available at the time). A WEL is the maximum concentration of an airborne substance in a given time, which workers may be exposed to by inhalation. These limits must not be exceeded and controls are put in place to safeguard this. Similarly, workplace exposure limits have been established for asbestos, lead, noise and vibration.

The requirement to carry out environmental monitoring of hazardous agents, such as substances and noise, will initially be based on the circumstances determined when health risk assessments are conducted. The risk assessment process may require environmental monitoring to be conducted because additional data is required to identify hazards, to establish the effectiveness of current controls, to decide on the level of risk or to determine suitable controls to improve risk. Environmental monitoring can assist with each of these aspects of the risk assessment process. The risk assessment may determine that one of the controls needed to manage the risk from the hazardous agents is that periodic environmental monitoring should be conducted to assess how well control measures are working. This can be used in conjunction with health surveillance.

Environmental monitoring is a specialised area of work and must be carried out by a competent person, for example, an occupational hygienist. Conducting environmental monitoring effectively will involve a level of technical expertise, for example, there are many different monitoring techniques for dusts, gases, vapours. There are several factors that complicate environmental monitoring for substances, including mixed exposure due to several different substances being present in the atmosphere together, and the need to determine the amount of respirable (particles that reach the alveoli of the lungs), rather than inhalable, particles (those breathed in through nose and mouth) in the work environment. Environmental monitoring requires knowledge of the appropriate technique, along with the expertise to interpret the results, to conduct the monitoring, provide a detailed report on findings and establish recommendations on how to reduce health risk.

The Control of Noise at Work Regulations (CNWR) 2005 require the employer to undertake a survey (initial environmental monitoring activity) of noise levels and this needs to be undertaken by a competent person, for example, an occupational hygienist or someone who has undergone special training in noise monitoring.

3.8 - Healthy working environment

Factors that might constitute a "healthy working environment"

The basic legal requirements for workplace health and welfare ("healthy working environment") are set out in the Workplace (Health, Safety and Welfare) Regulations (WHSWR) 1992 and the Approved Code of Practice (ACoP) to the regulations.

There are many factors that contribute to a 'healthy working environment', many of which have been found to be positive factors in research findings about work. These include:

ACCESS TO DRINKING WATER

Access to drinking water at anytime, for example, water fountains, containers and mains supplied water. This can provide workers with an opportunity to replace lost water, which is particularly important for those working in hot environments where they may lose water through sweating and evaporation. This in turn can help reduce fatigue, improve comfort and assist cooling.

VENTILATION

Good ventilation is important in providing an atmosphere that is not 'stuffy' or 'draughty', either by the provision of appropriate air conditioning or access to open windows. Good ventilation will enable the oxygen levels in the workplace to be maintained at a level that reduces fatigue and maintains alertness. It will also enable the removal of low level contamination, odours and carbon dioxide expelled by workers when they breathe.

REST FACILITIES

The provision of a healthy working environment includes appropriate rest facilities for workers to take breaks, to take food and drinks and where they might socialise with their fellow workers. The rest facilities should be free from workplace health risks and therefore will enable the worker to remove themselves from the various health risks that they may face as a normal part of their job, for example, noise or the pressure of having to deal with customers.

CLEANLINESS AND HOUSEKEEPING

A clean well maintained workplace, free from clutter, which provides a pleasant environment will contribute to the provision of a healthy workplace and establish a sense of well-being in workers.

TEMPERATURE

Temperature control is important and as different people like different levels of warmth it is better if workers can have some control over the temperature they experience. This may not be possible in some circumstances, for example, working in cold stores would not allow the worker to adjust the temperature of the environment. However, warm clothing would be provided under these circumstances and the amount of clothing used by a worker would allow some personal temperature control.

LIGHTING

Lighting must be sufficient to be able to do the job and must avoid glare. Where intricate work is carried out it will be necessary to provide individual lighting sources, which can be controlled by the worker.

FURNITURE, LAYOUT, DECORATION

As far as possible it is good practice to involve workers in how the workplace is laid out and for them to contribute to the selection of furniture, fittings and decoration. Colour plays an important part in the ambience of an environment and should be light and bright, but not too gaudy. The introduction of plants into the workplace has positive benefits. It increases oxygen levels and brightens up the workspace. Many offices have plants and some organisations have contracts with suppliers so that they are maintained and changed regularly. A similar benefit can be obtained by the introduction of wall fittings, such as photographs and pictures. It is useful to allow workers to select the pictures to provide them with an opportunity to influence the workspace and increase involvement.

Benefits of designing working environments with health in mind

The benefits of designing working environments with health in mind include:

- It creates an environment that makes workers feel valued by the employer demonstrating commitment to a pleasant workspace.
- If workers feel valued they are more likely to be committed to the business and give good, regular, loyal service.
- There is likely to be fewer accidents and cases of work-related ill-health.
- There will be a lower labour turnover and therefore a decreased cost of recruitment and training.
- The business will get a reputation for being a 'good place to work' and people will stay and want to work there.

Management of attendance

Learning outcomes

On completion of this element, candidates should be able to demonstrate understanding of the content through the application of knowledge to familiar and unfamiliar situations. In particular they should be able to:

4.1   Identity the main causes and types of sickness absence within organisations.

4.2   Outline the role and responsibilities of the health professionals, line-manager, human resources and the employee in the management of absence.

4.3   Outline effective techniques for the management of short and long term sickness absence and return to work.

4.4   Outline the principles and benefits of vocational rehabilitation including the role of outside support agencies.

Content

Sources of reference

Chartered Institute of Personnel and Development: Absence Guidance
http://www.cipd.co.uk/subjects/hrpract/absence.

Chartered Institute of Personnel and Development: Absence management Tools 1-4
http://www.cipd.co.uk/subjects/hrpract/absence/absmantool.htm.

Health and Safety Executive: Managing Sickness Absence & Return to Work Guidance:
http://www.hse.gov.uk/sicknessabsence.

Institution of Occupational Safety and Health: A Healthy Return - A Good Practice Guide to Rehabilitating
People at Work.

Managing attendance and employee turnover (ref B04) www.acas.org.uk/publications.

Working together to prevent sickness absence becoming job loss: Practical advice for safety and other trade
union representatives. HSE. http://www.hse.gov.uk/pubns/web02.pdf.

Relevant statutory provisions

Employment Act (EMA) 2002

Employment Act (EMA) 2008

Employment Equality (Repeals of Retirement Age Provisions) Regulations (EERAR) 2011

Employment Rights Act (ERA) 1996

4.1 - Main causes and types of sickness absence within organisations

Characteristics of absence

UNAUTHORISED ABSENCE OR PERSISTENT LATENESS

Unauthorised absence or persistent lateness may arise through home or family responsibilities, for example, looking after a sick child/parent or from a recurring medical condition, such as stress. They may also be caused by lifestyle factors and be linked to drugs and alcohol. These absence situations can be difficult to manage as they are often unexpected, sudden and have not been approved by designated individuals within an organisation.

AUTHORISED ABSENCES

The term 'authorised absences' is generally used where specific time off has been approved by a designated individual for activities such as jury service, reserve forces leave, maternity leave, annual holiday entitlement, trade union duties and compassionate leave. It is also extended to authorised absence to attend for medical diagnosis, tests and treatment. The term is also applicable to absence where a worker has used a sickness absence procedure to notify the employer of their wish to absent themselves from work due to ill-health and the employer has accepted their reason for absence.

SHORT TERM FREQUENT ABSENCE

Whilst there is no agreed definition of short term frequent sickness absence, the term is generally used to denote absence from work up to four weeks (28 days) and/or frequent short term absences of a few days, for example, 2 days absence every month or couple of months. When an employee has been absent from work for more than seven calendar days, an employer is entitled to ask the employee for a medical certificate, "Fit Note", signed by the employee's general practitioner doctor or other doctor.

LONG TERM ABSENCE

The term is generally used for absences from work, which are longer than four week (28 days).

Causes of sickness absence for manual and non-manual workers

According to the Chartered Institute for Personnel and Development (2009) the main causes of short-term absence in both manual and non-manual workers are from minor illnesses, such as a cold. The main cause of work-related sickness absence amongst manual workers is musculoskeletal disorders, particularly back pain, and stress remains the number one cause in non-manual workers.

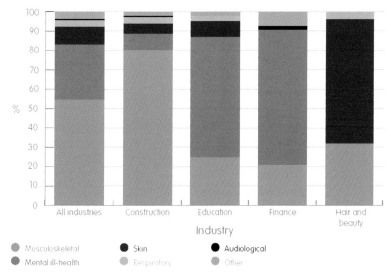

Figure 4-1: Work-related illness by industry. *Source: TSO, Working for a healthier tomorrow.*

Classification of absence into planned and unplanned

Planned absence is where an employee is able to give sufficient notification to their employer and negotiate authorised leave from work, for example, annual leave, jury service, and reserve forces commitment. In terms of sickness absence planned absence might be related to planned hospital treatment that has a recovery period following it, for example, hospitalisation for the removal of gall stones or for a vasectomy.

Unplanned absence can be due to unforeseen circumstances that require the employee to be absent from work, for example, compassionate leave. In terms of sickness absence this would relate to a sudden injury or illness that did not allow time to plan for absence, for example, a broken leg from a fall at home, food poisoning or glandular fever.

The effects on employees health of long term absence from work

The effects on an employee's health of long term absence from work will vary from individual to individual and will depend on the reasons for the absence and the pay and conditions of employment. There is strong evidence that, generally, work is good for health and the negative effects of not working can influence an employee's self esteem, lowering their confidence and resulting in a reduction in their health and well-being. The longer someone is absent from work due to sickness, the less likely they are to return to the workplace. Once a worker is absent from work for longer than four weeks they often have difficulty in returning to the working environment due to mental disengagement and as a consequence are less likely to return to work. If this situation becomes sustained it can lead to a state of "worklessness" where the individual no longer feels capable of engaging in work. The negative effects and social impact that sickness has on an individual, is well documented. In the long term, "worklessness" leads to poorer physical and mental health, increases social exclusion and increases poverty.

Cost implications of absence to the organisation and employees

Dame Carol Black's Review of the Health of Britain's working age population, "Working for a Healthier Tomorrow", highlights that 175 million working days were lost to illness in 2006. This represented an economic cost to the country of £13 billion, a loss of social standing and a risk of social exclusion for the worker. Following a survey conducted in conjunction with Pfizer, the CBI reported that the UK economy lost 190 million working days to absence in 2010, with each employee taking an average of 6.5 days off sick. The CBI state that 190 million days cost employers £17 billion and that nearly a third of the absences were of a long-term nature. This shows a significant increase since 2006.

The average direct cost of absence was £595 per employee in 2009, setting a new record high:

The cost of absence per employee tends to rise in step with the size of the workforce, so larger organisations experience the highest costs per head.

Absence cost varies considerably by sector, with direct costs in the public sector some 50% higher on average than in the private sector.

The indirect costs of absence are harder for organisations to measure but they are substantial, on average totalling £465 per employee.

Loss of productivity is seen as the single most important cost of absence, followed by the cost of sick pay itself and the cost of staff to cover for those who are absent.

Figure 4-2: Costs of absence.   *Source: CBI.*

The CBI survey identified that the direct costs of absence were higher for larger organisations, £717 per employee in organisations over 5,000 employees compared with £412 for organisations with 200 - 499 employees. The survey suggested that this was probably due to the larger organisations operating at higher rates of pay and providing more generous sick pay.

The financial implications for the organisations can often result from the cost of providing temporary replacement staff, or the payment of overtime for other staff members to cover the absence. In addition, the implications include administration costs such as finding a replacement worker, loss of productivity, interruptions to the flow of work, damage to the reputation of the organisation and high turnover of staff. Some employees, particularly those who are self employed, may not receive pay when they are off sick; as a consequence there are potential financial repercussions for the individual and their families who then have to rely on statutory sickness absence pay.

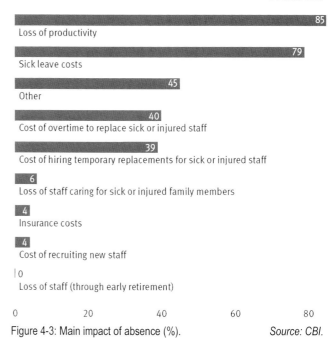

Figure 4-3: Main impact of absence (%).   *Source: CBI.*

For employees on long term absence from work the financial implications can have a steady worsening effect, causing the employee and their family to live off less money, with the potential to get behind with payments of utility bills or rent/mortgage payments.

Limited financial resource may mean that diet and home conditions become poor, creating an inappropriate condition for health improvement. The effect can remain in place for a considerable time after the employee has returned to work.

Effect on employees who cover for other employees absence

Sickness absence places an additional burden on other workers who have to cover for the worker that is absent. This has the potential to increase their stress and lower morale within the existing team. The need for the other workers to cover those that are absent can lead to them experiencing additional fatigue, which may have physical effects or psychological effects. Workers having to put in additional effort without rest or working longer hours may suffer from musculoskeletal injuries or stress. It may also create a work-life imbalance that could have consequential effects on the worker's family or others that depend on them. The long term effect may result in a further increase in absence as workers struggle to cope with the extra workload or individuals seeking work elsewhere, adding further to the workload of those who remain.

4.2 - Role and responsibilities of those involved in the management of absence

General practitioners

ROLE OF THE GENERAL PRACTITIONERS

General Practitioners (GPs) are primarily responsible for providing comprehensive health care to treat acute and chronic illnesses. They are responsible for promoting the health of their patients and are normally the first point of medical contact within the healthcare system for an employee. GP's have a pivotal role to play in supporting their patient to regain their health in order to help them return to the workplace, by offering simple advice. Whilst the GP has no responsibility to the employer the benefits of a tripartite approach between GP, employer and employee is that it helps to ensure that employees are able to obtain the support they need and to provide an opportunity to consider how an early return to work can be achieved.

BENEFITS TO THE EMPLOYER AND EMPLOYEE OF CLOSE LIAISON WITH THE GP

Close working and effective communication with the employee's GP is essential to support employees whose health may necessitate some adjustments within the workplace. However, it is important to remember that in order to maintain "patient confidentiality" the employee will have to consent under the Access to Medical Reports Act (AMRA) 1988 to allow the employer to contact their GP. The "Fit Note" encourages the commencement of this liaison, in that the note sets out considerations that the employer should take account of in the management of the employee's absence and their return to work.

Close liaison with the GP will provide the employer with a number of benefits, including information that helps them support the employee in their absence, a better understanding of the reasons for their absence and an early opportunity to prepare for and predict their return to work. In some cases, the liaison will provide the employer with confirmation of what they are being told by the employee and at other times it may challenge the perspective the employee is presenting. Similarly, the employee benefits from an independent party confirming and legitimising the reasons for the employee's absence. This can help to support the need for the employee to be absent and diminish any 'pressure' being asserted by the employer to return to work. Sometimes, the confirmation can be provided by the GP in a way that the employee may have difficulty expressing, perhaps because they want to avoid providing too much confidential information or do not have the means to express themselves.

Role and status of the "fit note" and how they can be used and if necessary questioned by employers

Fit notes, more correctly called Statement of Fitness for Work, are forms issued by doctors (mainly general practitioners) to employees for social security or statutory sick pay purposes. Their role is to provide evidence that an employee cannot work due to illness or injury and advice for those that could return to work with adjustments, for example, a phased return to work. The fit note focuses on what people "can do" rather then what they cannot and can provide a basis for the measures necessary to enable the employee's return to work. Should an employee wish to return to work before the date the fit note recommends, then they do not have to wait until that date, nor do they have to be signed back into work by the GP.

Any advice on a fit note is advice from a GP to an employee, not the employer. Therefore changes to the employee's work, such as "altered hours", would have to be agreed between the employer and employee. They cannot be imposed by GP's and if seen as excessive or unreasonable the employer may wish to discuss alternatives with the employee or question the basis for the advice with the GP, with the employee's consent. The legal status of fit notes remains to be tested in courts and tribunals, they may have some persuasive argument to support disability discrimination, unfair dismissal or subsequent personal injury claims. It is therefore appropriate that the employer consider the statement and advice it contains carefully and in the context of the work done by the employee.

Whilst the GP's comments on the fit note should be considered, their status is advisory and employers may need to consider the nature of the work that the employee undertakes, as there may be health and safety implications for a returning employee that the GP may not be aware of.

Under Section 2 of the Health and Safety at Work etc Act (HASAWA) 1974 the employer has a legal responsibility "to ensure so far as is reasonably practicable the health, safety and welfare at work of its employees".

Where there are concerns regarding an employee's ability to return to work it may be necessary, with the employee's consent, to consult with the employee's GP and request further clarification as to what work they can do. The employer should outline the employee's job role, hours of work, risks and job demands. In addition, it can be helpful to include information on any modifications, temporary of otherwise, that can be provided by the organisation to facilitate an early return to work.

COMPLETION OF THE STATEMENT OF FITNESS FOR WORK (FIT NOTE)

The following is based on the information on the NHS website, www.nhs.uk, and provides guidance on how the fit note works.

The GP can give advice to help an employee return to work. This is because work can play an important part in helping people to recover from illness or injury. When completing the fit note, the GP can choose one of two options:

- The person is 'not fit for work'.
- The person 'may be fit for work'.

The fit note also includes:

- Space for the GP to give general advice about the impact of the illness or injury.
- Tick boxes for the GP to suggest, where appropriate, common ways in which the employer could support the worker to return to work.

The GP will choose the 'may be fit for work' option if they think that returning to work, with support from the employer, will be achievable and will help. The GP can give general advice on the fit note about how the illness or injury may affect the worker's ability to work and can discuss this advice with the employer to see if the worker can return to work. For example, the GP may suggest possible changes, such as:

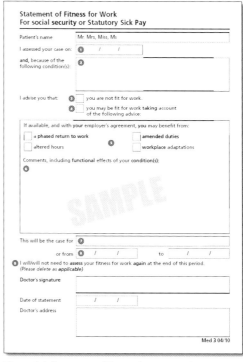

- Returning to work gradually, by starting back to work part-time.
- Working different hours temporarily, for example, avoiding 'rush hour' times.
- Performing different duties or tasks.
- Having other support to do the job, for example, if the employee has back pain, avoiding heavy lifting.

The employer needs to know what the worker can and cannot do. This does not mean stating what job, but providing advice on what functional activities can be carried out, for example, standing, sitting, walking, handling and lifting. Providing the manager with information like this will help them make a decision on the type of work the employee could do, based on what work is available.

Figure 4-4: Statement of fitness for work. *Source: DWP.*

If an employer has an occupational health service, the occupational health advisor should be consulted for advice and guidance on returning to work, and to provide support to the employee and manager. In order to achieve a successful return to work it is important that the employer and employee agree on:

- How the employee will return.
- What support will be provided?
- How long the support will last.

Information exchanged between the employer and GP

The information that should be provided to and can be requested by the GP relates particularly to the employee's duties, this will include:

- Job demands, for example, volume of work and time demands.
- The work environment, for example, stressors such as noise, heat humidity or cold.
- Health risks.
- Working time, for example, length of working day, rest breaks, shift working.
- Travel, whether the job require travel at home or overseas, for example, sales representative.
- Whether the employee is a lone worker, for example, security night watchman, social worker, district nurse, estate agent.

The information that should be provided to and can be requested by the employer, from the GP (with consent from the employee), includes:

- Asking the GP questions about the employee's functional capacity, for example, strength, physical and mental ability to cope with the job.
- What the employee can and cannot do, for example, work a full day, work shifts, and lift loads.
- How long their disability or medical condition might last.
- What suggestions the GP has regarding rehabilitation measures, for example, alternative duties, reduced hours, removed from direct contact with members of the public.

Throughout the process, the employer should emphasise the objective is to get the employee back to work as soon as possible and the employer's willingness to do all that is necessary to achieve this, including any required work routine adjustments to ease the process.

Occupational health practitioners

The occupational health practitioner's role in case management of sickness absence is to provide, in liaison with the human resources function, support to the co-ordination of effort and provision of information that centres on the individual and their return to work. It is important that case management is sensitive to individual cases and circumstances as they may vary greatly, for example, a worker may have particular needs related to their return to work following absence due to stress. An important part of the role of the occupational health practitioner is assessing fitness for work. This may be conducted as part of a return to work programme or by considering information provided by a GP within a fit note and through supplementary questions. The occupational health practitioner's role in case management will include providing reports to management related to an individual worker's fitness to work and actions to assist their return and continuation in work. The occupational health practitioner, in conjunction with human resources practitioners may also be involved in dealing with medico-legal issues.

There is no one specialised group that has all the necessary skills required to support workers therefore professional groups need to work collaboratively for the health and well-being of the client (worker). Multi-disciplinary teams can draw upon a wider range of professional expertise and experience for developing rehabilitation approaches. The role of occupational health is multifaceted covering many elements such as health promotion, co-ordinator, counsellor and the role of a clinician.

Occupational health practitioners have a pivotal role in relation to sickness absence by early intervention to avoid a short term absence becoming long term. Once a worker is absent from work for longer than four weeks they often have difficulty in returning to the working environment, due to metal disengagement and as a consequence are less likely to return to work. Occupational health can provide a route to early referral and have the expertise to advise on strategies to promote the health and well-being at work and occupational health. They will provide confidential support and guidance to workers regarding fitness for work. In addition, they will give advice to managers, and where relevant, trade unions, on how worker capability can be matched to employment and facilitate a return to work.

Human resources

One of the main roles of the human resources function of an organisation is to provide training, advice and support in managing absence. They will record sickness absence data, analyse the trends, causes and reasons for absence and will work with employees, managers, trade union representatives and occupational health practitioners in the co-ordination of the sickness absence management process. Human resources will ensure that the absence policies and procedures are being applied consistently across the organisation and will seek medical advice from either the employee's GP or specialist advice from an occupational health specialist where appropriate. Where necessary, they will ensure effective liaison with health professionals, managers and employees.

Line managers and employees

In order for the sickness absence management process to be effective it is important that both line managers and employees accept the agreed system. This is often best achieved by ensuring participation in the establishment of the system. This, in conjunction with the provision of information on the importance and value of the process can help encourage full co-operation and participation by line managers and employees.

Absence management processes will involve line managers in organising work to enable the employee to return to work, including part-time working, working different hours temporarily, performing different duties or tasks, for example, if the employee has back pain avoiding heavy lifting. This may involve the line manager in a lot of effort. Without their full co-operation communication with other employees affected may be poor and actions to support the employee's return to work will not be implemented or be ineffective. This will lead to the decline in the employees' confidence in the process and, in turn less willing participation.

It is important for the success of the absence management process that there is both co-operation and participation by line managers and all employees and operation of the agreed system by all parties.

It is essential that employees and managers are aware of their responsibilities under the sickness absence management process and that communication between both parties is maintained. Disengagement by employees who are off sick can be mitigated by the manager keeping in regular contact with them.

Training in the absence management system and soft skills

In order to establish co-operation and participation in the operation of the absence management system it is essential that all employees, including line managers, receive training. Line managers, in particular will need to be provided with information on the need to have an absence management system, how the system operates and their role in it. Employees will need to understand the reasons for the absence management system; this should include the motives behind it and benefits to employees and the organisation.

It should never be assumed that a line manager will know how to deal with sickness absenteeism. There is a myth that if someone is off sick that the manager cannot do anything about it: this is wrong. However, managers need training in how to deal with these situations as it requires special skills in communication and dealing with sensitive issues. It is essential to train line managers in the soft skills that support the absence management process, such as interviewing technique for return to work interviews.

> *The survey of 182 organisations, which together employ 705,000 people, shows that return-to-work interviews are highly regarded by human resources practitioners working in public sector organisations and companies of all types and sizes.*

Figure 4-5: Importance of return to work interviews.   *Source: Employment Review.*

Management training should include the following:

- Why people do not attend work; it is not always because of illness, but often other reasons, for example, child care, family commitments (extended family), hospital/dental appointments. They may be unhappy with the job or feel undervalued.
- Interviewing skills, particularly encouraging people to talk, empathy and listening skills.
- The importance of maintaining contact with absent employees, without being seen to be harassing the employee.
- Record keeping of absence of employees and interpreting results.
- Equality Act (EA) 2010 and the application of it within the workplace. The importance of treating everyone equally and being consistent in approach.
- Rehabilitation processes, understanding employee's needs, balanced with the needs of the organisation.

Consultation, communication and assessing the effectiveness of arrangements

An ongoing consultation process with employees or their representatives will ensure that the absence management policy and procedures do not discriminate against any particular employee. To this end communication with employees and the training of managers in the procedures is an essential part of the process. The employee must be comfortable to return to work and this will only be possible if the organisation creates the right working environment for that return, giving consideration to pre-existing conditions and modifying the work demand to accommodate the employee.

It is essential that the effectiveness of the arrangements made to facilitate the return to work of employees are assessed. This will involve consideration of the arrangements on a general and individual case basis. General arrangements may need to be adjusted to accommodate the needs of a specific case. This will ensure that arrangements are effective in enabling the efficient return to work of the employee and the minimum level of absence.

It is important to communicate the success of the absence management process as well as the need to modify or improve it. This will ensure its continued support and the long term effectiveness of the process.

Involving and consulting employee representatives

Union appointed representatives have long had a right to be consulted on health and safety matters, established under the Safety Representatives and Safety Committees Regulations (SRSC) 1977. The Health and Safety (Consultation with Employees) Regulations (HSCER) 1996 established the right of non-trade union employees to be consulted on health and safety issues. The need to consult was also emphasised in the Department of Health (2000) report "Improving working lives", which highlighted the need for collaboration with trade unions. Involvement and consultation of employee representatives is seen as vital for the successful implementation of workplace heath initiatives. Co-operation will ensure that employees are being treated fairly and a system of absence management is agreed between the employer and the employee representatives.

By involving employee representatives in the establishment and operation of the absence management process it will ensure that the process is seen as fair and appropriate. It will also help to avoid disagreement that might lead to the escalation of a particular issue relating to the application of the process that may result in dispute. The employee representatives may also be able to provide practical insight into the suitability of general and specific arrangements to facilitate the early return to work of employees.

They may also be able to provide an alternative to the line management processes that assess the effectiveness of the arrangements as they are applied to individual cases. Their involvement could also provide an additional strand of encouragement and support to the employee during the return to work process.

Role and function of investigating cases of work-related ill-health

Where an employee is absent due to a possible work related ill-health a thorough investigation should be carried out. This is particularly important where there are other employees who may be carrying out similar work that could have caused the ill-health. The investigation may involve carrying out a health risk assessment to identify areas of concern and recommend action to remove or control the causal factors. *(See also - Element 3 - Effects of work on health).* The *role* of the investigation of work related ill-health is the same as the investigation of injury accidents, which is to identify the causes in order to prevent a reoccurrence.

The *function* of ill-health investigation is:

- To establish the nature of the ill-health and worker affected.
- Identify immediate causes of the ill-health.
- Establish what the underlying causes are.
- Identify weaknesses in systems and standards.
- Recommend actions to prevent a reoccurrence.
- Determine how well post event ill-health interventions worked.
- Acquire data for statistics.
- Evidence the organisation's commitment to health.
- Prepare for civil and criminal action.

Meaning and scope of "health records" and the importance of confidentiality

The term "health records" has a number of meanings depending on the context of use. For example, in the context of workplace health the term "health record" relates to records kept concerning an individual's work that has involved exposure to specific health risks and the outcome of health surveillance related to those risks. A health record, in this context, is different from a medical record and should not include confidential clinical information. Clinical information that is used to make decisions on an individual's fitness to work is not held on a health record, but is kept in a medical record.

The Data Protection Act (DPA) 1998 establishes requirements for holding and access to personal data, including non-clinical and medical/clinical health records (as defined by Section 68 of DPA 1998), held by public and private organisations, regardless of the form in which it is held - electronic or paper (structured files relating to the individual). Section 1 of the DPA 1998 defines "personal data" as data that:

"Relate to a living individual who can be identified:

(a) From those data.

(b) From those data and other information which is in the possession of, or is likely to come into the possession of, the data controller, and includes any expression of opinion about the individual and any indication of the intentions of the data controller or any other person in respect of the individual".

Section 68 of the Data Protection Act (DPA) 1998 defines the meaning of "accessible record", one of the forms of personal data that are protected by the DPA 1998, and this definition includes health records. A "health record" means any record that:

"(a) Consists of information relating to the physical or mental health or condition of an individual.

(b) Has been made by or on behalf of a health professional in connection with the care of that individual".

The DPA 1998 establishes a wide scope to the meaning of the term "health record". This could be anything from the notes made by a GP to results of an MRI scan or X-rays conducted during routine health surveillance. In the context of health at work, health records under Section 68 of the DPA 1998 would not include records that do not contain confidential clinical information, for example, records of the number and duration of absence due to ill-health or the individual's restricted capacity to work due to health conditions. Medical records that contain confidential clinical data on an individual clearly fall within the term "health record" under Section 68. The occupational health practitioner must maintain clinical data in a confidential manner. This clinical data can only be accessed either by the employee approaching the holder of the record under the Data Protection Act (DPA) 1998, or by the employee giving their explicit written consent to another party for the information to be released.

Whilst the employer may own the records containing clinical data, they have no right of access to the information held in them. This is supported by a legal obligation under the DPA 1998 that all employee medical records are confidential. Should an occupational health nurse delegate record keeping duties to another member of the healthcare team, such as an occupational health technician, they must ensure that they have the knowledge and skills to undertake this aspect of confidential care. Computer held records are now regularly used and must comply with the Computer Misuse Act (CMA) 1990. Clear protocols should be written to specify who has access rights to the computer held medical records, taking into account the DPA 1998.

Under the DPA 1998 not only do the people on whom information is held have the right to access their records, they also have the right to have any inaccurate information corrected. Individuals have additional rights of access to their own health records. Under the DPA 1998 they are entitled to see all information relating to their physical or mental health that has been recorded by or on behalf of a 'health professional' in connection with their care. This applies not just to computerised data and structured files, but to 'unstructured' data as well. The right of access covers both NHS and private medical records, and information of any age, however long ago it was recorded.

The health professionals whose records can be seen are doctors, dentists, opticians, pharmacists, nurses, midwives, health visitors, clinical psychologists, child psychotherapists, osteopaths, chiropracters, chiropodists, dieticians, occupational therapists, physiotherapists, orthoptists, paramedics, radiographers, speech therapists, language therapists, music and art therapists, orthotists, prosthetists, medical laboratory technicians and clinical scientists.

Access rights are more limited if:

- Information about the individual's health is held by someone who does not fall within the definition of a 'health professional', such as records held by various kinds of psychotherapists (for example, counsellors) or alternative practitioners.
- Information is held by a health professional that is not, and never has been, responsible for the individual's care - such as a doctor conducting a fitness for work assessment.

In these cases, the individual is entitled to see computerised data and structured files, but not unstructured information. If details of a medical nature are disclosed to the employer following written consent then the medical information must be retained, but separate from the non-confidential health record.

This is because the medical information is confidential to the employee and should not be disclosed to a third party. Under the Data Protection Act 1998, employees must be informed that a health record is being kept regarding them and that they have a right to access that information and correct it.

Confidentiality of health records is important and must be assured by a systematic approach. The following confidentiality model illustrates the main features of such an approach, advocated by the NHS. Record holders must inform the employee of the intended use of their information, give them the choice to give or withhold their consent as well as protecting their identifiable information from unwarranted disclosures. These processes are inter-linked and should be ongoing to aid the improvement of a confidential service.

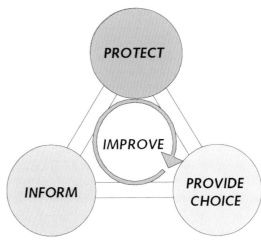

Figure 4-6: Confidentiality model.
Source: NHS, Confidentiality code of practice.

Action to take if an employee does not give consent

The Access to Medical Reports Act (AMRA) 1988 gives individuals right of access to any medical report prepared for the purposes of employment and insurance. An employer may not obtain a report from a doctor without the written consent of the individual to which the report applies. All organisations should ensure that part of their occupational health policy includes information regarding the requirements for 'medical examination', 'health assessments' and access to medical information and the procedures for these. An employee may withhold consent and if they do they must be made fully aware of the consequences of this action. Under the AMRA 1988 the employee has the right to see the report and to request alterations or amendments to be made before it is supplied to the employer.

There are implications if the employee unreasonably refuses to consent to the report being supplied as, without medical advice, the employer can only go on the evidence they have before them, which may be to the disadvantage of the employee. Without the full facts of the effects of the medical condition on the ability of the employee to work it is difficult for managers to make decisions regarding suitable work and rehabilitation requirements. If an employee claims that they have an underlying medical condition, but refuse to give their consent for the employer to obtain a medical report and the employer cannot establish to their satisfaction the legitimacy of the illness then the employer may apply the disciplinary and dismissal procedure.

It is important for the employer to be able to demonstrate a thorough investigation and this may mean considering other factors, such as bullying, that may cause the employee to feel they cannot bring the matter fully to the employer's attention. An industrial tribunal, when considering a case of dismissal, will look at the extent of an employer's investigation and will decide whether it genuinely looked into the employee's claims prior to taking disciplinary action. It is important to ensure that investigations are thorough and well documented.

4.3 - The management of short and long term sickness absence and return to work

Effective management of absence

The effective management of absence is an important issue that requires a co-ordinated response, drawn from the occupational health and human resources disciplines. It is influenced by both employment law and health and safety law. The Advisory, Conciliation and Arbitration Service (ACAS), Health and Safety Executive (HSE) and Chartered Institute of Personnel and Development (CIPD) all have perspectives on how absence should be managed.

They have collaborated to create a common perspective in the form of an absence management tool, which comprises guidance documents that provide insight into how absence may be managed.

The ACAS/HSE/CIPD absence management tool includes four guidance documents, entitled:

■ Do you have an absence problem?
■ How do you develop an absence strategy?
■ How do you deal with short-term absence?
■ How do you deal with long-term absence?

They are designed to give a good overview of some of the main issues that need to be considered in order to manage absence effectively, with links to a range of further resources.

Figure 4-7: Absence management tool. *Source: ACAS/HSE/CIPD.*

These are outlined below and cross referenced to where more detail is provided later in this section. More information on the absence management tool can be obtained from the websites of the three contributors.

DO YOU HAVE AN ABSENCE PROBLEM?

Do you have a problem with absence?

The first step is to collect data on absence in order to determine if there is a problem. This involves gathering, collating and analysing data on individual absences. This will mean data for each occurrence, including date of the first day of absence, cause of absence, whether the injury or illness is considered to be work-related, working days absent (updated regularly), date the employee was last contacted and the outcome, expected length of absence, and if known, return-to-work date. It is useful to categorise each incidence of absence in order to help with analysis and later management of incidence, for example:

■ Short-term or acute medical conditions (cold, influenza etc).
■ Musculo-skeletal injuries.

■ Long-term or chronic illness.
■ Work-related injury.
■ Stress-related.

See also - sickness absence recording and monitoring - later in this section - for further detail.

What is the nature of the absence problem(s)?

The data should be used to identify patterns or trends of individuals and groups. It is useful to establish data for overall levels of absence across the organisation and determine data on the nature of absence, the balance between long-term and short-term absence. If possible a comparison should be made with data for other similar organisations in order to 'benchmark' performance.

What are the likely causes of the problem(s)?

It is useful to use techniques like interviews, surveys and discussion to determine the causes of absence. Causes can generally be grouped into;

■ Role and organisational factors, for example, lack of clarity of job roles, workload and stress.
■ Medical factors, for example, work place injuries, lifestyle factors and recurrent health conditions.
■ External and social factors, for example, family problems, care commitments and travel difficulties.

What steps are likely to be most effective at addressing the problem(s)?

Solutions should be developed that are comprehensive, balanced and targeted. The overall approach needs to be supported by consistent policies and practice that are communicated clearly to employees and applied rigorously and consistently.

How do you prevent the problem(s) from recurring?

The absence management tool suggests that managers, in consultation with workers and their representatives, should try to ensure the following:

■ Good physical working conditions are provided.

- Ergonomic factors are taken into account when designing workplaces.
- Health and safety standards are rigorously maintained.
- New starters, especially young people, are given sufficient training and receive particular attention during the initial period in the job.
- The prevailing ethos is one of teamwork.
- Jobs are designed so that they give motivation and provide job satisfaction. They should provide variety, discretion, responsibility, contact with other people, feedback, some challenge, and have clear goals.
- Training, career development and promotion policies, communication procedures and welfare provision are examined to see if they can be improved.
- Policies on equal opportunities and discrimination are fair and observed.
- Supervisory training is adequate, and supervisors take an interest in their workers' health and welfare.

In addition, the absence management tool suggests management should consider the following as part of the overall approach to absence management:

- Introducing flexible working hours, or varied working arrangements, if this could assist workers without conflicting with production or other work demands.
- Providing crèche facilities.
- Authorising reasonable absences to cover business or medical appointments that have been notified in advance, including antenatal care - all pregnant employees, regardless of service, are entitled to reasonable, paid time off for antenatal care.
- Allowing for authorised absence whenever appropriate to cover specific religious observances of minority groups.
- Allowing special leave for all workers, not only employees.

HOW DO YOU DEVELOP AN ABSENCE STRATEGY?

Developing an absence strategy involves developing an absence policy and establishing the 'building blocks' of absence practice:

- Clear absence procedures.
- Rigorous monitoring.
- Use of 'trigger points' for action, for example, the number or duration of absences.
- Defined roles and accountabilities.

- Effective management processes, for example, home visits.
- Options for incentives and sick pay.
- Preventative initiatives - flexible working and occupational health.

See also - absence policies - later in this section - for further detail.

HOW DO YOU DEAL WITH SHORT-TERM ABSENCE?

The absence management tool emphasises that dealing with short-term absence will include the use of 'return to work' interviews for all absences, in order to:

- Establish the reason for the absence.
- Assess whether the reasons are consistent with other reliable evidence.
- Raise any doubts with the person that was absent.
- Allow the person to explain their absence.

The use of return to work interviews indicates to the employee that their absence was noticed and that it had consequences. In addition, it indicates that absence is a high priority along side other organisational priorities. When evaluating short term absence it is important to identify if there is a discernible pattern, for example, always on Monday, or whether the reason is the same for previous absences. If the investigation warrants it, an absence review meeting should be conducted by the line manager to consider the pattern and quantity of absence; this would usually be an informal opportunity to discuss the issue, not part of the disciplinary process.

The outcome of the discussion may lead to the involvement of other parties, such as occupational health practitioner or human resources staff; it may also be necessary to contact the employee's GP. It is important to take action when data has been obtained and evaluated, even if this is to confirm to the employee that the absence appears justified, for example, the absence may relate to a pregnancy that the employer had not been made aware of. Other practical steps to improve attendance may need to be taken, for example, temporary adjustment of hours of work, assistance in obtaining external help for home or encouragement/support in lifestyle changes. If absence does not improve it may be necessary to introduce disciplinary action.

See also - managing short term absence - later in this section - for further detail.

HOW DO YOU DEAL WITH LONG-TERM ABSENCE?

The absence management tool emphasises that research indicates that long-term absence is generally handled most effectively through early interventions and actions. The longer the period of absence, the less likely the employee is to return to work. When the employee has been absent for an extended period the employer should evaluate the situation and determine:

- When the employee is likely to return to work.
- What practical steps can be taken to help the individual return to work sooner, for example, keeping in touch?

- The level of support and contact that is appropriate while the individual is absent.
- The action to prepare for the individual's return to work at the appropriate time.
- What support the individual may need on their return.
- Although most long-term absence is attributable to genuine medical factors, the precise nature, extent and potential implications of a given medical condition may in practice be difficult to determine.

Advice on how to investigate the causes and background of long-term absence

In cases of long-term absence, employers should take reasonable steps to find out about the employee's true medical position. This is important in helping the employer clarify when the individual is likely to return to work, and to identify any practical steps that might be taken to accelerate their return. This may necessitate direct contact with the employee's GP; in order to do this explicit permission from the employee must be obtained. The employee may exercise their right to withhold consent to the application for a medical report from the GP or wish to see it before it is sent to the employer.

If the employee considers the report to be incorrect they can request that the GP amends it; if the GP refuses, the employee may have a statement attached to the report setting out their disagreement. Where there is reasonable doubt about the nature of the illness it would be appropriate to ask the employee to be examined by a doctor appointed by the organisation. If the employee refuses to co-operate, it will be necessary for the employer to take a decision on the appropriateness of the absence based on the information available.

Advice on how to develop appropriate responses to deal with the circumstances of the absence

Depending on the circumstances of the absence it may be appropriate to provide assistance to enable the employee to return to work. This could include phased return to work through part-time working or a short initial period to enable re-adjustment. It could also require specific work adjustments by the provision of special equipment or a person to assist with aspects of the work.

In order to ensure the effective return to work it may be necessary to provide medical and other interventions. The provision of physiotherapy or counselling may assist the employee's medical condition and financial support may make it easier to come to work, for example, by using a taxi to avoid driving. The circumstances of return, including any interventions or adjustments should be formally risk assessed.

If the employee does not appear likely to return to work within a 'reasonable time' it may be necessary to introduce dismissal processes. It is essential that if this is to be done that ACAS guidance be followed.

See also - managing long term absence - later in this section - for further detail.

Sickness absence recording and monitoring

The line manager should record every employee absence and must conduct 'return to work interviews' with the employee on their return to work. The aim of the interview is to identify the cause of the absence and to explore any problems that the employee may have. The manager must keep a record of the interview should this be required at a future date.

BENEFITS OF RECORDING AND MONITORING SICKNESS ABSENCE

The benefit of recording and monitoring sickness absence is that it enables an organisation to identify any trends and patterns that may occur. The fact that absence is recorded and monitored will emphasise the importance placed on it by the organisation and provide an opportunity to show the individual that absence is a significant issue. It may also help identify whether there are any workplace issues that are affecting absence, for example, bullying, poor management in a particular department, or work related ill-health. The data derived from recording and monitoring absence may also help to plan cover for absent employees. The data can also be used to 'benchmark' performance against other organisations. The recording and monitoring process will also help to identify employees whose return to work may not happen on a timely basis without intervention and those employees whose absence is disguising external factors affecting them, for example, family problems.

USE OF ABSENCE MEASUREMENT TECHNIQUES

The organisation will need to collect and record data on individual absence to ensure accurate payment of Statutory Sick Pay (SSP). Ideally, this data should be collected in a form that also enables the organisation to analyse absence types, trends and patterns.

This would involve collecting such data as listed below:

- Name or identification of the employee concerned.
- Location, department, team and job.
- Where they can be contacted.
- Date of the first day of absence.
- Cause of absence.
- Expected length of absence, if known.
- Whether the injury or illness is considered to be work-related.
- Working days absent (updated regularly).
- Date the employee was last contacted and the outcome.
- Return-to-work date.

The collected data on individual absence levels should be gathered on a daily basis and updated weekly. This will enable the identification of patterns or trends in absence at the individual and collective levels. To do this well it will be necessary to give responsibility to carry this out at appropriate levels, for example, in teams, departments and across the organisation as a whole. It is important to make sure that absence data is collated and presented on a consistent basis, i.e. like circumstances and methods are compared with similar sections of the organisation, for example, office workers with similar other office workers; and manual workers with others in similar occupations and circumstances.

The sickness absence data that is collected has to comply with the Data Protection Act (DPA) 1998. If an absence record contains specific medical information relating to an employee, this is deemed as sensitive data and it will be necessary to satisfy the statutory conditions for processing such data, for example, confidentiality. For this reason it is useful to separate data collected into general (non-confidential) and medical (confidential), so that appropriate control and confidentiality can then be assured.

Lost time rate

Organisations need to know their rates of absenteeism so that they can estimate the costs to the organisation of absence and to identify what needs to be done to reduce the cost. It is not just about the causes. Examples of common indices used for measuring absence are:

Lost time rate:
$$\frac{\text{Number of working days (hours) lost}}{\text{Total number of working days (hours)}^*} \times 100$$
(*excludes holiday and overtime)

Average length per absence: This will help to identify the type of absence, for example, long or short-term
$$\frac{\text{Number of days lost}}{\text{Number of absences}}$$

Days lost per person: This will identify the average number of days lost per person
$$\frac{\text{Number of days lost in a year}}{\text{Average number of employees per year}}$$

Frequency rate

Organisations also need information on how often employees are taking time off - individual frequency rates, for example:

Percentage of employees absent (individual frequency rate):
$$\frac{\text{Number of employees absent one or more times}}{\text{Average numbers employed}} \times 100$$

(This may also be calculated using figures per day, per month etc).

Frequency of absence rate:
$$\frac{\text{Number of separate absences per year (month)}}{\text{Average numbers employed during the year (month)}}$$

Bradford factor

The Bradford factor identifies persistent short-term absenteeism of individuals.

It measures the number of spells of absence and is a useful measure of the disruption caused by this type of absence. It is the unexpected frequent short-term absences that are most damaging and costly to organisations. It means either taking on temporary staff to do the work or expecting others to carry out two or more jobs, which is likely to mean that those people will eventually become affected as a result and also take time off.

It is measured by using the following formula:
$$S \times S \times D = B$$

B is the Bradford factor score.

S is the total number of instances of absence of an individual over a set period.

D is the total number of days of absence of that individual over the same set period.

The 'set period' is typically set as a rolling 52 week period.

Example: 8 one-day absences: $8 \times 8 \times 8 = 512$ points

1 ten day absence: $1 \times 1 \times 10 = 10$ points

5 absences of 3 days each: $5 \times 5 \times 15 = 375$ points

Total Bradford Factor score for worker: 897 points

If an organisation is using the Bradford factor as a method of recording absences then trigger points should be set as part of the attendance policy, so that managers know when and what action to take.

The results of the score should not immediately mean that disciplinary action is taken, as a full investigation of the circumstances of the absence should be undertaken. Care should be taken in interpreting the results; it is possible for an employee with a serious illness that is unknown to the employer to obtain a high score, for example, an employee with cancer attending for chemotherapy/radiotherapy once a week for several weeks. The Equality Act (EA) 2010 creates a duty on employers to make reasonable adjustments for disabled employees, which includes those undergoing such medical treatment. As certain disabilities may lead to a greater likelihood of short-duration absences or to a higher total of days of absence, a strong probability exists that disabled employees will be disproportionately disadvantaged by any non-individually tailored application of the Bradford factor.

Absence policies

Employee contribution is vital to the success of all businesses and therefore organisations must ensure a healthy working environment and support employees when they are ill to facilitate an early return to work. Therefore, good organisations, no matter how small or large must have an effective absence policy, which clearly outlines the responsibilities of employees and managers. From an organisational perspective effective absence policies and procedures can prevent short term absences from becoming long term and can help tackle any workplace issues.

POLICIES AND PROCEDURES FOR THE MANAGEMENT OF ILL-HEALTH AND ABSENCE

Managing attendance should be as much part of the business strategy as other issues such as production, services and finance and should be a major part of resource planning. It is imperative to any organisation to manage attendance effectively. This will include having a practical 'managing attendance policy', which should cover all aspects of non-attendance, including that due to ill-health and sickness absence. The **role** of the policy and its procedures is to set out the intent of the organisation with regard to attendance/absence, and the responsibilities and details of how these are to be fulfilled. Responsibilities will cover managers, employees, human resources and occupational health.

Attendance/absence needs to be accurately and effectively recorded, as the organisation must be able to assess if they have a problem and then take action to rectify it. The cost to organisations of absence attributed to sickness is significant *(see also - Element 2 - Effects on health at work)*, however, there are still a number of organisations who do not measure attendance/absence; they do not have any systems for collecting data and have no systems in place for monitoring or managing the problem. Good absence data can provide evidence to senior management on how absence is impacting on the 'bottom line' and encourage investment in programmes and resources to reduce the costs, for example, investment in occupational health provision, employee assistance programmes.

The **benefits** of having a policy and procedures are enormous, for example, managers and employees know what is expected of them. Clear policies and procedures will enable employees to see the importance placed on attendance and the need for their co-operation with regard to it. It will also enable managers to apply the policy appropriately to the variety of situations that might arise and guide its application so that it is applied consistently. The policy and procedures will ensure that there are systems for recording and monitoring so that problems can be addressed and absenteeism reduced, thus saving the organisation valuable resources such as good staff, reduction in recruitment and training of new staff, reduction in insurance claims for ill-health as well as the costs of employing casual labour to cover absences.

THE GENERAL CONTENTS OF AN ABSENCE MANAGEMENT POLICY

Providing details of contractual sick pay terms (if any) and its relationship to statutory sick pay

All organisations will have details regarding terms for sick pay within their contracts of employment for employees, for example, when it will be paid and under what circumstances. This will be different for each organisation. Details of this must be included within a managing attendance/absence policy, in order to ensure it is understood by both management and employees.

The process employees must follow if taking time off sick

The process for employees to follow when taking time off sick should be documented. This will include at what point they should report their sickness, for example, before 10am, to whom they should report and at what point they will be required to produce a completed self certification form and/or a GP's 'fit note'. The policy should also clearly state the organisation's requirements for employees to undergo medical/health examinations arranged by the organisation and the process for obtaining medical reports from GP's. The provision for return to work interviews should be stated, explaining how and when these interviews will be conducted.

After how many days employees need a self-certification form

This will be decided by the employer, but is normally after 3 days absence.

When they require a 'fit note' from the General Practitioner (GP)

This will be decided by the employer and should be clearly stated within the policy so that everyone is aware of the requirements. It is common practice for employers to request a 'fit note' after 5 days absence, but this can vary from 3 days to 7 days.

Mentioning that the organisation reserves the right to require employees to attend a medical examination and with consent to request a medical report from the employee's doctor

Details of when a medical/health examination may be required should be included and the process for this to be carried out by, for example, a company medical/nursing advisor or other outside health provider. The process for seeking consent for medical reports from other medical sources, such as a GP or hospital consultant should be explained.

The process should include information on the forms for completion to obtain consent, how this process will be managed, and who will have access to the report.

Provisions for return-to-work interviews

Information should be included within the attendance/absence policy on when and under what circumstances return to work interviews will be undertaken, for example, it may be policy that all absences require a return to work interview. These interviews help to identify short term absence problems at an early stage and it is advisable to carry out return to work interviews after every absence.

In doing this it provides the manager with an opportunity to discuss any underlying issues causing the absence and, when necessary, invoking disciplinary procedures for unacceptable absences, making it clear to the employee that unjustified absence is unacceptable, and may lead to dismissal.

Where the return to work follows an extended absence the interview may be used to confirm the record of absence held, establish that the employee has fully recovered or discuss any remaining health concerns the could affect work, discuss final details of the return to work plan and confirm any adjustments to working that have been made. Details of the scope of return to work interviews for longer term absences should be set out in the policy and procedures.

Managing short term absence

EFFECTIVE INTERVENTIONS MAY INCLUDE

Effective interventions may include:

- Proactive application of the absence policy.
- Return to work interviews to establish real reasons for absence.
- Clear procedures to deal with unacceptable absence levels and/or breach of the policy.
- Use of trigger mechanisms to instigate review of attendance, for example, Bradford Factor.
- Early intervention and involvement of occupational health professionals.

Proactive application of the absence management policy and procedures includes the use of interventions such as 'return to work interviews'. The policy should require the use of return to work interviews for all incidents of absence. This will convey to employees the importance placed on attendance and the need to limit absence. The interview may provide the employer with the opportunity to identify a cause of likely future absence at an early point and the chance to proactively respond to the circumstances, for example, making work adjustments to accommodate the employee's needs to provide care to a dependent relative or to allow a worker with back pain to recover. The requirement placed on the employee to account for their absence at time of interview may also serve as a deterrent for those wishing to take unjustified absence.

Although it's important to treat each case on its merits, it's also essential that employers apply the same standards to all staff. As a starting point, research indicates that the single most effective action to reduce absence is to consistently conduct return-to-work interviews for all staff who have been absent, however long or short the absence period.

Figure 4-8: Importance of return to work interviews.   *Source: CIPD.*

Managers find many competing pressures on their time and it may be tempting to overlook the requirement to carry out return to work interviews in all cases. It is therefore useful to require documentary evidence that the interview has taken place, such as a form provided to the human resources function on completion of the interview. This will also provide a written record for reference in subsequent absences and support formal disciplinary procedure, should they be necessary.

The attendance/absence policy should establish what are indications of unacceptable short term absence levels or patterns and this may be triggered by the use of the Bradford Factor points system to identify problem instances or other concerning patterns of absence, such as the same day within a specified period. When there are indications of unacceptable absence it is important that line managers do not draw immediate conclusions, particularly if supported by other anecdotal information.

Each individual case will require different treatment; it is important that the line manager starts by gathering as much information as possible about the nature and causes of the absence. This will involve reviewing the statistical and other data relating to the absence patterns, which will help to identify potential areas for discussion at the return to work interview that follows the absence triggering concern or a planned review of attendance/absence interview if this is more appropriate.

The review of attendance interview will provide the employee with an opportunity to recognise the organisation's perspective on the unacceptability of the absence and to comment on it. It is important that the review interview is non-judgmental, allows the employee to be open about the absences, provides discussion on what the causes of absence were, the likelihood of it recurring and what can be done to prevent it. The absences may relate to a variety of separate issues, but they may relate to a lifestyle/general health problem that will recur, for example, abuse of alcohol or high blood pressure. Although much absence is attributed to sickness, short term absenteeism can often be due to a managerial issue, such as poor motivation to work or excessive pressure of work and as such must be identified and 'managed' by the line manager.

Table 22: The most effective absence management approaches for short-term absence

% of organisations citing as a top three most effective approach for managing short-term absence

	All	Manufacturing and production	Private services	Non-profit organisations	Public services
Return-to-work interviews	64	67	63	66	59
Trigger mechanisms to review attendance	29	32	23	26	38
Disciplinary procedures for unacceptable absence	23	34	24	15	12
Restricting sick pay	16	18	24	11	2
Occupational health involvement	9	9	5	15	14
Managers are trained in absence-handling	9	11	7	7	10
Line managers take primary responsibility for managing absence	9	6	10	7	13
Sickness absence information given to line managers	8	4	8	6	12
Flexible working	6	4	7	10	5
Leave for family circumstances	5	1	5	6	8

Figure 4-9: Approaches for short term absence.   *Source: CIPD.*

The outcome of the absence review interview may lead to the involvement of other parties, such as an occupational health practitioner or human resources staff, it may also be necessary to contact the employee's GP. They may be able to provide additional support, advice or specific intervention that could help to prevent future absences.

Disciplinary action remains an option, if the circumstances warrant it. Disciplinary procedures and actions should be documented by stages so that everyone understands what is expected and to ensure that all employees are treated the same and fairly. The training of managers in absence management and providing up to date information on attendance of staff is essential if the procedure is to work.

Managing long term absence

OVERLAPS WITH MANAGING SHORT TERM ABSENCES

As with the management of short term absences it is important to apply the attendance/absence policy proactively in order to reduce the likelihood of recurring short term absence or absence becoming long term. When absence occurs, similar to short term absences, the policy should establish triggers that indicate action to prevent continued absence is required. This may be any absence over a set duration (often taken to be absence in excess of four weeks), a number of the same recurring absences or any absence linked to causes that often lead to long term absence, for example, back injuries or stress. This will enable the absence to be investigated and the opportunity to provide early intervention that allows return to work at an early point. The recurring absences may be identified and dealt with through the short-term absence strategies, including **return to work interviews**; however the potential long term absence incidents will require special attention. As part of a proactive strategy it would be useful to identify employees who might be more at risk of long term absence in advance. This would enable intervention to be taken at the earliest opportunity and may enable strategies to be put in place that enable them to stay in work.

The HSE, in their guidance document HSG 249 "Managing sickness absence and return to work" suggest the type of people that are likely to need help and support to stay in work include people:

■   Who are already in poor health, but whose condition might be made worse unless the system of working is changed.

■   Whose condition already affects their job performance and may begin to affect their attendance.

■   Who have already experienced long term absence or recurring short term absence for the same reason.

Managing long term absence is very important. The Chartered Institute of Personnel and Development (CIPD) estimate that absences of 8 days duration account for around 33% of absence, and absences of 4 weeks or more account for more than 15%. Therefore, it is important that organisations put into place a formal strategy to help workers return to work after extended periods of absence.

This should include the following:

- Line manager must be involved in the management process and take the lead.
- Early investigation of the circumstances surrounding the absence, including the causes and prognosis.

Line manager working with the human resources function to get occupational health advice and support as soon as possible, in order to put in place proactive measures to help the worker return to work. Early involvement of an occupational health professional can reduce the likelihood of lengthy absence, especially with issues such as stress and upper limb disorders.

Occupational health specialists can help put in pace bespoke treatment strategies and recommend adjustments to work and/or hours to help the individual remain in work or return to work at the earliest reasonable opportunity.

- Initial enquires with the individual regarding their absence.
- Maintaining contact with the absent worker and liaising with any worker representative.
- Referral to an occupational health specialist practitioner regarding the condition, its treatment and return to work strategies.
- Reviewing the worker's job and identifying what could be done to allow the worker back to work. This could include allowing a gradual return to work, changing work patterns/shifts, allowing flexible working to accommodate treatment or family demands.

Figure 4-10: Return to work guidance. *Source: HSE/CIPD.*

INITIAL ENQUIRIES

It is important that employees that are likely to be absent for a long term are contacted early in their absence, ideally between 2 - 6 weeks. These initial enquires will help to determine the current circumstances of their absence, their level of well-being and what factors are affecting their return to work. A similar approach may be taken for employees that have a pattern of recurring short or long term sickness absence.

Contact of this nature can be a sensitive issue as some employees may fear they are going to be pressurised to return to work before they are ready. However, without this contact employees that have been absent for some weeks start to feel disassociated with the workplace, become concerned about what people think of their absence and sometimes, particularly where sick pay is limited, feel of low value to the organisation. There is a serious risk that their mental health can diminish, leading to perceived barriers that prevent return to work.

Although the line manager should take the lead in applying the attendance/absence policy for long term absence it may not be appropriate for them to conduct initial enquires; they may not have the confidence to contact them as they may feel it intrusive. It may therefore be appropriate to ask someone else who is **suitably trained and impartial** to take on this role, for example, a trade union representative or worker representative or human resources manager (who may have more skills in dealing with sensitive issues than the line manager). Human resources or occupational health staff may be able to provide important impartiality where the absence relates to work that the line manger was responsible for managing, for example work-related stress.

KEEPING IN CONTACT WITH THE INDIVIDUAL

It is essential that contact be maintained with the individual at intervals after the initial contact. The frequency would depend on the circumstances, but it would be appropriate that the attendance/absence policy require a maximum period between contacts.

This can be quite important where the individual is not receptive to the contact and can establish an obligation on behalf of the employer and employee, which may reduce the impression that the contact is intrusive and only to the benefit of the employer. Periodic/regular contact can help support the well-being of the worker and provide opportunities to identify pathways to returning to work.

The contact with the individual should focus on their well-being and return to work, discussing what they can do as well as help they might need. An important aspect of the contact is to help the employee to maintain a relationship with work. It is useful to keep them in touch with both the formal and informal news related to the workplace.

As with the initial enquiries, although the line manager should generally take the lead in maintaining contact with the sick employee, it may be appropriate to ask someone else to take on this role if there are issues of conflict between the manager and the employee. It is important that the contact is supportive, encouraging and not intrusive. The line manager may not find this easy to maintain in circumstances where the employee's continued absence is causing the manager concern or they are implicated in the cause of the absence. In these circumstances, the contact could be made by another line manager from a different department, a trade union or employee representative, work colleague, human resources manager or occupational health practitioner. If the attendance/absence policy and procedures have been established in consultation with employees those that are absent should understand that keeping in contact is important in order to:

- Assess what help can be provided, including reasonable adjustments in the case of disabled employees.
- Find out when they will be able to return to work.
- Get information to help plan cover for their work in their absence.
- Explain pay rates for their absence.
- Check their understanding of your absence management procedures.

In situations where an employee refuses contact the HSE suggests in their guidance document HSG249:

- Making sure the employee knows who they can talk to other than their manager, for example, a human resources manager or occupational health provider.
- Using trade union or other employee representatives as intermediaries, especially if there is an established bond of trust between the employee and the representative.
- Enabling the employee to talk to someone of the same sex or religion, or at a neutral place, away from work and home.
- Making first contact in writing, offering help with any problems at work.
- Using an independent mediator.

FLEXIBILITY AND WHERE NECESSARY RESTRICTING SICK PAY

Where an employee is absent for a long period in order for them to return to work it is import to allow flexible working, particularly where there are issues regarding immediate and extended family commitments. Sick pay should only be restricted where there is evidence that the employee is fit to return to work, but is remaining off for other reasons, for example, having to face a disciplinary hearing, or they do not get on with their manager.

ARRANGING FOR A MORE DETAILED ASSESSMENT BY RELEVANT SPECIALISTS

If the employee asserts that they remain unwell and is absent from work it may be necessary to refer them to an occupational doctor or nurse for advice and guidance. This should include a complete health assessment in relation to the requirements of the job and provide advice to the manager on the functional capacity of the worker and what they can do.

CO-ORDINATION AND SUPPORT OF ANY HEALTH, OCCUPATIONAL OR REHABILITATION INTERVENTIONS

Planning and co-ordinating the return to work of an employee after long term absence needs to be a 'team activity' involving the occupational health practitioner, the worker, their manager, human resources and any relevant worker representative. Any actions must be agreed by all relevant parties. A typical plan could include:

- The goals to be achieved and by when.
- The type of work to be carried out, including modifications or restrictions.
- An agreed time period for the plan.
- Dates when the plan will be reviewed and how the worker and manager will deal with any problems, for example referring to occupational health or human resources for assistance.

It is helpful to appoint someone to co-ordinate the return to work process and act as a mentor for the worker, as well as liaising with the team and other co-workers to ensure the plan runs smoothly. This person needs to be someone trusted by all and could be an occupational health adviser, human resources person or worker representative.

CHANGE TO WORK PATTERNS OR ENVIRONMENT WHETHER TEMPORARY OR PERMANENT (REASONABLE ADJUSTMENT)

Identifying the need for reasonable adjustments is essential and must be paramount if organisations are to comply with the requirements of the Equality Act (EA) 2010 when enabling disabled people to work or when considering rehabilitation of a worker back to work following a period of sickness absence. Reasonable adjustments should be made to avoid them being put at a substantial disadvantage compared to people who do not have restricted capabilities. The need to make reasonable adjustments can apply to the working arrangements or any physical feature of the workplace. The HSE suggests in their guidance document HSG249 that the important steps in planning adjustments are:

- Discussion with the employee to form a view of their needs and capability.
- Seeking professional advice, when necessary, to help make informed decisions.
- Assessing the possible barriers to their return.
- Considering, with trade union or other employee representatives, the modifications or adjustments needed to overcome the barriers.
- Reviewing health and safety risk assessments in the light of the proposed modifications.
- Reviewing how well the modifications or adjustments work.

Reasonable adjustments

Adjustments to working arrangements

The adjustments to working arrangements may be temporarily applied while the individual regains strength, mobility or capacity to work or they may have to be introduced as a permanent arrangement for those employees that retain reduced capability.

- Allow a phased return to work, for example, building up from part-time to full-time hours over a period of weeks by changing work start and finishing times.
- Altering working hours, for example, not undertaking shift work, whilst undergoing a period of treatment or to allow travel at quieter times or allow flexible working to ease their work-life balance.
- Provide help with transport to and from work, for example, organising lifts to work or providing a taxi.
- Arrange home working.
- Transfer to another vacant job that better suits their long term capability.
- Assign to a different workplace, for example, someone with reduced mobility following an accident may not be able to work in an area where there is a lot of traffic activity.
- Allow absence for treatment, assessment or rehabilitation during working hours, for example, someone who is able to return to work, but requires continuing treatment such as cancer treatment, or someone requiring physiotherapy or counselling, should reasonably expect to be allowed time off for this.

Adjustments to premises

- Move tasks to more accessible areas and closer to washing and toilet facilities.
- Provide a ramp for people who find steps difficult.
- Improve lighting where sight-impaired employees work.
- Provide clear visual signs and alerts for deaf employees.
- Modify layouts and movement patterns.

Adjustments to the job

- Allocate some of the disabled persons work to another person, for example, someone who has had a heart attack may be unable to move heavy objects, which could be done by a co-worker.
- Provide a mentor while the individual gains confidence in being back at work.
- Acquire or modify equipment and tools, for example, a worker operating display screen equipment with visual impairment, might reasonably expect an employer to make modifications to the display screen equipment.
- Modify workstations, furniture, layouts and movement patterns.
- Provide additional training for employees to do their job, refresher courses.
- Modify instructions or work manuals, for example, Braille, or larger font size.
- Modify work patterns or management systems and styles to reduce pressures and give the employee more control.
- Arrange telephone conferences to reduce travel, or if face-to-face meetings cause anxiety.
- Provide additional supervision.

 Case Study - Customer service assistant

Paula was employed as a customer service assistant for a provincial newspaper when she was involved in a motorcycle accident on a day off. Her injuries meant she needed a wheelchair. Hers was a desk job dealing with customer queries, but it did involve her moving from office to office in a complex building. To enable Paula to return to work, her employer made adjustments to the glass panels in the doors on her routes at wheelchair height, changed the work surface area so that Paula's wheelchair could fit in and provided a suitable car parking space.

Source: HSE.

 Case Study - Residential home support worker

Mary was employed as a support worker in an NHS Trust residential home for adults with learning difficulties when she was diagnosed as having diabetes. Staff working at the home are required to provide cover on a 24 hour basis which means one member of staff remaining awake throughout the night and another asleep, but on call. Mary needs to be strict about her diet, blood sugar levels and medication. Doing the 'awake' shift would disrupt Mary's food intake and sleep patterns which could affect her blood sugar levels. If Mary did not do the 'awake' shifts then other members of the team would have to do more. The dilemma was discussed openly and Mary's managers and colleagues agreed that Mary would be 'excused' the 'awake' shifts but would take a greater share of the night 'sleep-in' and weekend day shifts. Mary, her colleagues and managers are happy with the arrangement.

Source: HSE.

See also - Element 2.3 -The Equality Act and Fitness for work.

RETURNING TO WORK

It is important that the employee's first day back after extended absence is a positive experience for them. Returning to work after this time may be seen by the employee as a challenging experience and an informal visit before the return date may enable them to adjust, catch up with changes and re-orientate themselves to the workplace.

In addition to conducting a return to work interview, when the employee returns it is important that someone welcomes them back, eases their induction to the workplace and any adjustments that may have been made for their benefit.

Fellow workers should be encouraged to make the return to work a positive, welcoming and encouraging experience. This may present challenges where it may be perceived that the employee returning to work is not likely to contribute fully to the work load, reduce bonuses and receive favourable treatment in the form of shorter hours. The negative feelings of the fellow workers can be reduced by explaining the return to work plan to them and encouraging a positive outlook.

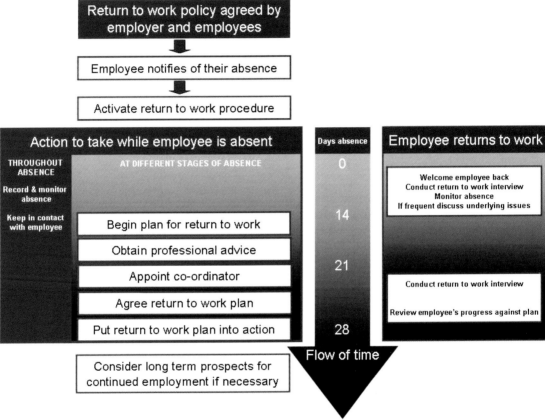

Figure 4-11: Managing sickness absence and return to work.   *Source: HSE, HSG249/RMS.*

The main findings of a CIPD absence survey conducted in 2009 included:

- The most commonly used approach to managing short-term absence was return-to-work interviews (83% of organisations), followed by trigger systems to review attendance (74%), and the provision of sickness absence information to line managers (73%) and the use of disciplinary procedures (73%).
- Return-to-work interviews were the most commonly used approach to managing long-term absence (74% of organisations), followed by risk assessments following return to work (61%), employee absence information for line managers (60%) and use of occupational health services (60%).
- The involvement of occupational health professionals was rated the most effective approach for managing long-term absence by all the main employer sectors.

Example of the content of a managing attendance policy

Introductory statement

A fair, but effective, control of absence depends on applying sound and consistent procedures. These procedures must be appropriate to the requirements of the organisation and take into account the circumstances of the worker. Managers must balance their responsibility for the control of sickness absence with their responsibility for staff welfare. Within the policy there is separate provision for managers to deal appropriately with:

- Frequent short term unrelated absences.
- A recurring medical condition.
- A long term absence.

Roles and responsibilities

The employee

Include responsibility to attend work as per their contract of employment, reporting of sickness and maintaining contact with the line manager, maintaining own health, informing line manager of problems, responsibility to return to work as soon as possible and to follow procedures for referral and rehabilitation.

The line manager/supervisor

Responsible for maintaining attendance records of their immediate reports, interviewing employees after any period of absence, educating employees on their responsibilities and ensure they follow procedures for reporting etc. The line manager must ensure that the employee has the necessary support to return to work, and support the rehabilitation process, which could include alternative work, reduced hours, changing work processes. They must maintain contact with employees during extended periods of absence and seek advice from occupational health and human resources when required.

Human resources department

Will monitor sickness absence of all employees and provide information to managers at trigger targets to prompt action by the line managers/supervisors. It will give the practical support and guidance to managers and supervisors to enable them to carry out their role in the policy, i.e. provide accurate and informative data promptly and consistently, information on disability discrimination and other employment law.

Occupational health

It is the responsibility of occupational health to provide clear advice and guidance to managers and human resources on individual cases and to work with management, general practitioner doctors and others to support early return to work. It has responsibility to provide support to the employee with rehabilitation and provide advice to enable them to improve their health in order to return to normal activity. This will include advice to managers on any job or workplace modifications which may resolve or help a problem and the provision of safe systems of work.

Management of short term sickness absence

Return to work interview. This section of the policy should include information on the process of the interview and what action should be taken by management and the employee following the interview. It will link, where appropriate, to disciplinary procedures. It may be necessary to refer the employee to occupational health for advice, but this should not be the first action. The employee must be informed in writing of the outcome of the interview and the agreed actions.

Management of a recurring medical condition

This procedure applies to employees who have an underlying health problem that causes recurring absences. Decisions on the management of a recurring medical condition will have been made following advice from occupational health.

Occupational health advice might include information on:

- If the condition is treatable and can a significant improvement in attendance be expected.
- The amount and duration of absences likely to be expected during the treatment, for example, hospital appointments.
- If the condition is not treatable, but is manageable, what is the likely level of absence to be expected?
- If the condition is work related and what the recommendations are, for example, alternative duties.
- If the condition or attendance at work can be improved by any modifications or alterations to the job, the hours, or the environment.
- Compliance with the Equality Act (EA) 2010.

The manager will need to consider:

- The effect of continued recurring illness on the work team and the organisation.
- If the recommendations made by occupational health can reasonably be implemented, for example, alternative duties, reduced hours etc.
- Compliance with the requirements of the Equality Act (EA) 2010.

Ideally the situation will be 'case managed' with discussions jointly involving the employee, the manager, the human resources, any worker representative and occupational health at regular agreed intervals.

Management of long term sickness absence

The policy would set out responsibilities for the investigation into the circumstances surrounding the absence, including the causes and prognosis. The requirement to conduct initial enquires should be set out and include information on the process of the initial enquiry and what action should be taken by management and the employee following the initial enquiry. The policy will set out the need to maintain contact, the goals of this and approach to be taken. It is important to set out the employee's responsibility to participate and their rights as to who will maintain contact. It may be necessary to refer the employee to occupational health for advice on the condition causing absence, rehabilitation and return to work strategies, the obligations and rights of the employee should be explained. The policy should set out the usual process of how a return to work plan is developed and the function of the return to work interview.

4.4 - The principles and benefits of vocational rehabilitation

Meaning of vocational rehabilitation

The generally accepted definition for vocational rehabilitation is:

> *"A process to overcome the barriers a worker faces in returning to employment which result from their injury, illness or disability".*

Figure 4-12: Definition for vocational rehabilitation.   *Source: RMS.*

It encompasses the support a worker and the employer needs to ensure the worker remains in or returns to work or can access work for the first time. It is an intervention to remove the barriers for a return to work, whilst providing therapeutic care.

Effective vocational rehabilitation depends on communication and co-ordination between the worker concerned, the employer and healthcare professionals.

Benefits of vocational rehabilitation

The detrimental impact that sickness has on a worker is well documented and early intervention can be effective in avoiding long term absence from work. The worker will feel valued by the organisation if investment in them is focused on them returning to work. There is strong evidence that it is a cost benefit for the organisation to retain skilled workers in work, rather than to replace them with someone who, whilst equally skilled, may take some time to achieve the level of performance required for the job.

Basic principles of the bio-psychosocial model and how it relates to the health of individuals

The bio-psychosocial model of health was developed in 1977 by George Engel, an American psychiatrist, and refers to the concept that biological, psychological, and social factors coalesce to play a significant role in the way human beings function. The biological part of the model relates to the medical aspects of injury and illness, psychological refers to the individual's personal beliefs and emotions. The social part of the model relates to the persons environment with which they live, including home and work. The health of individuals is best understood and managed in these terms.

 Case Study - Contact centre operative

Jane was 35 years old and worked in a contact centre as an operator. She did not enjoy her job and had been off sick with low back pain. She was waiting for an appointment with a physiotherapist and was in constant discomfort. She had not been sleeping and had become very tired and emotional. Her partner had encouraged her to rest and not to take any exercise. Jane was convinced she had a serious problem and that she would never be well enough to return to work.

 Case Study - Electrician

John was 47 years and an electrician. He had been experiencing low back pain and was finding some aspects of his job difficult. His GP had referred him for physiotherapy. John discussed the issues with his manager who was supportive and had temporarily re-arranged John's work to enable him to manage lighter tasks and attend for physiotherapy. John had a positive outlook and enjoys his job. He continued to undertake gentle exercise and his manager maintained contact with John.

The above two case studies illustrate how the bio-psychosocial model can be used to explain the influence that individuals belief and perceptions of illness can have upon the body and mind.

Jane was generally concerned that she was suffering from a serious medical illness (biological). Her perception was that any activity would make her condition more serious and she lacked motivation (psychological). Jane did not enjoy her job as she found it boring and did not have a good relationship with her manager (social). John was waiting for physiotherapy, but his GP reassured him that the majority of the population will suffer from back pain at some stage in their lives and there was nothing serious for him to be concerned about. He was encouraged to remain active and to take some mild analgesia, which helped to ease his discomfort (biological). He was motivated to get well and had a positive outlook on life (psychological). John enjoys his job and has a very good relationship with his manager who was very supportive (social).

Ensuring effective rehabilitation of the individual

Overall, there is strong evidence that effective rehabilitation depends on two features to be effective:

- Accommodating workplaces.
- Healthcare that is work-focused.

One of the barriers to successful return to work can be the worker's negative perception about their illness: "work will make their health worse". Or they may have social barriers, for example, lack of child care, looking after elderly relatives and the job demands itself. Addressing these barriers is an important aspect of any rehabilitation programme if it is to be successful. Organisations must support workplace interventions, and ensure they are tailored to support a safe return to work for the worker.

 Case Study - Warehouse operative

Brian was a 25 year old male with alcohol related problems. He had been having an increasing number of absences from work, was often late on duty and alcohol was smelt on his breath. The manger discussed the issues with Brian, who agreed that he required help to overcome his excessive drinking and advice from occupational health resulted in Brian being referred for alcohol counselling during the working day. With the full support of the manager Brian responded well, stopped drinking and his attendance improved. Further follow up by occupational health demonstrated that the early intervention and support provide for Brian prevented his excessive drinking.

Agencies that can support the employers and employees

There are a number of organisations that can provide support with vocational rehabilitation. It is important that the various forms of support and services the organisations provide are co-ordinated by some who can make the process of acquiring and providing these services effective. The co-ordinator should make sure relevant information is available on time, arrangements proceed smoothly and everyone concerned knows and understands what to expect from the service. The co-ordinator should be someone who is familiar with the employees' work environment, work activities and capabilities. In complicated cases a formal approach to the co-ordination, known as 'case management', may be taken to co-ordinate the effort of the range of services and people involved, for example, the GP, medical specialists, physiotherapists, counsellors, rehabilitation specialists, health and safety practitioners and worker representatives. In these complex circumstances, a case manger would often be qualified in a relevant medical area or be a specialist occupation health practitioner.

 Case Study - Driver recovering from stab wounds

An employee, working as a delivery driver, was assaulted by members of the public, which resulted in stabbing wounds to his back. The driver's employer notified their insurer, who also provided rehabilitation services, early in the case. Two days after the incident, a medical case manager from the insurer arranged counselling, which began within a week. In addition, the employee's GP recommended physiotherapy to treat complications resulting from the physical injury. The employee returned to work on light duties as recommended, within two months. The employer commented that they were impressed with his conduct throughout the recovery period and would keep him in mind for management positions. Four months after the incident, the employee began full duties in the same area where the assault took place. The medical case manager continued to liaise with the employer and employee throughout the process.

Source: HSE.

PRIMARY CARE

The purpose of the Primary Care Service Framework is to:

- Equip commissioners, providers and practitioners with the necessary background knowledge.
- Service and implement details to safely deliver the service for people with long term conditions.
- As a means of improving patient's health and quality of life by providing patient-centred, systematic and on-going support.
- To reduce the reliance on secondary care services and increase the provision of care in a primary, community or home environment.

In January 2005, the Department of Health published 'Supporting people with Long Term Conditions - an NHS and Social Care Model' which described three levels of appropriate long term *condition management* to help meet individual needs.

Level 3: Case management

Identifies the most vulnerable people, those with highly complex multiple long term conditions, and uses a case management approach to anticipate, co-ordinate and join up health and social care.

Level 2: Disease-specific care management

Involves providing people who have a complex single need or multiple conditions with responsive specialist services, using multi-disciplinary teams and disease-specific protocols and pathways, such as the National Service Frameworks and Quality and Outcomes Framework.

Level 1: Self care

Describes, the care and responsibility taken by the majority of individuals, towards their own health and well-being and the support provided to them.

It includes the actions people take for themselves, their children, and their families to stay fit and maintain good physical and mental health in order to ensure independence, self worth and the ability to lead as near a normal life as is possible. It ensures people will have the necessary skills and education, information, tools and devices and support networks to manage their own health. There are many support agencies such as The Shaw Trust and the Royal National Institute for the Blind that can provide targeted assistance. In addition, adaptations to the workplace may be paid for through the Governments "Access to Work Scheme".

NHS PLUS

NHS Plus is a network of NHS occupational health services across England who provide occupational health services to non-NHS employers on a fcc basis, mainly small and medium sized enterprises (SME's). It provides independent advice on staff unable to work due to health reasons, including referral to specialist doctors to assess staff and advice on rehabilitation and adjustments to help staff return to work.

ACCESS TO WORK

Access to Work is a Government initiative provided through *Jobcentre Plus* designed to keep or get back to work those who may have a disability or health conditions which prevent them being able to do parts of their job. There are Access to Work advisors who will provide advice and support to both employers and workers. Applicants may obtain payment towards:

- The equipment they need at work.
- Adapting premises to meet their needs.
- A support worker.
- The cost of getting to work if they cannot use public transport.
- A communicator at job interviews.

Access to Work may be available to those who are:

- In a paid job.
- Unemployed and about to start a job.
- Unemployed and about to start a Work Trial.
- Self-employed.

 Case Study - Worker with multiple sclerosis

A 23 year old female administration clerk with multiple sclerosis was finding her mobility problems made it difficult to access public transport. The Access to Work scheme funded the cost of a taxi to bring her to and from work, which meant she could continue in her job.

THE SHAW TRUST

The Shaw Trust believes everyone should have the right to work. They are committed to supporting disabled and disadvantaged people into employment, and enabling them to live more independent lives. Every year the trust works with over 75,000 clients many of whom face barriers due to disability, ill health or social circumstance. Thousands of employers and public sector organisations also benefit from the trusts range of services for business. According to the Office for National Statistics Labour Force Survey, Jan-March 2009 there are currently 1.3 million disabled people in the UK who are available for and want to work:

- Only half of disabled people of working age are in work (50%), compared with 80% of non-disabled people.
- Employment rates vary greatly according to the type of impairment a person has; only 20% of people with mental health problems are in employment.
- 23% of disabled people have no qualifications compared to 9% of non disabled people.
- Nearly one in five people of working age (7 million, or 18.6%) in Great Britain have a disability.
- The average gross hourly pay for disabled employees is £11.08 compared to £12.30 for non-disabled employees.

THE ROYAL NATIONAL INSTITUTE FOR THE BLIND (RNIB)

The RNIB work with the Government's Access to Work scheme to obtain up to 100% funding to pay for individually tailored sight disability support, whether it is adaptations to premises or equipment, accessible technology such as speech activated software or magnifying screen readers.

With each reader, any printed text is spoken out loud in a clear male or female, human-sounding voice.

See also - Element 8.2 - Workplace health services available to support organisations.

Figure 4-13: Quick reader. *Source: Verbalise Ltd SKU Qr2.*

This page is intentionally blank

Mental health at work

Learning outcomes

On completion of this element, candidates should be able to demonstrate understanding of the content through the application of knowledge to familiar and unfamiliar situations. In particular they should be able to:

5.1 Outline the common types of mental health disorders.

5.2 Outline the principles of managing and supporting individuals with mental health problems.

5.3 Explain the effects on employees of stress in the workplace.

5.4 Outline the role and likely content of a stress management policy.

5.5 Explain the application and use of the HSE Stress Management Standards in the management and control of stress at work.

5.6 Outline the role of line management competence in preventing and reducing stress.

Content

Sources of reference

Black, C, (2008) - Working for a Healthier Tomorrow, ISBN: 978 0-11-702-13-4, London TSO.

Department of Health (2006) - Action on stigma Promoting mental health ending discrimination at work, London: DoH.

DWP/DH Dec 2009 - 'Working our way to better mental health: a framework for action' - The Stationery Office.

Health and Safety Executive (2009) - Stress management competency indicator tool, HSE.

HM Government 4th Dec 2009 - 'Work, Recovery and Inclusion: employment support for people in contact with secondary mental health services, NMHDU, London.

Human Rights Act 2000 Faculty of Occupational Medicine (2006) - Guidance on ethics for occupational health physicians, London: FOM.

Lewis J. Thornbory, G (2006) - Employment law and Occupational Health, Oxford, Blackwell Publishing

National Institute for Health and Clinical Excellence (2009) - Promoting mental well-being at work, London: NICE.

Perkins R, Farmer P. and Litchfield P. Dec 2009 - 'Realising ambitions: better employment support for people with a mental health condition' - The Stationery Office.

Royal College of Psychiatrists (2008) - Mental Health and Work, London: Royal College of Psychiatrists.

Shift/Health, Work and Well-being Practical guide to managing and supporting people with mental health problems in the workplace.

The Sainsbury Centre for Mental Health (2007) - Policy Paper 8 Mental Health at Work: Developing the business case. London: The Sainsbury Centre for Mental Health.

Websites: www.hse.gov.uk and www.mind.org.uk.

Relevant statutory provisions

Access to Medical Reports Act (AMRA) 1988

Data Protection Act (DPA) 1998

Equality Act (EA) 2010

Health and Safety at Work etc Act (HASAWA) 1974

Management of Health and Safety at Work Regulations (MHSWR) 1999

5.1 - Common types of mental health disorders

Our health and well-being are affected by physical, psychological and or psychosocial factors. Although everyday fears and anxieties can affect our mental well-being, most of us would not consider ourselves "mentally unhealthy". However, our mental health may suffer, if the fears and anxieties became a major pre-occupation, affecting every aspect of our existence and preventing us from living our lives as we would wish. As with physical illness, a mental health problem can manifest itself as a range of signs and symptoms. It is important to understand that the inappropriate use of alcohol and other substances may be an indication of an underlying mental health disorder.

Mental well-being may also be connected to the amount of influence and control that a worker has over their home and work and most people experience times when they are not in control of all aspects of their lives. Therefore an employer has to take account of the needs of the whole person, both in and out of the workplace. The British Occupational Health Research Foundation (BOHRF) found that almost two thirds of remote and isolated workers reported a degree of psychological distress and therefore more attention needs to be paid to the impact of working alone on mental health. This may be linked to longer working hours, higher customer numbers, and feelings of isolation and lack of role clarity. The Management of Health and Safety at Work Regulations (MHSWR) 1999 places a duty on employers to assess and deal with risks to remote workers. The line manager must maintain contact and attention must be paid to the worker's general health and well-being.

The stigmatisation of individuals with mental health problems

Individuals suffering from mental health disorders can face fear and prejudice from society and yet 10% of the population will experience some form of mental illness during their lifetime. People with mental health problems are frequently not provided with full opportunities for employment. However, misconceptions of individuals with mental health issues are hard to remove and can influence occupational decisions for accessing work or for those who are already in employment and want to remain in work. This can lead to the stigmatisation of individuals with mental health problems.

It is important to understand that people with mental health problems do not pose more threats than others. There are myths to be quashed:

- People with mental health problems can (and do) work, most are in employment and the organisation employing them will not necessarily be aware if it.
- Work *does not* make mental health problems worse; in fact studies have shown that the opposite applies. People with mental health problems want to be treated the same as anyone else with a health problem.
- People with mental ill-health *do not* necessarily have more sickness absence.
- Having mental ill-health *is not* a sign of weakness. Some very famous people had mental ill-health namely Sir Winston Churchill, Ludwig Van Beethoven, Charles Dickens, Sir Isaac Newton, all of whom were high achievers and leaders in their work. Van Gogh suffered with depression all his life and eventually took his own life, but not before he had provided the world with wonderful paintings.

There is a perception that physical health is a separate entity from mental health and yet exercise can be effective in combating depression and physical ill-health can lead to depression, so the two elements are very much entwined. Strong evidence suggests that, generally, "good work" is good for health and well-being, whether this be paid or on a voluntary basis. Work is central to an individual's identity and meets important psychosocial needs.

This is supported by the work done by George Engel, an American psychiatrist, who developed the bio-psychosocial model of health in 1977. His work established the concept that biological, psychological and social factors have an effect on each other and the person as a whole.

"There is now broad agreement that human illness and disability can only be understood and managed according to a bio-psychosocial model that includes biological, psychological and social dimensions (Engel 1977; Waddell 2002). 'Bio-psychosocial' is a clumsy, technical term but it is difficult to find any adequate, alternative word. Put simply, this is an individual-centred model that considers the person, their health problem, and their social context".

Figure 5-1: Bio-psychosocial model. *Source: Gordon Waddell, Kim Burton "Concepts of rehabilitation for the management of common hlth problems".*

From the perspective of those with mental health problems work-related restrictions are often imposed by the way work is organised for those without mental health problems. A bio-psychosocial model approach should be adopted to help enable people with mental health problems to be accommodated in the workplace. This means that it is necessary to take a positive approach to the capabilities of the individual and what they can do in the workplace, considering the individual, their mental health condition and the social context. In this case, social factors include workplace interactions, for example, relationships with co-workers.

See also - Element 4 - Management of attendance - Basic principles of the bio-psychosocial model and how it relates to the health if individuals.

The Equality Act (EA) 2010 makes it unlawful to treat less favourably, on the grounds of disability, individuals with a physical and/or mental disability. The EA 2010 requires organisations to make reasonable adjustments to avoid putting workers with mental health issues at a significant disadvantage.

Recognition that most people with mental health problems can continue to work effectively

Mental health problems may cause fatigue, impaired cognitive ability and lead to poor concentration. Despite this most people can continue to work effectively and there is strong evidence that work is beneficial for their health and well-being. It may be necessary to provide the worker with enough time and rest periods in order to complete work, but the work should be done to a good standard. In the same way, in taking account of cognitive ability and concentration the worker may be provided with aids that prompt the right action or a co-worker that can assist when needed.

When considering mental health, account must be taken of any factors that may have contributed to a worker's mental ill-health and/or emotional distress, either from the worker's personal circumstances and/or the workplace, for example, work overload and poor co-worker relations. Workers may perceive that it is their workplace that has contributed to their poor mental status. Therefore a full assessment of the nature of their work and workplace may be required, leading to some form of temporary adjustment to support and enable the worker to remain in work.

> *"Work may be stressful and potentially psychologically detrimental to people with mental health problems. However, the evidence broadly shows that work is therapeutic for people with mental health problems (as for any other form of disability) in terms of symptom management, self-esteem, and selfidentity, 'normalisation' of activities and participation, improved social functioning and quality of life".*

Figure 5-2: Work is therapeutic. *Source: Gordon Waddell, Kim Burton "Concepts of rehabilitation for the management of common health problems".*

Categorisation of the effects of mental ill-health

Mental disorders are health conditions that are characterised by alterations in thinking, mood, or behaviour (or a combination of all three) associated with distress and/or impaired functioning. The main issues are associated with lack of concentration, feelings of isolation and in some situations inability to interact with others.

The majority of those suffering from mental ill-health conditions have what are classed as common mental health disorders, such as anxiety and depression, which tend to range in intensity from "mild to moderate". One in six of the working age population will suffer from a mental health condition that will meet diagnostic criteria such as anxiety or depression at any one time. Further evidence suggests that women aged 16-74 (59%), particularly those that are more socially disadvantaged, are more likely to show a prevalence in common mental health disorders.

"Mild to moderate" is a classification of the effects of mental ill-health and refers to the severity of the ill-health condition. This classification is usually characterised by mild or moderate symptoms. For example, mild or moderate symptoms of depression include depressed mood, lack of energy, sleep problems, anxiety, appetite disturbance, difficulty concentrating, and poor stress tolerance. Whereas, the classification *"severe and long term"* refers to mental ill-health that has a severe effect on the individual and the effects may be sustained in the long term. For example, severe and long term symptoms of depression include markedly depressed mood complicated by symptoms such as slowed speech, slowed (or agitated) responses, markedly impaired memory and concentration, excessive (or diminished) sleep, significant weight loss (or weight gain), intense feelings of worthlessness and guilt, recurrent thoughts of suicide and lack of interest in pleasurable activities. Doctors describe depression by how serious it is, including how seriously the symptoms affect the sufferer and others:

- Mild depression has some impact on the sufferer's daily life.
- Moderate depression has a significant impact on the sufferer's daily life.
- Severe depression makes the activities of daily life nearly impossible. A small proportion of people with severe depression may have psychotic symptoms. Psychosis is the medical term used to describe a severe mental disorder in which contact with reality is lost or highly distorted.

In some cases of mental ill-health the conditions in the category 'severe and long term' may be similar to those for 'mild to moderate' effects. However, those with long term ill-health will have had the symptoms for longer, in some cases all their lives, and may learn to live with the problems with the help of medication.

Examples of severe mental illness include schizophrenia and bi-polar disorder, major depression and post-traumatic stress disorder. Severe to long term conditions such as bi-polar disorder (manic depression) and schizophrenia account for less than 1:100, less than 2% of the population, but will require long term intensive treatment. Mental health problems can be compounded by inappropriate use of alcohol and drugs and a small minority will experience symptoms that result in a decline in their social functioning.

The effects on mental health of prolonged absence from work

There is strong evidence that, generally, work is good for health and the negative effects of not working can influence an employee's self esteem, lowering their confidence and resulting in a reduction in their health and well-being. The longer someone is absent from work due to sickness, the less likely they are to return to the workplace.

Once a worker is absent from work for longer than four weeks they often have difficulty in returning to the working environment due to mental disengagement and as a consequence are less likely to return to work. Prolonged absence can lead to depression or deep anxiety about their absence from work or returning to work.

In 2006 a review was conducted of more than 400 scientific studies on the relationship between work and health, entitled "Is work good for your health and wellbeing?" The review found that being out of work for long periods was generally bad for the worker's health, resulting in:

■ More consultations, higher use of medication and higher hospital admission rates than for the average population.

■ A two to three times increased risk of poor general health.

■ A two to three times increased risk of mental health problems.

■ 20% higher death rate.

"Many people out of work lose contact with who they are and what they are. When you meet someone in the pub, you may start by asking their name and then what they do. Work defines us. It gives people structure to their lives. Take that away and people lose their interaction with friends and colleagues, the mental stimulus, the daily activity. Worklessness is both a mental and physical decommissioning".

Figure 5-3: Effects of prolonged absence from work.   *Source: Professor Kim Burton, co-author of "Is work good for your health and well-being?"*

For those suffering from mental health problems their prolonged absence from work can:

■ Result in the mental health condition being made worse through lack of contact. The person will feel isolated and forgotten and if they are suffering with depression, they need to feel wanted and valued.

■ Result in high cost to the business in terms of lost skills and the need to employ casual/temporary staff to cover absences.

■ Result in high cost to the person's family as they will be supporting the individual. This also means a high cost to society as a whole as family members may have to take time off to care for the individual.

■ Can affect the reputation of the business as it may be regarded by society as uncaring and ruthless.

See also - Element 4 - Management of attendance - Causes and types of sickness absence within organisations.

Incidence of common types of mental ill-health and their effects

Research suggests that the cost of mental ill-health to employers in the UK is estimated at £28.3 billion (at 2009 pay levels). Among non-manual workers stress is the number one cause of mental health problems such as anxiety or depression. Positive steps to improve the management of mental health issues in the workplace could produce annual cost savings of around £8 billion from increased productivity, improved staff retention and reduced payments to cover sickness absence. Estimates from the Labour Force Survey show that there were 23.4 million working days lost in 2009/10 as a result of work-related ill health of which stress, depression or anxiety constituted 9.8 million working days, approximately 41% of the total days lost. The survey also estimated prevalence and rates of self-reported illness caused or made worse by work, by type of illness, for people working in the last 12 months, 2009/10 and found that stress, depression or anxiety illnesses had a prevalence of 435,000 and incidence of 1,450 per 100,000.

A CIPD absence survey conducted in 2009 found that almost four in ten employers said the recession had increased their organisation's focus on reducing absence levels and costs, with one in five seeing an increase in mental health problems, such as anxiety and depression in the past 12 months.

Those who experience enduring mental ill-health tend to become more disabled than those with a common mental health disorder. However, a person with anxiety can require intensive support, whereas someone with schizophrenia may be well stabilised on medication and require minimal intervention. People with physical problems are more likely to develop mental health problems and vice versa; therefore those who are off work with a physical problem may be worried about their job and experience anxiety in relation to this. Further evidence suggests that workers concerned about their job may attend work when they are not fit to do so resulting in them working below their capacity and potentially making their mental health problems worse. This gives rise to the phenomenon known as "presenteeism". The Sainsbury Centre for Mental Health suggests that presenteeism attributable mental health in the UK accounts for 1.5 times as many working days lost as absenteeism.

ANXIETY

Anxiety and panic disorders are common, but can cause extreme distress to individuals if left untreated. Symptoms that may manifest themselves at work may include loss of interest, poor concentration, low mood and irritability. There are a range of treatments available including medication, psychological therapies, for example, cognitive behavioural therapy (CBT) and self-help.

Cognitive therapy

Cognitive processes are our thoughts, which include our ideas, mental images, beliefs and attitudes. Cognitive therapy is based on the principle that certain ways of thinking can trigger, or exacerbate certain health problems, such as anxiety, depression and phobias.

The cognitive therapist helps the patient to understand their current thought patterns and in particular to identify any harmful, unhelpful, and 'false' ideas or thoughts. The aim is then to change the person's ways of thinking to avoid these ideas and to help the thought patterns become realistic and helpful.

Behavioural therapy

This aims to change any behaviour that is harmful or not helpful. Various techniques are used, for example, a common unhelpful behaviour is for people to avoid situations that can make them feel anxious. In some people with phobias the avoidance can become extreme and affect day-to-day life. In this situation a type of behavioural therapy called 'exposure therapy' may be used. This is where the person is gradually exposed to feared situations. The behavioural therapist teaches the person how to control anxiety and to face up to the feared situations, for example, by using deep breathing exercises and other techniques.

Cognitive-behavioural therapy (CBT)

This is a mixture of cognitive and behavioural therapies. They are often combined because how we behave often reflects how we think about certain things or situations. The emphasis on cognitive or behavioural aspects of therapy can vary depending on the condition being treated. There is often more emphasis on behavioural therapy when treating obsessive compulsive disorder (where repetitive compulsive actions are a main problem), whereas the emphasis may be more on cognitive therapy when treating depression. CBT has been shown to help people with various conditions - both mental health conditions and physical conditions. For example:

- Anxiety disorders - including phobias, panic attacks and panic disorder.
- Eating disorders - such as anorexia and bulimia.
- Depression.
- Obsessive-compulsive disorder (OCD).
- Anger.
- Post-traumatic-stress disorder.
- Sexual and relationship problems.
- Habits such as facial tics.
- Drug or alcohol abuse.
- Some sleep problems.
- Chronic fatigue syndrome/ME.
- Chronic (persistent) pain.

As a rule, the more specific the problem, the more likely CBT may help. This is because it is a practical therapy which focuses on particular problems and aims to overcome them. CBT is sometimes used alone, and sometimes used in addition to medication, depending on the type and severity of the condition being treated.

DEPRESSION

Depression is a broad and varied diagnosis and can be mild, moderate or severe. The main features are depressed mood and/or loss of pleasure in most activities, a feeling of helplessness: a *cognitive* state of mind. Certain physical illnesses can trigger depression in people of any age, but conversely people with depression may have symptoms that they think are caused by a physical illness, but are actually caused by depression. The severity of depression is determined by the number of symptoms, as well as the degree of functional impairment to undertake everyday tasks such as shopping, cleaning and going to work.

Psychological symptoms include:	Physical symptoms include:	Social symptoms include:
■ Continuous low mood or sadness. ■ Feelings of hopelessness and helplessness. ■ Low self-esteem. ■ Tearfulness. ■ Feelings of guilt. ■ Feeling irritable and intolerant of others. ■ Lack of motivation and little interest in things. ■ Difficulty making decisions. ■ Lack of enjoyment. ■ Suicidal thoughts or thoughts of harming yourself. ■ Feeling anxious or worried. ■ Reduced sex drive.	■ Slowed movement or speech. ■ Change in appetite or weight (usually decreased, but sometimes increased). ■ Constipation. ■ Unexplained aches and pains. ■ Lack of energy or lack of interest in sex. ■ Changes to the menstrual cycle. ■ Disturbed sleep patterns (for example, problems going to sleep or waking in the early hours of the morning).	■ Not doing well at work. ■ Taking part in fewer social activities and avoiding contact with friends. ■ Reduced hobbies and interests. ■ Difficulties in home and family life.

Figure 5-4: Symptoms of depression.

Source: NHS.

Treatment for depression usually involves a combination of drugs, talking therapies and self help. Treatment is based on the type of depression the individual is experiencing:

- Mild depression - the condition may improve by itself and the individual may only need monitoring and further assessment, usually after two weeks - known as 'watchful waiting'. Antidepressants are not usually recommended as a first treatment for mild depression.
- Moderate depression - a general practitioner (GP) doctor may recommend a talking treatment, for example, cognitive behavioural therapy (CBT) or prescribe an antidepressant.
- Severe depression - a GP may recommend taking an antidepressant along with talking therapy. A combination of an antidepressant and CBT usually works better than having just one of these treatments. The individual may be referred to a mental health team, comprising psychologists, psychiatrists, specialist nurses and occupational therapists. They often provide intensive specialist talking treatments, such as psychotherapy.

The effects of someone suffering depression on health and safety or their ability to perform their work would depend particularly on the type of work they were involved in. Work that involved high levels of social interaction with others, particularly if this includes thorough communication of important health and safety information may present a challenge to someone suffering from depression who was not receiving treatment. However, work that is low risk and relies on the person working on their own, for example, packing items in a warehouse, would present less difficulty. Some consideration of the person's condition may need to be taken if the work done by a sufferer of depression involved high risk activities working on their own, such as live electrical working, forestry activities or driving large goods vehicles (LGVs). Antidepressant medication can have side effects that cause drowsiness and this can affect a person's ability to drive or operate machinery and drinking alcohol can make these side effects worse.

BI-POLAR (MANIC DEPRESSION)

Bi-polar affective disorder is a psychotic condition (mental illness) that is characterised by fluctuations in mood, which can sometimes affect concentration and behaviour. These moods may range from feelings of severe depression to abnormally elevated mood swings (mania). According to the World Health Organisation it is the sixth leading cause of disability in the world. During the "manic" phases, sufferers of bi-polar disorder can loose their sense of judgement and perspective of what is "normal", they may develop fixed ideas and illusions of grandeur, for example, believing that they are related to Royalty. The depressive phase is characterised by severe sadness and sometimes suicidal tendencies. This condition can affect people from all walks of life and it may go undiagnosed and treated in sufferers where the symptoms are not so obvious. Treatment involves long term medication to stabilise the highs and lows of mood. However this medication can cause tremors. Even if mood swings are interspersed with periods of normality, the individual may not be aware of any changes affecting their actions and therefore may find it difficult to cope with relationships with colleagues, which has the potential to put both parties at risk. The problem is at its greatest for employers when the worker is experiencing the worst extremes of the spectrum. Therefore it can be helpful if co-workers are trained to report to managers problems they observe at the earliest opportunity. Occupational health specialists are likely to become involved in supporting a worker with this condition, particularly if the individual's work performance is affected, providing advice and support in return to work procedures.

SCHIZOPHRENIA

Schizophrenia results in a dramatic disturbance in an individual's thoughts and feelings. The person with schizophrenia may begin to experience the world differently to others and their behaviour may change and seem bizarre to others. Other symptoms may include an inability to concentrate, apathy, depression, delusions, hallucinations and ultimately social withdrawal. The individual may be affected by episodes of 'positive' symptoms, for example, delusions, and 'negative' symptoms, for example, social withdrawal. The delusions that people suffering from schizophrenia experience can be very powerful beliefs and even if evidence is produced to the contrary it will not alter the sufferer's belief. The person may also experience thought disturbances where they believe their thoughts are not their own and are being put into their mind by someone else. Another major symptom of schizophrenia is experiencing hallucinations, commonly in the form of hearing voices telling them to do things, though hallucinations can be in visual (see), tactile (feel) or olfactory (smell) form. Those suffering from schizophrenia may also present an apparent lack of emotional sensitivity, for example, not responding in an appropriate manner when hearing tragic news, but laughing instead.

Antipsychotic medicines are the main form of treatment for schizophrenia. These can help to control the condition, particularly positive symptoms. They have a calming effect, without necessarily causing sleepiness. The individual needs to take the medicine regularly to control the symptoms of schizophrenia. If they stop taking it the symptoms are likely to return within six months. About half of people with schizophrenia stop taking their medicines.

A worker suffering from schizophrenia, who is not being treated for it, could present challenges to health and safety related to their inconsistency, strong beliefs and lack of emotional sensitivity. However, a person receiving medical treatment may be able to conduct many forms of work without presenting a problem.

A particular difficulty arises where many sufferers believe they are cured after a period of time on medication and stop taking it, often without telling those that might be affected by their condition, with the risk of their condition expressing symptoms again and no one in the workplace being aware of it.

It is important to remember that only 1 in 100 people experience the more severe illnesses. Those who do will have regular contact from their medical, social or other support network and an agreed plan should their condition deteriorate (this is often referred to as a care plan or Care Programme Approach CPA).

Evidence shows that employment can be of great benefit, both to the employer and to the employee.

The vast majority of people with mental health problems are treated by their GP and most of these people are capable of continuing to work productively.

Figure 5-5: Mental ill-health and work. *Source: HSE/Shift Line Managers' Resource.*

Potential side effects and impact medication may have on work

There are many forms of therapeutic, medical interventions that are used to influence and control mental ill-health. Depending on the type of medication they may have side effects that could cause nausea, shakes and drowsiness. Where these side effects are likely the use of such medication may have an impact on work. For example, if an individual is taking medication that could cause drowsiness and their work may necessitate driving or working with machinery it could put the worker or others at risk of harm. Therefore, it may be necessary to ensure the situation is risk assessed. In order to do this it is important for the organisation to work with the worker, their general practitioner (GP) doctor (with consent) and, where appropriate, an occupational health practitioner in order to support the worker and adjust work where necessary.

5.2 - Managing and supporting individuals with mental health problems

Principles of the good management of an individual with mental ill-health in the workplace

The role of managers in supporting individuals with mental ill-health at work should not be underestimated. It is important that they are trained and equipped with the necessary skills and knowledge to enable them to effectively provide support. Employers have a duty under health and safety legislation to protect the health of their employees, including mental health. Mental ill-health is widespread within the workforce and the way they are managed is an important responsibility for managers. An organisation with a good reputation for supporting its workers when they are experiencing personal difficulties may offer an advantage over competitors; skilled staff will not be lost and staff morale may be enhanced when employees know that they will be sympathetically supported should they themselves experience any mental health or other problems. Managers need to recognise that physical and mental health can be interrelated and the worker may be absent from work with a physical problem, whereas the underlying cause may be psychological and vice versa. The worker's general practitioner (GP) doctor has a key role, but the management of workers with a mental health problem, is not a matter for healthcare professionals alone. There is strong evidence that medical treatment by itself has little impact on work outcomes, which emphasises the importance of the role of managers. Proactive organisational approaches to sickness, together with the temporary provision of modified work are effective and cost effective, particularly in large organisations. Early intervention is central to supporting workers to stay in work, preventing long term incapacity and early rehabilitation. The longer a person is absent from work the more difficult it becomes to return them to full employment. Mental ill-health is not a barrier to work and rehabilitation is about helping workers with health problems stay at, return to and remain in work. This should start with effective interventions, within the first six weeks, as most people with common mental health problems can be helped to return to work by following a few basic principles. These can be in the form of:

- Temporary modifications to work.
- Supportive environment.
- Directing them to appropriate help and considering the need for the provision of external resources, such as counselling, that may not be easy to access in a timely fashion via the NHS.

The HSE/Shift guidance document "Line Managers' Resource. A practical guide to managing and supporting people with mental health problems in the workplace" suggests that the approach to managing mental health problems should be to:

- Focus on mental well-being. A holistic approach to promoting the mental and physical well-being is most effective and beneficial. By presenting the issue of mental health in terms of well-being it is more likely to overcome barriers around stigma and to achieve involvement and commitment. ***Figure ref 5-7*** suggests ideas of a holistic approach.
- Engage with people. Over-emphasis on definitions and diagnoses may prove unhelpful, as a diagnostic 'label' can lead to preconceptions of what a person can or cannot do. The better approach, as with other health issues, would be to talk to the person and get a clear understanding of what they can do, rather than what they can not do, and work on the basis of the person's capabilities.

The main point behind **_figure ref 5-7_** is that mental health needs to be approached at different levels, corporate for policies and local interactions for the employee with the line manager.

> *The way forward is to bring mental well-being within the boundaries of normal working life , rather than focusing on it as out of the ordinary and thereby something 'different' or stigmatised.*

Figure 5-6: Approach to managing ill-health.   *Source: HSE/Shift Line Managers' Resource.*

Sources of external support available

The extent to which external agencies will be involved in the management and support of individuals with mental ill-health will depend on the reason they are required. Occupational health specialists will be able to provide independent advice on the impact of the worker's mental ill-health on their employment and can advise management on the intervention and support that is required to enable a return to the workplace.

In addition there are a number of organisations such as MIND, SHIFT, and Access to Work and the Shaw Trust who can provide information and support to managers on how to support an employee with mental health problems. **_See also - Element 8 - Workplace health support - for further information on these organisations._**

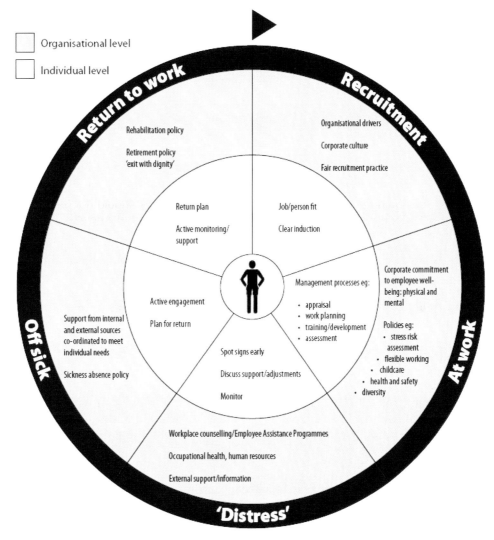

Figure 5-7: A holistic approach to managing an individual with mental ill-health. *Source: HSE/Shift "Line Managers' Resource".*

5.3 - The effects on employees of stress in the workplace

Meaning of "stress" and its effects on physical and mental health and work performance

MEANING OF STRESS

Stress is one of those concepts that has had several meanings in discussions and in the media and is widely abused and frequently misunderstood in the workplace. Stress is usually defined as a physiological and psychological response to the presence of a stressor.

The Health and Safety at Work European Commission (1999) defined stress as:

"A pattern of emotional, cognitive, behavioural and physiological reactions to adverse and noxious aspects of work content, work organisation and work environment. It is a state characterised by high levels of arousal and distress often by a feeling of not coping".

Figure 5-8: Definition of stress.   Source: The Health and Safety at Work European Commission (1999).

Whereas the HSE's formal definition of work-related stress is:

"The adverse reaction people have to excessive pressure or other types of demand placed upon them".

Figure 5-9: Definition of stress.   Source: HSE.

In other words stressors can be any demand, situation, internal stimulus or circumstance that threatens a person's personal security and balance, and everyone has a threshold where these stressors become unbearable. Stress is generally caused by an imbalance between the ability of an individual to cope with the demands placed upon them. Whilst stress in itself is not a medical condition, it can be a trigger for further mental health issues, such as anxiety and depression. Although people sometimes feel anxious or under pressure they usually cope with it.

Coping is any response to external life stressors that serves to prevent, avoid or control emotional stress. Coping strategies are ways to change the stressful situations, involving strategies that change the meaning of the stressor or strategies to help the person relax enough to take the stress in their stride. We all have ways of coping with stress, some are common to almost everyone and some can be individual in character. Stress can adversely affect work performance and can account for a high proportion of sickness absence.

EFFECTS OF STRESS

Feelings	Thoughts	Behaviour	Body
■ Irritable. ■ Anxious. ■ Low in self-esteem. ■ Low mood.	■ Racing thoughts. ■ Worry constantly. ■ Imagine the worst. ■ Go over and over things.	■ Having temper outbursts. ■ Drinking more. ■ Smoking more. ■ On the go all the time. ■ Talking more or faster. ■ Changing eating habits. ■ Feeling unsociable. ■ Being forgetful or clumsy. ■ Being unreasonable. ■ Struggling to concentrate.	■ Headaches. ■ Muscle tension and pain. ■ Stomach problems. ■ Sweating. ■ Feeling dizzy. ■ Bowel or bladder problems. ■ Breathlessness. ■ Dry mouth. ■ Sexual problems.

Figure 5-10: Symptoms of stress.   Source: NHS.

Effects	Short term	Long term
Head and mental health.	Anxious, changed moods, negative thoughts, more emotional, disturbed sleep patterns.	Anxiety, depression.
Heart, lungs and circulation.	Changes in heart rate, increased blood pressure 'palpitations'.	Hypertension (high blood pressure), heart disease.
Skin.	Sweating, reddening and blushing.	Eczema, psoriasis.
Metabolism.	Mobilisation of energy sources, increased cholesterol in blood, increased glucose availability.	Inefficient energy use, increased fat deposition, insulin resistance, metabolic syndrome.
Muscles and joints.	Increased blood flow to muscles, muscle tension.	Loss of muscle function and structure, stiffness, soreness, regional pain syndromes, osteoporosis.
Digestive system.	Butterflies in stomach, dry mouth, suppression of digestion/nausea.	Appetite suppression, impaired capacity to repair ulcers, chronic dysfunction of the gut, such as irritable bowel syndrome.

Reproduction and growth.	Suspension of reproductive and growth systems (hormones).	Reproductive abnormalities, male - decreased testosterone and erectile dysfunction, female - irregular menstrual cycle, loss of libido.
Immune system.	Enhancement of specific immune responses, for example, to deal with wounding.	Eventual immune suppression - increased susceptibility to infectious diseases.

Figure 5-11: Symptoms of stress.   Source: HSE.

Chronic (long term) stress can also contribute to anxiety and depression and can increase the risk of heart attack or stroke. The short and long term effects on work performance of work-related stress on groups of people at work include:

- Disputes and disaffection within the group.
- Poor performance.
- Increase in complaints and grievances.
- Increased reports of not being able to achieve.
- Customer dissatisfaction or complaints.
- Increased sickness absence.
- Increase in staff turnover.
- Difficulty in attracting new staff.

Stress is potentially problematic when work demands are high, the worker's influence over their work conditions are low and the rewards afforded to the work in terms of remuneration and esteem do not match the effort the worker invests in the organisation. Whilst occupational health specialists have a role to play in providing an impartial source of help and advice, ultimately it is the manager who holds the key to effective worker management.

ACUTE STRESS REACTION

Acute stress reaction is a transitory reaction to exceptional physical and psychological stressors. The reaction is immediate with the onset of symptoms taking place within one hour. The traumatising experience may be a serious threat to a person's own life or the life of someone close to them, such as an accident at work, a criminal attack, a rape or an unusual acute or threatening change in a person's social position. Symptoms of acute stress reaction are:

- Narrowing of attention.
- Apparent disorientation.
- Anger or verbal aggression.
- Despair or hopelessness.
- Inappropriate or purposeless over-activity.
- Uncontrollable and excessive grief.

POST-TRAUMATIC STRESS DISORDER (PTSD)

Post-Traumatic Stress Disorder (PTSD) is a complex and debilitating condition that can affect every aspect of a person's life. It is a psychological response to the experience of an event (or events) of an intensely traumatic nature. It is a condition that can affect anyone, regardless of age, gender or culture. It has been known for many years that there may be psychological consequences to traumatic events. In the First World War, Shell Shock became a recognised medical condition.

PTSD was first described in the Diagnostic Statistical Manual Version III of the American Psychiatric Association (DSM III) in 1980 as being a reaction to catastrophic trauma. In other words exposure to a threatening event that has provoked intense fear, horror or a sense of helplessness in the individual concerned. The type of traumatic event experienced may be witnessing the death or injury of others, physical assault, rape and accidents. The stressor (trauma) is outside the range of usual human experience and PTSD is characterised by three main symptom clusters:

Intrusive re-experiencing of the trauma: flashbacks, recurrence of trauma-related images. Individuals if they are reminded about their traumatic experience may experience palpitations, sweating, feeling tense or shaky.

Avoidance or numbing: a defence against memories and repetitions of the trauma. Individuals become less interested in activities that they used to enjoy and become isolated as they feel that nobody understands them.

Hyper-arousal: individuals experience increased physiological arousal and distress at events which symbolise the trauma. They may become hyper vigilant, have trouble concentrating and can become aggressive, both verbally and physically.

Other commonly associated symptoms associated with PTSD may relate to feelings of guilt about what the person should or should not have done during the traumatic exposure, and survivor guilt where others involved in the traumatic experience did not survive. In addition, individuals may show signs of depression, alcohol and/or drug dependency, all of which need to be addressed alongside treatment for PTSD.

Treatment of PTSD

The International Society for Traumatic Stress Studies Treatment Guidelines and the National Institute for Health and Clinical Excellence (NICE) Treatment Guidelines provide the evidence base to support specialised interventions such as Cognitive Behaviour Therapy (CBT), Eye Movement Desensitisation and Reprocessing (EMDR). EMDR is a relatively new therapy which involves prompting rapid eye movement with outside stimuli, while the patient reflects on the event that is causing distress.

The procedure can eliminate or lessen the negative associations of the traumatic event and it has a calming, self-affirming effect. Workers showing signs of problems at work that may have mental health overtones need to be directed to their general practitioner doctor or, where provided, occupational heath services. However employers may seek alternative support privately due to the lack of provision for approved therapies from within the NHS.

 Case Study - PTSD

A worker attended an occupational health clinic following a period of sickness absence for low back pain. Through a general discussion the worker broke down in tears, describing a traumatic incident that the worker had witnessed six years ago when one of his colleagues was seriously injured at work and subsequently had to have both his arms amputated. The occupational health nurse identified symptoms of PTSD and immediately referred the worker for supportive therapies via the worker health insurance scheme. Subsequent follow up demonstrated that the intervention had dramatically improved the worker's quality of life and the worker was no longer suffering from many of the associated symptoms. Had this worker's distress been identified earlier, then the associated difficulties and trauma suffered by the individual may have been mitigated.

Incidence of stress-related sickness absence in the working population

The Labour Force Survey, in 2009/10 estimated that 435,000 individuals in Britain, who worked at the time of the survey, believed that they were experiencing work-related stress at a level that was making them ill. This equates to a prevalence of 1,500 per 100,000 people (1.5%) of those who worked in the 12 months prior to the survey. Just over half of the cases were reported to be new cases, equating to an estimated incidence rate of 780 per 100,000 people (0.78%), which was consistent with previous annual survey results. The main findings of a CIPD absence survey conducted in 2009 included:

- Stress was the second biggest cause of short-term absence for non-manual workers.
- Stress was among the top four causes of long-term absence among manual staff, with stress being the number one cause of long-term absence among non-manual staff.

Table 17: Proportion of employers reporting increases or decreases in stress-related absence over the past year (%)				
	Increased	Stayed the same	Decreased	Don't know
All	35	36	15	14
Workforce size				
1–49	22	50	22	6
50–249	29	45	17	9
250–999	37	35	13	14
1,000–4,999	38	30	11	21
5,000+	51	15	13	21

Figure 5-12: Levels of stress in the workforce. *Source: CIPD Absence management survey 2010.*

Considering the presence of general stress in the working population, according to a Government mental health at work strategy 2009 "New Horizons" just over 20% of working age women and 17% of working age men are affected by stress and anxiety.

The number of working days lost through stress related issues was estimated to be 9.8 million in 2009/10 compared with 13 million in 2004; 6.5 million working days were lost in 1995. On average each person suffering work-related stress took an estimated 22.6 days off in 2009/10, which equates to 0.42 days lost per worker. This figure is statistically significantly lower than most years back to 2001/2; 2005/06 and 2008/09 were similar to 2009/10. The total number of working days lost through stress are 50 times greater than those lost through workplace accidents.

Causes of stress and relationship between work and other factors

There are many factors that contribute to stress within the workplace such as job insecurity, poor relationship with managers and peers, bullying and harassment, work overload or under load.

However, there may be other external factors that have a direct influence on whether a worker experiences stress, such as caring for children, elderly relatives and financial worries.

Work-related factors that can lead to stress include:

- Difficult journeys to and from work.
- Poor working conditions, for example, noise, extremes of temperature, poor lighting, uncomfortable seating or malfunctioning equipment.
- Long or unsociable working hours, for example, having to work overtime at short notice.

- Inflexible working hours.
- Excessively high workloads with unrealistic deadlines, leading to rushing, working under pressure and being overwhelmed.
- Mismatch between the requirements of the job and the worker's capabilities and needs.
- Unclear roles, leading to workers not knowing what to do in order to do the right thing.
- Inadequate support, for example, assistance with work, response to problems like defective equipment.
- Too much or too little responsibility
- Weak or ineffective management, leading to no sense of direction or over management to the extent that people are undervalued and self-esteem is affected.
- Multiple reporting lines with each asking for their work to be prioritised.
- Relationships with colleagues, including ridicule, intimidation, bullying, harassment, discrimination and lack of interpersonal contact in general.
- Threat of abuse or violence.
- Change, for example, an unfamiliar role or location of work.
- Lack of job security.

However, often there is no single cause of work-related stress. Although work-related stress can be triggered by sudden, unexpected pressures, it is often the result of a combination of stressful factors that build up over time.

Sometimes people may suffer from stress that is caused by external issues rather than work-related issues or the work-related issues add to already well established external stressors, which leads to stress.

Common external causes of stress include:

- Relationship difficulties, marriage or a divorce.
- Serious illness in the family, friends, pets or worker themselves.
- Bereavement.
- Caring for dependants, such as children or elderly relatives.
- Concerns about the schooling or career prospects of children or other relatives.
- Debt and other money problems.
- Involvement in disputes, complaints and legal action.
- Moving house or conducting significant work on the house.

The top causes of stress at work are workloads, external relationships, organisational change/restructuring and management styles.

Figure 5-13: Top causes of stress at work.   *Source: CIPD Absence management survey 2010.*

Table 18: The causes of work-related stress (top three causes, %)	All respondents	Manufacturing and production	Private sector services	Public services	Non-profit organisations
Workloads/volume of work	51	44	52	58	48
Non-work factors – relationships/family	49	50	55	39	48
Organisational change/restructuring	39	31	34	56	36
Management style	38	38	33	39	49
Relationships at work	30	28	26	34	34
Pressure to meet targets	17	16	21	18	7
Lack of employee support from line managers	16	20	15	14	16
Job insecurity	15	24	14	10	12
Non-work factors – financial concerns	15	22	14	10	10
Lack of control over how work is carried out	9	7	9	10	12
Long hours	8	8	10	4	7
Lack of consultation	4	3	4	4	1
Poorly designed jobs/poorly designed roles	3	3	2	6	4
Lack of training	2	3	3	1	1

Figure 5-14: Causes of work-related stress in the workplace.   *Source: CIPD Absence management survey 2010.*

5.4 - Stress management policies

The role and likely content of a stress management policy

The *role* of a stress management policy is to set out the organisation's approach to the management of stress in the workplace and to identify methods by which both managers and workers can seek to detect the presence of stress and to prevent its occurrence.

The policy must apply to everyone working for the organisation and should outline the responsibilities placed upon workers and managers. A comprehensive policy demonstrates a commitment by senior management to the health, safety and well-being of its workers and should recognise that there may be factors such as bullying, autocratic management styles and poor working conditions that may contribute to worker stress. The **content** of the stress management policy will:

■ Show a commitment to protecting the health, safety and welfare of workers, recognising that workplace stress is a health and safety issue. This is essential to demonstrate that the organisation recognises stress as a real issue, equal to other workplace matters to be managed.

■ Apply to everyone in the organisation and will detail responsibilities of all that are involved with its success, including that managers are responsible for implementation and the organisation is responsible for providing the necessary resources. Clear responsibilities will help ensure that the policy is translated into action by managers and workers.

■ Detail the role of any external support such as occupational health services. It is important that the policy recognises the extent and limit of internal means of managing stress. By detailing the role and availability of external support it recognises that it is acceptable to access this support to resolve issues.

■ Require the organisation to identify all workplace stressors and conduct risk assessments to eliminate stress or control the risks from stress. These risk assessment findings must be put into action and should be regularly monitored and reviewed. It will emphasise the need to take a proactive approach to managing stress risk.

■ Require consultation with worker health and safety representatives on all proposed action relating to the prevention of workplace stress. Solutions to risk issues may be observed by those that work with them, so it is important that workers are consulted, either directly or through worker representatives.

■ Require provision of training for all managers and supervisory staff in good management practices. It should not be assumed that managers and others know about stress and how to manage it; it is essential that they receive structured training in order that they have the correct understanding of the risk and actions necessary to manage it.

■ Require provision of necessary support programmes, such as confidential counselling for staff affected by stress caused by either work or external factors. The policy should include the plans for and provision of support programmes, where necessary. These support programmes should be organised in advance of their need so that they can be made available promptly.

■ Require adequate resources to enable managers to implement the organisation's agreed stress management strategy; this will include training managers in how to develop and implement the systems. Many of the stress risk management actions may be low cost but will invariable take time away from normal work routines to achieve. However, some may require significant resources, for example, the use of third party professional help. It is essential that the stress management policy does not remain good intentions and that the programme is implemented in agreed stages in accordance with an achievable time scale and within budget.

The stress management policy should take account of the Equality Act (EA) 2010. An employee suffering from a stress related illness may be protected by the Equality Act (EA) 2010 which defines that a person has a disability if:

■ They have a physical or mental impairment.
■ The impairment has a substantial and long-term adverse effect on their ability to perform normal day-to-day activities.

The term mental impairment could be interpreted to include stress. For the purposes of the Equality Act (EA) 2010, these words have the following meanings:

■ 'Substantial' means more than minor or trivial. In the context of stress, the condition would need to have a substantial adverse effect on the ability of the person concerned to carry out normal day-to-day activities. This includes situations where measures, such as medical treatment, are being applied to control the effects of the stress and the person is not showing symptoms at the time.

■ 'Long-term' means that the effect of the impairment has lasted or is likely to last for at least twelve months (there are special rules covering recurring or fluctuating conditions - treated as continuing if it is likely to recur) or for the rest of the life of the person affected.

■ 'Normal day-to-day activities' include everyday things like eating, washing, walking and going shopping.

People who have had a disability in the past that meets this definition are also protected by the Equality Act (EA) 2010. Most stress cases are associated with mental impairments of one form or another; it is reasonable to deduce that a clinically diagnosed stress condition would be recognised as mental impairment. The impairment also has to be "long-term", that is, lasting or likely to last 12 months or more. Temporary or short-term stress-related conditions do not attract the protection of the Equality Act (EA) 2010. It is also important to note that the impairment must be such that it affects normal day-to-day activities.

Many cases where people experience stress will not come under this classification. Those that do come under the classification of disabled are afforded protection from direct or direct discrimination, harassment and victimisation. In addition, the employer must make "reasonable adjustments" to enable the employee to continue with their existing job.

5.5 - Application and use of HSE stress management standards in the management and control of stress

Requirement to include stress in the risk assessment process

The Management of Health and Safety at Work Regulations (MHSWR) 1999 require employers to carry out risk assessments, which must also take account of the way work is organised and the effects this can have on health (including mental health).

When undertaking the risk assessment the way in which work is planned, organised and managed must be considered, especially in relation to job demand, control, support, relationships and roles. By using the Health and Safety Executive (HSE) stress management standards as a guide when conducting the risk assessment, any problems can be highlighted and action identified on the risk assessment records. The HSE Stress Management Standards cover the six primary sources of stress at work, which are *Demands, Control, Support, Relationships, Roles* and *Change*.

The standards set out positive conditions that will assist in the prevention or minimisation of stress; therefore, the absence of these positive conditions can lead to a risk of stress:

- Demands, for example, issues such as workload, work patterns and the work environment.
- Control, for example, how much say the person has in the way they do their work.
- Support, for example, the encouragement, sponsorship and resources provided by the organisation, line management and colleagues.
- Relationships, for example, promoting positive working to avoid conflict and dealing with unacceptable behaviour.
- Role, for example, whether people understand their role within the organisation and whether the organisation ensures that they do not have conflicting roles.
- Change, for example, how organisational change (large or small) is managed and communicated in the organisation.

Figure 5-15: Five steps approach to stress.   *Source: HSE, INDG43.*

The Stress Management Standards represent a set of conditions that, if present, reflect a high level of health, well-being and organisational performance. Management and control of stress within the workplace can be achieved by the application of three levels of intervention. These levels are known as *primary*, *secondary* and *tertiary* interventions.

 Case Study - Management of demands

Two employees work doing the same job as part of a small team. When a new manager arrives one of the employees is given the more difficult work, while the other is given the more routine repetitive tasks.

The employee with the challenging work begins to work longer hours in order to get his work completed on time. After a few weeks he is frequently off sick due to the pressure of work.

The other employee does the routine work easily and has time left with nothing to do. She soon feels bored and starts to make mistakes and not complete tasks due to lack of motivation.

The manager holds a meeting with the employees to discuss the problems. The manager agrees to look at the job design and reorganise work duties. Training is arranged so that both employees can undertake some of the more challenging work and the routine work is distributed more fairly.

Source: HSE, ACAS.

Primary prevention

Primary prevention is about introducing workplace strategies to avoid and minimise exposure to the sources of stress within the workplace, such as establishing fair employment policies, flexible working and re designing tasks and building cohesive supportive teams.

Every workplace is different and it can be helpful to carry out a stress audit using the HSE Stress Management Standards, as a comparator, to identify sources of stress and enable action to reduce workplace stressors.

Sixty-one per cent of organisations overall are taking steps to identify and reduce stress in the workplace, a figure that increases to 81% in the public sector.

Figure 5-16: Number of organisations taking action to control stress in the workplace.   *Source: CIPD Absence management survey 2010.*

The HSE Stress Management Standards are based on the 6 main stress factors of demands, control, change, relationships, role and support. Each standard defines a desired state (best practice) to be achieved in order to minimise the risk of stress in the workplace.

DEMAND

The standard is - "employees indicate they can cope with the demands of the job and there are systems in place locally to respond to any individual concerns".

Control measures to meet this include:

- Balancing the demands of the work to the agreed hours of work, consider shift working, the amount of additional hours worked and unsocial hours.
- Provision of regular and suitable breaks from work and rest periods.
- Matching worker skills and abilities to the job demands.
- Designing jobs so they are within the capability of workers.
- Minimising the work environment risks, such as noise and temperature.

CONTROL

The standard is - "employees indicate that they are able to have a say about the way they do their work and there are systems in place locally to respond to any individual concerns".

Control measures to meet this include:

- Providing, where possible, workers with control over their pace and manner of work; consider reducing the effects of repetitive and monotonous work by job rotation.
- Encouraging workers to use their skills and initiative to do the work.
- Encouraging workers to develop to enable them to do more challenging or new work.
- Providing workers with opportunity to influence when breaks are taken.
- Consulting workers regarding work patterns.

Figure 5-17: Stress at work. *Source: HSE/ACAS.*

SUPPORT

The standard is - "employees indicate that they receive adequate information and support from their colleagues and superiors and there are systems in place locally to respond to any individual concerns".

Control measures to meet this include:

- Establishing policies and procedures that provide support, particularly where workers may feel other factors are putting them under pressure.
- Provide systems that enable and encourage managers to identify where workers need support, consider where workers deal with the public in demanding environments, where new workers are introduced and times of high demand.
- Provide systems that enable and encourage managers to provide support to workers, consider particularly those working remotely by virtue of their location or time of working and new workers.
- Encourage co-workers to support each other.
- Ensure workers understand what resources and support is available and how they access it.
- Provide regular constructive feedback to workers.

WORK RELATIONSHIPS

Improving work relationships and attempting to modify people's attitudes and behaviour is a difficult and time-consuming process. Effective strategies include regular communication with staff, provision of accurate and honest information on the effect of organisational changes on them, adopting partnership approaches to problems, provision of support. The onus is on employers to promote a culture that respects the dignity of others - if it is left to employees to do this it will not happen.

The standard is - "employees feel able to indicate that they are not subjected to unacceptable behaviours, for example, bullying at work and there are systems in place locally to respond to any individual concerns".

Control measures to meet this include:

- Promote positive behaviour that avoids conflict and leads to fairness; consider co-workers, customers and suppliers.
- Establish policies and procedures that resolve unacceptable behaviour that leads to conflict.
- Encourage managers to deal with unacceptable behaviour, such as harassment, discrimination or bullying.

- Encourage workers to report unacceptable behaviour.
- Establish systems that ensure communication with managers and workers, consider timeliness of communication to those that work isolated by location or time.
- Establish systems that ensure involvement and consultation, such as regarding the process of conducting risk assessments.

ROLE

The standard is - "employees indicate that they understand their role and responsibilities and there are systems in place locally to respond to any individual concerns".

Control measures to meet this include:

- Ensure workers have the knowledge, skill and experience to conduct their role or are being supported appropriately; consider workers undertaking new or difficult work.
- Ensure role requirements are compatible, for example, that the need to manage costs does not conflict with health and safety.
- Ensure role requirements are clear.
- Ensure workers and their managers understand the roles and responsibilities.
- Provide systems to enable workers to raise concerns about role uncertainty or conflict, particularly consider the work/life balance for those workers that provide care for others outside their work.

CHANGE

The standard is - "employees indicate that the organisation engages them frequently when undergoing organisational change and there are systems in place locally to respond to any individual concerns".

Control measures to meet this include:

- Provide workers with timely information to help them understand the change, reasons for it and timing of effects.
- Ensure worker consultation on proposed changes.
- Provide workers with information on likely impacts of change on their jobs.
- Provide training and support through the period of change.

In addition to the six specific factors that relate to the HSE management standards for stress at work there are a number of general control measures that should form part of a stress management strategy. These include:

- Introducing a stress policy and procedures to demonstrate to managers, workers, worker representatives and enforcing authorities that the organisation recognises stress as a serious issue worthy of a commitment to manage the risk.
- Providing training and support for workers and all levels of management in the form of stress awareness and stress management training, as appropriate.
- Addressing the issue of work-life balance, which may include consideration of job-share, part-time work, voluntary reduced hours, home-working, flexitime etc.
- Promoting general health and well-being awareness initiatives within the organisation, such as diet, exercise and fitness programmes.
- Providing access to occupational health practitioners, counselling support or assistance programmes for those that may be affected by stress.

Secondary prevention

Secondary prevention involves responding to the likelihood that despite primary prevention methods stressors may still be present in the workplace and that different workers are affected by the presence of different levels of the stressors, for example, some workers may thrive on a particular level of workload and others see this as excessive pressure. Secondary prevention includes increasing awareness and education for both managers and workers in relation to the management of individual stressors and stress at work. However, organisations must ensure that this approach is accompanied by a systems (strategic) level approach, i.e. primary prevention, if the sources of stress are to be properly addressed.

Through greater awareness workers can utilise a number of ways to increase their ability to cope with demands, for example, examining the way they go about their work. They may be able to influence aspects that could reduce pressure and therefore the stress they experience. This could involve getting organised by tidying up, prioritising tasks and better time management.

In addition, raising awareness and education may enable workers to cope with stress; this may be by reducing the negative effects of stress, for example, by taking regular breaks and enabling the individual to re-assess their relationship with others. The education provided should also show the importance of changing the way a worker reacts to stressful circumstances and taking exercise, relaxation and social interaction, both within and outside work.

If necessary, the secondary prevention strategies should provide ready access to discussion of relationship issues with an independent person, such as an occupational health practitioner or someone from the human resources function.

Secondary prevention should also provide monitoring and supervision to identify where factors are having a negative influence on workers, providing an opportunity to talk about issues that affect and contribute to the pressures a worker may experience; these may be practical things like getting a defective chair replaced. Occupational health practitioners, health and safety practitioners and worker representatives contribute to this secondary prevention by observing these stress factors and obtaining intervention to get them resolved.

Tertiary provision of support

Tertiary provision of support generally consists of various forms of intervention to assist those affected by stress, which may include treatment, for example, medication or the provision of counselling. Counselling, such as Cognitive Behavioural Therapy (CBT), can be effective in helping workers deal with workplace and non-workplace stress, as the two are often interlinked. It can help the worker to challenge negative thought patterns and help them to react differently to events that may lead to stress. The National Institute for Health and Clinical Excellence (NIHCE) recommends CBT as the main intervention for anxiety disorders, depression and post traumatic stress disorder.

Furthermore, the British Occupational Health Research Foundation (BOHRF, 2005) advocates CBT as the treatment of choice for helping people with common mental health problems to remain in the workplace. However, the limited availability of these services in the NHS may delay timely intervention and employers may consider it cost effective to obtain counselling services through other health care providers outside the NHS, for example, employee action/assistance programmes (EAP) provided by private health care providers and insurance organisations.

The use of techniques to identify stress related issues

Work-related stress should be risk assessed in the same way as other hazards and processes in the workplace. The assessment should consider some of the causes of stress and identify the symptoms that may be exhibited, such as fatigue, loss of productivity, 'presenteeism' and negative attitudes to colleagues at work. The risk assessment must take account of worker perceptions of stress and include other factors, for example, job insecurity and workload issues.

Therefore, as part of the policy the risk assessment will contain both subjective and objective elements. *Subjective indicators* include data derived through techniques like stress audits, workplace satisfaction surveys and focus groups. *Objective indicators* can be ascertained from the levels of sickness absence, staff turnover and from accident statistics.

USE OF TECHNIQUES

There are several ways to assess the issues of work related stress, which will contribute as part of the risk assessment, for example:

- Carry out a survey of employees, enquiring about their perceptions of the work and workplace.
- Carry out focus groups. This is where a group of people meet for 1-2 hours to identify some of the workplace stressors, and, more importantly, getting them to develop workable solutions to reduce and/or eliminate the problem.

MANAGING THE RESULTS OBTAINED

If a survey or focus group activity is carried out it is important that this is followed through. Surveys have been carried out in some organisations and then no action has been taken on the findings, mainly because the management did not like or disagreed with the findings, and therefore decided to do nothing.

This is fraught with danger and likely to exacerbate the problems as the worker expectations will have been dashed. Surveys and focus group activities must only be carried out if they are going to be followed up and ideas put into action or reasons why they will not be put into action provided.

IMPLEMENTING IMPROVEMENTS

An action plan should be agreed following any survey or focus group activity. This needs to state what will be done, by whom and by when. It should be recognised that improvements may be easily made immediately or make take longer to implement. It is important that those actions that may take time and resource are supported and responsibilities given to those that can ensure completion. There should be someone (preferably a senior manager) who will take responsibility for monitoring the plan and ensuring that the actions are followed though.

COMMUNICATING THE RESULTS

The results of any survey or focus group activity must be communicated to the people who took part and all the workers affected by the results. This might be through the worker health and safety representatives (who should be involved in the activities from the beginning) and management briefings.

How results are communicated will depend on the organisation; some organisations place information like this on the company intranet, but whichever method is used there must also be a system set up for workers to comment or discuss any concerns they may have.

Table 19: Methods used to identify and reduce stress in the workplace (% of employers)					
	All respondents	Manufacturing and production	Private sector services	Public services	Non-profit organisations
Staff surveys	66	51	56	82	75
Flexible working options/improved work–life balance	62	36	61	77	69
Training for managers/staff	61	63	57	68	54
Risk assessments/stress audits	59	61	43	74	60
Written stress policy/guidance	48	39	41	66	40
Greater involvement of occupational health specialists	48	56	37	59	37
Employee assistance programme	47	37	47	51	54
Changes in work organisation	19	28	16	19	13
Focus groups	17	11	17	25	10

Figure 5-18: Methods used to identify and reduce work-related stress.

Source: CIPD Absence management survey 2010.

5.6 - Management competence

The importance of management competences

The role of managers in supporting individuals at work should not be underestimated. By equipping managers with the confidence and skills to address risk of stress amongst their workers, before problems escalate and lead to long-term absence, it will produce healthy and productive working environments and negate the cost of investing in appropriate training for managers.

The HSE line manager competency indicator tool was prepared in conjunction with the CIPD and takes the form of a questionnaire for managers to assess behaviour and their needs for competency. Depending on the sore achieved for the competency it will indicate whether development is needed (scores of below 75), reasonable competency is held (scores of 76-89%) or effective competency is held (scores of 90% and above).

It indicates the following areas of line management competencies that influence the prevention and reduction of stress in the workplace:

■ Respectful and responsible. This includes the manager's approach to managing their emotions and having integrity.
■ Managing and communicating existing and future work. This includes proactive work management, problem solving, participation and empowering.
■ Managing the individual within the team. This includes how accessible, sociable and empathetic the manager is.
■ Reasoning/managing difficult situation. This includes managing conflict, use of organisational resources and taking responsibility for resolving issues.

The use of the indicator tool is seen initially as a self reflection activity, providing insight an directions for self improvement. Some managers may feel that they are not able to acquire the competencies indicated without support from others, in the form of training, formal coaching or mentoring. It is important that the organisation support the development of these competencies as the line manager's role in minimising work-related stress is critical.

AREA 1
RESPECTFUL AND RESPONSIBLE: MANAGING EMOTIONS AND HAVING INTEGRITY

Behaviour/Competency	Strongly Disagree	Disagree	Slightly Agree	Agree	Strongly Agree
Integrity					
I am a good role model					
I treat my team members with respect					
I am honest					
I do what I say I will do					
I never speak about team members behind their backs					
Managing Emotions					
I act calmly in pressured situations					
I take a consistent approach to managing					
My moods are predictable					
I don't pass on my stress to my team					
I approach deadlines calmly					
I welcome suggestions for improvements from my team					
Considerate Approach					
I allow my team to plan their workloads					
The deadlines I create are realistic					
I give more positive than negative feedback					
I deal with problems myself rather than relying on others					
I allow my team to approach their work in their own way					
I show a consideration for my team's worklife balance					
Note down the total number of ticks in each column					
Now multiply each column total by the number indicated to calculate your column score	x 1 =	x 2 =	x 3 =	x 4 =	x 5 =
Add the column scores together and note the total score (maximum score is 85)					
Now divide your total score by 85 and multiply by 100	(........../85) x 100 =				

Figure 5-19: Line manager competency indicator tool for stress management.   *Source: HSE/CIPD.*

Management of people with musculoskeletal disorders

Sources of reference

Faculty of Occupational Medicine (2000) - Occupational Health Guidelines for the Management of Low Back Pain at Work, London: FOM.

Institute for Musculoskeletal Research and Clinical Implementation (2005) - Improved early pain management for musculoskeletal disorders, HSE Books.

Mckeown, C. and Twiss, M (2004) - Workplace ergonomics: a practical guide (Second edition) Wigston: Institution of Occupational Safety and Health Services Ltd.

Oakley Katie (2008) - 'Occupational Health Nursing' Chapter 11 (Third edition) Wiley, Chichester, UK.

Palmer, K. Cox, R.A.F. Brown, I. (2007) - Fitness for Work - the Medical Aspects, (Fourth edition) Oxford: Oxford University Press.

Royal College of General Practitioners, NHS Executive (2002) - The Back Book (Second edition), The Stationery Office.

Waddell, G. Burton, Kim A (2004) - Concepts of Rehabilitation for the Management of Common Health Problems, The Stationery Office, London.

Relevant statutory provisions

Health and Safety (Display Screen Equipment) Regulations (DSE) 1992, as amended in 2002

Manual Handling Operations Regulations (MHOR) 1992

6.1 - Types of musculoskeletal disorders (MSDs)

Work-related musculoskeletal disorders, their causes and prevalence in the working population

Musculoskeletal disorders (MSD's) is the term used to describe damage to muscles and soft tissues, which causes pain and discomfort of the back, shoulders, neck or lower arms and hands. MSD's are due to 'over use' of the affected muscles and soft tissues, which may be caused or made worse by work. Musculoskeletal disorders include conditions referred to as Upper Limb Disorders (ULD's), Work Related Upper Limb Disorders (WRULD's) and Repetitive Strain Injury (RSI). According to the Department for Work and Pensions (DWP), each year 3.5% of workers in the UK are affected by Work Related Musculoskeletal Disorders (WRMSD's), which are estimated to be costing the UK economy around £5.5 billion per year.

In the Labour Force Survey (LFS) for 2009/10, reported by the Health and Safety Executive (HSE), it was estimated that the prevalence of musculoskeletal disorders of all types that were caused or made worse by their current or past work in people in Great Britain who worked in the last 12 months was 572,000 and the incidence was 1,910 per 100,000 people (1.91%). The number of people that were suffering from a musculoskeletal disorder mainly affecting the back was 248,000 people and the incidence was 830 per 100,000 people (0.83%). The number of people suffering a musculoskeletal disorder mainly affecting the upper limbs or neck was 230,000 people and the incidence was 770 per 100 000 people (0.77%). Those suffering mainly lower limbs injuries represented 94,000, with an incidence of 320 per 100,000. Latest figures can be found on the DWP website (www.dwp.gov.uk) and the HSE website (www.hse.gov.uk).

MSD's are the second main cause of sickness absence in the UK (after mental health), and account for around 20% of long-term absenteeism. Therefore, there are good social and health reasons why these conditions should be prevented and reduced. There are also good economic arguments for putting in place positive preventive and control measures, in order to reduce the amount of suffering amongst individuals and reduce the costs to businesses, the NHS and society as a whole. Persuading management to take the problems of MSD's seriously is difficult. It is not life threatening nor does it cause critical injury, but the conditions can be very debilitating and the long term effects can be considerable, becoming chronic and permanent if not managed correctly.

BACK PAIN

Back pain is any form of pain in the spinal region, which is most commonly in the lower back; and is one of the most common of the conditions. Most people will admit to having back pain at some point in their lives. The pain may be as a result of a specific incident at work or elsewhere, or it may develop gradually over a period of time. Factors that influence the development of back pain are:

- Injury to the lower back.
- Poor lifting and handling techniques over a period of time.
- Poor posture, for example seating, standing, leaning over in top heavy postures.
- Obesity and poor physical fitness.
- Exposure to whole body vibration. *(See also - Element 3 - Effects of work on health).*

One of the causes of lower back pain is the strain of back muscles or other soft tissue (ligaments or tendons) connected to the vertebrae.

There are a number of risk factors that will predict when back pain will become long-term; these are older worker, poor (actual or perceived) general health, physical inactivity, low job satisfaction and psychological distress. There are also a number of psychosocial factors that may influence recovery from back pain:

- The person's attitudes and beliefs about back pain, their emotions and behaviours, for example a belief that they must be completely pain free, that pain is harmful and that work will make it worse. In addition, a belief that the pain is uncontrollable and that rehabilitation will not help.
- The person feels angry, depressed, and anxious and fears any movement because it will be painful.
- Diagnosis and treatment. This can be compounded by the attitudes of health professionals, with conflicting diagnosis or no diagnosis, 'medicalising' the problem and over use of investigations, for example, X-rays, Magnetic Resonance Imaging (MRI) scans.
- Advice or comments from health professions regarding the person's work, for example, "of course you will never be able to do that job again", without the health professional understanding the work or workplace.
- Attitudes of the family, such as lack of support and understanding or a partner ignoring the issue. Social isolation, family culture and the fear of ending up in a wheelchair, for example, someone they know now in wheelchair with arthritis of the spine leads to the fear factor of becoming the same.
- Compensation and work issues. How the individual feels about their work and if there is a compensation claim being pursued. There are also other factors such as a lack of incentive to return to work (some people can be better off on sick pay or benefits), or the individual is seeking ill-health retirement.
- There are also negative perceptions and attributions, such as job satisfaction, poor relationships with the manager and/or co-workers, low socio-economic status and a belief that the work is harmful and that the employer is responsible for the care, treatment and recovery.

■ The organisation's attitude to sickness absence will influence recovery. If there are no policies and procedures for supporting workers, such as lack of early access to occupational health services, poor return to work policies that provide little flexibility of working hours, no temporary work adjustments or temporary re-deployment. However, this should now be less of an issue since the introduction of the Equality Act (EA) 2010 and previous disability legislation.

■ Good sick pay entitlements and pension schemes can also have an influence on increasing the time off, particularly if the individual identifies with the negative aspects of work and recovery.

NECK AND SHOULDER PAIN

Neck and shoulder pain can be experienced following any activity where the individual is bending the head and neck forward or backwards and/or the arms are outstretched to undertake an activity. This will cause pain and discomfort in the neck and shoulders and is frequently experienced by computer operators, assembly and packaging workers, when the workstation/ assembly line has not been adjusted for the worker. The importance of assessing the workplace and ensuring the area is adjusted to suit the individual must be emphasised as many of these potential problems can be eliminated if correct ergonomic principles have been applied. For example, adjusting the height of the assembly line, adjusting the height of the computer screen, and avoiding overstretching the upper arms to reach objects by tilting the assembly line belt so that components fall towards the individual.

UPPER LIMB DISORDERS (TENOSYNOVITIS, CARPAL TUNNEL SYNDROME)

Work related upper limb disorders (WRULD) includes a number of conditions:

■ **Tenosynovitis** - pain and inflammation of the tendons in the wrist or lower arms or elbow. It can be very debilitating due to the pain, which can cause difficulty in grasping and holding objects.

■ **Carpal tunnel syndrome** - a condition of the wrist, where the tendon sheath has become enlarged compressing the nerves travelling through the 'carpal tunnel' in the wrist. Carpal Tunnel Syndrome affects the hands causing pain and numbness. Tingling sensations can occur from the arm to the shoulder and in severe cases loss of function of the lower arm and hand can occur.

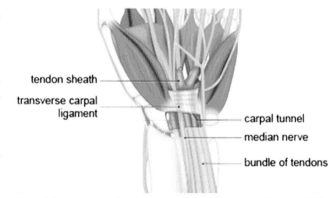

Figure 6-1: Carpal tunnel and median nerve.   Source: BUPA.

■ **Epicondylitis** - inflammation of the soft tissues of the elbow joint resulting in conditions such a 'tennis elbow' and 'golfers elbow'.

WRULDs can be caused by work that involves repetitive movement and awkward postures. An example of this type of work would be assembly line work where workers are putting together parts requiring a lot of manual dexterity and/or standing or sitting in poor postures. Similar conditions exist in computer work where workers are inputting data at a work station that is not adjusted to suit the person, such that the seat is too low/high, keyboard is at the wrong angle and poor posture results. Upper limb disorders can also be caused by other activities outside work such as playing computer games, housework, knitting, crocheting, painting and decorating, gardening, car repair and sports such as tennis, badminton, squash, and golf. Activities outside work must always be taken into account when reviewing the causes of an Upper Limb Disorder (ULD) as it may be caused by one of these activities, but is being made worse by work, or vice-versa.

WRULD's manifest themselves with persistent pain and discomfort in the muscles, tendons or soft tissues of the limbs. There is sometimes swelling and tenderness over the affected area and in some cases there is a 'crackling noise' (Crepitus) on movement. Tingling sensations and numbness can also be present. The work factors associated with the onset of WRULD's come under three main headings:

1) The **posture**, such as awkward positioning of the hands, wrists, arms and shoulders.

2) The **force** that is needed to undertake the task, for example grasping, pushing down, holding etc. This will also apply to hand tools, especially when the tool is not the correct size for the worker's hand.

3) The **frequency** and duration of the movement, for example rapid rates undertaking hand tasks such as typing or packing and/or a repetition of a single task.

It may be only one of these factors that are responsible for the increased risk. However, it is more likely to be an interaction between all of them.

LOWER LIMB DISORDERS

Lower limb disorders (LLD's) can also occur. The ill-health conditions are similar to ULD's, causing pain, tenderness, swelling and reduced function in the hips, knees, ankles, feet and toes. There is a causal association with kneeling, squatting, climbing, heavy lifting, walking/standing, and slip and trip hazards. There is also some effect on the knees, hips and feet for workers jumping from heights, for example, from a large goods vehicle (LGV), platforms or a tractor.

Effect that non-work related activities may have on MSDs

Non-work related activities can cause strain on specific parts of the worker's body. This may be prior to encountering workplace conditions that can then provide additional strain on these parts and leading to the worker suffering a musculoskeletal disorder (MSD). Depending on the extent of strain put on the body by these non-work related activities the additional strain from work activities may be sufficient to cause harm; even though it may be relatively small it may have a cumulative effect. In other situations, the organisation may identify a worker to have symptoms of MSD, take action to limit exposure to work activities that might lead to harm, but no improvement in symptoms take place. This could be because the non-work related activities the worker is engaged are not providing sufficient rest for the affected parts of the body to recover.

Examples of non-work related activities that may affect MSDs are:

- Sports where the player is holding a racquet or golf club. The action of holding the racquet or club to hit the ball places the tendons within the lower arm and elbow under extreme tension, which with overuse may cause pain in the wrist, forearm and/or elbow, for example, 'tennis elbow', 'golfers elbow'.
- Hobbies such as sewing, knitting, crocheting, painting, playing computer games may cause overuse of the tendons and soft tissue within the hand and arm.
- Housework and DIY activities like cleaning (using repetitive actions such as cleaning surfaces with the hands), painting and decorating (the individual may be painting a ceiling when the arms will be raised above the head, the head bent backwards, using a back and forward movement and pressure to apply the paint). The cumulative effect of these activities could cause damage to the tendons in the hand and arm, cumulative strain in the neck, shoulders and lower back strain.

Employer's role in effective management and treatment of MSDs

MSDs are a major cause of absenteeism. The conditions are very painful and can be debilitating and costly to both the organisation and to society. Therefore, early intervention is beneficial in that it will reduce the amount of suffering for an individual, as well as reduce sickness absence, loss of production and claims for disability, leading to reduced insurance premiums, which in turn will benefit everyone. In managing MSDs, there is a need for the employer to establish at the earliest time the help the worker needs and then prevent the situation becoming chronic. This has the aim of:

- Controlling the symptoms and restoring function as soon as possible.
- Preventing the pain becoming chronic, with long-term absence and disability.
- Identifying the obstacles to recovery.

There are often a number of things that can be obstacles to recovery from MSDs; it is not only the 'biological disease or injury', but the other psycho-social factors that influence recovery. *(See also - Element 4 - Management of attendance - for more information on the 'bio-psycho-social model of health').*

Effective management of MSDs means that there is a need to ensure the individual is properly assessed, in order to rule out possible serious back injury or disease. This will identify if there is nerve root pain or is it 'simple back pain'. This assessment should be carried out by a health professional competent to do so, normally an occupational health (OH) physician or occupational health nurse trained to carry out simple tests, with referral to a general practitioner doctor (GP) and/or orthopaedic specialist for further test and treatment.

- Early reporting of symptoms - the first complaint of pain or discomfort should be acted upon immediately. If this is done, the majority of cases of MSD's could be avoided and certainly prevented from becoming chronic. This will typically involve risk assessment, work organisation and ergonomic review.
- Control of the symptoms and restoration of function - this should be done as soon as possible to prevent it becoming chronic and/or disabling. It will include appropriate early intervention, with referral to a general practitioner (GP) doctor or occupational health provider, where this is necessary.
- Education of workers regarding work activities likely to contribute to MSD's - including how it might affect them and what they can do to prevent MSD, for example, keeping active, healthy diet, raising awareness of non-work activities that might worsen or cause MSD's.

Action that the individual can take to prevent or minimise re-occurrence of MSDs

In addition to the employer, the worker has a responsibility to maintain their fitness to carry out their job. This means the employer ensuring that workers are aware of the job requirements and the standard of fitness necessary to avoid or minimise their chances of getting an MSD. The following should form part of an educational programme for employees:

- Maintain or increase general physical activity, keeping the muscles active. This does not mean running miles each day, but keeping the body supple and active, not being a 'couched potato'.
- Avoid getting overweight, because a large stomach can prevent correct lifting procedures and it puts additional pressure on the muscles and spine.
- Consider the effects of hobbies and other activities away from work, for example, computer games, sporting activities, DIY - be aware that these could contribute to the onset of MSD's.

- Follow work procedures and adhere to instructions regarding handling, lifting and other tasks.
- Report to management at the earliest opportunity any symptoms of MSD's.

6.2 - Assessment and control of risk of musculoskeletal injury in the workplace

The factors which affect the risk of musculoskeletal injury

TASK, LOAD, INDIVIDUAL, ENVIRONMENT

The factors that affect the risk of musculoskeletal injury are the task, load, individual and environment. These factors may be reordered to make a useful word pneumonic to remember the factors:

- *L* oad.
- *I* ndividual.
- *T* ask.
- *E* nvironment.

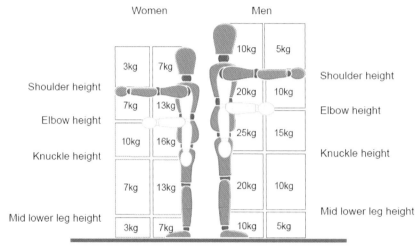

Figure 6-2: Guideline figures for lifting and lowering loads.   *Source: HSE INDG 143.*

Load

- The weight of the load can significantly affect the likelihood of musculoskeletal injury. The Health and Safety Executive (HSE) provides information that suggests that a load of more than 25 kg carried at knuckle height by a male close to the body may present a significant risk of injury.
- Bulky loads are hard to grip and can cause poor posture while lifting and moving the load.
- Similarly, unwieldy loads may cause the person to overbalance, causing strain on soft tissue and the spine.
- Loads that are difficult to grasp can cause the person holding them to lose grip and may lead to sudden strain of the body through snatching or compensating movements.
- When loads are unstable, like loads that are difficult to grasp, their sudden unexpected movement may cause a worker to move quickly to steady it putting parts of their body under sudden strain.
- Some loads may have contents that are likely to shift, for example, liquids in a container or loose items in a box. This movement may move the centre of gravity of the load causing sudden counteracting movement and unexpected strain on the body.
- The centre of gravity of a load may be uneven and set away from the natural points to grip a load. This can cause the effective weight of the load to be further away from the worker's body. This will cause extra leverage forces on the muscles and spine as the body seeks to counteract these forces.

Individual

- Personal characteristics may increase the risk of musculoskeletal injury. The strength of a worker will vary and establishes a limit of weight that they can lift, carry or handle. The average male has a greater strength than the average female. Some workers may have longer arms, which can make handling bulky loads easier. The height of a person will influence the centre of gravity of a person when bending over and if this posture is part of a necessary movement may cause extra leverage force on the back and muscles.
- The worker's health is a factor affecting risk of injury, for example, the worker may have pre-existing back or muscle injury which will increase the risk of injury from work.
- Pregnant females may be of increased risk of harm due to the tissue softening that occurs later in their term of pregnancy, ready for childbirth.
- Older workers may find it more difficult to handle objects due to conditions such as arthritis and their muscle tone may be reduced due to ageing. With the retirement age being raised this is likely to become a more common factor to consider.
- Young persons may not be fully physically developed and, if not properly introduced to the lifting tasks, may attempt to lift more than they are able to in an attempt to impress their new employer.

Task

■ Tasks that involve holding the load at a distance from the trunk will place the body under higher leverage forces and could lead to strain injuries to the spine or soft tissues.

■ The task may require unsatisfactory bodily movement or posture, such as twisting the trunk or stooping.

■ The task may require high levels of exertion, such as:

• Excessive lifting or lowering distances.

• Excessive pushing or pulling distances.

• Excessive carrying distances.

• Frequent or prolonged physical effort.

• Insufficient rest or recovery periods.

Environment

Environmental factors that affect the risk include:

■ Space constraints preventing good posture.

■ Uneven, slippery or unstable floors.

■ Variations in level of floors or work surfaces.

■ Extremes of temperature, humidity or air movement.

■ Poor lighting conditions.

Figure 6-3: Risks due to posture.   *Source: Speedy Hire Plc.*

The detailed consideration of each factor is necessary to achieve a suitable and sufficient risk assessment.

The process of risk assessing includes observing the task as it is actually done; recording the factors that contribute to risk; assessing the level of risk that each factor represents (taking account of the circumstances and controls in place); and considering if the risks are different at different times and for different people.

REPETITIVE MOVEMENT ACTIVITIES GIVING RISE TO MUSCULOSKELETAL RISKS

Keyboard operation

Keyboard operations, can involve small but very repetitive movement of the fingers when striking keys and using a mouse. A worker engaged in high levels of data entry may carry out a very large quantity of repetitive finger movements. This can lead to inflammation of the nerves and tendons that pass through the carpal bone in the worker's wrist, which in turn can lead to the condition known as carpal tunnel syndrome.

Similarly, this repetitive type of movement can lead to inflammation of the synovial lining of the tendon sheath, causing tenosynovitis.

Assembly of small components

Many repetitive light assembly tasks have a high risk of causing WRULDs. Tasks may include:

■ Inserting a spring into a car radiator cap using the worker's thumb to apply pressure.

■ Operating a hand power press to insert ball bearings into a component.

■ Folding the lid of a cardboard box.

■ Preparation and packaging of sandwiches.

These tasks may cause harm to the hands, arms, neck and shoulders. Where there is a high demand for a particular assembled piece of equipment the best method of production is to use robotic systems; they are faster more accurate and the risk of musculoskeletal injury to the assembly worker is removed.

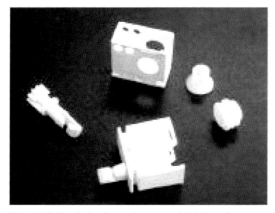

Figure 6-4: Small plastic gearbox assembly by hand presents musculoskeletal risk. *Source: Adm-Automation UK.*

Figure 6-5: Multi-function robotic cell eliminates musculoskeletal risk and provides rapid assembly of parts. *Source: Adm-Automation UK.*

Food preparation and packing

Many food preparation and packing tasks present significant risks of WRULDs, particularly due to the repetitive actions involved. In packing tasks the product is often delivered automatically, at a rate set by a conveyor, causing the workers arms to be moving continually.

The rate of packing may be as much as 20 times per minute, which presents a can present a significant risk. Though the product being handled is often light in weight the postures adopted to carry out packing tasks can cause elbows to be held in a raised position and significant gripping actions of the hand. Similar factors are present in many food preparation tasks.

Bricklaying

Many building site trades are associated with WRULDs. Plasterers, joiners, electricians and bricklayers are commonly affected. Bricklayers are often self-employed and therefore cannot afford to lose time from work. They will carry on working and ignore the warning signs of WRULD harm. The size of the bricks being laid, the number of bricks they are expected to lay (often several hundred per day), and the position of the wall or structure are factors that can particularly influence the risk.

Checkout operators

Risk factors in checkout operator work are particularly influenced by the duration and frequency of the tasks, as well as the design and layout of the workstation.

A number of factors can increase the risk of musculoskeletal injury to checkout operators, these include:

- Size, shape and weight of objects, which are moved/handled by checkout operators. The object being handled can range from a very small box of matches to a multi-pack of tins of beer.
- Awkward movements, such as twisting, bending, stooping and over-reaching, particularly in combination with handling articles and shopping bags.
- Individual characteristics such as age, gender, physical dimension, pregnancy and any disabilities or other conditions a person may have.
- Working height of the workstation.
- Type and position of equipment, such as bags, scanning equipment and scales.
- Type of floor surfaces whilst the operator is standing.
- Ergonomic design of chair.
- Leg room and the space around the workstation.

Avoiding hazardous manual handling operations and repetitive actions

The Manual Handling Operations Regulations (MHOR) 1992 place a duty on the employer, Regulation 4(1) requires:

Each employer shall, so far as is reasonably practicable, avoid the need for his employees to undertake any manual handling operations at work which involve a risk of their being injured.

Figure 6-6: Regulation 4(1) of MHOR 1992.   *Source: Manual Handling Operations Regulations (MHOR) 1992.*

When avoiding hazardous manual handling operations the first consideration is usually to try to eliminate the need for handling the load at all. This will include, for example, wrapping packs of goods 'in situ' or bringing equipment used to treat a patient to the patient, instead of manually handling the patient to the treatment.

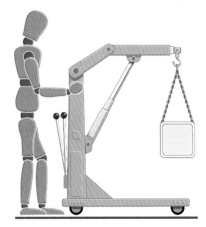

Figure 6-7: Mechanical aids. *Source: HSE Manual Handling (Manual Handling Operations Regulations 1992) Guidance L23.*

If the load must be handled then effort should be made to automate or mechanise the handling of the load. This may be by the use of conveyors and lift trucks or by pneumatic lifting devices. To avoid the handling of raw materials in sacks the materials may be obtained in bulk and provided to the workplace by gravity or pressure fed systems.

Similarly, repetitive actions may be avoided by the provision of automation of the whole or part of a processes, for example the automation of food packing or data readers to avoid the need to enter data manually.

Requirement to include MSDs in risk assessments

The Management of Health and Safety at Work Regulations (MHSWR) 1999, the Manual Handling Operations Regulations (MHOR) 1992 and the Display Screen Equipment Regulations (DSER) 1992 (amended 2002) apply to the prevention and management of MSD's.

These Regulations require a risk assessment to be carried out on work activities undertaken and, as in other risk assessments, action must be taken to reduce the risks as far as reasonably practicable. This will require the organisation to review all work activities involving manual handling operations, computer work, assembly work and any other work that has been identified as requiring repetitive movements, extreme forces, awkward postures and lifting activities.

MANUAL HANDLING OPERATIONS

Regulation 4 of MHOR 1992 requires:

"(1) Each employer shall:

(b) *Where it is not reasonably practicable to avoid the need for his employees to undertake any manual handling operations at work which involve a risk of their being injured.*

(i) *Make a suitable and sufficient assessment of all such manual handling operations to be undertaken by them, having regard to the factors which are specified in column 1 of Schedule 1 to these Regulations and considering the questions which are specified in the corresponding entry in column 2 of that Schedule".*

Figure 6-8: Manual handling. *Source: RMS.*

Schedule 1 of MHOR 1992 specifies that the risk assessment must include consideration of the task, loads, working environment, individual capacity and other factors. It also provides questions that should be considered related to these factors. Appendix 1 of DSER 1992 provides information on the factors to consider when analysing workstations to meet the risk assessment requirement set out in Regulation 2 of DSER 1992.

The Health and Safety Executive (HSE) has produced guidance to help with the assessment process - Manual Handling Assessment Charts, known as the 'MAC tool'. It can be downloaded from the HSE website and includes on-line training. It can be found at www.hse.gov.uk/msd. Special guidance has been produced for the NHS. A National Clinical Audit of 'Back pain management - occupational health practice in the NHS' was carried out by the Royal College of Physicians, The Faculty of Occupational Medicine and NHS Plus. The document can be downloaded from www.rcplondon.ac.uk or www.nhsplus.nhs.uk.

ASSESSMENT OF REPETITIVE TASKS (ART) TOOL

The assessment of repetitive tasks (ART) tool was designed by the Health and Safety Executive (HSE) to help health and safety inspectors assess repetitive tasks involving the upper limbs. The tool is freely available for general use from the HSE website and is useful for identifying repetitive tasks involving the upper limbs that present a high-risk of injury.

The ART tool is intended for people with responsibility for the design, assessment, management, and inspection of repetitive work. It enables the assessment of some of the common risk factors in repetitive work that contribute to the development of upper limb disorders. The ART tool is not intended for display screen equipment (DSE) assessments.

The ART tool helps to:

■ Identify repetitive tasks that have significant risks.
■ Identifies where risk reduction measures may be focused.
■ Prioritises repetitive tasks for improvement.
■ Consider options for risk reduction measures.

The ART process involves completing the task description form, following the flow chart and assessment guide to make an assessment, and completing the score sheet. The ART tool uses a numerical score and traffic light approach to indicate the level of risk for twelve factors, grouped into the following headings:

■ Frequency and repetition of movement.
■ Force.
■ Awkward postures of the neck, back, arm, wrist and hand.
■ Additional factors, including breaks and duration.

Figure 6-9: Beef packing - a repetitive task. *Source: HSE.*

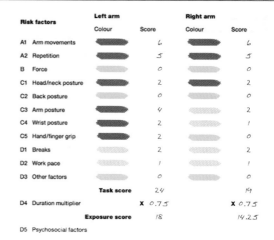

Figure 6-10: The ART tool score sheet. *Source: HSE.*

DISPLAY SCREEN EQUIPMENT

The Health and Safety (Display Screen Equipment) Regulations (DSE) 1992, as amended in 2002, aim to reduce risks from display screen equipment work, include WRULDs, such as carpal tunnel syndrome.

They apply where there are employees who 'habitually use display screen equipment as a significant part of their normal work'. Such people are called users. Employers are required to analyse workstations to assess and reduce risks, including consideration of the following factors:

- Equipment - display screen, keyboard, work desk, work surface and work chair.
- Environment - lighting levels, reflection and glare, noise, temperature and humidity.
- Interface between computer and user - software, work rate and work rate.

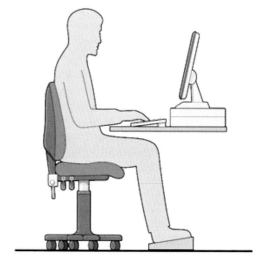

Figure 6-11: Seating and posture for DSE tasks. *Source: HSE, L26.*

Seating and posture should be assessed to determine if it provides:

- Seat back adjustment, lumbar support, seat height adjustment, no excessive pressure on thighs and knees.
- Space for postural change, no obstructions.
- Forearms approximately horizontal, minimum extension, flexion or deviation of wrists.
- Space in front of keyboard to support wrists.
- Screen height and angle providing comfortable head position.

Controls to prevent the risk of musculoskeletal injury

CONTROL OF RISK OF MUSCULOSKELETAL INJURY

Management should ensure that good ergonomic principles are applied to the workplace if MSD's are to be prevented. This means ensuring that tasks, equipment and workstations are designed to suit the individual, which is fitting the task to the person.

People vary in height, weight, strength and ability to take in information and instructions. Designing the workplace with the worker in mind is paramount to preventing ill health, injury and errors. Ergonomics can help to solve a number of problems. Consider the size of a worker working at an assembly bench. If they are very tall they may not be able to place their legs under the bench and may be bending forward in a 'top heavy' posture, which will cause back and knee problems.

Conversely, a short person may have difficulties reaching across a bench and could develop shoulder, neck and upper arm problems. The layout of control panels can influence risks particularly where they requiring the worker to bend, stretch and twist in order to read them. The use of hand tools must be considered. Many hand tools require a wide grip, for example, pruning shears, which will put severe strain on the hands and arms, particularly for people with smaller hands. The handles and grip of hand tools should be designed so that they do not dig into the hand, but spread the load over the hand.

General issues to be considered in order to reduce MSD's include:

- Reduce the amount of manual handling, for example, use of mechanical aids.
- Modify the work station to suit the worker, for example, work bench raised or lowered.
- Seating, for example, adjusted to suit the worker, ensure where possible the worker can sit to do the job rather than stand.

- Seek advice on hand tools and equipment: are there alternatives available? Which are more suitable to the workers that need to use them?
- Ensure the lighting is suitable for the job, for example, not too bright, not to dim. Provide individual lighting if required.
- Rotate the work done by workers so that they are not doing the same job all the time, ideally within a normal work period.
- Ensure proper rest breaks are taken or alternative work activities, for example, break from computer work to carry out filing or printing etc.
- Ensure workers are educated and trained to carry out their role; they should understand the risks and the controls to minimise them, correct work procedures and the need to report any early symptoms.

The load

- Consideration should be given to reducing the weight of an individual load, although this may mean increasing the frequency of handling.
- If there is a great variety of weight to be handled it may be possible to sort the loads into weight categories so that precautions can be applied selectively.
- Where the size, surface texture or nature of a load makes it difficult to grasp, consideration should be given to the provision of handles, hand grips, indents etc. to improve the grasp.
- Loads in packages should be such that they cannot shift unexpectedly while being handled.
- Any loads to be handled should not have sharp corners, jagged edges, rough surfaces and the like.

Individual capability

- It is important to match the work activity to the state of health, fitness and strength of the individual. This is particularly so where the worker is disabled.
- An individual's physical capacity can also be age-related, typically climbing until the early 20's and declining gradually from the mid 40's.
- If a load is bulky, unwieldy or heavy consider the use of more than one person to move it.
- Specific arrangements should be made to assess, and if necessary adjust, the work conducted by pregnant workers.
- Provide personal protective equipment to enable the worker to hold the load close to their body, for example, overalls for dirty or dusty items.
- Provide training on safe posture, movement and lifting technique.

Figure 6-12: Manual handling technique. *Source: HSE, L23.*

The task

- Ensure work and components in regular use are stored at waist height. Storage above or below this height should be used for lighter or less frequently used items.
- Layout changes should avoid the necessity for frequent bending, twisting, reaching, etc. and the lessening of any travel distances.
- Pay attention to the work routine; consider fixed postures dictated by sustained holding or supporting loads, frequency of handling loads, with particular emphasis on heavy and awkward loads.

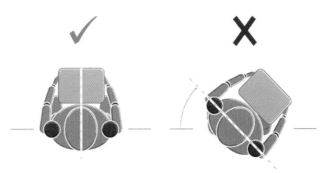

Figure 6-13: Avoid twisting movement. *Source: HSE, L23.*

- Fixed breaks are generally less effective than those taken voluntarily within the constraints of the work organisation.
- Handling while seated also requires careful consideration. Use of the powerful leg muscles is precluded and the weight of the handler's body cannot be used as a counterbalance. For these reasons, the loads that can be handled in safety by a person who is seated are substantially less than can be dealt with while standing.
- Team handling could be a solution for some tasks that are beyond the capability of one person. However, team handling can create additional problems. The proportion of the load carried by each member of the team will vary; therefore, the load that can be handled in safety will be less than the sum of the loads with which an individual could cope.

The working environment

- Adequate gangways, space and working area should be provided in order to allow room to manoeuvre during handling.
- Lack of headroom could cause stooping and constrictions caused by a poor workstation; adjacent machinery etc. should also be avoided.
- In many cases, problems are simply caused by lack of attention to good housekeeping.
- Whenever possible all manual handling tasks should be carried out on a single level. If tasks are to be carried out on more than one level, access should preferably be by a gentle slope, or failing that, properly positioned and well maintained stairs/steps. Steep slopes should be avoided.
- Workbenches should be of a uniform height, thus reducing the need for raising or lowering loads.
- Finally, look at the general working environment. A comfortable working environment, for example, heating, ventilating and lighting, will help to reduce the risk of injury.

Workplace health promotion

Learning outcomes

On completion of this element, candidates should be able to demonstrate understanding of the content through the application of knowledge to familiar and unfamiliar situations. In particular they should be able to:

7.1   Outline the scope and nature of workplace health promotion.

7.2   Outline the main factors influencing the health and performance of working age people.

7.3   Outline the benefits of health promotion in the workplace.

7.4   Outline the organisational approaches to support the health of the workforce.

Content

Sources of reference

Naidoo and Wills (2009) - Foundations for Health Promotion, (Second/Third edition) Bailliere Tindall.

National Institute for Health and Clinical Excellence website http://www.nice.org.uk.

Oakley Katie (2008) - 'Occupational Health Nursing' Chapter 12, (Third edition) Wiley, Chichester, UK.

World Health Organisation (1998) - Health promotion glossary WHO/HPR/HEP/98.1.

Relevant statutory provisions

The Employment Equality (Repeals of Retirement Age Provisions) Regulations (EERAR) 2011

7.1 - The scope and nature of workplace health promotion

Meaning of the term "health promotion"

The World Health Organisation's (WHO) "Health for all" declaration heralded a global movement for improving the health of all peoples of the world by the year 2000. This aspiration was not realised, but was justified as a means of initiating action. The definition of health promotion shown in *figure ref 7-1* was issued after 38 countries met in Ottawa, Canada and issued a call for action to achieve the goal of "Health for all".

"Health promotion is the process of enabling people to increase control over, and to improve, their health. To reach a state of complete physical, mental and social well-being, an individual or group must be able to identify and to realize aspirations, to satisfy needs, and to change or cope with the environment. Health is, therefore, seen as a resource for everyday life, not the objective of living. Health is a positive concept emphasizing social and personal resources, as well as physical capacities. Therefore, health promotion is not just the responsibility of the health sector, but goes beyond healthy life-styles to well-being".

Figure 7-1: Definition of health promotion. *Source: WHO, Ottawa Charter for Health Promotion.*

Workplace health promotion may involve one to one help, group discussion and therapy, provision of information and positive peer pressure from colleagues. All of these can make a valuable contribution to a health behaviour change initiative.

The workplace as a positive setting for health promotion

The workplace provides a positive setting in which to provide health promotion to a high proportion of the working age people. It enables the working age population, approximately 37 million people, to be involved in health promotion in an accessible way, allowing systematic and opportunistic health related messages to be conveyed, particularly as workers spend 60% of their waking hours in work. Males are one group of individuals that are considered to be difficult to involve in preventative health care and are known to visit their General Practitioner (GP) doctor less often than females, but in the workforce, they are more likely to take the opportunity to seek health advice. The workplace presents an opportunity for health related interaction with the male members of the workforce to discuss and check their health and well-being in relation to their work duties.

Because the organisation has control of the worker's activities and time, it enables people who may not usually have an interest in health to receive health promotion information during the working day. The workers may be balancing a complex work-life mix, which does not allow a lot of time to receive fresh health promotion information and to reflect on it. By presenting the health promotion at work it can be considered without it affecting the work-life balance. A health promotion message received within a work context may be more acceptable than receiving it from a GP practice, which may be seen by some as a more formal authoritarian setting. Health promotion in a workplace has the potential to be a more positive setting, offering the opportunities for support and follow up.

In addition, the workplace makes it easier to conduct follow up on any health and well-being activities that take place. The organisation can align their health promotions with national health awareness days, such as quit smoking and breast awareness, through the active promotion and engagement with these health messages. Promotion can be achieved through the provision of information on the organisation's intranet, one to one help, group meetings, presentations from colleagues and health specialists and the organisation of charity fun walks. Group events can encourage more physical activity by workers and provide opportunity for family involvement. This might include such events as sponsored family walks, marathons and abstinence from certain foods or drinks for a limited period.

Historically, during and immediately post the Victorian era, many organisations made great efforts to improve the health and well-being of workers through the provision of parklands, social clubs, sports grounds and many other facilities, typically encouraging worker participation after work hours through such activities as the company football and cricket teams, badminton and so on. The ethos was to include everyone, including past and present workers, by mixing those who had retired with younger members of the workforce in such activities as dominos and crown green bowling teams. The more successful organisations secured their future workers by encouraging the parents of children approaching school leaving age to apply for work. Families were not forgotten, day trips to coastal resorts were organised for the families of workers and trips to pantomimes for children. A strong culture of health and well-being was established through this process.

In more recent years, many organisations have rediscovered the benefits of improved social interaction between and with their workers through the provision of leisure facilities or activities. This may be through the introduction of relaxation areas, such as Japanese water gardens or another similar place of tranquillity away from the worker's normal busy or noisy workplace. Gymnasiums and saunas, for exercise and relaxation can often be provided at relatively low financial cost to the organisation, usually utilising space not normally used for work to locate the facilities, such as basements or atriums. Some organisations, particularly those who employ a significant number of females at a location, now provide crèche facilities to support working parents or carers.

All these factors characterise the workplace as a positive setting for health promotion. The workplace offers a potential for colleagues to act as positive role models and influence their peers.

For those engaged in health promotion activities the workplace also provides an opportunity to access peer support from colleagues and occupational health practitioners.

"Employers are in a unique position of being able to educate, motivate and support their employees in understanding and actively maintaining their fitness and well-being".

Figure 7-2: Employer's role in health promotion.   *Source: DWP, DoH, HSE (2006) Health, Work and Well-being - Caring for our future.*

The employers' role is to create a supportive environment where health and well-being are part of the core business of the organisation. Heath and safety in the workplace has often had an overemphasis on safety aspects; whilst this is important, it is only one feature of creating the vision for a healthy workplace. An environment that supports health and well-being will address not only issues of safety, such as the operation of machinery or equipment and the wearing of protective personal equipment, but will incorporate the engagement of the workforce in strategies to improve and maintain their health in a supportive culture. An awareness of the importance of promoting heath at work and supporting employees to improve their own health has the potential to make a more productive workforce and help them make the "right lifestyle choices throughout their working lives".

7.2 - The health and performance of working age people

"For the purpose of data analysis, the working age population is taken to be females aged 16 to 59 and males aged 16 to 64. This is consistent with the current school-leaving age and State Pension age at 2011. With this definition the current working age population is 36.6 million people".

Figure 7-3: Definition of working age population.   *Source: TSO, Working for a Healthier Tomorrow.*

The minimum legal age for a person to work is 14 years and then only in a part time capacity; therefore they and those aged 15 years are not normally included when considering the range of working age people. For data analysis purposes, at the time of going to press, all females aged 16 - 59 and all males 16 - 64 are considered to be the working age population. However, as life expectancy increases and the state pension age rises this definition will need to be adjusted to reflect the actual working age of the population. The Employment Equality (Repeals of Retirement Age Provisions) Regulation (EERAR) 2011 removes the general right of the employer to operate a compulsory retirement age, unless it can be objectively justified. Men and women can now work past the age when the state pension is normally paid. Employers now have to have a flexible approach to retirement age and support those that wish to continue to work regardless of age.

Increasing prosperity has enabled working people to spend money above the basic needs for survival. The extra disposable income has led to more people changing from walking or using public transport to the use of private cars, with the resultant reduction in physical exercise. This extra income has resulted in an exponential growth in the availability of non-essential consumer goods, promoted by mass direct marketing and advertising to individuals. The psychological impact of this for many is to create a feeling that their lives are not complete if they do not purchase that which is on offer. These feelings are further increased when such individuals observe their friends, relatives and neighbours purchasing things that they do not own themselves, leading them to want to do the same. In itself, this may be a positive influence, but if the increased financial resource needed to purchase these extra items is not available, there may be a tendency to reduce the money spent on essential items to provide the finance for that which they now desire. This will often result in a reduction in the quality of their diet, with the substitution of less healthy, hunger satisfying foods that typically contain high salt, sugar, fat or carbohydrate and few vitamins. This diet can lead to an increased risk of obesity, stroke, heart disease or diabetes. These effects will often not only affect the worker's health, but the diet and health of other family members, such as their children.

In a similar way, the ease of availability of financial credit has influenced the consumer's purchasing power, greatly encouraging many to spend many times their disposable income and resulting in the creation of large personal debts. When debt exposure becomes too great it becomes more difficult to meet the minimum repayments and the harassment from the lender to repay greatly increases personal concerns, leading to worry, anxiety and the feelings of low esteem. This in turn can result in increased consumption of alcohol and tobacco, and depression leading to increased absence from work or poor work performance. In extreme cases, this could lead to inflicting self-harm, harm to other family members or loss of contact with family and friends resulting in personal isolation or suicide.

The life expectancy is the most commonly used measure of health for the population and has the advantage of allowing comparisons across the United Kingdom and for international ranking. For example, the UK is ranked 22 out of 195 countries behind many European countries. Life expectancy for women is about 81% and for men 77% (Office for National Statistics 2009). Subjective measures of how people feel about their health are obtained from the General Household Survey.

"Health can also be assessed by asking people how they feel. One such measure is derived from the General Household Survey (GHS), which asks people in Britain about self-perceived general health. In 2005, 89% of the working age population reported being in good or fairly good health, leaving 11% in poor health".

Figure 7-4: Level of health of working age population in the UK.   *Source: TSO, Working for a Healthier Tomorrow.*

Lifestyle factors

Lifestyle factors are about how people live their lives and the habits and behaviours that contribute to or challenge their health status. All these personal choices are part of the life of the workers that make up an organisation. Some examples are diet, exercise, smoking, alcohol and the increasing use of "recreational" drugs - drugs taken for personal pleasure as opposed to medical necessity.

"Smoking rates have fallen over recent decades, but are still at 22%. Levels of obesity are increasing dramatically and, if current trends continue, around 90% of men and 80% of women will be overweight or obese by 2050".

Figure 7-5: Smoking and obesity rates in the UK.   *Source: TSO, Working for a Healthier Tomorrow.*

DIET

Obesity is a huge public health challenge and in the workplace could have an adverse effect on the safety and comfort of individuals. For example, obesity may affect a worker's ability to work in a confined space and office furniture may need to accommodate overweight individuals.

"The percentage of people aged 45 to 64 and 65 to 74 who were obese increased by 10 per cent to about 30 per cent between 1995 and 2007 in England. A smaller percentage of people aged 75 and over were obese in 1995 (15 per cent) but by 2007 this had also increased by 10 per cent to 25 per cent. In the period 1995 - 2007, the increase in the percentage of people with obesity in the age groups 45 to 64, 65 to 74 and 75 and over was twice the percentage increase (5 per cent) seen among the younger age group 16 - 44".

Figure 7-6: Obesity rates in the UK.   *Source: National Statistic Office 2009.*

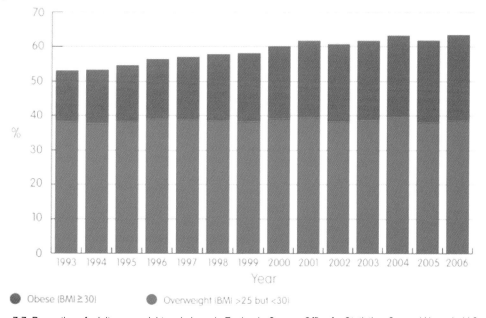

Figure 7-7: Proportion of adults overweight and obese in England. *Source: Office for Statistics, General Household Survey.*

The figure above illustrates the proportion of people who are overweight, which has remained consistent at approx 38%, but those in the obese category has increased by over 10% in a thirteen year period. The diet of working age people can affect their general health. Diet relates to the quantity and quality of food eaten. As a general comment, poor diet can cause the worker to become lethargic, reduce their mobility and lead to longer-term harm that could cause sickness absence.

People who do not eat enough food may lack enough energy or mental concentration to perform adequately in work, which can lead to rapid fatigue and result in errors. Their muscles may become wasted, leaving them to become incapable of work that requires some physical strength. Those that continue with this diet may find that their body's immunity to common diseases in society becomes reduced and their general health can decline, resulting in absence from work. Young females are the most likely group in the working age population to suffer effects from not eating enough food, but older people living alone may also have this pattern of diet.

People who eat too much food or less healthy food may find that they put on weight, which can reduce mobility or diminish capability for sustained exertion. Both effects can impact on people that regularly or occasionally have to conduct manual handling tasks or take up a restricted posture, such as may be required when doing maintenance or construction work. In some cases, the level of obesity can cause high levels of lethargy and lapses of attention, which in jobs that are safety critical or with inherent demands, such as large goods vehicle driver, train driver or call centre operative, the diminished performance can have serious effects.

As previously discussed, less healthy foods can lead to a higher risk of diabetes, cardiovascular disease or a stroke, all of which may cause the individual to have significant single or repeated absence from work and may limit their ability to continue the full range of activities associated with their job.

> *"The combined cost of cardiovascular disease (CVD) to the NHS and the UK economy is £30 billion annually (Luengo-Fernandez et al. 2006).*
>
> *The cost of CVD to the UK healthcare system in 2006 was £14.4 billion (around 48%); productivity losses accounts for £8 billion annually (26%) and the cost of informal care of people with CVD is also £8 billion annually (26%) (Allender S et al. 2008)".*

Figure 7-8: Cost impact of CVD to the UK economy and health service. *Source: NICE, Prevention of CVD - costing report June 2010.*

Cardiovascular disease is the UK's biggest killer. In 2007, over 100,000 women died from CVD in the UK - almost 24,000 more than died from cancer. The total annual cost of all coronary heart disease related burdens is £7.06 billion, the highest of all diseases in the UK for which comparable analyses have been done.

Diet during working time can have both short and long-term effects that may be positive or negative. For some workers the food they have from their workplace may be the main meal of the day and its content can therefore greatly influence the health of the worker.

EXERCISE

The health issue of exercise relates to obtaining an optimum of exercise. It is possible to over or under exercise. People in the working age population that lead an essentially sedentary work and personal life may find that their food intake is not utilised by body activity, thus leading them to accumulate fat in the body. In addition, their muscles and other soft tissue can become less used to physical activity, increasing the risk of injury when tasks involving physical exertion are made. Progressively, suppleness, flexibility and dexterity of movement may become diminished. Lack of exercise may lead to inefficient functioning of the metabolism and gradual strain on the cardio-vascular system. This in turn may limit the amount of oxygen available to parts of the body like the brain and lead to reduced mental and physical performance. This may influence safety critical decision making and the ability to carry out highly pressured tasks or work under emergency situations.

Those that exercise too much may place their body under significant strain, with the potential for them to suffer from problems that can affect their ability to carry out their work. For example, someone that plays a large amount of tennis may put their upper limbs under significant strain, and whilst their job may include some small effect on upper limbs, the combined effect of exercise and work could be too much, leading to the worker suffering an upper limb disorder.

> *"Trends in our dietary and exercise habits also threaten health. Only 30% of adults eat at least five portions of fruit and vegetables a day. We are becoming more sedentary in our lifestyles, with participation in physical activity at low levels. Twenty per cent of men and around 40% of women meet recommended physical activity guidelines".**
>
> **Health Survey from England (2006).*

Figure 7-9: Diet and exercise rates in the UK. *Source: TSO, Working for a Healthier Tomorrow.*

The NHS Information Centre for Health and Social Care report "Statistics on Obesity, Physical Activity and Diet: England, 2011" (the report) described that the Chief Medical Officer (CMO) had established physical activity guidelines based on a frequency-duration scale. The guidelines take into account the time spent participating in physical activities together with the number of active days over a period of four weeks. In the Health Survey for England (HSE) for 2008, the summary levels are divided into three categories:

- High activity - defined as 20 or more occasions of moderate or vigorous activity of at least 30 minutes duration over a four-week period (i.e. at least 5 occasions per week on average). This category corresponds to the minimum activity level required to gain general health benefits, including reduction in the relative risk for cardiovascular morbidity, as recommended by the Chief Medical Officer.
- Medium activity - defined as 4 to 19 occasions of moderate or vigorous activity of at least 30 minutes duration over a four-week period (i.e. 1 to 4 occasions per week on average).
- Low activity - defined as fewer than 4 occasions of moderate or vigorous activity of at least 30 minutes duration over a four-week period (i.e. less than 1 per week on average).

The report established that the Health Survey for England (HSE) for 2008 found that 39% of men and 29% of women aged 16 and over met the government's recommendations for physical activity, compared with 32% and 21% respectively in 1997. In addition, the "Active People Survey 2009/10" found that 6.938 million adults aged 16 and over (4.176 million men and 2.761 million women) in England participated in sport and active recreation three times a week for 30 minutes, equating to medium activity level. The report confirmed that the HSE 2008 survey studied adults aged 16 to 74 who had worked (paid or voluntary) at the time of the survey.

They were asked about their moderate intensity physical activity during work, which includes time spent sitting or standing, walking around, climbing stairs or ladders and lifting, carrying or moving heavy loads. The survey established:

■ Men spent slightly more time than women sitting and/or standing, climbing stairs and/or ladders and carrying or moving heavy loads. Men and women spent similar amounts of time walking around.

■ 24% of men and 11% of women reported doing at least 30 minutes of moderate or vigorous activity whilst at work each day, thus meeting the government recommendations for physical activity solely from their work.

■ Most men (62%) and women (59%) considered themselves to be very or fairly active at work.

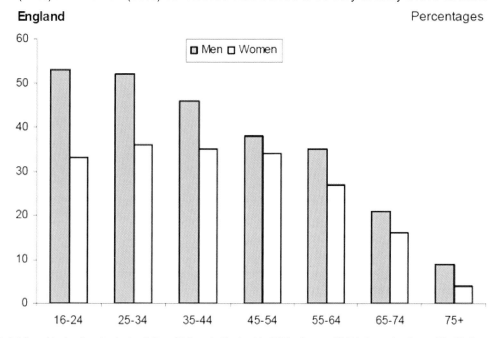

Figure 7-10: Adults achieving the physical activity guidelines in England in 2006. *Source: NHS Information Centre/Health Survey for England.*

SMOKING

Smoking tobacco involves the respiration of nicotine and carbon monoxide, which is associated with temporary increase in heart rate and blood pressure, straining the heart and blood vessels. In time, smoking causes fat deposits to narrow and block blood vessels, limiting blood flow through the body.

Workers that smoke may find that their endurance level when carrying out physical work activities is reduced. Reduced blood flow can lead to poor oxygen flow to feet and hands, which may affect the comfort of workers that smoke and limit their ability to stand or be on their feet without a rest.

Smoking increases the risk of cancer (for example, the lungs, larynx, oral cavity or oesophagus), heart disease, strokes and respiratory disease (for example, chronic bronchitis, emphysema or chronic obstructive pulmonary disease). This is true whether the worker smokes cigarettes, bidi (thin cigarettes of tobacco wrapped in brown tendu leaf) or shisha (also known as a water pipe or hookah).

Whilst smoking rates in the UK have reduced since the introduction of smoking legislation that banned smoking in public places (from 50% for men to 23% and from 40% for women to 21% for women) there persists a social gradient of those who continue to smoke. Those in higher socio economic groups smoke less than those in lower social classes. This is important for workplace health promotion, as these groups will require additional support.

"Cigarette smoking is lower among households classified as professional and managerial (15 per cent) than among those classified as routine and manual (26 per cent). Smoking is highest in the 20 - 24 age group (31 per cent) and lowest among those aged 60 and over (12 per cent)".

Figure 7-11: Smoking rates in the UK.   *Source: National Statistic Office 2009.*

"Smoking rates are higher among Bangladeshi men (40%) and Pakistani men (29%) than in the general population (21%), while Indian men and south Asian women are less likely to smoke".

Figure 7-12: Smoking rates in the UK.   *Source: NHS.UK, Living well.*

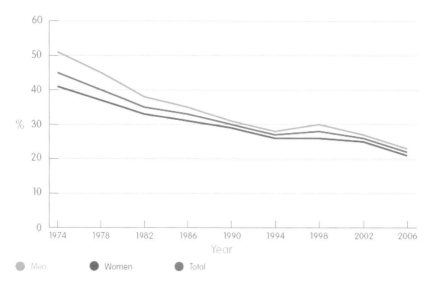

Figure 7-13: Proportion of adults who smoke in the UK. *Source: Office for Statistics, General Household Survey.*

Tobacco smoking continues to be the largest single preventable cause of ill-health and is a major contributing factor to the gap in life expectancy between rich and poor. Smoking has a cost to organisations through working days lost. The chronic effects of smoking can cause severe debilitation of workers, leading to potential sudden major loss of performance due to medical absence. These workers may not be readily replaced and reliance on them may create a major knowledge or skill gap at the time of their absence.

ALCOHOL AND DRUGS

Alcohol and drugs can have both short and long-term effects on health and performance at work. If consumed outside the workplace they can still have an acute affect on the person at work. For example, someone may drink alcohol or take recreational drugs in their personal time and be suffering from the effects when they present themselves for work. Examples of this might be:

- A group of night workers may meet in the evening before their shift and drink alcohol.
- Someone may drink at a party after work through into the early hours of the morning and present themselves for an early shift to courier parcels.
- Drinking or taking drugs as part of a mid-work break can mean the worker returning to work under the influence of the drugs or alcohol.

Drugs and alcohol may suppress reasoning, balance and co-ordination, leading to personal injuries due to errors or at times unnecessary disagreement with co-workers and management. The more safety critical the job a worker holds the more significant the possible effects on performance. A forklift truck operator under the influence of drugs or alcohol could drive the truck below acceptable performance standards and harm people or damage equipment.

Similarly, a worker may be a user of drugs for medication that may affect their performance. Some medications carry a warning not to drive or operate machinery when they have been taken. Workers should identify to management that they are taking drugs for medication that may affect their work so that arrangements can be made to take account of it. The chronic effects of moderate drugs and alcohol consumption can include depression, schizophrenia, liver damage and increased risk of heart disease, all of which could cause an otherwise reliable worker to be absent from work for sustained periods.

Cannabis

Amphetamines

Alkyl nitrates

Figure 7-14: Types of alcohol and drugs.

Source: www.fantazia.org.uk/drugs.

The organisation can help by providing a health enhancing environment, such as the provision of support programmes, including counselling on the effects of alcohol, smoking and drugs and how to reduce dependency on such stimulants.

Focusing too much on single issues, such as smoking or alcohol, is not always the best approach. Often it is better in the workplace to take a holistic approach that encourages a general increase in awareness of pursuing a more healthy work style, which in turn supports a healthy lifestyle. This would include diet and the availability of healthy eating options in worker canteens or restaurants and encouraging more physical activities through the provision of a gym or subsidised gym membership of a nearby health club.

Ongoing support and encouragement is an essential part of the process, including the use of someone to act as a lifestyle coach to help in explaining the benefits of adopting a healthier lifestyle. Risk assessment methodologies should consider how the job or task can be structured to reduce stress, fatigue and boredom, but improve posture and mental alertness. Particular attention should be given to the provision of suitable rest periods or breaks.

> *"Through their lifestyles, individuals can have a significant impact on their own long-term health status. The most important indicators of healthy living relate to how and what people eat and drink, how active they are and whether they smoke or not. Unhealthy lifestyles can be threatening to the working age population as the onset of poor health might impact on the ability to work.*
>
> *This can eventually lead to worklessness which further exacerbates health problems".*

Figure 7-15: Effect of lifestyle on health.   *Source: TSO, Working for a Healthier Tomorrow.*

Although the workplace has the potential to create an environment that supports changes in behaviour that can contribute to an individual's health and well-being, organisations must also consider the outside influences that can impact upon employees' health. These include low income, poor housing and education and the cultural influences on them. These outside factors must be considered; otherwise the focus on individuals could be seen as judgemental and unfair.

Individual factors

INDIVIDUAL DIFFERENCES

The ways in which people differ are many and various and this is important to bear in mind from the point of view of work performance, health and well-being. It is vital to know what a particular job entails (the job description) and to specify the characteristics required to enable a person to perform that job effectively (the person specification).

Physical differences will need to be considered carefully when establishing controls for work activities as some differences may limit or prohibit individuals from certain tasks. A person with colour blindness may not be suitable for electrical work where it is essential to differentiate colours and a person with asthma may be unsuitable for work with chemicals that are respiratory sensitisers. Similarly, a person with a large build may not be capable of accessing a confined space safely.

AGE

The health and performance of the working population may vary with age. As people get older, the physical effects of their life may cause progressive restrictions in movement and capability due to effects of the ageing process on bones, joints and soft tissue. The performance of older workers may become limited and the worker may need more frequent rest periods. Conditions such as arthritis, limited eyesight or hearing are characteristics that may become apparent with older workers.

These characteristics may not limit the worker from all work, but may specifically prohibit them from some work. Because age and its effects are progressive, it is necessary to observe aging and monitor its effects to ensure workers' abilities match the work they are expected to do. Progressive arthritis may limit the performance of a worker to lift items from a low level, which may mean adapting the work to eliminate the need to do this. Similarly, developing glaucoma, a condition affecting eyesight, may cause a forklift truck driver to be re-deployed to other work.

Young people, between the ages of 16 and 18, are seen as vulnerable to health harm and diminished well-being, in particular because they are still developing physically and mentally. Regulation 19 of the Management of Health and Safety at Work Regulations (MHSWR) 1999 requires employers to pay attention to particular risks that could harm young people, such as working with agents hazardous to their health or work in extremes of cold, heat, noise or vibration.

One of the ways the employer can manage this is by not exposing young persons to the risks at all. As such, performance may be affected by the need to remove the young person from the risk by a change of work. At the very least exposure should be controlled to a higher standard than for an adult worker.

PREGNANCY

"Pregnancy should be regarded not as an illness but as part of everyday life. Protection of health and safety in respect of pregnant women can often be achieved by applying existing rules and procedures in the relevant areas. Many women work while they are pregnant, and many return to work while they are still breastfeeding. However, some hazards in the workplace may affect the health and safety of new and expectant mothers and of their children. A pregnancy entails great physiological and psychological changes. The hormonal balance is very sensitive and exposures capable of disrupting it can lead to complication, possibly resulting, for example, in miscarriage".

Figure 7-16: Pregnancy. *Source: EU Commission, Communication 52000DC0466.*

The condition of the pregnant worker changes through the stages of pregnancy, which can have a variety of effects on their health and in turn their work performance. Regulation 16 of MHSWR 1999 expects the pregnant worker's employer to take account of these factors by making an assessment and putting in place actions to manage risks that have a bearing on pregnancy.

This includes chemicals that can affect the foetus in its development, for example, lead, and those that can affect the newborn child through transfer from blood to milk consumed during breast-feeding, for example, organic mercury. Aspects of the work that relate to physical exertion, extremes of posture and where long periods of stamina are required must also be considered. Over exertion may bring on a miscarriage in the early term of pregnancy and in later term high levels of activity without rest can bring on fatigue and raise blood pressure.

Pregnancy may increase the need for rest periods, changes to shift working and increased absence for regular attendance at health clinics. The MHSWR 1999 requires that facilities for rest and for nursing mothers must be provided by the employer, as necessary.

For further information see also - Health and Safety Executive (HSE) guidance INDG 373 "A guide for new and expectant mothers who work" and HSG122 "New and expectant mothers at work. A guide for employers".

 Case Study - Health care worker

A care worker notified her employer of her pregnancy. The employer looked back at the outcome of the initial risk assessment, which had identified that a possible risk for pregnant women was exposure to acts of violence (for example, difficult patients). The employer then conducted a specific risk assessment for the pregnant worker, who dealt with patients who were difficult and on occasion violent. As a result the employer offered the care worker suitable alternative work at the same salary and reviewed the assessment at regular intervals. The employee accepted the alternative work and had a risk free pregnancy. Following her maternity leave the employee returned to work.

Source: HSE.

Domestic factors

Domestic factors are a significant influence on the health and well-being of working age people. These factors may have negative effects on the worker and thus on their contribution to the organisation. Conversely, a happy and fulfilled family and personal life will benefit the motivation of the worker and their state of well-being, thereby enhancing their contribution to the workplace. Negative domestic factors may include:

- Debt.
- Physical/mental abuse from partners.
- Need to make provision for dependent children or caring for relatives.
- Family illness, disability or death.

These negative domestic factors may lead to anxiety or stress, which may be brought into the workplace and have a significant effect on the performance of the worker. *Debt* can become a dominant force affecting all aspects of a person's life. At home, debt can limit the provision of necessities such as food, heat and light, leading to the worker not getting the rest and recuperation needed to return to work and fulfil a productive working day. The responsible adult within a family group will often forgo their own well-being to ensure other dependents do not go without such things as food. This situation is aggravated by the anxiety that the debt may cause, leading to poor sleep.

Fatigue may become sustained and the health and well-being of the individual continue to decline. The workplace may have a positive influence on such a situation as it can be a place to put the debt out of the worker's mind, giving a feeling of worth, and may provide a source of cheap nourishing food and warmth. Alternatively, it may just emphasise the effects of debt by showing what the individual does not have compared to other workers.

Case Study - Female office worker

She was so far in debt that bailiffs called to the house frequently to remove any items of value. Electricity and gas were provided on pre-payment card systems, which meant the heating/lighting could be lost at any time. The children's main meal was provided at school. She had run out of friends to borrow from, as money was not returned. She frequently absented herself from work at short notice to talk with advisors, banks, courts and others about her debt. Her day was interrupted with telephone calls from organisations seeking money. She became more anxious, she was always tired and her diet suffered to the extent that on occasion she would faint. She began to suffer from hair loss and was constantly distracted. The issue was becoming a regular distraction to other workers who wanted to show concern. Her employer provided a confidential discussion and helped to develop a plan, arranging for critical payments to be made directly from her salary. This started to stabilise her finances and meant she was able to re-structure the debt and continue to make payments. Her performance improved and was sustained and she was able to have the benefit of an increase in salary related to her performance.

Abuse can take many forms and may be physical or mental. The effects on the worker can similarly be physical and mental, and may limit their ability to carry out effectively the full range of their work. This may be due to sudden physical harm that limits mobility, appearance, or a steady decline in the worker's confidence to deal with aspects of their work, for example, an abused female no longer able to deal with male customers. In addition, abuse of a worker can also influence the performance of co-workers when they spend time trying to find out what and how the abuse happened or showing concern.

Caring issues are a growing aspect that influences the working age population. People are living longer and medical science has enabled more people to survive disabling conditions. These factors, together with the societal move to providing more care in the community, have caused more challenges for workers and employers to deal with. The acute aspect of this issue can mean that the employee is suddenly required to provide care to someone and be absent from work for a short time or some weeks. The need for them to absent themselves to provide care may happen repeatedly and, depending on the work, limit the worker in the full range of their job. It could be hard for a delivery driver to respond easily to a carer if their deliveries took them away from their locality and delivery contracts required fulfilment. This may cause the delivery driver to become re-deployed or to find a different job.

Caring of this nature can cause a build up of fatigue and lead to workers paying little attention to their own well-being when away from work. This can have a long-term degenerative effect on the health and well-being of the worker, leading to poor performance over time.

Similar issues can be present when a carer is caring for children. A school may suddenly want the carer to collect their child due to such things as the child's ill-health or school closure due to poor weather. The illness of children can mean that the absence becomes sustained for a period, particularly in situations where other children in the family then contract the same illness.

By removing the worker from the workplace to deal with care issues will have a detrimental effect on work performance. The additional burden of the organisation and individual organising to deal with care issues can put the worker under both physical and mental pressure, particularly where the effect of their absence has a significant effect on the organisation, for example, in the nursing profession.

Behavioural factors

Behavioural factors will influence how the employee performs in the workplace. All individuals are different. These differences will influence patterns of work behaviour and may limit the performance of a worker in their job. These individual behavioural differences arise from an interaction between the 'inherited characteristics' (passed on from the parents) and the various 'life experiences' through which the individual passes from the moment of conception. Some individuals tend to be hardworking and well disposed to work, whereas others may need more encouragement and supervision to enable them to achieve the organisational goals.

ATTITUDE

"Attitude - The tendency to respond in a particular way to a certain situation".

Figure 7-17: Attitude. *Source: RMS/NEBOSH.*

Attitudes are not directly observable and can only be assessed by observing behavioural expression (physical or verbal behaviour). A person's attitudes will govern the way in which they view health and well-being and will dictate the resultant response or pattern of behaviour. Attitudes, like other aspects of individual differences, are formed (not necessarily consciously) from a lifetime of experiences and as such are not easily changed. A person's attitudes are not simply an aid to coping with their environment, but may determine how they wish to change the environment they are in. Any attempts to change such a fundamental part of an individual's personality will be resisted.

Attitudes to work, health and well-being will greatly reflect the many factors affecting people when they develop their attitudes. Attitudes to work may reflect how they see their personal responsibility, rights, morals and values. Some people of working age may have developed attitudes to work that see it as unnecessary, 'not for them' or a burden. These people may quickly absent themselves from work for what they see as justifiable reasons that someone with a different attitude would not. Those in this category, if they are out of work for a period of time due to ill-health, may quickly slide into 'worklessness'. It is possible for people to develop a hyper-sensitivity relating to health and work, seeing that it is essential to be in 100% health in order to be at work. This can lead to early absence from work for minor ill-health or fear of the onset of ill-health.

Other people may hold attitudes that mean they will work through minor illness because they see the responsibility to those that will be affected by their absence. Clearly, an attitude that means a worker will come to work at all costs, in all circumstances of ill-health, would be undesirable if it presented significant risk of harm to the worker or others. For most people of working age experiencing ill-health it is possible to continue work, even if it involves light or alternative duties. This is an aspect reflected by the introduction of the Statement of Fitness to Work - 'fit note'. This reflects a societal change of attitude to work and health that moves the balance back from sickness absence towards trying to continue work, even in a restricted or limited way.

PERCEPTION

"Perception - The process by which people interpret information that they take in through their senses".

Figure 7-18: Perception. *Source: RMS/NEBOSH.*

The process of perception involves something getting the attention of someone and their interpretation of that thing. In the context of health and well-being, it means that a portion of the working age population may not perceive the importance of health simply because the topic does not have their attention or if it does they have not interpreted the importance of it. It is very easy for important health messages to have been lost in the perception process by as appearing to be "too complicated", having "too much jargon" or just "not apply to me". This can mean that some people reject the importance of health and its effect on performance at work right from the beginning and may continue to perceive the issue in this way. This can lead to health messages, for example, those regarding diet displayed in an organisation's eating area, not to be perceived at all. One of the advantages of promoting health in the workplace is that the organisation has a high degree of control over the worker and may use this to present health issues in a way that gets the attention of the worker and ensures the correct interpretation. This is helped by the opportunity to engage in two-way communication, which can explore the perception of the worker and ensure the health message is understood.

MOTIVATION

The motivation of people will vary at different stages of their working life and be influenced by their personal priorities. Some people may feel motivated to ignore minor ill-health because if they were to take time off work they would lose income. Others who are less dependent on their income may be more inclined to absent themselves from work. If someone was in employment where 'sick pay' was provided for all ill-health absences there would be no financial penalty for taking time off for minor illness and this could provide sufficient motivation for the worker to maximise their opportunities for absence. Some workers in this type of employment might not take advantage of the opportunities to absent themselves because they may be motivated to not let other workers down or by the potential loss of self-esteem that would be created if they were absent. The peer group influences can be very strong with regard to health, absence and work, which could be a very positive influence on worker behaviour or very negative. A culture of absence may prevail and include senior people in the organisation, leading to a large scale loss of performance.

"Working sets an example to family members and children such that worklessness is less likely to be seen as the norm".

Figure 7-19: Effect of lifestyle on health. *Source: Local Government Employers/TSO, Working for a Healthier Tomorrow.*

Why individuals may wish to make a positive change in their health

The reasons for an individual to wish to make a positive change in their health are likely to be many and varied and very personal to that individual. An episode of ill-health can act as a catalyst to reappraise their life and there may be a direct link between how they live their life and the illness. The illness may not be their own, but may be a parent, sibling, friend or co-worker. The factor that leads an individual to wish to make a positive change in their health may be that they reach an age in their life that causes them to become more aware of their health and mortality. Sometimes small events can cause this re-appraisal, for example, meeting school friends at a school reunion, the need to get into clothes that have not been worn for a time or not being able to play football with children without feeling untoward effects.

The workplace can also act as that trigger, acting before an ill-health experience by creating a positive environment to support health related change. In environments where the individual constitutes a 'norm', for example, if everyone in their family has a poor diet, then there is less likely to be influencers for positive change. The positive environment of the workplace may cause the individual to review the 'norm' and self-reflect, along with other members of the workforce. This is why "Making the healthy choice easy" is an important maxim for the workplace and will include:

- Healthy canteen food choices.
- Healthy workplace conditions and working practice enabled and facilitated.
- Workers valued, respected and part of a team.
- Clear objectives and goals, including health and well-being, with fairness and rewards transparent.
- Facilities for rest and relaxation.

7.3 - Benefits of health promotion in the workplace

Health promotion in the workplace will have a direct effect by reducing work-related ill-health and sickness absence. In addition, the reduction in short term and long-term ill-health will reduce the costs of benefits that the State has to pay to offset the effects of ill-health. By promoting health and the management of ill health in the workplace, sickness absence can be reduced, which can have a direct and immediate reduction in the cost of 'sick pay', whether the worker's employer or the State pays this.

A systematic approach to the health and well-being of the workforce and to improving the working environment will increase the commitment and satisfaction of the workers. This will result in greater efficiency and effectiveness and will contribute to reduced absenteeism and staff turnover, resulting in an increase in productivity. Morale will be enhanced by the knowledge that workers are working for a caring, supportive employer. This is summarised and illustrated by the World Health Organisation (WHO) table from Regional Guidelines for the Development of Healthy Workplaces.

Benefits of health promotion	
To the organisation	*To the employee*
■ A well-managed health and safety programme.	■ A safe and healthy work environment.
■ A positive and caring image.	■ Enhanced self-esteem.
■ Improved staff morale.	■ Reduced stress.
■ Reduced staff turnover.	■ Improved morale.
■ Reduced absenteeism.	■ Increased job satisfaction.
■ Increased productivity.	■ Increased skills for health protection.
■ Reduced health care/insurance costs.	■ Improved health.
■ Reduced risk of fines and litigation.	■ A healthier family and community.

Figure 7-20: Benefits of a healthy workplace. *Source: WHO, Regional Guidelines for the Development of Healthy Workplaces 1999.*

A healthy workplace contributes to the success and long-term survival of the organisation and contributes to overall well-being of society.

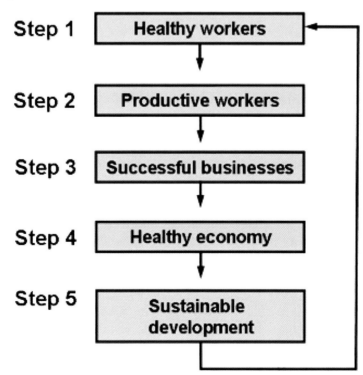

Figure 7-21: Benefits of a healthy workplace. *Source: RMS/WHO, Regional Guidelines for the Development of Healthy Workplaces.*

7.4 - Organisational approaches to support the health of the workforce

Creating an organisational culture to support health

INFLUENCING SENIOR MANAGEMENT AND DECISION MAKERS

The workplace as a setting for promoting health and well-being and reducing health inequalities is well recognised. When creating an organisational culture to support health and well-being it is essential to influence senior management and other decision makers, for example, trustees, governors, shareholders or members of council. Without their commitment it is very difficult to make progress in establishing an organisational structure that is supportive to health and well-being. It is important that the organisation's formal goals, objectives and policies that are set by senior managers and other decision makers, include health and well-being as a specific item. In this way, the senior managers will need to engage with the goal in a professional way and allocate resource to meet it. They will then be more likely to set a strategy to meet the goal and monitor progress to its fulfilment. Senior managers work with competing goals and will tend to support the creation of a positive health culture only if they see a value in it. If they are to be influenced a strong, clear case for commitment to support the health and well-being of the workforce will need to be made.

It will be necessary for those with understanding of the costs and benefits of health and well-being to establish the case for commitment. In order to influence senior management and decision makers as a whole it is often best achieved by identifying someone from within the group that can act as a 'champion' for the topic of health and well-being. This will help to ensure that senior management and other decision makers understand the business case for health and well-being and have clear goals that the strategy will deliver. The strategy must encompass measurable actions that take the organisation towards the goals. It is important that outcomes are planned to be measured as part of the strategy in order to maintain continued influence of senior managers and decision makers.

Creating an organisational culture to support health will be an endeavour that will involve the workplace from top to bottom. It will be an all encompassing ethos and philosophy that values the workers and places their health and well-being at the centre of the organisation's operations. The organisational culture will continue to influence senior management and decision makers and will facilitate the production and maintenance of a health and well-being strategy.

THE IDENTIFICATION AND ROLE OF A "HEALTH CHAMPION"

The identification of a "health champion" from the senior management team who will lead the implementation of the health and well-being plan is an important step in a successful strategy. This can be done by the most senior executive selecting a suitable person, the team voting for someone or someone volunteering to take the role because they have an interest in the issue. It is important that the person is committed to health and well-being as an organisational goal.

The role of the "health champion" will be to actively observe and encourage that health and well-being are included in all senior management decisions to the extent necessary to ensure that the strategy succeeds. They will report back to the senior management team at intervals on the progress and effectiveness of the strategy and ensure that an annual review is conducted, reported and considered by senior management.

PRIORITISATION OF HEALTH INTERVENTIONS BASED ON HEALTH NEEDS ASSESSMENT

The supportive culture of the organisation must be demonstrated by the health and well-being of workers being central to the organisation's goals and part of its overall operation. In order to do this the organisation needs to place resource where it is going to have the best effect on meeting the strategy. This will include the support of a number of health interventions. Which health intervention is selected to be part of the strategy over a given period should be based on a formal analysis and justification. The prioritisation of health interventions should therefore be based on a health needs assessment - *see also Element 8.1.* This formal, structured health needs assessment (HNA) will help to ensure that resources are targeted to good effect and not wasted on interventions that have little effect. In addition, the health needs assessment will provide an opportunity to involve those that are going to benefit from the strategy and those that will have to implement it, which will increase the likelihood that the strategy will be effective. This can stimulate the development of new understanding, experience and communication relating to health and well-being.

"Health needs assessment (HNA) is a systematic method for reviewing the health issues facing a population, leading to agreed priorities and resource allocation that will improve health and reduce inequalities".

Figure 7-22: Health needs assessment.   *Source: HDA/NICE, HNA - a practical guide.*

THE ROLE OF ORGANISATIONAL POLICIES

Organisational policies create structure and momentum to the strategy, setting out the agreed position and processes to meet the goals for health and well-being. All organisational policies should be redesigned to include health and well-being assessment and management. This will include determining the impact the policy will have on the health and well-being of the workforce and will seek to maximise the health benefits. For example, home working, driving, shift working and lone working policies may have significant elements that relate to health and well-being.

In addition, purchasing and maintenance/replacement policies could greatly influence health and well-being. Specific policies that have a direct bearing on health and well-being include tobacco, alcohol and drugs, healthy eating, physical activity, breastfeeding and mental health and well-being. These specific policies should seek to clarify the organisation's position, goals and arrangements to assess and manage these important health and well-being issues.

Tobacco

The statutory no smoking inside workplaces requirement forces the employer to have a role in supporting a smoking cessation strategy as employees can no longer smoke in the workplace. The employer's policy in response to this may simply be to state the legal requirements and its prohibitions or it could include a commitment to support the worker in their efforts to give up the habit.

The policy may set out health interventions, including promotion, habit dependency control and professional support, which will help the worker and meet the legal prohibition.

Alcohol and drugs

Organisations need a clear policy and procedure on alcohol and drugs, which is communicated to the workforce, commencing at induction. The policy should include strategies to support the employee who is using alcohol and drugs inappropriately. It is important for the policy to establish the boundaries of what the organisation will 'tolerate but discourage' and what they 'require as mandatory compliance'.

For example, there may be a mandatory requirement that those conducting safety critical work are not working under the influence of alcohol and drugs and co-operate with the organisation to enable workers to confirm they are not under the influence.

Diet/lifestyle

If food is provided or made available at work the organisation can promote healthy options, providing information on food values and calories in order to aid worker weight management. Exercise may be encouraged with such things as a "use the stairs" policy and a policy to encourage workers to take a mid-work period break involving exercise, for example, a short walk or exercise class.

In addition, policies may encourage walking to work, in conjunction with public transport if required, and the provision of cycle racks and changing facilities, where possible, to encourage cycling. This may also work to support the organisation's aspirations and policies for the environment.

Breastfeeding

Arrangements for breastfeeding have implications that affect health and well-being as well as work performance. Therefore, they should be covered within policies to ensure clarity and consistency.

Mental health and well-being

It is important that policies include aspects of mental health and well-being related to selection and recruitment of workers, as well as how they are accommodated with regard to training and other activities. In addition, policies should recognise stress as an important work-related health and well-being issue.

Techniques which promote empowerment of individuals to make change

Strategies for health and well-being improvement will include the provision of information, work-based campaigns and seminars. In order to empower individuals to improve their health and well-being it helps if they have been involved in the development of the promotion.

This can be achieved through the use of the usual consultation and involvement mechanisms the organisation has in place, for example, the health and safety committee and team briefings. This will help the organisation to introduce health and well-being interventions with the minimum negative impact on individuals.

An example of this approach could be involving them in a healthy eating day by letting them choose a named country to theme the food on, such as Malaysia or China. Alternatives could include involving them in producing a healthy eating poster to support diet promotion and weight monitoring. Part of the empowerment is to provide the knowledge, understanding and means to make changes.

For example, the provision of seminars and information could convey the effects of smoking, workers could be provided with charts to monitor their smoking profile and they could be offered interventions or motivations to help them engage with the campaign and reduce or give up smoking.

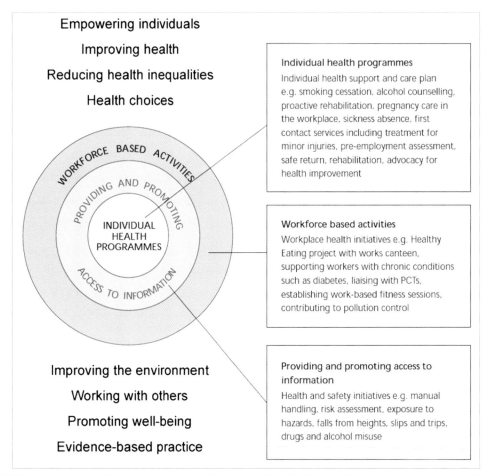

Figure 7-23: Elements of a health programme. *Source: Department of Health, Taking a Public Health Approach in the Workplace.*

Activities and events

Comprehensive health and well-being strategies could include activities and events such as **well persons' clinics** that provide opportunities for workers to have general health screening to assess their overall state of health, such as blood pressure checks and weight assessment. Other tests may be carried out, depending on the risk factors identified during the assessment.

These can be a particularly important part of an holistic approach to health and well-being, where effort is made to target groups of highest risk. The positive label - 'well person' - helps to encourage those that do not feel they have a health problem to attend and confirm their current status.

These clinics provide an environment to identify at an early point conditions that could lead to long-term health issues and sometimes enable wider well-being issues to be discussed. **Immunisation programmes**, organised and offered by the organisation, such as for periodic influenza inoculations, enable workers to gain access to services free of charge that may otherwise cause them to be absent from work to obtain.

There is a mutual, positive benefit in offering these arrangements in an organised way during work hours or just after. In the same way, the organisation may support health and well-being related issues like giving blood to the transfusion service or **smoking cessation clinics**. These could be supplemented by developing local links with GP practices and other community based health facilities.

Support for employees

In order to make a health and well-being strategy a success it may be necessary to help to reduce the barriers for worker participation.

This can be done by providing support to the things that lead to health and well-being. For example, if the organisation would like workers to exercise more they may negotiate and provide **subsidised gym** membership at a local gym and **shower facilities** for those that cycle or run to work or take exercise as a break. Developing links with local providers of **healthy food and drinks**, such as the local organic fruit and vegetable supplier, is a service that may benefit the workers and encourage them to take up of a good diet.

Debt management advice could also be provided as a support for employees, initially by financial experts arranged by the organisation, workers could then be directed to external sources of help and support.

Workplace health support

Learning outcomes

On completion of this element, candidates should be able to demonstrate understanding of the content through the application of knowledge to familiar and unfamiliar situations. In particular they should be able to:

8.1 Explain the main principles in carrying out an occupational health needs assessment.

8.2 Outline the types of workplace health services which are available to support organisations.

8.3 Outline the role of the different professionals involved with occupational health provision.

Content

Sources of reference

Lewis J, Thornbory G (2006) - Employment Law and Occupational Health a practical handbook, Oxford, Blackwell Publishing.

Nursing and Midwifery Council (NMC) 2008 - The Code: Standards of conduct, performance and ethics for nurses and midwives, London: NMC.

Oakley Katie (2008) - 'Occupational Health Nursing' Chapters 1 and 3 (Third edition), Wiley, Chichester, UK.

Relevant statutory provisions

Health and Safety at Work etc Act (HASAWA) 1974

Management of Health and Safety at Work Regulations (MHSWR) 1999

8.1 - Main principles in carrying out an occupational health needs assessment

General principles of health needs assessments

The workplace provides an ideal setting for improving the health and well-being of the working population as there is access to a populace that is relatively constant. "Saving Lives - Our Healthier Nation" (Department of Health, 1999) acknowledges that "the workplace provides opportunities both to improve the health of the workforce and to address health inequality". This view has been reinforced by the publication in 2008 "Working for a Healthier Tomorrow"; Dame Carol Black's review of the health of Britain's working age population.

"Health needs assessment (HNA) is a systematic method for reviewing the health issues facing a population, leading to agreed priorities and resource allocation that will improve health and reduce inequalities".

Figure 8-1: Definition of health needs assessment.   *Source: NICE 2005.*

An occupational health needs assessment enables organisations to identify the health requirements of the workforce, by involving employers, workers, worker health and safety representatives and other relevant stakeholders for the protection and promotion of health and well being within the workplace.

A health needs assessment provides an opportunity to:

- Identify health problems as well as strengths.
- Identify those groups most at risk, for example, from occupational related exposure to noise greater than 85dB.
- Analyse the social and organisational influences on worker health.
- Understand local problems and tailor solutions.
- Involve the workforce and managers in planning.
- Prioritise and target resources effectively.
- Demonstrate the reasons for decisions.
- Evaluate the effectiveness of policies and interventions.

"A workplace Health Needs Assessment means systematically looking at the health needs of the workforce and the workplace using health information and involving colleagues, employees and employers".

Figure 8-2: Health needs assessment.   *Source: Department of Health, Taking a Public Health Approach in the Workplace.*

The National Institute for Clinical Excellence (NICE) suggests a 5 step approach:

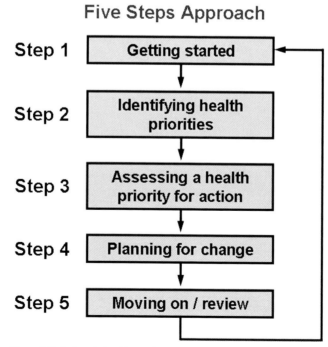

Figure 8-3: 5 steps to health needs assessment.   *Source: RMS/NICE.*

STEP 1

Getting started

- Identify the population to be reviewed - the whole organisation or just a section of it.
- Define the objective of the assessment.

- Decide who needs to be involved - consider management, workers, human resources, health and safety practitioners, worker health and safety representatives and occupational health staff.
- Establish what resources are required to conduct the assessment.
- Identify the risks - consider what the organisation does, for example, production, retail or health care. Identify the risks to health using the information provided in Element 3 - Hazards to health.

STEP 2

Identifying health priorities

- Population profiling - young, old, female, male, disabled, migrant workers. Number of population at risk.
- Gather data - relating to health, for example, absence statistics, causes of absenteeism and injuries, insurance claims for ill-health or injury, any reported symptoms of ill-health such as upper limb disorders, stress or skin problems.
- Perceptions of needs - talk to workers and managers to find out what they think the health priorities are for the organisation.
  - Perceptions and expectations of the profiled population, for example, what the workers feel their health priorities are.
  - Perceptions of occupational health practitioners.
  - Perceptions of the organisation, based on available data about size and severity of health issues of the population, and inequalities compared with other populations. Perception is affected by the priorities of the organisation and perhaps corporate priorities.
- Identifying and assessing health conditions and determinant factors - establish evidence of workers being smokers, obese, having related health problems such as high blood pressure, heart disease, musculoskeletal disorders (MSD's). Go through in a methodical way as set out in Element 3 to identify the potential health problems and match this with the findings of causes of absenteeism or reported work related ill-health.

STEP 3

Assessing a health priority for action

Choosing health conditions and determinant factors with the most significant size and severity impact for action first - refer to the information on absenteeism and the associated work being carried out. Assess whether the health priority is significant, if so why and what makes it significant.

- Some health conditions may have legal mandatory actions associated with them.
- Some may have well established causal links that mean failing to make them a priority is very likely to lead to harm, for example, exposure to sensitising dusts leading to asthma, exposure to vibration when using vibrating tools leading to hand arm vibration syndrome and exposure to high levels of noise causing noise induced hearing loss.
- Consider the general health of the workforce, for example, smokers, overweight, inactive; what impact might they have on the organisation in relation to absenteeism.

STEP 4

Planning for change

- Decide what interventions might be appropriate - for example, work rotation and breaks, worker education, introduction of audiometric testing, improving the canteen food with better healthier choices and providing support to stop smoking.
- Risk management strategy - interventions should fit within a cohesive risk management strategy. Where possible, giving priority to collective protective measures over individual protective measures.
- Clarifying aims of intervention - when interventions have been decided they should be set out as a clear aim, with measurable outcomes.
- Action planning - present a prioritised action plan, which sets out what needs to be done, by whom and by when. Ensure these are cost effective solutions, which will define the health and well-being strategy and effectively reduce risk. Provide time frames for completion, with someone appointed to make the change happen.
- Monitoring and evaluation of the strategy - monitor the actions and look to evaluate the outcomes, for example, review absenteeism to determine whether it has changed (improved), whether insurance claims have reduced and whether workers have observed a positive impact on their lives.

STEP 5

Moving on/review

- Learning from the changes - what worked well, what did not and why, what needs to be changed.
- Measuring impact - review all information and data to see what impact has been made, for example, reduced absenteeism attributed to work-related ill-health, question workers and managers and get their

opinions. Always make sure what is being done is benefiting the workers and the organisation; if it is not then it should not continue and it will be necessary to move onto something that will. It is important not to be afraid to admit that interventions are ineffective.

■ Choosing the next priority - establish what has been achieved, set the next priorities and repeat the process of setting an action plan, ensure the health and well-being programme remains dynamic. When the organisation's priorities change, ensure that health and well-being is reviewed to meet the changes. This may be achieved through the implementation of an audit system.

"A Health Needs Assessment is not just looking for health problems and threats to health. All employees and employers have strengths and assets that promote health and well-being such as knowledge, resources, ability to self-care, family support.

Health Needs Assessment is a continuous process of profiling and determining priorities for the workforce. It involves looking at:

• Workforce profile and structure i.e. demographics

• Workplace lifestyle and socio-economic status

• Incidence and prevalence of disease and disability

• Uptake of services both preventive, treatment and rehabilitation

• The workforce's own assessment of their health needs and the impact of work on their health

• Analysis of social and organisational influences on health".

Figure 8-4: Health needs assessment process.   *Source: Department of Health, Taking a Public Health Approach in the Workplace.*

Job roles, work processes and their associated potential hazards, links to risk assessment

Health needs may be influenced, and therefore identified, by the specific job role of the worker. Needs can be identified by taking the approach that all workers with a given role will have the same fundamental needs. A worker may be a foundry operative, large goods vehicle driver or baker. These job roles have specific features that can influence the health of all workers that do these jobs. In a similar way, the health needs may be defined by the work process that is carried out, for example, operating display screen equipment or carrying out manual handling tasks. There are specific features of these tasks that may give rise to hazards that can impact on the health of all workers that carry out the work process. In each case, whether it is the job or work process classification it will be the associated hazards of the job or work process that establishes the occupational health needs. Many of the occupational health needs may be identified within the general risk assessments conducted by organisations while managing health and safety.

Distinction between hazard and risk

It is important that the person assessing occupational health needs understands the difference between hazard and risk.

HAZARD

"Something that has the potential to cause harm".

Figure 8-5: Definition of hazard.   *Source: RMS.*

Health hazards exist in a number of forms and can be broadly grouped as chemical, physical, biological, psychosocial and ergonomic. ***(See also - Element 3 - Effects of work on health).***

RISK

"The likelihood that someone will be harmed by the hazard".

Figure 8-6: Definition of risk.   *Source: RMS.*

Many things have the potential to cause harm, but it depends on what we do with the hazard that can increase or decrease the likelihood of harm. For example, sealed asbestos presents a low risk; it is only when we start to move it, drill it or do similar things to it in a way that makes it into dust that can be inhaled that it presents a high risk to health.

Demands of the job - physical and psychological

The job may place physical and psychological demands on the worker. These demands can be due to exposure to a range of hazards that can have a physical or psychological effect on the worker's health. It is important that an occupational health needs assessment identify the full range of demands arising from a job. This includes assessing the effects of all potential hazards to health including the physical, chemical, biological, psychosocial, and ergonomic issues. It is important to identify the demands that exist when the job is being conducted under normal conditions and abnormal conditions, such as peaks of work demand or breakdown/emergency situations. *(See also - Element 3 - Effects of work on health - for more detail).*

 Case Study - Female office worker

The physical demands of the job of a baker could include working in high temperatures, conducting repeated dexterous movements of the lower limbs, standing for long periods, manual handling of flour in sacks, and exposure to flour dust. The psychological demands could include constant pace of work with little breaks, and demands for high levels of concentration and fatigue.

Assessing how an individual's health may affect the job

Someone's state of health could put their own health and safety at risk if they are working in an environment where they might be exposed to hazards likely to make an existing health condition worse. Also someone with an existing health problem could endanger the health and safety of others. This is an essential aspect of an occupational health needs assessment and is linked to the concept that certain jobs may carry features that have intrinsic health needs due to the fact that a worker may have conditions that might affect their health and safety performance and endanger themselves and others.

A good example of this might be the job of driving a large goods vehicle, where the assessment would seek to identify and manage conditions that could cause a driver to perform unsafely, such as sudden loss of consciousness due to an uncontrolled diabetic condition leading to a hypoglycaemic attack. *(See also - Element 2 - Effects of health on work - for more detail).*

Assessing how work might affect health

For most organisations this will be the largest part of the occupational health needs assessment as it will take account of the full range of health hazards that may arise from the work. Many may be identified through the general risk assessment process. The risk assessment process should identify those groups of workers that will be of particular risk from a health hazard, including vulnerable groups. In doing so it is important to remember that a person with an existing health condition, who works in an unsuitable environment, may find that it makes the existing condition worse, for example, work in a very cold environment may have an adverse effect on a worker with asthma. The occupational health needs assessment should seek to identify health needs for this class of worker and not be limited to identifying those needs that affect all workers. This class of worker may have additional health needs to those of other workers. *(See also - Element 3 - Effects of work on health - for more detail).*

Identifying when specific fitness standards are required and why

Fitness standards are required when there is a legal requirement, for example, drivers of large goods vehicle (LGV's) and some railway workers. In addition, an organisation may adopt industry fitness standards or may develop their own. Fitness standards should be established by a systematic health needs assessment that not only defines what the standard is but why it is needed.

The process of conducting an occupational health needs assessment should naturally lead to identifying positive and negative health characteristics of particular work and can therefore indicate when specific fitness standards are required and why. *(See also - Element 2 - Effects of health on work - for more detail).*

Special cases - age, pregnancy, disability

It has been recognised that certain categories of worker may be at higher risk; these specifically include pregnant or nursing mothers and young persons. This recognition is reflected in the Management of Health and Safety at Work Regulations (MHSWR) 1999. Also, Schedule 1 of Regulation 4 of the Manual Handling Operations Regulations (MHOR) 1992 (as amended) requires that risk assessments take account of individual capability, including the effects of pregnancy. Any workers who may have suffered physical deterioration with age may need special consideration to enable them to carry out tasks safely. This is an aspect that must be considered when conducting manual handling risk assessments.

In the same way, special cases must be considered as an integral part of a comprehensive occupational health needs assessment. Some data needed to conduct the occupational health needs assessment for this category of worker can be drawn from risk assessments conducted to satisfy the above legislative requirements. The occupational health needs of workers with disabilities may not differ from the general worker population being assessed, depending on the work they conduct. If their disability presents a vulnerability to the health effects of some of the work they do, this must be taken into account.

Similarly, if their disability may lead to health and safety effects on others this too should be taken into account when conducting the occupational health needs assessment. The Equality Act (EA) 2010 prohibits the discrimination, harassment or victimisation of workers with regard to their age. This means employers will need to continue to provide support and training for older workers, in the same way that they might younger workers.

The Employment Equality (Repeals of Retirement Age Provisions) Regulations (EERAR) 2011 remove the general right of the employer to operate a compulsory retirement age, unless it can be objectively justified. Because of this legislation, there is likely to be a greater number of older workers in employment, which will lead to the need to consider their specific occupational health needs where these vary from the general workforce.

(See also - Element 2 - Effects of health on work - for more detail).

8.2 - Workplace health services available to support organisations

The role, function and benefits of occupational health services

The role of the occupational health service is to provide support to the management of an organisation in order that health at work is managed with a positive outcome.

The functions of an occupational health service include:

- Identify occupational risks to health through risk assessment.
- Assess the health of the working population.
- Provide input to the health needs assessment.
- Provide on-going advice to management on matters of health.
- Provide health promotion.
- Support management with absence management and providing early intervention.
- Assess fitness for work following illness and injury.
- Providing advice to management and workers on rehabilitation.
- Advising management on requirements for first aid provisions and monitoring the service.
- Providing medical and health surveillance.

"Referral to OH is often regarded by staff as a punishment, this image needs to be changed and a more positive and enabling one created. This requires a more enlightened vision of the role of OH by management".

Figure 8-7: Role of occupational health (OH) services.   *Source: Royal College of Nursing/TSO.*

The benefits of occupational health services are that they will:

- Help protect the health of employees.
- Help employers make sure that they are complying with the legal requirements for a safe workplace.
- Enable the identification of health risks.
- Enable the establishment of workplace health standards.
- Enable detection of any adverse health effects at an early stage.
- Assist in the evaluation of control measures.
- Provide information useful in the detection of hazards and assessment of risks.
- Promote good health and well-being.
- Improve the level of general health of the workforce and reduce the level of ill-health absence.

Applying the findings of the workplace health needs assessment to determine level and types of service needed

Conducting an occupational health needs assessment will lead to the identification of health hazards relating to the work, the evaluation of current controls and identification of interventions to support health. From this process it is possible to determine the level and types of occupational health services needed to meet the objectives identified. Meeting the objectives will require the development of an action plan and the assignment of individuals to enable the plan to be implemented. If the organisation has a low level of health risk, such as an office environment, then the plan will be relatively simple. More complex organisations with complex risks to manage, such as within a chemical processing environment, will often choose to engage external assistance to complement their own occupational health department or contract the service to a third party.

If an occupational health service is to be provided it must be integrated into the organisation's operation. It should be clear how it will contribute to the success of the organisation and how this will be known. Therefore the following should be addressed:

- Establish the purpose of the occupational health service.
- Identify the goals, objectives, which are based on the occupational health needs of the organisation.
- Determine how the performance of the occupational health service will be measured.
- Report the outcomes of the occupational health service to the top management.

This establishes direction for the occupational health service, defines the organisation better, and determines long term goals and what outcomes are to be achieved. It will set the context for development of the occupational health service, based on the needs of the organisation and its risks. It should also be the basis of corporate identity and will make health and well-being more visible. The type of health services provided will depend on the resources available and the outcome of the occupational health needs assessment.

Types of generalist occupational health services

Occupational health services provide an independent advisory service for management and workers. In order to ensure that occupational health provision meets the needs of the organisation and its workforce a health needs assessment (HNA) should be undertaken to identify the level and range of services required. There are legal requirements that necessitate the engagement of an occupational health provider where health surveillance is required under Control of Substances Hazardous to Health (COSHH) 2002, such as lung function testing, but there is no legal requirement to provide a service when there are no specific identifiable hazards.

However, an occupational health service will encompass looking after the general health and well-being of all workers and the promotion of health at work. An occupational health service should be part of the overall strategy of the organisation and have the ability to influence and recommend changes to enhance the success of the organisation. The person who leads the occupational health service must have access to a level of management where they can have an impact and be empowered to bring about change. This means access to top management level, where there is accountability for the health of the workforce and the occupational health service provided. The occupational health service should report to top management on the actions and benefits that the service is giving to the organisation.

IN-HOUSE

Occupational health services can be in-house, where occupational health staff are employed directly by the organisation. The responsibility for ensuring appropriate nursing and medical personnel are recruited and up to date on their professional register rests with the organisation employing them.

EXTERNAL PROVIDER

Organisations may decide to engage an outside contracted occupational health service or a sole practitioner to provide their occupational health service. However the employing organisation must ensure that the contactor they engage is fit for practice and meets the same professional criteria as for in-house provision.

Larger organisations may engage a specialist occupational health provider to manage the whole service. The recruitment and personnel management of occupational health personnel will then rest with the contracted provider. However, the organisation employing the contracted occupational health service should ensure that there are systems in place to audit the performance of the service and check that those carrying it out are competent to do so.

Public providers

Organisations can sometimes access workplace health support from Local Authorities (LA), for example, healthy lifestyle and food hygiene. There may be a charge for this; however, some services are part of the local authority strategy for health and will be funded by the local authority. Also, some local authority occupational health services offer contracted services to local organisations in a similar way to external providers. The same standards should apply to them in relation to staff and auditing the performance of the service.

Private provider organisations

These will be 'external providers' such as AVIVA and BUPA who provide occupational services. They operate on a contract for services and will operate the same as described earlier for the external provider. Their services should be contracted on what is required by the organisation to address the issues identified through the occupational needs assessment. Some of the services may be provided as part of an insurance package in order to assist the organisation in reducing workplace risk and therefore claims on their insurance policy. The organisation should ensure that they are providing the required services and set a system of audit and review.

Sole providers

There are an increasing number of individuals, for example, doctors and occupational nurses, that provide independent occupational health services on a contract or as needed basis. It is important that any organisation using these services ensures the competence of the people providing the service.

Specialist support services

There are a number of organisations providing specialist support services for organisations regarding improving the health of the workforce. The main ones and their roles are outlined as follows.

BACKCARE

BackCare is a national charity that aims to reduce the impact of back pain on society by providing information, support, promoting good practice and funding research. BackCare acts as a connection between patients, healthcare professionals, employers, policy makers, researchers and all others with an interest in back pain. More information is available at www.backcare.org.uk.

BUSINESS LINK

Business Link is a Government organisation that provides businesses of all sizes with access to information from the government. Its content was developed in partnership with subject experts within government and relevant business-support organisations to help businesses comply with regulations and improve performance.

Advice is available on health and well-being and includes:

- How to prevent and manage illness.
- How to improve health and well-being.
- Work hours and rest periods.
- Employing young people.
- Recruiting and employing disabled people.
- How to deal with stress.
- Preventing upper limb disorders.
- Understanding regulations.

More detail can be obtained from www.businesslink.gov.uk.

CONSTRUCTING BETTER HEALTH (CBH)

CBH is responsible for delivering the National Scheme for the management of occupational health in the construction industry. It focuses on five key areas:

- Setting industry standards for both work-related health issues and competency of occupational health provision.
- Building a construction-specific knowledge portal.
- Centralising the collection of work-related health data.
- The transmission of fit-for-task data to enable employers to manage work-related health risks at site level.
- A referral route through to specialists in the field of return to work and rehabilitation.

More information can be obtained at www.constructingbetterhealth.co.uk.

JOBCENTRE PLUS

This is a Government agency that provides advice and support to people of working age who are out of work. A number of its schemes and programmes focus on help for disabled people and those with a health condition.

Access to Work

Access to Work is a Government initiative designed to keep or get back to work those who may have a disability or health condition which prevents them being able to do parts of their job. There are Access to Work advisors who will provide advice and support to both employers and workers. Applicants may obtain payment towards:

- The equipment they need at work.
- Adapting premises to meet their needs.
- A support worker.
- The cost of getting to work if they cannot use public transport.
- A communicator at job interviews.

Access to Work may be available to those who are:

- In a paid job.
- Unemployed and about to start a job.
- Unemployed and about to start a work trial.
- Self-employed.

Pathways to Work

Helps people to get work if they are receiving allowances or benefits because of a condition or disability. The programme is tailored to the individual and may include:

- Work-focused interviews to identify needs, opportunities and support.
- Condition Management Programmes to help the person to better understand and manage their condition.
- Return to Work Credit to provide financial support.

Work Choice

Work Choice helps people with disabilities whose needs cannot be met through other work programmes like Access to Work or workplace adjustments. This might be because they need more specialised support to find employment or keep a job once they have started work. It will also ensure that employers get the support they need to employ more disabled people.

The Work Choice programme has three different modules:

Module 1:   Work Entry Support - provides help with personal skills and work-related advice to get people into supported or unsupported work.

Module 2:   In-Work Support - provides help to start work and stay in a job.

Module 3:   Longer-term In-Work Support - provides help people to progress in a job and where appropriate, help move into unsupported work.

New Deal for Disabled People (NDDP)

This is a national programme of advice and practical support for people with disabilities, which helps them move into paid employment. Programmes and their names change from time to time. More detail can be obtained from www.direct.gov.uk.

MIND

Mind helps people to take control over their mental health. They do this to make it possible for people who experience mental distress to live full lives, which includes working and to play their full part in society. They provide information and advice and training programmes, in all areas of the country. MIND's vision is of "a society that promotes and protects good mental health for all, and that treats people with experience of mental distress fairly, positively and with respect".

More information can be obtained from www.mind.org.uk.

NHS PLUS

NHS Plus is a network of NHS occupational health services across England who provide occupational health services to non-NHS employers on a fee basis, mainly small and medium sized enterprises (SME's). It is part of the Government's Health, Work and Well-being Strategy, and seeks to promote the benefits of good health at work with the aim to build healthy and productive workforces.

Health, Work and Well-being is a Government-led initiative to protect and improve the health and well-being of working age people.

NHS Plus's support and services include:

- Prevention and removal of health risks in the workplace - through the provision of risk assessments such as those for display screen equipment and immunisation programmes for work-related infectious diseases such as hepatitis B.
- Screening and surveillance - by providing pre-employment health screening, specific health screening for workers who handle food, drive or work at night.
- Independent professional advice on staff unable to work due to health reasons - referral to specialist doctors to assess staff and advice on rehabilitation and adjustments to help staff return to work.
- Lifestyle and well-being - well person health screening, work related health promotion and counselling support for staff experiencing issues affecting their ability to work.

NHS Plus also runs the Health at Work Advice Line for small businesses in England. The objectives of this national advice line include:

- Helping businesses retain staff without a period of absence.
- Supporting businesses in helping staff back to work following a period of sickness absence.
- Improving productivity as a result of actions taken by small businesses related to advice received from the helpline.

The advice line particular focuses on businesses employing less than 49 staff, as they are less likely to have access to occupational health advice and most likely to benefit from problem solving support. The advice line operates across England through a single national telephone number operated by NHS Direct: www.health4work.nhs.uk or telephone 0800 077 8844.

More information about NHS Plus can be found at www.nhsplus.nhs.uk.

RNIB

Royal National Institute of Blind People (RNIB) is the UK's leading charity offering information, support and advice to almost two million people with sight loss. It provides helps anyone with a sight problem in the form of braille and Talking Books, as well as practical solutions to everyday challenges. It provides information on eye conditions and provides support and advice for people living with sight loss.

More information is available at www.rnib.org.uk.

ACTION ON HEARING LOSS

Action on Hearing, formerly known as RNID, offer a range of services for deaf and hard of hearing people and provides information and support on all aspects of deafness, hearing loss and tinnitus. This can include interpreter training, lip speakers and speech to text operators.

More information is available at www.actiononhearingloss.org.uk.

SHAW TRUST

The Shaw Trust is a not for profit employment organisation. It offers support in the form of training and work opportunities for people who suffer ill health or are disabled or disadvantaged through social circumstances. They also help employers recruit and rehabilitate people with disabilities and will help employers with problems of sickness absence.

More information is available at www.shaw-trust.org.uk.

SHIFT

Shift is an initiative to tackle stigma and discrimination surrounding mental health issues in England. Their aim is to create a society where people who experience mental health problems enjoy the same rights and opportunities as other people. Shift is working in a number of areas to reduce and remove the stigma and discrimination directed towards people with experience of mental health problems. It has a number of initiatives specific to the workplace, including the Action on Stigma initiative, which is for people with an interest in reducing the stigma and discrimination directed towards people in the workplace.

As part of Action on Stigma, Shift has published the "Line Managers' Resource". The "Line Managers' Resource" is a booklet and website that gives advice and information for managing and supporting people with mental health problems in the workplace.

More information is available at www.shift.org.uk.

The potential role of primary care

PRIMARY HEALTH CARE (PHC)

Primary health care (PHC) is the term for the health services that play a central role in the local community, for example, GPs, practice and community nurses, pharmacists, dentists and midwives. Primary care providers are usually the first point of contact for a patient and follow a patient throughout their care pathway. They provide care for the local community, which includes families and people who work.

Primary care workers should be encouraged to get involved in workplace health and well-being, particularly in providing health promotion support. This means everyone working together to provide access to health care that is seamless, preventing ill-health, promoting positive health and ensuring that those needing support are cared for with the aim of returning the person to as active a life as possible - which includes contributing to the community through employment.

Linking with the PHC team organisations could develop various health promotion activities, which the PHC will help with. They will provide advice and support with issues such as smoking cessation, diet and healthy eating, drug and alcohol abuse, stress and anxiety. PHC's will also provide health educational materials and information.

Resources needed

BUDGETING FOR SERVICE PROVISION

It is important for employers to work with their workers to set the strategy for workplace health and well-being, to encourage good healthy living and make it possible for workers to access the help and support that is needed to promote health.

The focus of the health and well-being strategy must be to meet the needs of the specific organisation. Therefore, the first step must be to develop a 'plan of action' based on an occupational health needs assessment, which must be linked to the overall business strategy of the organisation. The objectives of the plan should be defined, for example, what service is to be provided in order to achieve a reduction of absenteeism. *(See also - Element 8 - Workplace health support).*

The type of health and well-being services provided will depend on the outcome of the occupational health needs assessment of the resources available. It is essential that a budget for this should be identified and managed appropriately, based on the priorities defined in the health needs assessment. Without clear budgets, relating to specific objectives, it is hard to compete with other organisational needs that will demand resources. It is also important to develop data on the cost as well as the benefits of prevention of ill-health.

BENEFIT OF PROVIDING SERVICES IN EXCESS OF STATUTORY MINIMUM

Though an organisation's occupational health services must provide for and meet the minimum statutory needs there is a benefit in providing services in addition to this. Statutory minimum provision would limit the influence of occupational health services to addressing a small number of specific risks and would not address the wider issue of managing general ill-health and well-being.

Workplace ill-health can be expensive. *(See also - Element 2 - Effects of health on work and Element 4 - Management of attendance).* The effect on an organisation of absence due to illness or injury may mean replacing staff, additional supervision, recruitment, reduced productivity and output, higher insurance and compensation claims, and damage to the businesses reputation, all of which could cost millions of pounds.

Therefore, organisations need to take the wider context of health and well-being as seriously as protecting it against any other risks to the business, such as financial, production or service delivery risks. The smaller the business the bigger the impact will be if a worker has a serious injury, or is off sick for an extended period of time. It could put the organisation out of operation.

The main aim of any organisation must be to stop ill-health happening, which will save time and money. There are good sources of advice and guidance on the HSE website, which employers should be encouraged to use. It provides case studies and looks at methods available to improve and maintain the health of the workforce and can be found at www.hse.gov.uk/business/business-benefits.htm.

8.3 - The different professionals involved with occupational health provision

The potentially conflicting role of health professionals who work with both employee and organisation

Situations of conflict may arise where a health professional involved in health provision identifies a health condition that a worker is suffering from that could be made worse by the work the worker does. For example, a worker who had severe asthma may work in a job that exposes them to a respiratory sensitiser; this could affect the workers short and long term health. The health professional may feel that it would be in the best interest of the worker if the employer was made aware of the condition, but the employee may feel that this could jeopardise their job. The health professional would be left in a conflicting role of wanting to represent the interests of both the worker and the employer. In this situation health professionals are bound by confidentiality restrictions, which would prevent them releasing the information to the worker's employer without their express permission.

There is also a potential for conflict for health professionals working within the occupational health setting regarding the issues of confidentiality of medical records. There are times when a manager may ask to see a worker's medical record, but this is not permitted without the worker's consent.

Employee health information is protected by legislation:

■ Human Rights Act 1998 - protection of personal life, which includes data.

■ Data Protection Act 1998 - that any data must be fairly and lawfully processed, is not kept longer than is necessary and is secure, particularly 'sensitive data' like medical records. *See also Element 4.2 "Role and responsibilities of the health professionals, line-managers, human resources, and the employee in the management of absence" - The meaning and scope of "health records", the importance of confidentiality.*

■ Access to Medical Reports Act 1998 - this gives people the right of access to their medical and health records given for the purpose of insurance or employment. *See also Element 4.2 "Role and responsibilities of the health professionals, line-managers, human resources, and the employee in the management of absence" - Action to take if employee does not consent.*

There are also professional codes of practice that require medical and nursing staff to protect confidentiality.

The code of professional practice for doctors is described in 'Duties of a doctor' by the General Medical Council (GMC) and stipulates when information can and cannot be divulged.

The nursing profession is controlled by the Nursing and Midwifery Council (NMC) the statutory body for nurses and the specific 'Code'.

This states that "nurses must respect people's right to confidentiality and ensure that people are informed about how and why information is shared".

However, in all of the Codes, there is a requirement for the disclosure of information if the nurse/doctor believes someone may be at risk of harm.

Figure 8-8: Code of conduct. *Source: NMC.*

An example of this might be someone who has developed a condition that means they are unfit to drive; this must be reported to the Driver and Vehicle Licensing Authority (DVLA) for the health and safety of the individual and others.

In all aspects of occupational health practice these codes apply and managers must be made aware of them and understand the need for confidentiality. Information and advice to management can be supplied without breaching confidentiality legislation/codes and it is advice on of the work capability of the worker that is paramount, not what illness or condition the individual may have.

Likely makeup of the workplace health service delivery team

REGISTERED MEDICAL PRACTITIONER

Highest qualification

Fellow of the faculty of occupational medicine (FFOM)

This is an accredited specialist who has made a significant contribution to the discipline. They should be competent to deal with any occupational health problem and provide authoritative advice.

Member of the faculty of occupational medicine (MFOM)

This is an accredited specialist who is a doctor who has completed an approved course of higher professional training at consultant level. They should be competent to deal with the majority of occupational health problems or know who can provide an expert opinion when necessary.

Associate of faculty of occupational medicine (AFOM)

This is a medical doctor, who has passed the required occupational health examinations, but has not yet completed the specialist training; they are generally competent to practice in occupational health.

NURSING

Registered nurse

The title 'nurse' is protected in the UK and to be entitled to use it a person must be registered with the regulatory body for nursing, the Nursing Midwifery Council (NMC), on part 1 of their register, they are then a Registered Nurse (RN). There is no professional or statutory requirement for a registered nurse to hold a post-registration qualification in occupational nursing, although many nurses do. Health and safety legislation makes reference to "competence" and therefore it is advisable to engage "suitably qualified" practitioners. Occupational health nurses have an important public health role in the prevention of ill-health at work and in the promotion of health and well-being in the workplace. They therefore should hold as a minimum of a certificate/diploma in occupational health nursing, or be working towards a qualification.

In 2004 the NMC opened up another part of the register for registered specialist community public health nurses; existing occupational health nurses were allowed to migrate onto this part of the register, along with health visitors and school nurses. The opportunity to migrate across has now closed. Should registered nurses working in occupational health wish to be on this part of the register, then they have to undertake a programme of education at degree level which is validated by the NMC and will accord them with a Specialist Practitioner Qualification on part 3 of the register. Those entering the profession with formal occupational health qualifications that meet NMC competency requirements can also be registered on part 3 of the register. Those nurses registered on part 3 of the NMC register are known as a Registered Specialist Community Public Health Nurse (RSCPHN (OH)).

Expert occupational health nurse

This is a nurse with over 5 years experience with an occupational qualification and registered on part 3 on the Register as a Registered Specialist Community Public Health Nurse (RSCPHN (OH)). The Expert Occupational Health Nurse is competent to develop, and lead an occupational health service and to develop protocols and procedures for operational activities and strategies. This nurse will be a competent practitioner, who can supervise others and ensure that professional standards are maintained.

Experienced occupational nurse

This is a nurse with two years experience in occupational health with an occupational health qualification and working towards registration on Part 3 of the NMC Register.

Figure 8-9: Part 7 of Working for a healthier tomorrow.
Source: TSO.

The Experienced Occupational Health Nurse is competent to develop protocols and procedures and to carry out the full occupational health role.

Competent occupational health nurse

This nurse has two years post registration experience and training equivalent to diploma level or working towards degree level qualification. They are competent to work under the guidance of established protocols and procedures. The Competent Occupational Health Nurse is competent to carry out the occupational health role under the supervision of an Experienced Occupational Health Nurse.

AFFILIATE OF FACULTY OF OCCUPATIONAL MEDICINE

Diploma in occupational medicine (DOccMed)

This is a diploma in occupational medicine held by a medical doctor, such as a General Practitioner, who has completed a basic training course in Occupational Medicine and obtained the Diploma by examination. Holders have a general grounding in occupational health, but should seek the advice of a Consultant in Occupational Medicine for more complex cases.

Occupational health technician

Occupational health technicians are a relatively new discipline in occupational health. Qualified technicians may be trained to diploma level and have to pass theory and practical examinations in order to qualify. Many occupational health technicians receive in-house training, are able to carry out audiometry, spirometry, venepuncture and have attended travel health, immunisation and hand arm vibration syndrome (HAVS) courses. Some have gained further qualifications in health related subjects. They are competent to carry out most practical procedures and some take on extra vocational training.

They are not qualified to provide advice on sickness absence management policies, develop occupational health strategies and they must work under the supervision of a registered Nurse or Doctor.

ALLIED HEALTHCARE PROFESSIONAL

Chiropractor

They provide services to manage any musculoskeletal and neurological conditions that require intervention. Chiropractic treatment may also be beneficial in treating other conditions such as migraines. Practitioners will have undertaken a four year training programme at degree level and must be registered with the General Chiropractic Council.

More information about the work of Chiropractors can be found on www.chiropractic-uk.co.uk.

Physiotherapists

Physiotherapy uses physical methods, such as massage and manipulation, to promote healing and wellbeing. Physiotherapy treatments are used to help restore a person's range of movement following injury or illness and for people with neurological conditions (those affecting the brain and nervous system) and chronic (long-term) health conditions. Practitioners will have undertaken a three year training programme at degree level and must be registered with the Health Professions Council (HPC).

More information is available on the Chartered Society of Physiotherapy (CSP) website: www.csp.org.uk.

Occupational therapists

Occupational therapy promotes health by enabling people to return to and obtain work and undertake other activities. These include work as well as leisure and domestic activities. Occupational therapists work with individuals, families, companies, groups and communities to facilitate health and well-being through engagement or re-engagement in occupation. They are also involved in assessing people to return to work following a period of extended absence through ill health or injury, and many are now employed as part of the occupational health team. Occupational therapists are becoming increasingly involved in addressing the impact of social, political and environmental factors that contribute to exclusion and occupational deprivation. Occupational therapists and support workers help people engage as independently as possible in the activities (occupations) which enhance their health and well-being.

The work of the College of Occupational Therapy can be viewed on www.cot.co.uk.

Occupational psychologists

Psychology is involved with how we think, how we act, how we react and interact, both individually and as groups, and the thoughts and feelings behind such behaviours. Psychologists work in many different areas of society and many are employed by companies to provide advice and guidance on mental health problems such as depression and stress. They also provide help with performance issues to ensure people are working to the best of their abilities. They will support workers with issues such as stress and depression, bullying and harassment, as well as all aspects of personal life that may be impacting on the worker's ability to work effectively.

More information of the role of the psychologist can be found of the website www.bps.org.uk.

Counsellors

Counsellors are often employed by companies to provide a confidential counselling service to employees. Counselling provides a private and confidential opportunity to explore a difficulty a person is having; this may be related to pressure or stress or difficulties adjusting to work after a long absence.

By listening attentively and patiently the counsellor can begin to perceive the difficulties from the person's point of view and can help them to see things more clearly, possibly from a different perspective. Counselling is a way of enabling choice or change or of reducing confusion. It does not involve giving advice or directing a person to take a particular course of action. Counsellors do not judge or exploit their clients in any way. Companies should ensure that any counsellor is qualified and has a recognised qualification in counselling or psychotherapy.

More information can be found on the British Association of Counselling and Psychotherapy website www.bacp.org.uk.

Importance of identifying and proving competence when selecting workplace services

It is important to identify and prove competence when selecting workplace services in order to ensure that assessment and treatment services are correct and effective. Services, such as health surveillance, must be conducted to accepted standards as they can have both legal and practical effects on the employer and worker. Those providing occupational health services should have occupational competence. It is not sufficient for individuals providing occupational health services to only have competence in general health, as this will not provide sufficient, relevant competence. For example, occupational health doctors and nurses are expected to have skills and expertise that include:

- Understanding of the health hazards that can arise at work.
- Ability to assess risks relating to the health of individuals and groups.
- Knowledge of the law relating to workplace issues.
- Awareness and understanding of the way business operates.

In the same way, organisations that provide occupational health services should be able to authenticate their occupational competence. Occupational Health Service Standards for Accreditation is a system of voluntary accreditation to promote safe, appropriate and quality services by occupational health providers in the United Kingdom. It aims to:

- Enable services to identify the standards of practice to which they should aspire.
- Credit good work being done by high quality occupational health services.
- Providing independent validation that they satisfy standards of quality.
- Raise standards where they need to be raised.
- Help purchasers differentiate occupational health services to select the service which is most appropriate to their needs.

"The standards apply to core clinical occupational health services, i.e. services provided by doctors, nurses and occupational health technicians and do not apply to non-clinical services that may sometimes be provided as part of more comprehensive occupational health services, for example occupational hygiene and ergonomics".

Figure 8-10: The standards of practice - scope.   *Source: The Faculty of Occ. Medicine of the Royal College of Physicians.*

The Faculty of Occupational Medicine (of the Royal College of Physicians) published 'Standards for Occupational Health Services' (2010), which is a quality system intended to lead to accreditation.

These standards have been produced in collaboration with a number of stakeholders including the RCN, DoH, EEF, NHS Plus, Associations of NHS OH Nurses and Physicians, Association of OH Nurse Practitioners AOHNP (UK), Commercial Occupational Health Providers Association (COHPA) and Society of Occupational Medicine (SOM).

The standards cover 6 main domains:

- Business probity for example, integrity and financial propriety.
- Information Governance for example, records, reports, confidentiality.
- People for example, levels of competence, experience and professional development.
- Facilities and equipment for example, facilities for the provision of services, use of and calibration of equipment.
- Relationship with purchasers for example, dealing fairly with customers, to be customer focused.
- Relationships with workers for example, ensure that workers are treated fairly and that they are involved.

Figure 8-11: Standards for occupational health services.
Source: TSO.

Minimum requirements have been set under each of these domains. Organisations seeking occupational health service provision should use these standards as the benchmark for their services.

'Safe Effective Quality Occupational Health Service - Standards for Accreditation' January 2010 can be downloaded from the Faculty of Occupational Medicine. www.facoccmed.ac.uk.

Role of the occupational hygienist, health and safety advisor, and ergonomist

OCCUPATIONAL HYGIENIST

"Occupational hygiene is the discipline of anticipating, recognising, evaluating and controlling health hazards in the working environment with the objective of protecting worker health and well-being and safeguarding the community at large".

Figure 8-12: Definition of occupational hygiene. *Source: Occupational Hygiene Association, 1988.*

The work of the occupational hygienist is about the prevention of ill-health from work, through recognising, evaluating, and controlling the risks. Occupational hygienists have a technical expertise in measuring exposure levels such as dusts, gases, vapours and noise, the interpretation of the results and provision of advice on practical solutions that can be put in place to prevent and/or control the hazard.

Hygienists work in all types of organisations, both public and private, from offices to factories, with many working as self-employed consultants. They have a range of expertise, can advise on regulatory compliance and the investigation of short to long term health issues arising from exposure, these being both acute and chronic, such as noise levels and monitoring.

More information on the role of the Occupational Hygienist is available on: www.bohs.org.

HEALTH AND SAFETY PRACTITIONERS

Their role is to help employers reduce risks. They promote awareness of health and safety within the workplace with the main focus on preventing accidents and injuries and work related ill-health. They help managers for create, and maintain a safe and healthy working environment.

In more recent years Health and safety practitioners have become more involved in workplace health and well-being and work closely with other members of the occupational health team. Although their main focus has been on safety they play a big role in promoting a healthy working environment. Their contribution to health and well-being is essential in areas such as training and rehabilitation, especially where issues of a safety nature may be a barrier to getting a worker back to work.

More information on the role and qualifications of health and safety practitioners is available on the IOSH website www.iosh.co.uk.

ERGONOMIST

Ergonomics is an applied science that takes account of physical and psychological capabilities and human limitations.

Figure 8-13: Definition of ergonomics. *Source: Raistrick Claire, 2008.*

The International Ergonomics Association defines ergonomics as follows:

Ergonomics (or human factors) is the scientific discipline concerned with the understanding of interactions among humans and other elements of a system, and the profession that applies theory, principles, data and methods to design in order to optimize human well-being and overall system performance.

Figure 8-14: Definition of ergonomics. *Source: International Ergonomics Association.*

In general terms ergonomics is the fit between the workers, their tools and their working environment.

Ergonomists are employed in some large organisations and provide advice and practical solutions to the design, layout and adaptation of tools and machinery to people. Many ergonomists are employed on a consultancy basis.

More detail on ergonomists is available on the Institute of Ergonomics and Human Factors website www.ergonomics.org.uk.

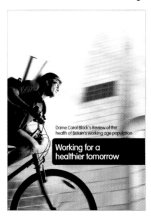

Figure 8-15: Working for a healthier tomorrow. *Source: TSO.*

Relevant statutory provisions

Content

RMS technical publications refer to the principal legislation relevant to the subjects covered by the publication. This is provided in context in the sections that comprise the publication. In addition, an outline of the main points of the legislation is provided in this relevant statutory provisions section. Here the outline relates to the main points of the legislation relevant to health and well-being. This is provided to aid understanding and 'signpost' further reading and research.

RMS publications are widely used by students to support their professional studies and by qualified practitioners to maintain their continual professional development or to develop new skills.

This section to the guide provides an excellent reference source for those undergoing the following learning programmes:

- To meet the requirements of the NEBOSH National Certificate in the Management of Health and Well-being at Work syllabus, in particular.
- To develop knowledge of occupational health practice for nurses working in occupational health situations.
- To develop and enhance competency and skills needed of occupational health technicians.
- Chartered Institute of Personnel and Development (CIPD) qualifications and certificates.
- Chartered Institute of Managers (CIM) qualifications and certificates.

The source documents used in this section may be obtained, free of charge, from www.legislation.gov.uk and www.hse.gov.uk/pubns/books.

Access to Medical Reports Act (AMRA) 1988

Outline of main points

Access to medical reports is governed by the Access to Medical Reports Act (AMRA) 1988. The AMRA 1988 is relevant in the context of recruitment, health screening during employment, time off for medical reasons and dismissal for medical reasons.

The AMRA 1988 covers medical records held by employers as well as records held by doctors. More accurately, it gives an individual the right to have access "to any medical report relating to the individual which is to be, or has been, supplied by a medical practitioner for employment purposes or insurance purposes" (Access to Medical Reports Act 1988 s.1). It also gives individuals the right to refuse consent for any medical report (as defined) to be supplied by a doctor to an employer or insurer, plus other rights.

Employees and prospective employees should not be sent for medical examination without first being informed of their rights under the AMRA 1988.

Rights under the AMRA 1988 are enforceable through the normal courts, not through employment tribunals.

Control of Asbestos Regulations (CAR) 2006

Law considered in context/more depth in Element 4.

Outline of main points

SUMMARY

The Control of Asbestos Regulations (CAR) 2006 came into force on 13th November 2006 (Asbestos Regulations - SI 2006/2737). These Regulations bring together the three previous sets of Regulations covering the prohibition of asbestos, the control of asbestos at work and asbestos licensing:

- Asbestos (Licensing) Regulations (ASLIC) 1983 (and as amended).
- Asbestos (Prohibitions) Regulations 1992 (and as amended).
- Control of Asbestos at Work Regulations (CAWR) 2002.

CAR 2006 prohibits the importation, supply and use of all forms of asbestos. They continue the ban introduced for blue and brown asbestos 1985 and for white asbestos in 1999. They also continue the ban the second-hand use of asbestos products such as asbestos cement sheets and asbestos boards and tiles; including panels which have been covered with paint or textured plaster containing asbestos.

The ban applies to new use of asbestos. If existing asbestos containing materials are in good condition, they may be left in place; their condition monitored and managed to ensure they are not disturbed.

Duty to manage asbestos in non-domestic premises (regulation 4)

CAR 2006 also includes the 'duty to manage asbestos' in non-domestic premises. Guidance on the duty to manage asbestos can be found in the "Approved Code of Practice, The Management of Asbestos in Non-Domestic Premises", produced by the Health and Safety Executive (HSE) as publication L127.

Information, instruction and training (regulation 10)

CAR 2006 requires mandatory training for anyone liable to be exposed to asbestos fibres at work. This includes maintenance workers and others who may come into contact with or who may disturb asbestos (e.g. cable installers) as well as those involved in asbestos removal work.

Prevention or reduction of exposure to asbestos (regulation 11)

When work with asbestos or which may disturb asbestos is being carried out, CAR 2006 requires employers and the self-employed to prevent exposure to asbestos fibres. Where this is not reasonably practicable, they must make sure that exposure is kept as low as reasonably practicable by measures other than the use of respiratory protective equipment. The spread of asbestos must be prevented. CAR 2006 specifies the work methods and controls that should be used to prevent exposure and spread.

Control limits

Worker exposure must be below the airborne exposure limit (Control Limit). CAR 2006 has a single Control Limit for all types of asbestos of 0.1 fibres per cm^3. A Control Limit is a maximum concentration of asbestos fibres in the air (averaged over any continuous 4 hour period) that must not be exceeded. In addition, short term exposures must be strictly controlled and worker exposure should not exceed 0.6 fibres per cm^3 of air averaged over any continuous 10 minute period using respiratory protective equipment if exposure cannot be reduced sufficiently using other means.

Respiratory protective equipment

Respiratory protective equipment is an important part of the control regime but it must not be the sole measure used to reduce exposure and should only be used to supplement other measures. Work methods that control the release of fibres such as those detailed in the **Asbestos Essentials Task Sheets** (available on the HSE website) for non-licensed work should be used. Respiratory protective equipment must be suitable, must fit properly and must ensure that worker exposure is reduced as low as is reasonably practicable.

Asbestos removal work undertaken by a licensed contractor

Most asbestos removal work must be undertaken by a licensed contractor but any decision on whether particular work is licensable is based on the risk. Work is only exempt from licensing if:

- The exposure of employees to asbestos fibres is sporadic and of low intensity (but exposure cannot be considered to be sporadic and of low intensity if the concentration of asbestos in the air is liable to exceed 0.6 fibres per cm3 measured over 10 minutes).
- It is clear from the risk assessment that the exposure of any employee to asbestos will not exceed the control limit.
- The work involves:
    - Short, non-continuous maintenance activities. Work can only be considered as short, non-continuous maintenance activities if any one person carries out work with these materials for less than one hour in a seven-day period. The total time spent by all workers on the work should not exceed a total of two hours*.
    - Removal of materials in which the asbestos fibres are firmly linked in a matrix. Such materials include: asbestos cement; textured decorative coatings and paints which contain asbestos; articles of bitumen, plastic, resin or rubber which contain asbestos where their thermal or acoustic properties are incidental to their main purpose (e.g. vinyl floor tiles, electric cables, roofing felt) and other insulation products which may be used at high temperatures but have no insulation purposes, for example gaskets, washers, ropes and seals.
    - Encapsulation or sealing of asbestos-containing materials which are in good condition.
    - Air monitoring and control, and the collection and analysis of samples to find out if a specific material contains asbestos.

It is important that the amount of time employees spend working with asbestos insulation, asbestos coatings or asbestos insulating board (AIB) is managed to make sure that these time limits are not exceeded. This includes the time for activities such as building enclosures and cleaning.

Under CAR 2006, anyone carrying out work on asbestos insulation, asbestos coating or AIB needs a licence issued by HSE unless they meet one of the exemptions above.

Although you may not need a licence to carry out a particular job, you still need to comply with the rest of the requirements of CAR 2006.

Licensable work - additional duties

If the work is licensable there are a number of additional duties. The need to:

- Notify the enforcing authority responsible for the site where you are working (for example HSE or the local authority).
- Designate the work area (see regulation 18 for details).
- Prepare specific asbestos emergency procedures.
- Pay for your employees to undergo medical surveillance.

Source: HSE website: www.hse.gov.uk.

Control of Lead at Work Regulations (CLAW) 2002

Law considered in context/more depth in Element 3.

Outline of main points

The **Control of Lead at Work Regulations (CLAW) 2002** aims to protect people at work exposed to lead by controlling that exposure. CLAW 2002, which is summarised below, apply to any work which exposes people to lead.

Exposure to lead must be assessed by employers so that they may take adequate measures to protect both employees and anyone else who may be exposed to lead at work. Once the level of exposure has been assessed, then adequate measures can be taken ranging from simple maintenance of good washing facilities through to the provision of control measures such as respiratory equipment and constant medical surveillance. CLAW 2002 prohibits the employment of young persons and women of reproductive capacity from some manufacturing, smelting and refining processes (specified in Schedule 1).

WORK WITH LEAD

The Regulations apply to any work which exposes employees or others to lead. In practical terms, this means any work from which lead arises:

a) In the form of lead dust, fume or vapour in such a way as it could be inhaled.
b) In any form which is liable to be ingested such as powder, dust, paint or paste.
c) In the form of lead compounds such as lead alkyls and compounds of lead, this could be absorbed through the skin.

Employers' duties under CLAW 2002 extend to any other people at work on the premises where work with lead is being carried on.

LEAD ASSESSMENT

Before employers (or a self employed person) can take adequate measures to protect people from lead at work, they need to know exactly what the degree of risk of lead exposure is. The level of risk dictates the measures to be taken. The employer's first duty, therefore, is to assess whether the exposure of any employee is liable to be significant. The next step is to determine the nature and degree of exposure. The assessment must be made before the work is commenced and revised where there is a reason to suspect that it is incorrect.

The purpose of the assessment is to determine whether or not exposure to lead is significant. Where exposure is significant then the employer must, so far as is reasonably practicable, ensure the prevention or adequate control of exposure by means other than the provision of personal protective equipment (PPE).

Where control measures are not sufficient on their own and PPE is issued then it must comply with the PPE Regulations or be of a type approved by the Health and Safety Executive (HSE). When deciding controls the employer must take reasonable steps to ensure that they are being used and employees are under a duty to make full and proper use of control measures, PPE or any other measures dictated by CLAW 2002.

CONTROL MEASURES

Employers must, so far as is reasonably practicable, provide such control measures for materials, plant and processes as will adequately control the exposure of their employees to lead otherwise than by the use of respiratory protective equipment or protective clothing by those employees. Again, personal protective equipment and clothing should be used as a last resort. Employers are under a duty to restrict access to areas to ensure that only people undertaking necessary work are exposed.

If other control measures are inadequate, respiratory protective equipment must be provided for employees exposed to airborne lead. Employees must also be provided with protective clothing where they are significantly exposed to lead. Respiratory protective equipment (RPE) or protective clothing should comply with any UK legislation which implements relevant EU 'design and manufacture' Directives. Employers must also carry out an assessment before selecting RPE or protective clothing to ensure it will satisfy the necessary requirements and provide adequate protection.

The assessment should define the characteristics required by the RPE or protective clothing in order to be suitable, and compare these characteristics against those of the protective equipment actually available. RPE must be examined and tested at appropriate intervals and records kept for a minimum period of 5 years.

Control measures, respiratory equipment and protective clothing must be maintained in an efficient state, in efficient working order and good repair. Employers should ensure that employees use the measures provided properly and employees must make full and proper use of all respiratory protective equipment or protective clothing provided, report defects immediately to the employer and take all reasonable steps to ensure RPE or protective clothing is returned to its storage accommodation after use.

Eating, drinking and smoking are prohibited in any place that is, or is liable to be, contaminated with lead.

OCCUPATIONAL EXPOSURE LIMITS

Control limits for exposure to lead in atmosphere are:

- For lead other then lead alkyls, a concentration of lead in air which any employee is exposed of 0.15 mg per m^3 (8 hour TWA).
- For lead alkyls a concentration of lead of 0.10 mg per m^3 (8 hour TWA).

Air monitoring in relevant areas must be carried out at least every 3 months. This interval can be increased to 12 months providing that there are no material changes to the workplace and lead in air concentrations have not exceeded 0.10 mg per m^3 on two previous consecutive occasions.

MEDICAL SURVEILLANCE

Employees subject to, or liable to be, significantly exposed (or for whom a relevant doctor has certified that they should be) must be placed under medical surveillance by an employment medical adviser or appointed doctor. The Regulations set down action levels for blood-lead concentrations, which are:

- 20 g/dl for women of reproductive capacity.
- 35 g/dl for any other employee.

Levels for urinary lead concentration are also specified. The adviser or doctor can certify that employees should not be employed on work which exposes them to lead or can only be employed under certain conditions. An investigation must be made when blood-lead action levels are exceeded. Employees exposed to lead at work are under a duty to present themselves, in normal working hours, for medical examination or such biological tests as may be required. Employers and employees have a right to appeal against decisions made by relevant doctors.

INFORMATION, INSTRUCTION AND TRAINING

Every employer must ensure that adequate information, instruction and training is given to employees who are liable to be exposed to lead so that they are aware of the risks from lead and the precautions which should be observed. Information must also be given about the results relating to air monitoring and health surveillance and their significance.

Adequate information, instruction and training must also be given to anyone who is employed by the employer to carry out lead assessments, air monitoring, etc.

RECORDS

Adequate records must be kept of assessments, examination and testing of controls, air monitoring, medical surveillance and biological tests. Those records should be made available for inspection by employees (although not health records of identifiable individuals).

Specific recording requirements are made in respect of female employees who are, or who are likely to be, exposed to significant levels of lead. Air monitoring records must be kept for at least 5 years and individual medical records for 40 years.

Control of Noise at Work Regulations (CNWR) 2005

Law considered in context/more depth in Element 3.

The implementation of the European Physical Agents (Noise) Directive as the Control of Noise at Work Regulations 2005 came into force on 06 April 2006. These regulations replaced the Noise at Work Regulations 1989. The main changes were the reduction, by 5dB, of the exposure levels at which action has to be taken, the introduction of a new exposure limit value and a specific requirement on health surveillance.

Outline of main points

CHANGES TO THE ACTION LEVELS

The values of the actions levels associated with noise at work have been lowered and their names have been changed. The first action level is reduced from *85 dB(A) down to 80 dB(A)* and will be known as the *lower exposure action value.* Meanwhile, the section level is reduced from *90 dB(A) down to 85 dB(A)* and will be known as the *upper exposure action value*. The Regulations also allow the employer to average out the exposure to noise over a one week period instead of the previous normal eight hour period, in situations where the noise exposure varies on a day-to-day basis. When determining noise levels for the purposes of determining exposure action levels, the noise exposure reducing effects of hearing protection may not be taken in to account.

Where exposure is at, or above, the *lower exposure action value* (80 dB(A)) the employer has a duty to provide hearing protection to those employees that request it. The employer also has a duty to information, instruction and training on the risks posed by exposure to noise and the control measures to be used. Where the exposure it at, or above, the *upper exposure action value* (85 dB(A)) the employer is also required to introduce a formal programme of control measures. The measures to be taken as part of this programme of control measures will depend on the findings of the noise risk assessment (see below).

The CNWR 2005 also introduced a new value known as the *exposure limit value*. When evaluating the risks to employees from noise, the employer needs to take account of the exposure limit values. These are limits set both in terms of daily (or weekly) personal noise exposure (LEP,d of 87 dB) and in terms of peak noise ($LCpeak$ of 140 dB). The exposure action values, take account of the protection provided by personal hearing protection. *If an employee is exposed to noise at or above the exposure limit value, then the employer must take immediate action to bring the exposure down below this level.*

Summary of exposure limit values and action values

The lower exposure action values are: A daily or weekly personal noise exposure of 80 dB (A-weighted)

A peak sound pressure of 135 dB (C-weighted)

The upper exposure action values are: A daily or weekly personal noise exposure of 85 dB (A-weighted)

A peak sound pressure of 137 dB (C-weighted)

The exposure limit values are: A daily or weekly personal exposure of 87 dB (A-weighted)

A peak sound pressure of 140 db (C-weighted)

NOISE RISK ASSESSMENT AND CONTROL MEASURES

The requirement for a noise risk assessment was carried through from the Noise at Work Regulations 1989 into the Control of Noise at Work Regulations 2005. Employers are required (in accordance with the general risk assessment and control measure hierarchy contained in Schedule 1 to the Management of Health and Safety at Work Regulation 1999) to ensure that the risks associated with employees' exposure to noise are eliminated where this is reasonably practicable. Where elimination is not reasonably practicable, then the employer must reduce the risks down to as low a level as is reasonably practicable. Regulation 6(2) of the Control of Noise at Work Regulations 2005 introduced the requirement for a formal programme of control measures and states:

"If any employee is likely to be exposed to noise at or above an upper exposure action value, the employer shall reduce exposure to a minimum by establishing and implementing a programme of organisational and technical measures, excluding the provision of personal hearing protectors, which is appropriate to the activity and consistent with the risk assessment, and shall include consideration of:

(a) Other working methods which eliminate or reduce exposure to noise.

(b) Choice of appropriate work equipment emitting the least possible noise, taking account of the work to be done.

(c) The design and layout of workplaces, work stations and rest facilities.

(d) Suitable and sufficient information and training for employees, such that work equipment may be used correctly, in order to minimise their exposure to noise.

(e) Reduction of noise by technical means including:

(i) In the case of airborne noise the use of shields, enclosures, and sound-absorbent coverings.

(ii) In the case of structure-borne noise by damping and isolation.

(f) Appropriate maintenance programmes for work equipment, the workplace and workplace systems.

(g) Limitation of the duration and intensity of exposure to noise.

(h) Appropriate work schedules with adequate rest periods."

If the risk assessment indicates an employee is likely to be exposed to noise at or above an upper exposure action value, the employer must ensure that:

■ The area is designated a Hearing Protection Zone.

■ The area is demarcated and identified by means of the sign specified for the purpose of indicating "ear protection must be worn" (to be consistent with the Health and Safety (Safety Signs and Signals) Regulations 1996).

■ The sign must be accompanied by text that indicates that the area is a Hearing Protection Zone and that employees must wear personal hearing protectors while in that area.

■ Access to the area is restricted, where this is technically feasible and the risk of exposure justifies it, and must make every effort to ensure that no employee enters that area unless they are wearing personal hearing protectors.

MAINTENANCE

There is a duty on the employer to maintain controls introduced to protect employees. This will include maintenance of acoustic enclosures and the maintenance of machinery (as required under the Provision and Use of Work Equipment Regulations 1998) to control noise at source.

HEALTH SURVEILLANCE

Under the CNWR 2005, employees who are regularly exposed to noise levels of 85 dB(A) or higher must be subject to health surveillance, including audiometric testing. This constitutes a big change from the previous Regulations that only required an employer to carry out health surveillance where the employee was subject to noise levels of 95 dB(A) or higher. Where exposure is between 80 dB and 85 dB, or where employees are only occasionally exposed above the upper exposure action values, health surveillance will only be required if information comes to light that an individual may be particularly sensitive to noise induced hearing loss.

Control of Substances Hazardous to Health Regulations (COSHH) 2002

Law considered in context/more depth in Elements 1 and 3.

Amendments to COSHH 2002 were made by the Control of Substances Hazardous to Health (Amendment) Regulations 2004. The main change being that MELs and OESs were replaced by workplace exposure limits (WELs).

Outline of main points

REGULATIONS

Reg. 2   *Interpretation*

"Substance hazardous to health" includes:

1) Substances which under The Chemicals (Hazard Information and Packaging) Regulations (CHIP 4) 2009 are in categories of very toxic, toxic, harmful, corrosive or irritant.

2) A substance listed in Schedule 1 to the Regulations or for which the HSE (*formerly HSC*) have approved a maximum exposure limit or an occupational exposure standard.

3) A biological agent.

4) Dust in a concentration in air equal to or greater than:

■ 10 mg/m3 inhalable dust as an 8hr time weighted average (TWA).

■ 4 mg/m3 respirable dust as an 8hr TWA.

5) Any other substance which creates a health hazard comparable with the hazards of the substances in the other categories above.

Reg. 3   *Duties*

Are on employer to protect:

■ Employees.

Any other person who may be affected, except:

■ Duties for health surveillance do not extend to non-employees.

■ Duties to give information may extend to non-employees if they work on the premises.

Reg. 4   *Prohibitions on substances*

Certain substances are prohibited from being used in some applications. These are detailed in Schedule 2.

Reg. 5   *Application of regulations 6-13*

Regulations 6-13 are made to protect a person's health from risks arising from exposure. They do not apply if:

The following Regulations already apply:

■ The Control of Lead at Work Regulations (CLAW) 2002.

■ The Control of Asbestos Regulations (CAR) 2005.

The hazard arises from one of the following properties of the substance:

■ Radioactivity, explosive, flammable, high or low temperature, high pressure.

■ Exposure is for medical treatment.

■ Exposure is in a mine.

Reg. 6   *Assessment*

Employers must not carry out work that will expose employees to substances hazardous to health unless they have assessed the risks to health and the steps that need to be taken to meet the requirements of the Regulations. The assessment must be reviewed if there are changes in the work and at least once every 5 years.

A suitable and sufficient assessment should include:

■ An assessment of the risks to health.

■ The practicability of preventing exposure.

■ Steps needed to achieve adequate control.

An assessment of the risks should involve:

■ Types of substance including biological agents.

■ Where the substances are present and in what form.

■ Effects on the body.

■ The people that might be affected.

■ Existing control measures.

Reg. 7   *Control of exposure*

1) Employer shall ensure that the exposure of employees to substances hazardous to health is either prevented or, where this is not reasonably practicable, adequately controlled.

2) So far as is reasonably practicable (1) above except to a carcinogen or biological agent shall be by measures other than personal protective equipment (PPE).

3) Where not reasonably practicable to prevent exposure to a carcinogen by using an alternative substance or process, the following measure shall apply:

- Total enclosure of process.
- Use of plant, process and systems which minimise generation of, or suppress and contain, spills, leaks, dust, fumes and vapours of carcinogens.
- Limitation of quantities of a carcinogen at work.
- Keeping of numbers exposed to a minimum.
- Prohibition of eating, drinking and smoking in areas liable to contamination.
- Provision of hygiene measures including adequate washing facilities and regular cleaning of walls and surfaces.
- Designation of areas/installations liable to contamination and use of suitable and sufficient warning signs.
- Safe storage, handling and disposal of carcinogens and use of closed and clearly-labelled containers.

4) If adequate control is not achieved, then employer shall provide suitable PPE to employees in addition to taking control measures.

5) PPE provided shall comply with The Personal Protective Equipment at Work Regulations (PPER), 2002 (dealing with the supply of PPE).

6&7) For substances which have a maximum exposure limit (MEL), control of that substance shall, so far as inhalation is concerned, only be treated if the level of exposure is reduced as far as is reasonably practicable and in any case below the MEL.

Where a substance has an occupational exposure standard (OES), control of that substance shall, so far as inhalation is concerned, only be treated as adequate if the OES is not exceeded or if it is, steps are taken to remedy the situation as soon as reasonably practicable.

8) Respiratory protection must be suitable and of a type or conforming to a standard approved by the HSE.

9) In the event of failure of a control measure which may result in the escape of carcinogens, the employer shall ensure:

Only those who are responsible for repair and maintenance work are permitted in the affected area and are provided with PPE.

Employees and other persons who may be affected are informed of the failure forthwith.

Reg. 8 Employer shall take all reasonable steps to ensure control measures; PPE, etc. are properly used/applied.

Employee shall make full and proper use of control measures, PPE etc. and shall report defects to employer.

Reg. 9 *Maintenance of control measures*

Employer providing control measures to comply with Reg.7 shall ensure that it is maintained in an efficient state, in efficient working order and in good repair and in the case of PPE in a clean condition, properly stored in a well-defined place checked at suitable intervals and when discovered to be defective repaired or replaced before further use.

- Contaminated PPE should be kept apart and cleaned, decontaminated or, if necessary destroyed.
- Engineering controls - employer shall ensure thorough examination and tests.
- Local exhaust ventilation (LEV) - Once every 14 months unless process specified in Schedule 4.
- Others - At suitable intervals.
- Respiratory protective equipment - employer shall ensure thorough examination and tests at suitable intervals.
- Records of all examinations, tests and repairs kept for 5 years.

Reg. 10 *Monitoring exposure*

Employer shall ensure exposure is monitored if:

- Needed to ensure maintenance of adequate control.
- Otherwise needed to protect health of employees.
- Substance/process specified in Schedule 5.

Records kept if:

- There is an identified exposure of identifiable employee - 40 years.
- Otherwise - 5 years.

Reg. 11 *Health surveillance*

1) Where appropriate for protection of health of employees exposed or liable to be exposed, employer shall ensure suitable health surveillance.
2) Health surveillance is appropriate if:
- Employee exposed to substance/process specified in Schedule 6.
- Exposure to substance is such that an identifiable disease or adverse health effect can result, there is a reasonable likelihood of it occurring and a valid technique exists for detecting the indications of the disease or effect.
3) Health records kept for at least 40 years.
4) If employer ceases business, HSE notified and health records offered to HSE.
5) If employee exposed to substance specified in Schedule 6, then health surveillance shall include medical surveillance, under Employment Medical Adviser (EMA) at 12 monthly intervals - or more frequently if specified by EMA.
6) EMA can forbid employee to work in process, or specify certain conditions for him to be employed in a process.
7) EMA can specify that health surveillance is to continue after exposure has ceased. Employer must ensure.
8) Employees to have access to their own health record.
9) Employee must attend for health/medical surveillance and give information to EMA.
10) EMA entitled to inspect workplace.

11) Where EMA suspends employee from work exposing him to substances hazardous to health, employer of employee can apply to HSE in writing within 28 days for that decision to be reviewed.

Reg. 12   Information etc

Employer shall provide suitable and sufficient information, instruction and training for him to know:

- Risks to health.
- Precautions to be taken.

This should include information on:

- Results of monitoring of exposure at workplace.
- Results of collective health surveillance.

If the substances have been assigned a maximum exposure limit, then the employee/Safety Representative must be notified forthwith if the MEL has been exceeded.

Reg. 13   Arrangements to deal with accidents, incidents and emergencies

To protect the health of employees from accidents, incidents and emergencies, the employer shall ensure that:

- Procedures are in place for first aid and safety drills (tested regularly).
- Information on emergency arrangements is available.
- Warning, communication systems, remedial action and rescue actions are available.
- Information made available to emergency services: external and internal.
- Steps taken to mitigate effects, restore situation to normal and inform employees.
- Only essential persons allowed in area.

These duties do not apply where the risks to health are slight or measures in place Reg 7(1) are sufficient to control the risk. The employee must report any accident or incident which has or may have resulted in the release of a biological agent which could cause severe human disease.

Note: The main impact of the latest version of the COSHH Regulations concerned the control of substances that cause occupational asthma.

APPENDIX 3 CONTROL OF SUBSTANCES THAT CAUSE OCCUPATIONAL ASTHMA

This relates certain regulations specifically to substances with the potential to cause asthma.

- Regulation 6 - assessment of risk to health created by work involving substances hazardous to health, (i.e. substances that may cause asthma).
- Regulation 7 - prevention or control of exposure to substances hazardous to health, (i.e. substances that may cause occupational asthma).
- Regulation 11 - health surveillance, (for employees who are or may be exposed to substances that may cause occupational asthma).
- Regulation 12 - information, instruction and training for persons who may be exposed to substances hazardous to health, to include: typical symptoms of asthma, substances that may cause it, the permanency of asthma and what happens with subsequent exposures, the need to report symptoms immediately and the reporting procedures.

Training should be given, including induction training before they start the job.

SCHEDULE 3 ADDITIONAL PROVISIONS RELATING TO WORK WITH BIOLOGICAL AGENTS

Regulation 7(10)

Part I Provision of general application to biological agents.

1   Interpretation

2   Classification of biological agents

The HSC shall approve and publish a "Categorisation of Biological Agents according to hazard and categories of containment" which may be revised or re-issued. Where no approved classification exists, the employer shall assign the agent to one of four groups according to the level of risk of infection.

Group 1 - unlikely to cause human disease.

Group 2 - can cause human disease.

Group 3 - can cause severe disease and spread to community.

Group 4 - can cause severe disease, spread to community and there is no effective treatment.

3   Special control measures for laboratories, animal rooms and industrial processes

Every employer engaged in research, development, teaching or diagnostic work involving Group 2, 3 or 4 biological agents; keeping or handling laboratory animals deliberately or naturally infected with those agents, or industrial processes involving those agents, shall control them with the most suitable containment.

4   List of employees exposed to certain biological agents

The employer shall keep a list of employees exposed to Group 3 or 4 biological agents for at least 10 years. If there is a long latency period then the list should be kept for 40 years.

5   Notification of the use of biological agents

Employers shall inform the HSE at least 20 days in advance of first time use or storage of Group 2, 3 or 4 biological hazards. Consequent substantial changes in procedure or process shall also be reported.

6   Notification of the consignment of biological agents

The HSE must be informed 30 days before certain biological agents are consigned.

Part II Containment measures for health and veterinary care facilities, laboratories and animal rooms.

Part III Containment measures for industrial processes.

Part IV Biohazard sign.

The biohazard sign required by regulation 7(6) (a) shall be in the form shown.

Part V Biological agents whose use is to be notified in accordance with paragraph 5(2) of Part I of this Schedule.

■ Any Group 3 or 4 agent.
■ Certain named Group 2 agents.

Figure RSP-1: Biohazard sign. *Source: COSHH 2002.*

Control of Substances Hazardous to Health (Amendment) Regulations 2004

See also - COSHH 2002 and CLAW 2002.

These Regulations make minor amendments to the Control of Substances Hazardous to Health Regulations (COSHH) 2002.

Outline of main points

The main change is that maximum exposure limits (MELs) and occupational exposure standards (OESs) were replaced by workplace exposure limits (WELs).

Control of Vibration at Work Regulations (CVWR) 2005

Law considered in context/more depth in Element 3.

Hand-arm vibration (HAV) and whole body vibration (WBV) are caused by the use of work equipment and work processes that transmit vibration into the hands, arms and bodies of employees in many industries and occupations. Long-term, regular exposure to vibration is known to lead to permanent and debilitating health effects such as vibration white finger, loss of sensation, pain, and numbness in the hands, arms, spine and joints.

These effects are collectively known as hand-arm or whole body vibration syndrome. CVWR 2005 introduced controls that aim substantially to reduce ill-health caused by exposure to vibration.

Outline of main points

Regulation 4 states the personal daily exposure limits and daily exposure action values normalised over an 8-hour reference period.

	Daily exposure limits	Daily exposure action values
Hand arm vibration	5 m/s^2	2.5 m/s^2
Whole body vibration	1.15 m/s^2	0.5 m/s^2

Regulation 5 requires the employer to make a suitable and sufficient assessment of the risk created by work that is liable to expose employees to risk from vibration. The assessment must observe work practices, make reference to information regarding the magnitude of vibration from equipment and if necessary measurement of the magnitude of the vibration.

Consideration must also be given to the type, duration, effects of exposure, exposures limit / action values, effects on employees at particular risk, the effects of vibration on equipment and the ability to use it, manufacturers' information, availability of replacement equipment, and extension of exposure at the workplace (e.g. rest facilities), temperature and information on health surveillance. The risk assessment should be recorded as soon as is practicable after the risk assessment is made and reviewed regularly.

Regulation 6 states that the employer must seek to eliminate the risk of vibration at source or, if not reasonably practicable, reduce it to a minimum. Where the personal daily exposure limit is exceeded the employer must reduce exposure by implementing a programme of organisational and technical measures. Measures include the use of other methods of work, ergonomics, maintenance of equipment, design and layout, information, instruction and training, limitation by schedules and breaks and the provision of personal protective equipment.

Regulation 7 states that health surveillance must be carried out if there is a risk to the health of employees liable to be exposed to vibration. This is in order to diagnose any health effect linked with exposure to vibration. A record of health shall be kept of any employee who undergoes health surveillance. If health surveillance identifies a disease or adverse health effect, considered by a doctor to be a result of exposure to vibration, the employer shall ensure that a qualified person informs the employee and provides information and advice. In addition, the employer must also review risk assessments and the health of any other employee who has been similarly exposed and consider alternative work.

Regulation 8 states that employers must provide information, instruction and training to all employees who are exposed to risk from vibration. This includes any organisational and technical measures taken, exposure limits and values, risk assessment findings, why and how to detect injury, health surveillance entitlement and safe working practices. The requirement for information, instruction and training extends to persons whether or not an employee, but who carries out work in connection with the employers duties.

Data Protection Act (DPA) 1998

The Data Protection Act (DPA) 1998 came into force early in 1999 and defines the ways in which information about living people may be legally used and handled. The main intent is to protect individuals against misuse or abuse of information about them.

Outline of main points

The DPA 1998 contains eight 'data protection principles', which specify that personal data must:

- Be processed fairly and lawfully.
- Be obtained only for lawful purposes and not processed in any manner incompatible with those purposes.
- Be adequate, relevant and not excessive.
- Be accurate and current.
- Not be retained for longer than necessary.
- Be processed in accordance with the rights and freedoms of data subjects.
- Be protected against unauthorised or unlawful processing and against accidental loss, destruction or damage.
- Not be transferred to a country or territory outside the European Economic Area unless that country or territory protects the rights and freedoms of the data subjects.

Employment Act (EMA) 2002

Law considered in context in Elements 3 and 5.

Outline of main points

The Employment Act, which reached the UK statute book in July 2002, introduced new provisions concerning 'family-friendly' working, the resolution of individual disputes at the workplace, equal treatment for fixed-term employees and other matters. The Employment Act (EMA) 2002 is a major piece of legislation. Its main themes are the enhancement of statutory rights designed to help parents balance work and family commitments and the reform of employment tribunal procedures and workplace dispute resolution mechanisms in response to the rising number and cost of employment tribunal claims in recent years. It also includes provisions on a range of other issues, including equal treatment for fixed-term employees and time off for trade union learning representatives. Most of the provisions of EMA 2002 came into force in April 2003. The following changes were made under the Act:

- Employees on fixed-term contracts must be treated as favourably as permanent workers - this came into effect on 1st October 2002. (See Fixed-Term Employees (Prevention of Less Favourable Treatment) Regulations 2002).
- All employers, regardless of size, must operate a minimum standard compulsory disciplinary and grievance procedure. This came into force on 1st October 2004.
- An increase in statutory maternity leave to six months paid leave and a further six months unpaid leave. This came into force on 6th April 2003.
- Introduction of leave for adoptive parents of six months paid leave following the adoption of a child and a further six months unpaid leave. This came into force 6th April 2003.
- Introduction of two weeks paid paternity leave for working fathers. This is at the same rate as maternity pay. This came into force on 6th April 2003.
- Requests by working parents of young or disabled children to work flexibly must be considered by their employers. This came into force on 6th April 2003.
- Reimbursement by the government of maternity, paternity and adoptive payments made by employers. Small employers can reclaim 100% reimbursement.
- Establishment of union learning representatives with a right to paid time off work.
- A questionnaire procedure in Equal Pay cases in employment tribunals. This is intended to provide comparable information to be used in the process of disclosure and gives access to details of other employee's pay rates. This came into force on 6th April 2003.

Employment Act (EMA) 2008

Law considered in context in Element 3.

Outline of main points

The Employment Act 2008 strengthens, simplifies and clarifies important aspects of UK employment law. The EMA 2008 represents a significant change in disciplinary and grievance procedures - procedures of companies are now guided by a code of practice and the principles of fairness and transparency. Although a failure to follow the code is not illegal, employment tribunals are required to take it into account when considering cases. In addition, the principles in the code should be considered when looking at redundancies or dismissals, as unfair dismissal falls within the jurisdiction of the code.

The main features of the ***Employment Act (EMA) 2008*** are that it:

- Repeals the existing statutory procedures for dealing with discipline, dismissal and grievance issues, as set out in the Employment Act 2002.
- Removes the regime which rendered dismissal of an employee automatically unfair where the employer did not follow the prescribed statutory disciplinary and dismissal procedures.
- Permits employment tribunals to increase or reduce awards by up to 25% if an employer or employee unreasonably fails to act in accordance with a relevant ACAS Code of Practice.

Other provisions of the 2008 Act include:

- Abolition of the set timescale for ACAS conciliation.
- Provision for tribunals to deal with certain claims and issues without a hearing - these include determining the compensation to be awarded when the employer has admitted liability for unfair dismissal.
- Sections dealing with new rules on the national minimum wage, changes to trade union law and provisions applying to employment agencies.

Employment Equality (Repeals of Retirement Age Provisions) Regulations (EERAR) 2011

Law considered in context in Element 1, 2 and 7.

Outline of main points

The Employment Equality (Repeals of Retirement Age Provisions) Regulations (EERAR) 2011 removes the general right of the employer to operate a compulsory retirement age, unless it can be objectively justified. Men and women can now work past the age when the state pension is normally paid.

Employment Rights Act (ERA) 1996

Law considered in context in Element 3.

Outline of main points

The Employment Rights Act 1996 deals with rights that most employees can get when they work, including unfair dismissal, reasonable notice before dismissal, time off rights for parenting, redundancy and more. It was amended substantially by the Labour government since 1997, to include the right to request flexible working time.

EMPLOYMENT PROTECTION

All employees are protected by the Employment Rights Act 1996, as amended, against suffering any harm because of any reasonable actions they take on health and safety grounds. This applies regardless of their length of service.

NEW AND EXPECTANT MOTHERS

The Employment Rights Act requires employers, when offering suitable alternative, to ensure that the work is:

- Suitable and appropriate for her to do in the circumstances.
- On terms and conditions no less favourable than her normal terms and conditions.

TIME OFF WORK

The Employment Rights Act 1996 also covers the time off from work to which an employee is entitled. One such entitlement is maternity leave. An employee cannot be dismissed for taking maternity leave.

If an employer were to do so, they would be guilty of pregnancy discrimination. Other provisions related to time off include those concerning training, public duties and medical problems.

DISMISSAL AND REDUNDANCY

Two major topics covered by the Employment Rights Act 1996 are dismissal and redundancy. The Act makes unfair dismissal illegal. Unfair dismissal occurs when an employer terminates an employee without a legitimate and lawful reason for doing so. It is also the Employment Rights Act 1996 that provides for a redundancy payment.

EMPLOYMENT TRIBUNAL

The process by which disputes related to a violation of your employment rights are resolved is outlined within the Employment Rights Act 1996. It provides aggrieved employees with the right to take their case before an Employment Tribunal. The cases which entitle you to make an application to an Employment Tribunal are outlined on what is known as a "jurisdiction list." A jurisdiction list can be obtained from the local tribunal office.

Equality Act (EA) 2010

Law considered in context in Element 1, 2, 4, 5 and 6.

Arrangement of relevant Parts, Chapters and Sections of the Act

Chapters

1) Protected characteristics.

2) Prohibited conduct.

Discrimination.

Adjustments for disabled.

Discrimination: supplementary.

Outline of main points

PART 2 EQUALITY: KEY CONCEPTS

Chapter 1 Protected Characteristics

Section 4 the following characteristics are protected characteristics:

- Age.
- Disability.
- Gender reassignment.
- Marriage and civil partnership.
- Pregnancy and maternity.
- Race.
- Religion or belief.
- Sex.
- Sexual orientation.

Section 5 Age

(1) In relation to the protected characteristic of age:

(a) A reference to a person who has a particular protected characteristic is a reference to a person of a particular age group;

(b) A reference to persons who share a protected characteristic is a reference to persons of the same age group.

(2) A reference to an age group is a reference to a group of persons defined by reference to age, whether by reference to a particular age or to a range of ages.

Section 6 Disability

(1) A person (P) has a disability if:

(a) P has a physical or mental impairment, and

(b) The impairment has a substantial and long-term adverse effect on P's ability to carry out normal day-to-day activities.

(2) A reference to a disabled person is a reference to a person who has a disability.

(3) In relation to the protected characteristic of disability:

(a) A reference to a person who has a particular protected characteristic is a reference to a person who has a particular disability;

(b) A reference to persons who share a protected characteristic is a reference to persons who have the same disability.

(4) This Act (except Part 12 and section 190) applies in relation to a person who has had a disability as it applies in relation to a person who has the disability; accordingly (except in that Part and that section).

(a) A reference (however expressed) to a person who has a disability includes a reference to a person who has had the disability, and

(b) A reference (however expressed) to a person who does not have a disability includes a reference to a person who has not had the disability.

(5) A Minister of the Crown may issue guidance about matters to be taken into account in deciding any question for the purposes of subsection (1).

(6) Schedule 1 (disability: supplementary provision) has effect.

Section 9 Race

(1) Race includes:

(a) Colour;

(b) Nationality;

(c) Ethnic or national origins.

(2) In relation to the protected characteristic of race:

(a) A reference to a person who has a particular protected characteristic is a reference to a person of a particular racial group;

(b) A reference to persons who share a protected characteristic is a reference to persons of the same racial group.

(3) A racial group is a group of persons defined by reference to race; and a reference to a person's racial group is a reference to a racial group into which the person falls.

(4) The fact that a racial group comprises two or more distinct racial groups does not prevent it from constituting a particular racial group.

(5) A Minister of the Crown may by order:

(a) Amend this section so as to provide for caste to be an aspect of race;

(b) Amend this Act so as to provide for an exception to a provision of this Act to apply, or not to apply, to caste or to apply, or not to apply, to caste in specified circumstances.

(6) The power under section 207(4)(b), in its application to subsection (5), includes power to amend this Act.

Section 11 Sex

In relation to the protected characteristic of sex:

(a) A reference to a person who has a particular protected characteristic is a reference to a man or to a woman;

(b) A reference to persons who share a protected characteristic is a reference to persons of the same sex.

PART 2: PROHIBITED CONDUCT

Section 13 Direct discrimination

(1) A person (A) discriminates against another (B) if, because of a protected characteristic, A treats B less favourably than A treats or would treat others.

(2) If the protected characteristic is age, A does not discriminate against B if A can show A's treatment of B to be a proportionate means of achieving a legitimate aim.

(3) If the protected characteristic is disability, and B is not a disabled person, A does not discriminate against B only because A treats or would treat disabled persons more favourably than A treats B.

(4) If the protected characteristic is marriage and civil partnership, this section applies to a contravention of Part 5 (work) only if the treatment is because it is B who is married or a civil partner.

(5) If the protected characteristic is race, less favourable treatment includes segregating B from others.

(6) If the protected characteristic is sex:

(a) Less favourable treatment of a woman includes less favourable treatment of her because she is breast-feeding;

(b) In a case where B is a man, no account is to be taken of special treatment afforded to a woman in connection with pregnancy or childbirth.

(7) Subsection (6)(a) does not apply for the purposes of Part 5 (work).

(8) This section is subject to sections 17(6) and 18(7).

Section 15 Discrimination arising from disability

(1) A person (A) discriminates against a disabled person (B) if:

(a) A treats B unfavourably because of something arising in consequence of B's disability, and

(b) A cannot show that the treatment is a proportionate means of achieving a legitimate aim.

(2) Subsection (1) does not apply if A shows that A did not know, and could not reasonably have been expected to know, that B had the disability.

Section 19 Indirect discrimination

(1) A person (A) discriminates against another (B) if A applies to B a provision, criterion or practice which is discriminatory in relation to a relevant protected characteristic of B's.

(2) For the purposes of subsection (1), a provision, criterion or practice is discriminatory in relation to a relevant protected characteristic of B's if:

(a) A applies, or would apply, it to persons with whom B does not share the characteristic,

(b) It puts, or would put, persons with whom B shares the characteristic at a particular disadvantage when compared with persons with whom B does not share it,

(c) It puts, or would put, B at that disadvantage, and

(d) A cannot show it to be a proportionate means of achieving a legitimate aim.

Section 20 Duty to make adjustments

(1) Where this Act imposes a duty to make reasonable adjustments on a person, this section, sections 21 and 22 and the applicable Schedule apply; and for those purposes, a person on whom the duty is imposed is referred to as A.

(2) The duty comprises the following three requirements.

(3) The first requirement is a requirement, where a provision, criterion or practice of A's puts a disabled person at a substantial disadvantage in relation to a relevant matter in comparison with persons who are not disabled, to take such steps as it is reasonable to have to take to avoid the disadvantage.

(4) The second requirement is a requirement, where a physical feature puts a disabled person at a substantial disadvantage in relation to a relevant matter in comparison with persons who are not disabled, to take such steps as it is reasonable to have to take to avoid the disadvantage.

(5) The third requirement is a requirement, where a disabled person would, but for the provision of an auxiliary aid, be put at a substantial disadvantage in relation to a relevant matter in comparison with persons who are not disabled, to take such steps as it is reasonable to have to take to provide the auxiliary aid.

(6) Where the first or third requirement relates to the provision of information, the steps which it is reasonable for A to have to take include steps for ensuring that in the circumstances concerned the information is provided in an accessible format.

(7) A person (A) who is subject to a duty to make reasonable adjustments is not (subject to express provision to the contrary) entitled to require a disabled person, in relation to whom A is required to comply with the duty, to pay to any extent A's costs of complying with the duty.

(8) A reference in section 21 or 22 or an applicable Schedule to the first, second or third requirement is to be construed in accordance with this section.

(9) In relation to the second requirement, a reference in this section or an applicable Schedule to avoiding a substantial disadvantage includes a reference to:

(a) Removing the physical feature in question,

(b) Altering it, or

(c) Providing a reasonable means of avoiding it.

(10) A reference in this section, section 21 or 22 or an applicable Schedule (apart from paragraphs 2 to 4 of Schedule 4) to a physical feature is a reference to:

(a) A feature arising from the design or construction of a building,

(b) A feature of an approach to, exit from or access to a building,

(c) A fixture or fitting, or furniture, furnishings, materials, equipment or other chattels, in or on premises, or

(d) Any other physical element or quality.

(11) A reference in this section, section 21 or 22 or an applicable Schedule to an auxiliary aid includes a reference to an auxiliary service.

(12) A reference in this section or an applicable Schedule to chattels is to be read, in relation to Scotland, as a reference to moveable property.

(13) The applicable Schedule is, in relation to the Part of this Act specified in the first column of the Table, the Schedule specified in the second column.

Section 26 Harassment

(1) A person (A) harasses another (B) if:

(a) A engages in unwanted conduct related to a relevant protected characteristic, and

(b) The conduct has the purpose or effect of:

(i) Violating B's dignity, or

(ii) Creating an intimidating, hostile, degrading, humiliating or offensive environment for B.

(2) A also harasses B if:

(a) A engages in unwanted conduct of a sexual nature, and

(b) The conduct has the purpose or effect referred to in subsection (1)(b).

(3) A also harasses B if:

(a) A or another person engages in unwanted conduct of a sexual nature or that is related to gender reassignment or sex,

(b) The conduct has the purpose or effect referred to in subsection (1)(b), and

(c) Because of B's rejection of or submission to the conduct, A treats B less favourably than A would treat B if B had not rejected or submitted to the conduct.

(4) In deciding whether conduct has the effect referred to in subsection (1)(b), each of the following must be taken into account -

(a) The perception of B;

(b) The deriving from these hazards and the health and safety policy of their employer and the organisation and arrangements for fulfilling that policy. other circumstances of the case;

(c) Whether it is reasonable for the conduct to have that effect.

Section 27 Victimisation

(1) A person (A) victimises another person (B) if A subjects B to a detriment because:

(a) B does a protected act, or

(b) A believes that B has done, or may do, a protected act.

(2) Each of the following is a protected act:

(a) Bringing proceedings under this Act;

(b) Giving evidence or information in connection with proceedings under this Act;

(c) Doing any other thing for the purposes of or in connection with this Act;

(d) Making an allegation (whether or not express) that A or another person has contravened this Act.

(3) Giving false evidence or information, or making a false allegation, is not a protected act if the evidence or information is given, or the allegation is made, in bad faith.

(4) This section applies only where the person subjected to a detriment is an individual.

(5) The reference to contravening this Act includes a reference to committing a breach of an equality clause or rule.

Health and Safety (Display Screen Equipment) Regulations (DSE) 1992 (as amended)

Law considered in context/more depth in Elements 6.

Outline of main points

- Every employer must carry out suitable and sufficient analysis of workstations.
- Employers must ensure that equipment provided meets the requirements of the schedule laid down in these Regulations.
- Employers must plan activities and provide such breaks or changes in work activity to reduce employees' workload on that equipment.
- For display screen equipment (DSE) users, the employer must provide, on request, an eyesight test carried out by a competent person.
- Provision of information and training.

WORKSTATION ASSESSMENTS (REGULATION 2)

Should take account of:

Screen	-	positioning, character definition, character stability etc.
Keyboard	-	tilt able, character legibility etc.
Desk	-	size, matt surface etc.
Chair	-	adjustable back and height, footrest available etc.
Environment	-	noise, lighting, space etc.
Software	-	easy to use, work rate not governed by software.

INFORMATION AND TRAINING (REGULATIONS 6 & 7)

Should include:

- Risks to health.
- Precautions in place (for example the need for regular breaks).
- How to recognise problems.
- How to report problems.

Health and Safety at Work Act (HASAWA) 1974

Law considered in context/more depth in Elements 1, 2, 5 and 8.

HASWA 1974 was amended by Article 2 of the Legislative Reform (Health and Safety Executive) Order (LRHSEO)2008. LRHSEO 2008 abolishes the Health and Safety Commission and Executive. Article 4 establishes the new Health and Safety Executive and amends reference to the Commission in HASWA 1974 to "the Executive".

Outline of main points

OVERALL AIMS OF THE ACT

1) To protect people.
2) To protect the public from risks which may arise from work activities.

THE MAIN PROVISIONS - SECTION 1

a) Securing the health, safety and welfare of people at work.
b) Protecting others against risks arising from workplace activities.
c) Controlling the obtaining, keeping, and use of explosive and highly flammable substances.
d) Controlling emissions into the atmosphere of noxious or offensive substances (Repealed).

Duties are imposed on:

a) The employer.
b) The self-employed.
c) Employees.
d) Contractors and subcontractors.
e) Designers, manufacturers, suppliers, importers and installers.
f) Specialists - architects, surveyors, engineers, personnel managers, health and safety practitioners, and many more.

EMPLOYER'S DUTIES - [TO EMPLOYEES]

Section 2(1)

To ensure, so far as **reasonably practicable**, the health, safety and welfare at work of employees.

Section 2(2)

Ensuring health, safety and welfare at work through:

- Safe plant and systems of work e.g. provision of guards on machines.
- Safe use, handling, storage and transport of goods and materials e.g. good manual handling of boxes.
- Provision of information, instruction, training and supervision e.g. provision of induction training.
- Safe place of work including means of access and egress e.g. aisles kept clear.
- Safe and healthy working environment e.g. good lighting.

Further duties are placed on the employer by:

Section 2(3)

Prepare and keep up to date a written safety policy supported by information on the organisation and arrangements for carrying out the policy. The safety policy has to be brought to the notice of employees. If there are fewer than five employees, this section does not apply.

Section 2(4)

Recognised Trade Unions have the right to appoint safety representatives to represent the employees in consultations with the employer about health and safety matters.

Section 2(6)

Employers must consult with any safety representatives appointed by recognised Trade Unions.

Section 2(7)

To establish a safety committee if requested by two or more safety representatives.

EMPLOYER'S DUTIES - [TO PERSONS NOT HIS EMPLOYEES]

Section 3

a) Not to expose them to risk to their heath and safety e.g. contractor work barriered off.
b) To give information about risks which may affect them e.g. location induction for contractors.

SELF EMPLOYED DUTIES

Section 3

a) Not to expose themselves to risks to their health and safety e.g. wear personal protection.
b) Not to expose other persons to risks to their health and safety e.g. keep shared work area tidy.

Some of the practical steps that an organisation might take in order to ensure the safety of visitors to its premises are:

- Identify visitors by signing in, badges etc.
- Provide information regarding the risks present and the site rules and procedures to be followed, particularly in emergencies.
- Provide escorts to supervise visitors throughout the site.
- Restrict access to certain areas.

CONTROL OF PREMISES

Section 4

This section places duties on anyone who has control to any extent of non-domestic premises used by people who are not their employees. The duty extends to the provision of safe premises, plant and substances, e.g. maintenance of a boiler in rented out property.

MANUFACTURERS, DESIGNERS, SUPPLIERS, IMPORTERS, INSTALLERS

Section 6

This section places specific duties on those who can ensure that articles and substances are as safe and without risks as is reasonably practicable. The section covers:

- Safe design, installation and testing of equipment (including fairground equipment).
- Safe substances tested for risks.
- Provision of information on safe use and conditions essential to health and safety.
- Research to minimise risks.

EMPLOYEES' DUTIES

Section 7

a) To take reasonable care for themselves and others that may be affected by their acts/omissions e.g. wear eye protection, not obstructs a fire exit.

b) To co-operate with the employer or other to enable them to carry out their duty and/or statutory requirements e.g. report hazards or defects in controls, attend training, provide medical samples.

Additional duties created by the Management of Health and Safety at Work Regulations 1999 employees' duties:

- Every employee shall use any equipment, material or substance provided to them in accordance with any training and instruction.
- Every employee shall inform (via supervisory staff) their employer of any (a) risk situation or (b) shortcoming in the employer's protection arrangements.

OTHER DUTIES

Section 8

No person to interfere with or misuse anything provided to secure health and safety - e.g. wedge fire door open, remove first aid equipment without authority, breach lock off systems.

Section 9

Employees cannot be charged for anything done or provided to comply with a specific legal obligation e.g. personal protective equipment, health surveillance or welfare facilities.

THE EMPLOYMENT MEDICAL ADVISORY SERVICE

Section 50

The HSE operates the Employment Medical Advisory Service (EMAS), which assists in the investigation of work-related ill-health.

Through the HSE Info Line, EMAS also offers advice on general enquiries regarding fitness for work, medical aspects of employment, health in the workplace, and general and specific complaints of ill-health attributable to work. EMAS' main function is to assist in the investigation of ill-health attributable to work, and help to bring enforcement, action or prosecution of employers, if appropriate.

Health and Safety (Miscellaneous Amendments) Regulations (MAR) 2002

See also - MHOR 1992 and WHSWR 1992.

MAR 2002 made minor amendments to UK law to come into line with the requirements of the original Directives and came into force on 17th September 2002. The Regulations related to health and well-being that are affected by the amendments are detailed below.

Outline of main points

REGULATION 3 - AMENDMENT OF THE HEALTH AND SAFETY (FIRST AID) REGULATIONS 1981

The Health and Safety (First Aid) Regulations 1981 are amended by adding the additional requirements that any first-aid room provided under requirements of these regulations must be easily accessible to stretchers and to any other equipment needed to convey patients to and from the room and that the room be sign-posted by use of a sign complying with the Health and Safety (Safety Signs and Signals) Regulations 1996.

REGULATION 3 - AMENDMENT OF THE HEALTH AND SAFETY (DISPLAY SCREEN EQUIPMENT) REGULATIONS 1992

The Health and Safety (Display Screen Equipment) Regulations 1992, Regulation 3 - Requirements of workstations, was amended to remove transitional arrangements relating to the introduction of the regulations and provide a simpler requirement for workstations, removing reference to who may use the workstation:

"3. Every employer shall ensure that any workstation which may be used for the purposes of his undertaking meets the requirements laid down in the Schedule to these Regulations, to the extent specified in paragraph 1 thereof".

The requirement "used for the purposes of his undertaking" includes workstations provided by the employer and others and to workstations provided by the employer to others (including members of the public) as part of the undertaking. The Health and Safety (Display Screen Equipment) Regulations 1992, Regulation 5 - Eyes and eyesight tests, was amended to clarify the requirement for eye and eyesight tests to ensure that those who may become employed as users are provide for and receive eye and eyesight tests before they become users.

The Health and Safety (Display Screen Equipment) Regulations 1992 Regulation 6 - Provision of training, was similarly amended with regard to health and safety training for those who may become employed as users, such that they receive training before they become a user.

REGULATION 4 - AMENDMENT OF THE MANUAL HANDLING OPERATIONS REGULATIONS 1992

Regulation 4 of the Manual Handling Operations Regulations 1992 were amended by adding the requirement to, when determining whether manual handling operations at work involve a risk of injury and the appropriate steps to reduce that risk, have regard to:

- Physical suitability of the employee to carry out the operations.
- Clothing, footwear or other personal effects they are wearing.
- Knowledge and training.
- Results of any relevant risk assessment conducted for the Management of Health and Safety at Work Regulations.
- Whether the employee is within a group of employees identified by that assessment as being especially at risk.
- Results of any health surveillance provided under the Management of Health and Safety Regulations.

REGULATION 5 - AMENDMENT OF THE PERSONAL PROTECTIVE EQUIPMENT AT WORK REGULATIONS 1992

The Personal Protective Equipment at Work Regulations 1992 were amended so that personal protective equipment (PPE) must also be suitable for the period for which it is worn and account is taken of the characteristics of the workstation of each person.

Provision of personal issue of PPE needs to take place in situations where it is necessary to ensure it is hygienic and free of risk to health.

Where an assessment of PPE is made this must consider whether it is compatible with other personal protective equipment that is in use and which an employee would be required to wear simultaneously.

The amendments require that information provided to satisfy regulation 9 for the provision of information, instruction and training must be kept available to employees. A new, additional duty is created requiring the employer, where appropriate, and at suitable intervals, to organise demonstrations in the wearing of PPE.

REGULATION 6 - AMENDMENT OF THE WORKPLACE (HEALTH, SAFETY AND WELFARE) REGULATIONS 1992

The Workplace (Health, Safety and Welfare) Regulations 1992 have been amended to improve clarity, include additional regulations and make provision for the disabled. An additional regulation (4A) sets out a requirement where a workplace is in a building, the building shall have stability and solidity appropriate to the nature of the use of the workplace. The range of things requiring maintenance under these regulations is extended to equipment and devices intended to prevent or reduce hazards. A new duty requires workplaces to be adequately thermally insulated where it is necessary, having regard to the type of work carried out and the physical activity of the persons carrying out the work. In addition, excessive effects of sunlight on temperature must be avoided.

The regulations were amended with regard to facilities for changing clothing in that the facilities need to be easily accessible, of sufficient capacity and provided with seating. Requirements were amended such that rest rooms and rest areas must include suitable arrangements to protect non-smokers from discomfort caused by tobacco smoke. They also must be equipped with an adequate number of tables and adequate seating with backs for the number of persons at work likely to use them at any one time and seating which is adequate for the number of disabled persons at work and suitable for them.

A new regulation (25A) was added requiring, where necessary, those parts of the workplace (including in particular doors, passageways, stairs, showers, washbasins, lavatories and workstations) used or occupied directly by disabled persons at work to be organised to take account of such persons.

Human Rights Act (HR) 2000

Law considered in context/more depth in Element 5.

Outline of main points

Human rights legislation exists to safeguard individual rights in the UK and expand individual awareness of the basic values and standards we share. Anyone in the UK for any reason has fundamental rights that government and public authorities are legally bound to respect. The first human rights legislation was drafted after World War II by the Council of Europe and is called the European Convention on Human Rights. The Convention came into force in 1953 to ensure the cruelties carried out during the war were never repeated.

The Convention is made up of a series of short Articles. Each Article is a short statement defining a right or freedom, together with any exceptions. These Rights affect matters of life and death, such as freedom from torture as well as rights that exist in everyday life. The Human Rights Act came into effect in the UK in October 2000. The Act enabled people in the UK to take human rights cases to court in the UK, whereas before they had to be taken to Strasbourg.

There are 16 basic rights in the Human Rights Act (HR) 2000, all taken from the European Convention on Human Rights. Public authorities have a duty to treat people in accordance with their Convention (law or standard) rights and must not breach the rights unless there is a legitimate reason. The main rights related to health and well-being are expressed in Articles 8 to 10 and 14.

ARTICLE 8: RIGHT TO RESPECT FOR PRIVATE AND FAMILY LIFE

This right states that everyone has a right to respect for their private and family life, their home and correspondence. People have the right to live their own life and have personal privacy.

ARTICLE 9: FREEDOM OF THOUGHT, CONSCIENCE AND RELIGION

This right protects people's rights in relation to their thoughts and beliefs. The state is not permitted to interfere with a person's right to hold a particular belief.

ARTICLE 10: FREEDOM OF EXPRESSION

This right states that everyone has the right to express their views and receive opinions with out interference from a public authority.

ARTICLE 14: PROHIBITION OF DISCRIMINATION

This right states that discrimination cannot occur on the grounds of particular attributes such as a person's sex, race, or religion. It also protects people from discrimination on the grounds of, for example, disability or marital status. A public authority should ensure policies and decisions do not involve any form of discrimination on any ground.

PROTOCOL 1, ARTICLE 1: PROTECTION OF PROPERTY

This article has three elements to it: a person has the right to a peaceful enjoyment of their property; a public authority cannot take away what someone owns and cannot impose restrictions on a person's use of their property. This article refers to possessions such as land, houses, leases and money.

PROTOCOL 1, ARTICLE 3: RIGHT TO FREE ELECTIONS

This right means that people are entitled to free elections, which must be held at reasonable intervals and conducted by secret ballot. A public authority must respect the rights of voting individuals and ensure elections are conducted freely and fairly.

A pubic authority must always be alert to policies or actions that might interfere with these rights. Any interference with someone's rights must be justified and pursue one of the legitimate aims, which vary according to the right and must be proportionate to that aim.

Management of Health and Safety at Work Regulations (MHSWR) 1999 (as amended)

Law considered in context/more depth in Elements 1, 2, 3, 5, and 8.

Outline of main points

Management of Health and Safety at Work Regulations (MHSWR) 1999 set out some broad general duties that apply to almost all kinds of work. They are aimed mainly at improving health and safety management. MHSWR 1999 was amended by the Management of Health and Safety at Work (Amendment) Regulations (MHSWR) 2006. The principal regulations of MHSWR 1999 (as amended) are discussed below.

RISK ASSESSMENT (REGULATION 3)

The regulations require employers (and the self-employed) to assess the risk to the health and safety of their employees and to anyone else who may be affected by their work activity. This is necessary to ensure that the preventive and protective steps can be identified to control hazards in the workplace. Where an employer is employing or about to employ young persons (under 18 years of age) he must carry out a risk assessment which takes particular account of:

- The inexperience, lack of awareness of risks and immaturity of young persons.
- The layout of the workplace and workstations.
- Exposure to physical, biological and chemical agents.
- Work equipment and the way in which it is handled.
- The extent of health and safety training to be provided.
- Risks from agents, processes and work listed in the Annex to Council Directive 94/33/EC on the protection of young people at work.

Where 5 or more employees are employed, the significant findings of risk assessments must be recorded in writing (the same threshold that is used in respect of having a written safety policy). This record must include details of any employees being identified as being especially at risk.

PRINCIPLES OF PREVENTION TO BE APPLIED (REGULATION 4)

Regulation 4 requires an employer to implement preventive and protective measures on the basis of general principles of prevention specified in Schedule 1 to the Regulations. These are:

1) Avoiding risks.
2) Evaluating the risks which cannot be avoided.
3) Combating the risks at source.
4) Adapting the work to the individual, especially as regards the design of workplaces, the choice of work equipment and the choice of working and production methods, with a view, in particular, to alleviating monotonous work and work at a predetermined work-rate and to reducing their effect on health.
5) Adapting to technical progress.
6) Replacing the dangerous by the non-dangerous or the less dangerous.
7) Developing a coherent overall prevention policy which covers technology, organisation of work, working conditions, social relationships and the influence of factors relating to the working environment.
8) Giving collective protective measures priority over individual protective measures.
9) Giving appropriate instructions to employees.

HEALTH AND SAFETY ARRANGEMENTS (REGULATION 5)

Appropriate arrangements must be made for the effective planning, organisation, control, monitoring and review of preventative and protective measures (in other words, for the management of health and safety).

Again, employers with five or more employees must have their arrangements in writing.

HEALTH SURVEILLANCE (REGULATION 6)

In addition to the requirements of other specific regulations, consideration must be given to carrying out health surveillance of employees, where there is a disease or adverse health condition identified in risk assessments.

HEALTH AND SAFETY ASSISTANCE (REGULATION 7)

The employer must appoint one or more competent persons to assist him in complying with the legal obligations imposed on the undertaking. The number of persons appointed should reflect the number of employees and the type of hazards in the workplace. If more than one competent person is appointed, then arrangements must be made for ensuring adequate co-operation between them.

The competent person(s) must be given the necessary time and resources to fulfil their functions. This will depend on the size the undertaking, the risks to which employees are exposed and the distribution of those risks throughout the undertaking.

The employer must ensure that competent person(s) who are not employees are informed of the factors known (or suspected) to affect the health and safety of anyone affected by business activities. Competent people are defined as those who have sufficient training and experience or knowledge and other qualities to enable them to perform their functions. Persons may be selected from among existing employees or from outside. Where there is a suitable person in the employer's employment, that person shall be appointed as the 'competent person' in preference to a non-employee.

PROCEDURES FOR SERIOUS AND IMMINENT DANGER AND FOR DANGER AREAS (REGULATION 8)

Employers are required to set up emergency procedures and appoint *competent persons* to ensure compliance with identified arrangements, to devise control strategies as appropriate and to limit access to areas of risk to ensure that only those persons with adequate health and safety knowledge and instruction are admitted. The factors to be considered when preparing a procedure to deal with workplace emergencies such as fire, explosion, bomb scare, chemical leakage or other dangerous occurrence should include:

- The identification and training requirements of persons with specific responsibilities.
- The layout of the premises in relation to escape routes etc.
- The number of persons affected.
- Assessment of special needs (disabled persons, children etc.).
- Warning systems.
- Emergency lighting.
- Location of shut-off valves, isolation switches, hydrants etc.
- Equipment required to deal with the emergency.
- Location of assembly points.
- Communication with emergency services.
- Training and/or information to be given to employees, visitors, local residents and anyone else who might be affected.

CONTACTS WITH EXTERNAL SERVICES (REGULATION 9)

Employers must ensure that, where necessary, contacts are made with external services. This particularly applies with regard to first-aid, emergency medical care and rescue work.

INFORMATION FOR EMPLOYEES (REGULATION 10)

Employees must be provided with relevant information about hazards to their health and safety arising from risks identified by the assessments. Clear instruction must be provided concerning any preventative or protective control measures including those relating to serious and imminent danger and fire assessments. Details of any competent persons nominated to discharge specific duties in accordance with the regulations must also be communicated as should risks arising from contact with other employer's activities (see Regulation 11).

Before employing a child (a person who is not over compulsory school age) the employer must provide those with parental responsibility for the child with information on the risks that have been identified and preventative and protective measures to be taken.

CO-OPERATION AND CO-ORDINATION (REGULATION 11)

Employers who work together in a common workplace have a duty to co-operate to discharge their duties under relevant statutory provisions. They must also take all reasonable steps to inform their respective employees of risks to their health or safety which may arise out of their work. Specific arrangements must be made to ensure compliance with fire legislation.

PERSONS WORKING IN HOST EMPLOYERS' OR SELF EMPLOYED PERSONS' UNDERTAKINGS (REGULATION 12)

This regulation extends the requirements of regulation 11 to include employees working as sole occupiers of a workplace under the control of another employer. Such employees would include those working under a service of contract and employees in temporary employment businesses under the control of the first employer.

CAPABILITIES AND TRAINING (REGULATION 13)

Employers need to take into account the capabilities of their employees before entrusting tasks. This is necessary to ensure that they have adequate health and safety training and are capable enough at their jobs to avoid risk. To this end, consideration must be given to recruitment including job orientation when transferring between jobs and work departments.

Training must also be provided when other factors such as the introduction of new technology and new systems of work or work equipment arise.

Training must:

- Be repeated periodically where appropriate.
- Be adapted to take account of any new or changed risks to the health and safety of the employees concerned.
- Take place during working hours.

EMPLOYEES' DUTIES (REGULATION 14)

Employees are required to follow health and safety instructions by using machinery, substances, transport etc. in accordance with the instructions and training that they have received.

They must also inform their employer (and other employers) of any dangers or shortcoming in the health and safety arrangements, even if there is no risk of imminent danger.

TEMPORARY WORKERS (REGULATION 15)

Consideration is given to the special needs of temporary workers. In particular to the provision of particular health and safety information such as qualifications required to perform the task safely or any special arrangements such as the need to provide health screening.

RISKS ASSESSMENT IN RESPECT OF NEW OR EXPECTANT MOTHERS (REGULATION 16)

Where the work is of a kind which would involve risk to a new or expectant mother or her baby, then the assessment required by regulation 3 should take this into account.

If the risk cannot be avoided, then the employer should take reasonable steps to:

- Adjust the hours worked.
- Offer alternative work.
- Give paid leave for as long as is necessary.

CERTIFICATE FROM A REGISTERED MEDICAL PRACTITIONER IN RESPECT OF NEW OR EXPECTANT MOTHERS (REGULATION 17)

Where the woman is a night shift worker and has a medical certificate identifying night shift work as a risk then the employer must put her on day shift or give paid leave for as long as is necessary.

NOTIFICATION BY NEW OR EXPECTANT MOTHERS (REGULATION 18)

The employer need take no action until he is notified in writing by the woman that she is pregnant, has given birth in the last six months, or is breastfeeding.

PROTECTION OF YOUNG PERSONS (REGULATION 19)

Employers of young persons shall ensure that they are not exposed to risk as a consequence of their lack of experience, lack of awareness or lack of maturity.

No employer shall employ young people for work which:

- Is beyond his physical or psychological capacity.
- Involves exposure to agents which chronically affect human health.
- Involves harmful exposure to radiation.
- Involves a risk to health from extremes of temperature, noise or vibration.
- Involves risks which could not be reasonably foreseen by young persons.

This regulation does not prevent the employment of a young person who is no longer a child for work:

- Where it is necessary for his training.
- Where the young person will be supervised by a competent person.
- Where any risk will be reduced to the lowest level that is reasonably practicable.

Note: Two HSE publications give guidance on these topics. HSG122 - New and expectant mothers at work: a guide for employers and HSG165 - Young people at work: a guide for employers.

EXEMPTION CERTIFICATES (REGULATION 20)

The Secretary of State for Defence may, in the interests of national security, by a certificate in writing exempt the armed forces, any visiting force or any headquarters from certain obligations imposed by the Regulations.

PROVISIONS AS TO LIABILITY (REGULATION 21)

Employers cannot submit a defence in criminal proceedings that contravention was caused by the act or default either of an employee or the competent person appointed under Regulation 7.

EXCLUSION OF CIVIL LIABILITY (REGULATION 22)

The effect of these Amendment Regulations is to limit the right of action in civil proceedings against an employer. Breach of a duty under MHSWR 1999 does not confer a right of civil action to a third party. Employees have a right of civil action related to breaches of MHSWR 1999. The amendments also afforded to employees protection against claims by third parties in the circumstance where employees may owe a duty to third parties under regulation 14 of the 1999 Regulations.

Manual Handling Operations Regulations (MHOR) 1992 (as amended)

See also - Health and Safety (Miscellaneous Amendments) Regulations (MAR) 2002.

Law considered in context/more depth in Element 6.

Outline of main points

1)   *Citation and commencement*

2)   *Interpretation*

   "Injury" does not include injury caused by toxic or corrosive substances which:

   Have leaked/spilled from load.
   Are present on the surface but not leaked/spilled from it.
   Are a constituent part of the load.

   "Load" includes any person or animal.

   "Manual Handling Operations" means transporting or supporting a load including:

   Lifting and putting down.
   Pushing, pulling or moving by hand or bodily force.
   Shall as far as is reasonably practicable.

3)   *Disapplication of regulations*

4)   *Duties of employers*

4) (1)(a)   *Avoidance of manual handling*

The employer's duty is to avoid the need for manual handling operations which involve a risk of their employees being injured - as far as is reasonably practicable.

4) (1)(b)(i)   *Assessment of risk*

Where not reasonably practicable make a suitable and sufficient assessment of all such manual handling operations.

4) (1)(b)(ii)   *Reducing the risk of injury*

Take appropriate steps to reduce the risk of injury to the lowest level reasonably practicable.

4) (1)(b)(iii)   *The load - additional information*

Employers shall provide information on general indications or where reasonably practicable precise information on:
The weight of each load.
The heaviest side of any load whose centre of gravity is not central.

4) (2)   *Reviewing the assessment*

Assessment review:

Where there is reason to believe the assessment is no longer valid.
There is sufficient change in manual handling operations.

5)   *Duty of employees*

Employees shall make full and proper use of any system of work provided for his use by his employer.

6)   *Exemption certificates*

7)   *Extension outside Great Britain*

8)   *Repeals and revocations*

Schedule 1   Factors to which the employer must have regard and questions he must consider when making an assessment of manual handling operations.

Schedule 2   Repeals and revocations.

Appendix 1   Numerical guidelines for assessment.

Appendix 2   Example of an assessment checklist.

Thus MOHR 1992 establish a clear hierarchy of measures:

1. Avoid hazardous manual handling operations so far as is reasonably practicable.
2. Make a suitable and sufficient assessment of any hazardous manual handling operations that cannot be avoided.
3. Reduce the risk of injury so far as is reasonably practicable.

Misuse of Drugs Act (MDA) 1971

Law considered in context/more depth in Element 2.

Outline of main points

The Misuse of Drugs Act 1971 aims to control the possession and supply of numerous drugs and drug-like substances, as listed under the MDA 1971. It also enabled international co-operation against illegal drug trafficking. In addition to establishing a list of drugs and penalties the MDA 1971 establishes the Home Secretary as an important player in a drug licensing system. Therefore, for example, various opiates are available legally as prescription-only Controlled Drug medicines and hui and cannabis (hemp) may be grown under licence for 'industrial purposes'. The MDA 1971 creates three classes of "controlled substances". The ranges of penalties for illegal or unlicensed "possession" and "possession with intent to supply" are graded differently within each class. The lists of substances within each class can be amended "by order", so the Home Secretary can list new drugs and upgrade, downgrade or delist previously controlled drugs with less of the bureaucracy and delay associated with passing an Act through both Houses of Parliament. The MDA 1971 does not cover all drugs or drug-like substances. Offences under the MDA 1971 include:

■ Possession of a controlled drug unlawfully.
■ Possession of a controlled drug with intent to supply it.
■ Supplying or offering to supply a controlled drug (even where no charge is made for the drug).
■ Allowing premises you occupy or manage to be used unlawfully for the purpose of producing or supplying controlled drugs.

Reporting of Injuries, Diseases and Dangerous Occurrences Regulations (RIDDOR) 1995

Law considered in context/more depth in Element 3.

Outline of main points

The Reporting of Injuries, Diseases and Dangerous Occurrences Regulations (RIDDOR) 1995 cover the requirement to report certain categories of injury and disease sustained at work, along with specified dangerous occurrences and gas incidents, to the relevant enforcing authority. These reports are used to compile statistics to show trends and to highlight problem areas in particular industries or companies.

REPORTING

1)   When a person **dies or suffers any serious condition** specified in Schedule 1 **(Reporting of Injuries)** and Schedule 2 **(Reporting of Dangerous Occurrences)** a responsible person is to notify by the quickest possible means (usually by telephone) the enforcing authorities and must send them a written report within 10 days (F2508).

2)   In cases of diseases that are linked to work activities listed in Schedule 3 *(Reporting of Diseases)* a responsible person is required to notify, without delay, the enforcing authorities and must send them a written report forthwith (F2508A).

3)   If personal injury results in **more than 3 days incapacity** from work off from normal duties, but does not fall in the category of "major", the written report alone is required. The day of the accident is not counted.

4)   The enforcing authority is either the Health and Safety Executive or the Local Authority. The approved form for reporting is F2508 for injuries and dangerous occurrences and F2508A for diseases.

"Accident" includes:

- An act of non-consensual physical violence done to a person at work.
- An act of suicide which occurs on or in the course of the operation of a relevant transport system.

ROAD TRAFFIC ACCIDENTS

Road traffic accidents only have to be reported if:

- Death or injury results from exposure to a substance being conveyed by a vehicle.
- Death or injury results from the activities of another person engaged in the loading or unloading of an article or substance.
- Death or injury results from the activities of another person involving work on or alongside a road.
- Death or injury results from an accident involving a train.

NON EMPLOYEE

The responsible person must not only report non-employee deaths, but also cases that involve major injury or hospitalisation.

RECORDING

In the case of an accident at work, the following details must be recorded:

- Date.
- Name.
- Nature of injury.
- Brief description of the event.
- Time.
- Occupation.
- Place of accident.

Copies of F2508, or suitable alternative records, must be kept for at least 3 years. This may be held electronically provided it is printable.

DEFENCES

A person must prove that he was not aware of the event and that he had taken all reasonable steps to have such events brought to his notice.

Typical examples of major injuries, diseases and dangerous occurrences

MAJOR INJURIES (RIDDOR - SCHEDULE 1)

The list of major injuries includes:

- Any fracture, other than the finger or thumbs or toes.
- Any amputation.
- Dislocation of the shoulder, hip, knee or spine.
- Permanent or temporary loss of sight.
- Chemical, hot metal or penetrating eye injury.
- Electrical shock, electrical burn leading to unconsciousness or resuscitation or admittance to hospital for more than 24 hours.
- Loss of consciousness caused by asphyxia or exposure to a harmful substance or biological agent.
- Acute illness or loss of consciousness requiring medical attention due to any entry of substance by inhalation, ingestion or through the skin.
- Acute illness where there is a reason to believe that this resulted from exposure to a biological agent or its toxins or infected material.
- Any other injury leading to hypothermia, heat-induced illness or unconsciousness requiring resuscitation, hospitalisation greater than 24 hours.

DISEASES (RIDDOR - SCHEDULE 3)

Conditions due to physical agents and the physical demands of work

- Inflammation, ulceration or malignant disease of the skin due to ionising radiation.
- Decompression illness.
- Subcutaneous cellulitis of the hand (beat hand).
- Carpal tunnel syndrome.
- Hand-arm vibration syndrome.

Infections due to biological agents

- Anthrax.
- Hepatitis.
- Legionellosis.
- Leptospirosis.
- Tetanus.

Conditions due to chemicals and other substances

- Arsenic poisoning.
- Ethylene Oxide poisoning.
- Cancer of a bronchus or lung.

- Folliculitis.
- Acne.
- Pneumoconiosis.
- Asbestosis.
- Occupational dermatitis.

DANGEROUS OCCURRENCES (RIDDOR - SCHEDULE 2)

Dangerous occurrences are events that have the potential to cause death or serious injury and so must be reported whether anyone is injured or not.

Note: This information is a brief summary only. For full details consult HSE document L73 A Guide to RIDDOR 95.

Road Traffic Act (RTA) 1988

Law considered in context/more depth in Element 2.

Outline of main points

SECTION 3 - DRINK AND DRUGS

This section concerns causing death by careless driving when under the influence of drink or drugs. A person will be guilty of an offence if they cause the death of another person by driving a mechanically propelled vehicle on a road or other public place without due care and attention, or without reasonable consideration for other persons using the road or place, and:

(a)   They are, at the time when they are driving are, unfit to drive through drink or drugs, or

(b)   They have consumed so much alcohol that the proportion of it in their breath, blood or urine at that time exceeds the prescribed limit, or

(c)   They have within 18 hours after that time, required to provide a specimen in pursuance of section 7 of this Act, but without reasonable excuse fails to provide it, they are guilty of an offence.

For the purposes of this section a person shall be taken to be unfit to drive at any time when his ability to drive properly is impaired.

Working Time Regulations (WTR) 1998 (as amended)

Law considered in context/more depth in Elements 3.

The Working Time Regulations (WTR) 1998 came into effect on 1st October 1998 to implement the European Working Time Directive into UK law.

Since their introduction the WTR 1998 have been updated and amended through additional legislation to cover an even wider range of workers, and granted additional rights to young workers. While special rules apply in respect of young workers and junior doctors, the core rights at the heart of the WTR 1998 remain the same.

Outline of main points

The WTR 1998 protect workers from being forced to work excessive hours. They also make the provision of paid annual leave mandatory, and include rights to rest breaks and uninterrupted periods of rest. The Regulations apply to "adult workers" (over 18) and to "young workers" (over compulsory school age), and some of the detailed provisions are slightly different for each of these two groups. There are exceptions to some of the Regulations, primarily for employees working in transport (air, road, rail, sea etc.), sea-fishing, work at sea, doctors in training, certain activities of the armed forces, police and civil protection workers.

The Regulations have 4 principal effects that are, in summary:

- To place a 48 hour limit on the average working week.
- To place an 8 hour limit on average night work for each 24 hours and provide night workers with the right to a health assessment.
- To guarantee rest breaks during the day and daily and weekly rest periods.
- To guarantee the right to four weeks paid holiday per year.

Workplace (Health, Safety and Welfare) Regulations (WHSWR) 1992

See also - Health and Safety (Miscellaneous Amendments) Regulations (MAR) 2002.

Law considered in context/more depth in Element 3.

Outline of main points

SUMMARY

The main requirements of the Workplace (Health, Safety and Welfare) Regulations 1992 are:

1)   *Maintenance* of the workplace and equipment.

2)   *Safety* of those carrying out maintenance work and others who might be at risk (e.g. segregation of pedestrians and vehicles, prevention of falls and falling objects etc.).

3)   Provision of *welfare* facilities (e.g. rest rooms, changing rooms etc.).

4)   Provision of a safe *environment* (e.g. lighting, ventilation etc.).

ENVIRONMENT

Regulation 6   Ventilation - enclosed workplaces should be ventilated with a sufficient quantity of fresh or purified air (5 to 8 litres per second per occupant).

Regulation 7   Temperature indoors - This needs to be reasonable and the heating device must not cause injurious fumes. Thermometers must be provided. Temperature should be a minimum of 16°C or 13°C if there is physical effort.

Regulation 8 Lighting - must be suitable and sufficient. Natural light if possible. Emergency lighting should be provided if danger exists.

Regulation 10 Room dimensions and space - every room where persons work shall have sufficient floor area, height and unoccupied space (min 11 cu.m per person).

Regulation 11 Workstations and seating have to be suitable for the person and the work being done.

SAFETY

Regulation 12 Floors and traffic routes must be of suitable construction. This includes absence of holes, slope, uneven or slippery surface. Drainage where necessary. Handrails and guards to be provided on slopes and staircases.

Regulation 13 Tanks and pits must be covered or fenced.

Regulation 14 Windows and transparent doors, where necessary for health and safety, must be of safety material and be marked to make it apparent.

Regulation 15 Windows, skylights and ventilators must be capable of opening without putting anyone at risk.

Regulation 17 Traffic routes for pedestrians and vehicles must be organised in such a way that they can move safely.

Regulation 18 Doors and gates must be suitably constructed and fitted with any necessary safety devices.

Regulation 19 Escalators and moving walkways shall function safely, be equipped with any necessary safety devices and be fitted with emergency stop.

HOUSEKEEPING

Regulation 5 Workplace and equipment, devices and systems must be maintained in efficient working order and good repair.

Regulation 9 Cleanliness and waste materials - workplaces must be kept sufficiently clean. Floors, walls and ceilings must be capable of being kept sufficiently clean. Waste materials shall not be allowed to accumulate, except in suitable receptacles.

Regulation 16 Windows etc. must be designed so that they can be cleaned safety.

FACILITIES

Regulation 20 Sanitary conveniences must be suitable and sufficient and in readily accessible places. They must be adequately ventilated, kept clean and there must be separate provision for men and women.

Regulation 21 Washing facilities must be suitable and sufficient. Showers if required (a table gives minimum numbers of toilets and washing facilities).

Regulation 22 Drinking water - an adequate supply of wholesome drinking water must be provided.

Regulation 23 Accommodation for clothing must be suitable and sufficient.

Regulation 24 Facilities for changing clothes must be suitable and sufficient, where a person has to use special clothing for work.

Regulation 25 Facilities for rest and eating meals must be suitable and sufficient.

Assessment

Content

Assessments of understanding

It is understood that those using this publication may be doing so to broaden their understanding of this important topic, health and well-being, and others will be studying in order to obtain a specific health related award. The approach taken by those assessing such awards will vary.

This element provides information on how one such award is assessed, the NEBOSH National Certificate in the Management of Health and Well-being at Work. The questions and related answers provided in this element may prove useful for those that want to assess their understanding for this award and for more general reasons.

The questionnaire and accompanying report, provided in the section 'health and well-being workplace review' below, will be of great use to those studying for the NEBOSH award and will prove particularly useful to those that wish to develop and use their own means of assessing health and well-being in the workplace.

Assessment questions

NEBOSH PAPER NHC1

To assist students understanding of the assessment requirements for the NEBOSH National Certificate in the Management of Health and Well-being at Work award, paper NHC1, some short answer questions that are typical of the type used in an award at this level have been included. This is accompanied by the following observations related to the success of candidates taking examinations of this type.

At every examination a number of candidates - including some good ones - perform less well than they might because of poor examination technique. It is essential that candidates practice answering both essay-type and short answer questions and learn to budget their time according to the number of marks allocated to questions (and parts of questions) as shown on the paper.

A common fault is that candidates may fail to pay attention to the action verb (e.g. outline, identify, explain, describe) in each question.

The need to understand the meaning of the 'action verb' and to read the question carefully is emphasised in the comments below that are taken from recent NEBOSH examiner's reports:

"… many answers were too brief to satisfy the requirement for an outline or description. Points made should have been supported by sufficient reasoning to show their relevance to the question".

"Some candidates, even though they identified many of the relevant factors, could not be awarded the full range of marks available because they produced a truncated list that did not properly outline the relationship between each factor and the corresponding risks".

"…some candidates could not be awarded high marks as their responses did not include adequate and appropriate description of the practical measures…

"While answers to this question were generally to a reasonable standard, many were too brief to attract all the marks that were available".

"Some answers were extremely brief answers are expected to be proportionate to the marks available".

Answers to assessment questions

Typical answers are provided on pages 203-206.

General confirmation of understanding

Those not taking examinations related to health and well-being may find the questions and answers useful to check and confirm their understanding of some of the issues covered by this publication.

HEALTH AND WELL-BEING WORKPLACE REVIEW

NEBOSH Unit NHC2

The aim of this unit is to assess a candidate's ability to complete successfully a health and well-being review of their workplace and to provide a report to management with justified recommendations.

The questionnaire has been produced by NEBOSH as part of their practical assessment of the above award, their origination and copyright is acknowledged. In order to understand how the questionnaire may be used and the type of report produced by candidates studying this award, a completed questionnaire and report is provided.

In summary the proforma and report should clearly identify:

- The nature, and if appropriate, the location of each health and well-being at work issue.
- Review findings with prioritisation and justification.
- Clear links to strengths and weaknesses in the way that health and well-being at work is managed, with relevant prioritisation.

Creating workplace templates

The NEBOSH template is an excellent starting point for those wishing to develop and create their own templates to carry out reviews of their health and well-being standards at work.

Sample assessment questions

NHC1 - Managing health and well-being in the workplace

ELEMENT 1

1. **Outline** two benefits to the employer resulting from a proactive health and wellbeing policy. **(8)**

2. **Explain**, with examples, the expression "good work is good for your health and wellbeing". **(8)**

ELEMENT 2

1. (a)   When is it appropriate to carry out pre-employment screening? **(2)**

    (b)   **Outline** why employers should conduct pre-employment screening assessments. **(6)**

2. The Disability Discrimination Act 1995 defines what is classed as 'reasonable adjustments'.
    Outline FOUR examples of reasonable adjustments which an employer might need to make. **(8)**

ELEMENT 3

1. **Identify FOUR** agents that can cause skin disease and give an example for each type identified. **(8)**

2. **Explain** with examples how allergic contact dermatitis may be caused. **(8)**

ELEMENT 4

1. (a)   **Explain** the meaning of the term 'may be fit for work'. **(2)**

    (b)   **Outline** the role and status of the 'fit note'. **(6)**

2. (a)   **Define** the term vocational rehabilitation. **(2)**

    (b)   **Outline** the benefits of vocational rehabilitation within the context of the employee and the employer. **(4)**

ELEMENT 5

1. (a)   **Explain** with examples what is mean by the terms **'subjective and objective indicators'** when assessing work related stress. **(4)**

    (b)   **Outline** who should be informed of the outcome following any stress survey or focus group action. **(4)**

2. **Outline** with examples the effects of prolonged absence from work on the mental health of individuals. **(8)**

ELEMENT 6

1. **Explain**, **with examples** why good ergonomic principles should be applied to the workplace if musculoskeletal injury is to be prevented. **(8)**

2. **Outline TWO** factors which should be included when assessing a proposed manual handling operation. **(8)**

ELEMENT 7

1. (a)   **Outline** with examples the main life style factors which affect the health and wellbeing of individuals. **(4)**

    (b)   **Explain** how diet can have an affect on general health. **(4)**

2. **Outline** why it is important to take a balance approach to regular exercise. **(8)**

ELEMENT 8

1. **Distinguish** between the terms hazard and risk using an appropriate example. **(8)**

2   **Outline** the role of the occupational hygienist. **(8)**

Any resemblance to NEBOSH examination questions is coincidental; the questions have been created to illustrate the type of question which may be asked at examination to check understanding of the relevant element learning outcomes.

PLEASE REFER TO THE BACK OF THIS ASSESSMENT SECTION FOR ANSWERS.

Health and well-being practical application

NATIONAL CERTIFICATE IN THE MANAGEMENT OF HEALTH AND WELL-BEING AT WORK
UNIT NHC2 - HEALTH AND WELL-BEING PRACTICAL APPLICATION

Candidate report template

Student number:	HAW001		
Location:	Acme Systems Plc, Tyne and Weir	Date of review:	18/10/20XX

Structure report under the following headings:

Introduction including overview of area reviewed and activities taken place

Acme Systems' call centre is based in Tyne and Weir and the Company operates a 24/7 shift system, with reduced numbers in the evenings, shifts are 6-8hours and a permanent night shift is used two thousand staff are employed in the call centre. Staff ages range from 16 to 66, 2 staff are registered disabled and 4 are expectant mothers.

The building consisted of an E shape design with reception and training and IT facilities on the ground floor and call centre work on the first and second floor. The workplace consisted of a modern office facility, taken over from a previous occupier (i.e. the premises were not specifically designed for use as a call centre).

Call centre staff are arranged in groups of five and use computers and telephones continuously during their shift, opportunities are available for staff to break out from their work, but a bonus scheme conflicts with this opportunity to take a break. Back ground noise from call centre staff telephone use was evident and it was difficult to have a clear conversation in their vicinity.

Review summary

A gap analysis was conducted using the following questionnaire to review the current health and well being status of the company.

The review has confirmed the company's commitment to health and well being, as there was a well resourced programme, some important policies had been established and basic health screening was in place. However, it has highlighted areas where there are opportunities to extend the current good practices and for further improvement. The most significant ones being:

1. Conducting an occupational health needs assessment to establish what is required to extend the programme from dealing with life style issues to embrace the full range of occupational health affecting employees.

2. Evaluating the risk from noise in the call centre and establishing interventions to deal with it.

3. Evaluating the risk from manual handling operations and establishing interventions to deal with it.

4. Providing training to managers on how to implement company policies and manage health and well being issues.

Though most of the above items will require support from our OH contracted provider, at their usual fee, this will provide the company with the means to move the health and well being strategy to the next step and focus better on occupational health issue that have a risk of long term health effects on employees. This will make the investment of the moderate sum of money involved worthwhile and will reduce the likelihood of claims for compensation. Recommendations number 2 and 3 are actions that we must take to comply with specific regulations.

NATIONAL CERTIFICATE IN THE MANAGEMENT OF HEALTH AND WELL-BEING AT WORK UNIT NHC2 - HEALTH AND SAFETY PRACTICAL APPLICATION

			Candidate's proforma
	Sheet number:		of
Student name:	Emily Bishop	Student number:	
Place inspected:	Acme Systems Plc. Tyne and Weir	Date of inspection:	18/10/20XX

Section 1 - Organisational Support

1.1 Is your initial impression that the senior management of the organisation are committed to health and well-being at work and it is embedded in the core values of the business?	Yes	No	N/A
	√		

Comments:

The health and safety policy statement makes a clear commitment to deal with a wide range of issues which affect the health and wellbeing of employees, for example health screening at pre-employment, with ongoing help and support counselling to reduce employee dependency on smoking and alcohol where requested.

Management demonstrate a commitment to health and well-being through procedures for dealing with health related issues such as skin care, reducing noise exposure, substance misuse, bullying and harassment. The company has delegated responsibilities for health to all managers and this forms part of the managers' performance targets and review. Support is provided through access to appropriately trained OH & S professionals when required.

1.2 Are there health and well-being at work recommendations featured with targets in the organisations strategy/business plan?	Yes	No	N/A
	√		

Comments:

The company has set targets to reduce absence due to sickness and have clear policies to support this. Smoking, obesity, exercise and diet are all topics included as targets in the business plan. This is demonstrated by the company providing healthy foods through the canteen and vending machines. Employees have access to a gym at reduced rates, which is subsidised by the company, and employees are actively encouraged to undertake activities such as walking at lunch time and using stairs. The business plan requires managers to attend quarterly away days chaired by senior management; which are held at Centre Park resorts. Issues of exercise are discussed and ways to improve both activity levels at work and at home are invited from the team.

1.3 Are specific resources identified and made available for health and well-being at work activities?	Yes	No	N/A
	√		

Comments: (please give examples)

Yes a Feng Shui garden facility is provided for staff breakout.

A small gymnasium with professional instructors is also provided at reduced rates.

The company have organised healthy lifestyle campaigns in conjunction with their local authority health promotion unit. Lunch time sessions have also been introduced for employees to try samples of healthy foods and to learn more about healthy eating to lose weight and maintain the weight loss. Stop smoking courses have also been introduced.

The OH service has carried out training sessions for employees on stress prevention, skin care, back care and exercise.

1.4	Is there any evidence of manager training in health and well-being at work?	Yes	No	N/A
			√	

Comments:

No formal, assessed training courses have been organised, but some aspects have been included in more general training, but mainly to deal with issues concerning display screen assessment and use.

Specifically, there is no formal training for managers in absence management or the application of the substance misuse policy. Although there are clearly stated policies and procedures, there is little evidence that management are adequately trained to deal with situations arising from frequent absenteeism or substance misuse in the workplace. There was a recent example of this where an employee had an accident, albeit minor and no one was seriously injured, but he had been drinking and although the manager sent the employee home, there was no proper investigation as the manager did not know how to apply the policy.

1.5	Are health and well-being at work issues/plans/targets regularly reviewed by senior management?	Yes	No	N/A
		√		

Comments:

Yes, but evidence suggests they focus more on smoking, alcohol, and diet issues, but do not fully address assessment of hazards from work activities such as noise in the call centre.

There is a need for the company to focus on work related issues such as stress and noise. Employees have to deal with some very difficult customers at times and there is no system to provide support through de-briefing sessions with managers so that their problems are fully understood and the proper support provided. Counselling support is available, but this is not always accessed as there is a fear of being seen as not coping.

Management could review working shifts with reference to nuisance noise as it is important that employees can get away from the constant noise of the call centre activities, through regular breaks.

1.6	Has the organisation been accredited against a specific health at work standard (e.g. Welsh Corporate Health Standards) or one which includes health as a core component e.g. IIP?	Yes	No	N/A
			√	

Comments:

No externally audited standard is in place. The systems that have been introduced in the company could be assessed for IIP and or the Workplace Health Awards, management seem reluctant to do this as they see it as additional work. However, the value of such recognition could be enormous to the company, by raising its profile as a good employer, which could help recruitment and retention of staff as well as a potential reduction in insurance premiums.

1.7	Has the organisation been accredited against a specific health at work standard (e.g. Welsh Corporate Health Standards) or one which includes health as a core component e.g. IIP?	Yes	No	N/A
			√	

Comments:

No externally audited standard is in place. The systems that have been introduced in the company could be assessed for IIP and or the Workplace Health Awards, management seem reluctant to do this as they see it as additional work. However, the value of such recognition could be enormous to the company, by raising its profile as a good employer, which could help recruitment and retention of staff as well as a potential reduction in insurance premiums.

1.8 Has the organisation been accredited against a specific health at work standard (e.g. Welsh Corporate Health Standards) or one which includes health as a core component e.g. IIP?	Yes	No	N/A
		√	

Comments:

No externally audited standard is in place. The systems that have been introduced in the company could be assessed for IIP and or the Workplace Health Awards, management seem reluctant to do this as they see it as additional work. However, the value of such recognition could be enormous to the company, by raising its profile as a good employer, which could help recruitment and retention of staff as well as a potential reduction in Insurance premiums.

1.9 Is there a health and well-being at work champion in the work place? If so, are they in a position to effectively influence changes?	Yes	No	N/A
	√		

Comments:

Yes for each Section there is a H&S advisor with training to NEBOSH National General Certificate level. They are able to make recommendations, observations to the site health and safety committee, but the committee does not have the ability to provide resources to meet their recommendations. The limited health and well-being knowledge of the safety advisors means their input to issues and solutions could be better. The company should consider nominating and training a manager/employee in each working area as a champion, as this would have a greater impact because he/she will understand the needs of the workers more and be able to fight their corner for improved facilities.

1.10 Has the organisation carried out an overall occupational health needs assessment?	Yes	No	N/A
		√	

Comments:

No comprehensive occupational needs assessment as been carried out, the site use an external health provider AAF Staff Wellbeing Development Corporation (AFF), but as stated previously (1.5) their emphasis is more on social health issues (eating, drinking, smoking) rather than work related issues such as screening for work related noise induced hearing loss. The company should, as a matter of urgency, undertake a full OH needs assessment, which includes a full risk assessment of all potential risks to health e.g. noise, stress, upper limb disorders and set out how these issues are to be managed. This should include access to a qualified OH Nurse, to help with the health needs assessment, provide advice on prevention and control measures and to undertake health surveillance where appropriate. The well-being programme, although important, should not be carried out instead of addressing the workplace health risks, which must take priority.

Section 2 - Communication and employee involvement

2.1 Is there evidence that health and well-being at work issues are communicated to employees through a range of means; e.g.(i) communication at meetings, (ii) notice board, (iii) displays, (iv) leaflets, (v) newsletters etc.	Yes	No	N/A
	√		

Comments:

Communication at meetings: Occasional communication of health and wellbeing issues at general meetings, though the quarterly away day meetings do include consideration of exercise. Notice board: some evidence, names and contact numbers for AFF to follow up on some health and well being activities such as no smoking advice. Displays: drinking water 'igloo' display encouraging staff to dink more water at work + additional drinking fountains installed. Leaflets: Concerning breast cancer, dyslexia, weight watchers available in reception Newsletters: occasional mention of activities, such as fun runs for raising money for charities, such as the British Heart Foundation, and photographs from the quarterly away days.

2.2 Is this communication effective?	Yes	No	N/A
		√	

Comments:

Most staff do not take an interest in the limited promotions. The company should set up a small working group of employees, H & S and management to develop systems for communicating health issues. Employee involvement is vital to success and will demonstrate the high priority the company place on health. It could be part of the H&S committee remit, so that it becomes part of the normal business of the H&S committee.

2.3 Is there any evidence that employees are involved, consulted and can raise any views on health and well-being at work issues in the organisation? For example through staff suggestions schemes with feedback to employees; staff surveys etc.	Yes	No	N/A
		√	

Comments:

No evidence that employees are involved other than through their Union Safety Representatives, who raise matters at the H&S committee from time to time. This could be improved by implementing 2.2 above, as well as encouraging suggestions from employees or carrying out a staff survey. However, if a staff survey is carried out it will be important that the findings of such a survey are taken seriously and managed, and changes implemented as required.

2.4 Is the communication in a form which is accessible to everyone who may need it, for example, for the visually impaired, languages other than English?	Yes	No	N/A
		√	

Comments:

No survey of need for alternate language signs has been carried out. Brail signs are used for toilets and emergency exit direction signs. No alternative language signs are displayed.

Leaflets on health are available from the local health protection agency or local authority and they are available in other languages.

2.5 Do you think employees are actively engaged in any health at work activities? Consider:	Yes	No	N/A
		√	

- **How many would you say were involved?**
- **Are there any barriers to participation e.g. shift work, home workers?**
- **Are there activities inclusive for all staff e.g. disabled?**
- **Have there been any special arrangements made for these activities e.g. showers, timing of events, paid to attend or in own time?**

Comments:

Healthy lifestyle campaigns for employees and managers have been organised in conjunction with their local authority health promotion unit. Lunch time sessions have also been introduced for employees to try samples of healthy foods and to learn more about healthy eating to lose weight and maintain the weight loss. Stop smoking courses have been introduced and well supported by managers and employees.

The OH service has carried out training sessions for employees on stress prevention, skin care, back care and exercise, these have been affected by shift working and to date not enough employees have attended. Shifts can be a barrier to employee involvement in general interventions for lifestyle health and well being, however, this could be alleviated if the company would consider re-introducing a social 'club' with activities such as football, tennis, swimming.

2.6	Is the participation of employees in health and well-being activities recorded?	Yes	No	N/A
			√	

Comments:

No system for recording has been identified. This could be undertaken by keeping a simple register, where employees sign in when they take part in any activities, however, this may be seen as prying and should be managed sensitively as they may say "why would the company want to know who is using facilities?"

2.7	Do employees actively take responsibility for health and well-being at work activities themselves? e.g. organise walking clubs, keep fit classes?	Yes	No	N/A
		√		

Comments:

Approximately sixty staff have established a regular week-end walking club. This has proved to be very successful and has helped to develop a more social environment into the company. There are a group of employees who want to set up a 'weight watchers' club and a 'keep fit' class, but they are finding difficulty in getting someone to lead these activities. The Local Health Authority may be able to help with this and should be contacted.

Section 3 - Policies and procedures

3.1	Is there an overall policy for the management of health and well-being at work which has been communicated to employees?	Yes	No	N/A
		√		

Comments:

The policy has been included in the staff hand-book which is updated and issued annually. The policy is communicated and discussed in the induction session conducted for new employees.

3.2	Is there a policy that incorporates the management of musculoskeletal disorders which is communicated to employees?	Yes	No	N/A
		√		

Comments:

Risk controls are established and a facility to report any early symptoms, such as pain or swelling to the wrists of DSE operators is in place. If the company had access to an OH Nurse on a more frequent basis they could provide advice to employees and help to prevent potential problems, with lost time. This could include education and personal advice on use of the work station. A system is in place which requires key board operators to take frequent rest breaks and this has been communicated to all relevant employees. Though, there is still a need for employees to receive further training on workstation use e.g. chair adjustment, screen positioning and keyboard use.

3.3	Is there any assessment of risk of musculoskeletal injury to employees in the organisation?	Yes	No	N/A
		√		

Comments:

DSE work station assessments are up to date, though there is some further work to be done regarding manual handling operations.

3.4	Is there a policy that incorporates the management of mental health which is communicated to employees?	Yes	No	N/A
			√	

Comments:

No evidence has been found within the policy that considers mental health issues or its management. There is a bullying and harassment policy, but this has not been fully implemented into actions, especially in relation to potential stress. There is also no clear indication from the company regarding their attitude to the employment of people with mental ill health. This could be addressed with the introduction of a mental health policy.

3.5	Is there any assessment of risk to the mental health of employees in the organisation?	Yes	No	N/A
			√	

Comments:

No evidence has been found. Mental health is still a taboo subject and both management and employees are fearful of this. This could be improved with education, which could be undertaken by an OH Nurse with the local Community Mental Health Nurse. This would help to break down barriers and improve managers' and employees' understanding of mental health and that it should not be feared or people shunned. There is research evidence available that demonstrates how good management and support for people with mental ill health has helped keep people in work and to return to work.

3.6	Have other relevant health issues been included in risk assessments in the organisation e.g. hazardous substances; noise; vibration?	Yes	No	N/A
			√	

Comments:

No, noise has not been assessed and may well be a significant risk to workers in the call centre. A noise assessment should be carried out by a competent person. The main issue is one of nuisance noise, which can be very distracting and stressful, however, there may also be areas where noise levels exceed the legal limits.

3.7	Are there any policies and procedures on work-life balance?	Yes	No	N/A
		√		

Comments:

Hours of work are limited, employees are encouraged to take regular exercise and flexible working is available to Carers.

3.8	Are there any relevant policies and procedures that reflect the needs of staff who undertake shift work, night working, and extended hours of work, part-time or remote working?	Yes	No	N/A
		√		

Comments:

Policies are in place, and work procedures for out of hours working were available. Employees are offered health assessment for night working. There is also a policy in place for staff working off site/remotely. These are mostly sales people visiting customers.

3.9	Are there organisational policies which include the following issues? Tobacco, alcohol and drugs, health eating, physical activity, new and expectant mothers?	Yes	No	N/A
		√		

Comments:

There is strong evidence for 3.9, but more emphasis on work place issues needs to be addressed. There is a substance misuse policy, but this is not well implemented due to the lack of management training. This needs to be addressed as previously mentioned.

3.10	Is there a policy that deals with disability discrimination?	Yes	No	N/A
		√		

Comments:

A policy which addresses disability discrimination has been established and is current with the requirements of the Equality Act 2010 and guidance. The company still needs to educate management regarding disability. This should include information on the definition of disability and what 'reasonable adjustments' means. This should form part of the training programme for managers regarding attendance management and rehabilitation.

Section 4 - Management of ill-health and absence, monitoring, health assessment and review

4.1 Are there any clear policies and procedures for the management of ill-health and absence? Consider the following:	Yes	No	N/A
	√		

- Whether there are any policies in place to manage sickness absence?
- Whether the policy includes direction on communication with an absent employee, and appropriate others?
- Does the policy include direction on return to work procedures?
- Does the policy include clear guidance on issues relating to confidentiality (record keeping)?

Comments:

Policies are in place to manage sickness absence, managers have been trained and employees are fully aware of the notification procedures they should follow when unfit for work. The policy includes direction on return to work procedures and includes clear guidance on issues relating to confidentiality and storage of records.

4.2 Is there a system for the recording of sickness absence data?	Yes	No	N/A
	√		

Comments:

All sickness absence is recorded and generalised information is made available to the H&S committee for analysis and to identify any trends.

4.3 Are managers made aware of the sickness absence data?	Yes	No	N/A
	√		

Comments:

Yes, monthly statistics are produced that include types of reason for each category of absence. Each manager receives information on sickness absence performance of the company and for the area they are responsible for.

4.4 Has there been an analysis of sickness absence data? If yes, what are the main work-related causes and does there appear to be any pattern to the absences?	Yes	No	N/A
	√		

Comments:

Yes, this was something that I was personally involved in. Though no work related causes were identified the analysis showed non attendance by some groups of employees and managers, following their week-end breaks. Significant absence patterns were also identified following the quarterly away days.

4.5 Does the organisation carry out any health surveillance or biological monitoring?	Yes	No	N/A
	√		

Comments:

Regular and annual hearing and lung function tests carried out on workers exposed to noise or Dust in the workplace.

4.6 Does the organisation carry out any monitoring, e.g. atmospheric, thermal and noise which has been identified in risk assessments or by law?	Yes	No	N/A
		√	

Comments:

No evidence was observed or recorded with regard to workplace monitoring. As was identified earlier, there is a need to conduct noise assessments in the call centre. Though the majority of the problem is anticipated to be nuisance noise there may be some areas that have noise levels above those set out in the Control of Noise at Work Regulations. The need for other monitoring may become more apparent after the health needs assessment has been conducted.

4.7 Does the organisation undertake any form of pre-employment screening (pre-placement assessment)?	Yes	No	N/A
	√		

Comments:

Yes basic physical health checks are made after the person is offered a job and before they start employment. This includes weight, sight, and blood pressure. At this time no pre-employment assessment of hearing is made. Similarly no pre-employment questionnaire is used to identify other specific pre-existing conditions that may need to be taken into account. These should be considered as part of the health needs assessment. As should be the setting out of health standards to assist with the screening process.

4.8 Is there a procedure for formal reporting of diagnosed occupational diseases?	Yes	No	N/A
	√		

Comments:

The requirements of RIDDOR are fully in place and understood.

Section 5 - Competence and interventions

5.1 Does the organisation have any access to informed advice on health and well-being issues e.g. occupational health providers? Has the competence of this advice been verified?	Yes	No	N/A
	√		

Comments:

AFF employee wellbeing corporation (AFF) have been appointed, and are currently contracted for a three year period (until 1st January 20XX). All staff employed by AFF are qualified medical professionals, including occupational hygienists and medical practitioners. The extent of advice needed should be evaluated as part of the health needs assessment.

5.2 Has the organisation carried out any form of health and well-being training to employees e.g. posture, skin awareness, stress awareness etc?	Yes	No	N/A
	√		

Comments:

Some health and wellbeing training has been conducted by the contracted OH staff, this focused on stress, skin and back care. Some informal training on DSE issues was also conducted at the same time as the workstations were assessed. There is scope for general health and well being training to be conducted and for this to be extended to specific health and well being topics including stress and noise.

5.3 Have employees and managers received information and training on the sickness absence management procedures?	Yes	No	N/A
	√		

Comments:

All managers have received information and the information is updated by Human Resources whenever a change is implemented. This has had limited effect and managers need training on absence management to make the implementation of procedures more effective.

5.4 Have any employees who use equipment such as personal protective equipment (PPE) received information and training on its correct use?	Yes	No	N/A
	√		

Comments:

Contract cleaners are fully conversant with the requirements to use personal protective equipment (PPE); typically this would include gauntlet gloves. They are also made aware that they must report any damaged equipment and not to use any that is defective. No other employees are required to use PPE.

5.5 Have any of the following health and well-being interventions been undertaken or are planned?	Yes	No	N/A
	√		

- Well-person clinics
- Immunisation programmes
- Stop smoking groups
- Physical activity or relaxation classes
- Health food and drink provision e.g. fresh fruit, salad, etc
- Screening
- Subsidised gym membership
- Other

Comments:

Well-person clinics: yes, but limited to social health issues. Immunisation programmes: None in place. Stop smoking groups: Groups have been established and are progressing well. Physical activity or relaxation classes: Yes gym and instructors are made available. Health food and drink provision e.g. fresh fruit, salad, etc: Alternate healthy options are available in the staff restaurant. Screening, some limited screening in place: Weight, eye sight and blood pressure screening available. Subsidised gym membership is provided.

5.6 Do you know if there has been any evaluation of the effectiveness of these interventions?	Yes	No	N/A
		√	

Comments:

None determined. This is an aspect that could be developed, this could include surveys and questionnaires as well as specific monitoring. However, there is no facility for OH nurse monitoring of these types of thing at this time.

5.7 Based on your review do you now feel that overall the organisation is committed to health and well-being at work?	Yes	No	N/A
	√		

Comments:

The organisation is committed to health and well-being at work, but some areas have not been address adequately such as noise. Audiometric testing for call centre staff has not been carried out. Also staff use hand held telephones and complain that they have difficulty hearing callers due to the office background noise level. Consideration should be given to trialling the use of head 'phones to reduce the effect of background noise.

Main findings of the health and well-being at work review

The review identified that the company was not new to health and well being issues and had some established good practices. In particular, these related to lifestyle health and well being issues, absence management, promotion of non-work related health, encouragement of staff to develop their own programmes and provision of advice from contracted health and well being specialists. However, the review also identified that there were opportunities for improvement. These related to widening the perspective of health and well-being so that it included more work related issues, improving communication.

Specifically the review identified the following main strengths and weaknesses.

1 Organisational support

Strength

The company and managers were committed to a range of items that they felt had an important influence on health and well-being. This was mainly focused on exercise, healthy eating, and limiting alcohol and smoking dependency. It is clear that the effort put into the health and wellbeing issues selected for attention to date has had an effect.

Weaknesses

Though this focused organisational support has had a significant positive effect, it remains limited. The topics selected for attention were not obtained by structured analysis and no formal needs assessment had been conducted.

It is essential that a detailed occupational health needs assessment be conducted to validate the work done to date and establish what other needs exist. This should be conducted by utilising the services of a qualified occupational health nurse to help with the health needs assessment and provide advice on prevention and control measures. The assessment should encompass a full risk assessment of all potential occupational risks to health. In order to ensure legal compliance with the Manual Handling Operations Regulations 1992 and Control of Noise at Work Regulations 2005 assessments for these risks must be conducted as a matter of priority.

The company and managers should widen the scope of their commitment to manage health and well being issues and this should include greater emphasis on work related issues. It is important that this is done without having a detrimental effect on the issues currently being focused on. In addition, it is important that others in the company play a more active part in managing health and well being issues. It would be helpful if a 'champion' could be established for each section, from managers or employees, to help ensure that interventions are applied, remain relevant and are effective.

In order to establish a wider scope it will be necessary to organise the inclusion of such work place issues as 'back care', DSE, noise, bullying/harassment by customers and stress within the business plan and targets. The specific detail of these should be derived from the work done when conducting the detailed occupational health and well-being needs assessment.

Because no general health and well being training had been provided to managers their perspective of the topic has been limited, effort has tended to focus on lifestyle issues rather than workplace health. Managers would benefit from general training, which would improve their perspective and help them understand the need to widen the scope of issues addressed. Specific training was also needed to support the implementation of specific policies, such as absence and bullying/harassment.

2 Communication and employee involvement

Strengths

A H&S committee was in place and H&S advisors were available to each section. There was some evidence that their work had included a small range of health issues, though well being was not usually included.

Communication of non-workplace health and well being issues had been effective to the extent that it has stimulated employees and managers to use exercise facilities and establish groups focusing on exercise and smoking cessation. This has provided a strong and effective opportunity for joint working.

Weaknesses

The informal and unstructured approach to communication will not lend itself to a wider scope of issues. The current approach to communication should be evaluated and longer-term approaches to communication and involvement established. It would be best if the evaluation could be done by putting together a working party of employees and managers as a subgroup of the H&S committee. This would maximise acceptance of recommendations and serve as an opportunity to widen the remit and understanding of the H&S committee with regard to health and well being.

3 Policies and procedures

Strengths

The company had established some policies and procedures that support the health and well being issues that had been the main focus of the company strategy to date. These had been supported by targets and plans to improve health and well being and specialist, contracted, health and well being advice established to support the targets.

The policies had been communicated to managers and employees and they have had some effect on sickness absence, though policies have not been supported by the provision of training.

Weaknesses

However, the policy on bullying and harassment had not been fully implemented into actions, especially in relation to its effect on stress. Similarly, the policy on substance misuse had not been well implemented due to lack of management training. This had led to some difficulty in applying the policy following a recent accident involving an employee who had been drinking. Unfortunately the incident was not properly investigated from a health and well being perspective, which means an opportunity to identify the cause of the drinking was lost and there remains a possibility of a reoccurrence.

As there were no clear indications from the company regarding its attitude to the employment of people with mental ill health it is essential that policies are established that addresses this topic. Health risk assessments of exposure to noise had not been conducted and there may well be a significant risk to workers in the call centre, this should be conducted as a matter of priority as it is also a specific requirement of the Control of Noise at Work Regulations 2005. Following this assessment, it is essential that a clear policy and procedure be established for this risk.

4 Management of ill health and absence, monitoring, health assessment and review

Strengths

The sickness absence programme had been firmly established. Trends of sickness absence had been identified and individuals given programmes for improvement.

Weaknesses

Though there was some evidence of ill health absence management for situations covered by general sickness the lack of manager training had limited its use for wider, often underlying, ill health issues. Absence management is an aspect of health and well-being that can have a significant effect on the company and the principles established for sickness should be widened to identify and mange work related causes of absence.

It was noted that there was no system in place to conduct pre-employment assessments of hearing, this should be addressed as part of the measures introduced to assess and respond to this health risk.

5 Competence and interventions

Strengths

The company had access to competent health and well being services through a contracted company, it is important that these are evaluated following the health needs assessment. The contracted OH service had provided training to employees on stress, skin and back care.

A significant number of interventions were in place related to life style aspects of health and well being.

Weaknesses

Though information on the sickness absence management procedures was provided by Human Resources managers had not been provided with formal training, which had led to its limited use for health and well being management.

Few interventions had been established for occupational health issues. Notably, none of the workers in the call centre have received an audiometric test as part of their pre-employment assessment or subsequently. The company should include audiometric testing in the pre-employment screening for prospective call centre employees, to establish a base line hearing level. Annual audiometric testing should be carried out for all call centre staff and any deterioration should be investigated. Work should be carried out to reduce noise levels in the call centre and a review of the suitability of telephones should be considered.

Conclusions

Significant progress had been made in establishing commitment to a selected number of issues that focus on life style health and well-being. This had led to effective plans and targets for improvement resulting in the motivation and involvement of managers and employees in successful campaigns. The enthusiasm of employees had been surprisingly good. It is essential that this is used as a basis to move to wider, particularly workplace based, health and well being issues.

The failure to identify and manage work based health risks can have a major impact on the health of employees and lead to their short and long-term absence from work. The risks that workers are exposed to could lead to chronic health harm, such as deafness, back injury or disorders affecting their wrists. These types of harm cause severe debilitation of workers for the remainder of their life. The identification and management of these risks is essential to minimise their effects on the workforce and to limit any costs to the company due to their absence or for compensation for harm done. This will require a health needs assessment to be conducted. The needs assessment will help to establish clear direction, which will involve setting out and clarifying policies related to health risks and support this with general and specific training for managers.

The work to improve health and well-being will require specific interventions to be taken, some of these should not wait until the completion of the health needs assessment as they have specific legal requirements related to them, this includes noise and manual handling risks. Assessment of the source and level of these health risks must be conducted as a priority in order to avoid the company being prosecuted. Following this, interventions for noise risk should include the introduction of audiometric testing of call centre employees at pre-employment (to establish a base line hearing level) and annually (to identify any deterioration). This will enable the company to provide early intervention, which will minimise harm to employees and reduce the risk of compensation claims.

By continuing effort and improving the management of health and well being in the company it will provide the wide range of benefits that Dame Carol Black identified in her review "Working for a healthier tomorrow", which included reduced lost time of employees, more productivity, reduced recruitment and training costs, improved moral and reputation of the company. The improvements recommended should be carried out, not only because they will improve the company's moral legal and economic position but also because it is right to do.

The progress so far and that planned should not go unrecognised, the work done by managers and employees should be commended and recognition sought from external organisations like Investors in People (IIP) or Workplace Health Awards.

Recommendations - include as a table in the following format:

Recommendation	Likely resource implications	Priority	Review date
Review current health and wellbeing provider suitability, since they had not identified any workplace health and wellbeing issues.	1 day of HR's time to discuss and consider responses by OH providers, including current one.	High	2 weeks Follow up review at three monthly intervals
Conduct full health and well being needs assessment	OH provider, including OH nurse. Estimate of 10 days £5,000	High	2 months Review annually for changes of need
Current OH provider to provide additional services relevant to all health risks affecting staff at the location.	Estimate of 20 days £10,000 over 12 months period, 10 days each year thereafter	High	3 months – review progress and effectiveness of service
Assess noise levels in the call centres	Outside consultant 5 days assessment £2500	High	1 month Review against audiometric results
Establish clear policy and procedure on noise risks	HR time to draft about 2 days, comment from OH provider (at no additional cost as it is within contract) and review by selected managers (approximately 1 hour per manager and 3 hours for HR to review and amend)	High	1 month Review 3 months after introduction
Include pre employment audiometric screening for new employees	£35 per person	High	1 month Review results at 3 month intervals and service annually
Establish annual audiometric screening for all call centre employees	£70,000 £23,333 Staff with longest service first	High	Phased in over 36months, review results at 3month intervals and service annually
Conduct manual handling risk assessments	H&S Advisors, estimate of 10 days total, spread over each section	High	2 months Review at H&S committee after 3 months and then after changes
Establish 'champion' for health and well being	Volunteers, training, time for them to be active, 1-2 days per month	Medium	3 months
Establish working party to evaluate health and well being communication	Use of H&S committee members, likely to be 2 meeting a month apart	Low	6 months Discuss at next meeting
Conduct general and specific training for managers - including absence management, disability, mental health, noise, musculoskeletal risks	OH provider 5 times one day to cover shifts, run as formal training session in meeting room £2500	Medium	3 months Review after first session and at end of training to identify need for further training or support
Establish clear policy and procedure on mental health	HR time to draft about 2 days, comment from OH provider (at no additional cost as it is within contract) and review by selected managers (approximately 1 hour per manager and 3 hours for HR to review and amend)	Medium	3 months Review 3 months after introduction
Review frequency of actual breaks taken by call centre staff against break policy	Three person days, could use H&S Advisors, to include shift workers	Medium	3 months

Sample assessment questions - answers

NHC1 - Managing health and well-being in the workplace

ELEMENT 1

1. **Outline** two benefits to the employer resulting from a proactive health and wellbeing policy. **(8)**

Any two outlines from the following:

Reduced absenteeism

The employer's management of workplace ill-health cases will ensure that absence is reduced to a minimum, which will control direct and indirect costs arising from the ill-health. Often the positive co-operation that such programmes provide can make the worker feel more valued. A workforce that feels valued is more likely to enjoy their work and feel loyalty to their employer. Being part of a team and not wishing to let that team down will have an effect on the attendance behaviour of the workers.

Reduction in staff turnover

Organisations that maintain and promote health are seen as positive employers, with values that workers can relate to. This can encourage people to want to work for the organisation and can lead to reduced turnover of workers, as they feel valued and recognise what they may loose by moving to another organisation

Reduction in recruitment and training costs

By retaining workers and making the organisation a desirable place to work these recruitment costs will be reduced. Instead of advertising, the method of recruitment may become by worker recommendation to others and waiting lists of potential applicants. Reduced turnover will mean that direct and indirect costs of training will not be required.

Increased productivity

By maintaining and promoting health, organisations establish a positive workplace where health and well-being are normal and this will greatly reduce staff turnover. The team which is not constantly disrupted, with people leaving the organisation and new members joining, will function well and achieve the overall objectives of the organisation, as a result efficiency and effectiveness will be increased.

Seen as a caring employer

A "Caring Employer" label will mean that the best recruits are drawn to the company and so the quality of work and the volume of output should be increased with evident increase in success and worker satisfaction.

2. **Explain**, with examples, the expression "good work is good for your health and wellbeing". **(8)**

Strong evidence suggests that work provides a structure for day to day living, enhances self esteem and creates opportunities for social interaction. Work is crucial in personal identity terms, for example, the individual is able to provide for the needs of their family. In terms of their place in society and within their own community work is a marker of social standing and status. The economic benefit from work-related income allows the individual to have control over economic choice, for example, paying to use leisure facilities and suitable housing provision. Conversely, individuals who are economically inactive have a decrease in life expectancy and many experience an increase in ill-health from issues such as, smoking, obesity and heart disease; resulting in an increase in the need for health care provision. Many individuals,' not working, experience low self-esteem and low financial state, which magnifies the social and economic stability of this country.

ELEMENT 2

1. (a) When is it appropriate to carry out pre-employment screening? **(2)**
   (b) **Outline** why employers should conduct pre-employment screening assessments. **(6)**

Part (a)

A pre-employment health assessment should be undertaken once the individual has been offered the job and they have met all the other criteria for undertaking the role.

Part (b)

- *To ensure someone is fit to do the job - assessed against specific fitness standards.*
- *To ensure that those with known health problems are not put at risk, or they put others at risk.*
- *It provides a baseline of health for the individual entering the workplace e.g. hearing. Lung function, vision. Both the employee and business need to know this in case there is any future claims, for example, noise induce hearing loss or occupational asthma.*
- *It can also be used to inform employees of any specific health requirements and/or the positive health initiatives the business has in place that the employee can access.*

2. The Disability Discrimination Act 1995 defines what is classed as 'reasonable adjustments'.
   Outline FOUR examples of reasonable adjustments which an employer might need to make. **(8)**

Any outline from four of the following:

- *Adjustments to premises e.g. installing ramps for wheelchair access*
- *Allocating some of the disabled persons work to another person*
- *Transferring to another vacancy.*
- *Altering working hours e.g. not undertaking shift work*
- *Assigning to a different workplace*

- *Allowing absence for treatment*
- *Acquiring or modifying equipment e.g. someone with visual difficulty may require modifications to the DSE*
- *Opportunities for re-training and/or developing new skills.*
- *Modifying work manuals e.g. Braille, or larger font size.*
- *Modifying procedures for testing or assessment e.g. someone with learning or reading difficulties may require a more practical assessment*
- *Providing a reader or interpreter e.g. the visually impaired may require a reader and/or voice activated equipment.*
- *Providing supervision.*

ELEMENT 3

1. **Identify FOUR** agents that can cause skin disease and give an example for each type identified. **(8)**

Acceptable answers would include:

Mechanical	*Friction, pressure, trauma*	*e.g. callosities*
Physical	*Heat, cold, radiation*	*e.g. rashes, chilblains, frostbite, burns, cancer*
Chemical	*Acids, alkalis, solvents, oils, pitch, tar*	*e.g. dermatitis, rashes, dry skin, blistering.*
Plants	*Flowers, wood*	*e.g. dermatitis, rashes*
Biological	*Organisms, insects, mites, scabies*	*e.g. infection, infestation*

2. **Explain** with examples how allergic contact dermatitis may be caused. **(8)**

It is usually caused by one specific agent and the skin reaction can be immediate or may be delayed for up to a week or more after exposure. The initial reaction is normally following exposure to high concentrations and/or long exposure to a substance. Following this initial reaction it may then only take small, short exposures to get a reaction.

Commonly used examples of contact allergens are:

- *Epoxy resins e.g. found in adhesives, cement and surface coating agents.*
- *Rubber latex e.g. found in rubber gloves, tubes - health care workers, hairdressers.*
- *Gluteraldahyde e.g. used as a sterilising agent in health care.*
- *Nickel salts e.g. used to coat other metals to prevent rusting as in electroplating.*
- *Dyes e.g. used in hairdressing.*

ELEMENT 4

1. (a) **Explain** the meaning of the term 'may be fit for work'. **(2)**
   (b) **Outline** the role and status of the 'fit note'. **(6)**

Part (a)

The doctors (mainly general practitioners) will choose the 'may be fit for work' option if they think that the employee returning to work – with support from the employer – will help. The doctor can give general advice on the fit note about how the illness or injury may affect the workers ability to work.

Part (b)

Fit Notes are forms issued by doctors (mainly general practitioners) for statutory sick pay purposes. They provide evidence where an employee cannot work due to illness or injury and advice for those that could return to work with adjustments; for example a phased return to work. The fit note focuses on what people "can do" rather then what they cannot. Should an employee wish to return to work before the Fit Note date, then they do not have to wait until that date, nor do they have to be signed back into work by the GP. Whilst the GP's comments on the fit note should be considered, they are advisory and employers may need to consider the nature of the work that the employee undertakes; as there may be health and safety implications for a returning employee that the GP may not be aware of.

2. (a) **Define** the term vocational rehabilitation. **(2)**
   (b) **Outline** the benefits of vocational rehabilitation within the context of the employee and the employer. **(4)**

Part (a)

The generally accepted definition is:

Vocational rehabilitation is a process to overcome the barriers an individual faces in returning to employment which result from injury, illness or disability. It encompasses the support for an individual either new to employment for the first time.

Part (b)

Early intervention can be effective in avoiding long term absence. The employee will feel valued by the organisation if investment in them is focused in them returning to work and there is strong evidence that it is a cost benefit for the business to retain skilled employees in work rather than to replace them with someone who whilst equally skilled may take some time to achieve the level of performance required for the job.

ELEMENT 5

1. (a) **Explain** with examples what is mean by the terms '**subjective and objective indicators**' when assessing work related stress. **(4)**
   (b) **Outline** who should be informed of the outcome following any stress survey or focus group action. **(4)**

Part (a)

Subjective indicators *for example stress audits, workplace satisfaction surveys and focus groups.* **Objective indicators** *can be ascertained from the levels of sickness absence, staff turnover and from accident statistics.*

Part (b)

The results of any survey or focus group activity must be communicated to the people who took part and all the employees. This might be through the Trade Union or employees representatives (who should be involved in the activities) and management briefings. How results are communicated will depend on the business, Some organisations place information like this on the company intranet, but whichever method is used there must also be a system set up for employees to comment or discuss any concerns they may have.

2. **Outline** with examples the effects of prolonged absence from work on the mental health of individuals. **(8)**

- *The mental health condition may be made worse through lack of contact. The person will feel isolated and forgotten and if they are suffering with depression, they need to feel wanted and valued.*
- *Result in high cost to the business in terms of lost skills and the need to employ casual/temporary staff to cover absences.*
- *Result in high cost to the person's family as they will be supporting the individual, this also means a high cost to society as a whole as family members may have to take time off to care for the individual.*
- *Can affect the reputation of the business – it may be regarded by society as uncaring and ruthless.*

ELEMENT 6

1. **Explain**, **with examples** why good ergonomic principles should be applied to the workplace if musculoskeletal injury is to be prevented. **(8)**

People vary in height, weight, strength and ability to take in information and instructions. Designing the workplace with the worker in mind is paramount to preventing ill health, injury and errors.

Ergonomics can help to solve a number of problems. Consider the size of a worker working at an assembly bench, if they are very tall they may not be able to place their legs under the bench and may be bending forward in a 'top heavy' posture, which will cause back and knee problems. Conversely, a short person may have difficulties reaching across a bench and could develop shoulder, neck and upper arm problems. This means ensuring that tasks, equipment and workstations are designed to suit the individual, which is fitting the task to the person.

The use of hand tools must be considered. Many hand tools require a wide grip, for example, pruning shears, which will put severe strain on the hands and arms, particularly for people with smaller hands. The layout of control panels can influence safety and reduce error rates. Switches that can be inadvertently turned on or off; controls that are difficult to understand; displays that are difficult to read, requiring the worker to bend, stretch and twist in order to read them; controls that are difficult to reach or badly labelled so that errors can occur.

2. **Outline TWO** factors which should be included when assessing a proposed manual handling operation. **(8)**

Any two outlines from the following:

Load

- *The weight of the load*
- *Bulky loads*
- *Unwieldy loads may cause the person to overbalance*
- *loads that are difficult to grasp*
- *Some loads may have contents that are likely to shift, for example liquids in a container*
- *The centre of gravity of a load may be uneven and set away from the natural points to grip a load*

Individual

- *Strength of a worker will vary and establishes a limit of weight that they can lift, carry or handle.*
- *The workers, for example the worker may have pre-existing back or muscle injury which will increase the risk of injury from work.*
- *Pregnant females may be of increased risk of harm*
- *Older workers as they may find it more difficult to handle objects due to conditions such as arthritis and their muscle tone may be reduced due to ageing.*
- *Young persons may not be fully physically developed.*

Task

- *Holding the load at a distance from the trunk will place the body under higher leverage forces*
- *bodily movement or posture, such as twisting the trunk or stooping.*
- *The task may require high levels of exertion, such as: Excessive lifting, lowering, carrying distances, frequent physical effort, insufficient rest or recovery.*

Environment

- *Space constraints preventing good posture.*
- *Uneven, slippery or unstable floors.*
- *Variations in level of floors or work surfaces.*
- *Extremes of temperature, humidity or air movement.*
- *Poor lighting conditions.*

ELEMENT 7

1. (a) **Outline** with examples the main life style factors which affect the health and wellbeing of individuals. **(4)**
    (b) **Explain** how diet can have an affect on general health. **(4)**

Part (a)

Lifestyle factors are about how people live their lives and the habits and behaviours that contribute to or challenge their health status. All these personal choices are part of the life of the workers that make up an organisation. Some examples are diet, exercise, smoking, alcohol and the increasing use of "recreational" drugs, drugs taken for personal pleasure as opposed to medical necessity.

Part (b)

The diet of working age people can affect their general health, diet relates to the quantity and quality of food eaten. As a general comment, poor diet can cause the worker to become lethargic, reduce their mobility and lead to longer term harm that could cause sickness absence. People who do not eat enough food may lack enough energy or mental concentration to perform adequately in work, this can lead to rapid fatigue and result in errors. Their muscles may become wasted, leaving them to become incapable of work that requires some physical strength. Those that continue with this diet may find that their body's immunity to common diseases in society becomes reduced and their general health can decline resulting in absence from work.

People who eat too much food or less healthy food may find that they put on weight, which can reduce mobility or diminish capability for sustained exertion such as manual handling tasks or take up a restricted posture in some cases, the level of obesity can cause high levels of lethargy and lapses of attention, which in jobs that are safety critical or with inherent demands, such as heavy goods vehicle / train driver or call centre operation, the diminished performance can have serious effects.

2. **Outline** why it is important to take a balance approach to regular exercise. **(8)**

People in the working age population that lead an essentially sedentary work and personal life may find that the food intake is not utilised by body activity, thus leading them to accumulate fat in the body. In addition, their muscles and other soft tissue can become less used to physical activity, increasing the risk of injury when tasks involving physical exertion are made. In addition, supplety, flexibility and dexterity of movement may become diminished. Lack of exercise may lead to inefficient functioning of the metabolism and gradual strain on the cardio-vascular system. This in turn may limit the amount of oxygen available to parts of the body like the brain and lead to reduced mental and physical performance. This may influence safety critical decision making and the ability to carry out highly pressured tasks or under emergency situations.

Those that exercise too much may place their body under significant strain, with the potential for them to suffer from problems that can affect their ability to carry out their work. For example, someone that plays a large amount of tennis may put their upper limbs under significant strain, and whilst their job may include some small effect on upper limbs the combined effect could be too much, leading to the worker suffering an upper limb disorder.

ELEMENT 8

1. **Distinguish** between the terms hazard and risk using an appropriate example. **(8)**

Any appropriate specific health hazards from chemical, physical, biological, psychosocial, and ergonomic categories.

'Hazard' is anything that can cause harm. Many things have the potential to cause harm, but it depends on what we do with the hazard e.g. sealed asbestos is safe, it is only when we start to move it, drill it etc and make it into dust, which can be inhaled, that it will damage health.

'Risk' is the likelihood that someone will be harmed by the hazard. This is the measure of the risk. Using the example of asbestos, if it is known that asbestos is hazardous to health when inhaled, and therefore, the likelihood of someone being harmed by exposure to asbestos dust is high and they are likely to develop serious respiratory problems, including lung cancer.

2. **Outline** the role of the occupational hygienist. **(8)**

Occupational hygienists play an important role in the prevention of ill-health from work, through recognising, evaluating, and controlling the risks. Occupational hygienists have a technical expertise in measuring exposure levels such as dusts, gases, vapours and noise, and the interpretation of the results and advice on practical solutions that can be put in place to prevent and/or control the hazard. Hygienists work in all types of organizations both public and private from offices to factories with many working as self employed Consultants. They have a range of expertise and can advise on regulatory compliance and the investigation of short to long term health issues arising from exposure both acute and chronic, such as noise levels and monitoring.

Index

Y